AF539517

# CROSSROADS

Drawing the Dutch Landscape

# CROSSROADS

# Drawing the Dutch Landscape

**Selections from the Harvard Art Museums and the Maida and George Abrams Collection**

Edited by Joanna Sheers Seidenstein and Susan Anderson
With contributions by Susan Anderson, Yvonne Bleyerveld, Anne Driesse, Joseph Leo Koerner, William W. Robinson, and Joanna Sheers Seidenstein
Afterword by George S. Abrams

Harvard Art Museums
Cambridge, Mass.

Distributed by Yale University Press
New Haven and London

CONTENTS

Depictions of the land have much to teach us about cultures and communities. Landscape drawings have a place in almost every civilization, representing natural beauty but also speaking to economics, politics, and a shared sense of nostalgia. Between the second half of the sixteenth and the early eighteenth century, artists working in the Netherlands produced an extraordinary number of landscapes in a variety of media, with drawing serving a foundational and expressive role. In sketches made outdoors and finished sheets produced in the studio, Dutch draftsmen adopted, revised, and invented a wide range of conceptual and technical approaches to the representation of their surroundings, often choosing to depict specific, recognizable sites within their local landscape. *Crossroads: Drawing the Dutch Landscape* explores this surge in landscape production—one of the most remarkable communal meditations on the physical environment in the history of art—through a selection of more than eighty-five works from the holdings of the Harvard Art Museums and the Maida and George Abrams Collection.

George Abrams (Harvard College '54, Harvard Law '57), a tireless champion and supporter of the museums, has over the past four decades given or pledged more than 450 drawings to our collection, in addition to placing a significant number on long-term loan. His generosity has made our institution home to the most comprehensive gathering of early modern Dutch drawings in North America, encompassing every genre and type of drawing produced in the period, with noted strengths in figure studies, Mannerism, works by Rembrandt and his school, and landscapes. Focusing on the last category, *Crossroads* was prompted by the announcement in 2017 of a promised gift of more than three hundred drawings from the Abrams Collection. This project, developed in part to honor the museums' longstanding relationship with George and his late wife, Maida, demonstrates how such passionate partnerships can generate powerful opportunities for scholarship and learning: as a major site for the study not only of Dutch drawings from this period but of works on paper more generally, the museums serve as a place of inspiration for students, scholars, and the public, as well as a launching pad for future investigations that will bring these objects to still wider audiences. We extend our deepest thanks to George for helping us illuminate the potent connections between the art of the past and the concerns of our day.

The history of Old Master drawings at Harvard originates in the collecting and commitment of the Fogg Museum's first associate director, Paul J. Sachs (1878–1965), who gave generously to the museum both during his life and upon his death. In addition to inspiring successive benefactors with his largesse, Sachs was renowned for his teaching and advocacy of the next generation of curators. In this spirit, the Abrams Collection has time and again supported scholarship within and beyond Harvard's walls. William W. Robinson, curator of drawings from 1988 until his retirement in 2015, devoted much of his career to researching, exhibiting, and publishing sheets from the Abrams Collection; he adds to his extraordinary scholarly record an essay in the present volume. Edouard Kopp served as Maida and George Abrams Curator of Drawings from 2015 to 2018, bringing his energy to countless projects, several of them related to Dutch drawings, and initiating this exhibition before his departure. Joachim Homann, who assumed the role in 2019, leads the drawings department with remarkably innovative thinking around the study and display of drawings from all regions and periods, offering yet new ways of accessing and exploring the Abrams Collection and sharing its treasures with the university and with audiences around the world. In addition, thanks to the Stanley H. Durwood Foundation, a fellowship dedicated to the study of Dutch drawings will also continue at the museums for years to come. The 2018–22 Durwood Fellow, Joanna Sheers Seidenstein, spearheaded this project with Susan Anderson, curatorial research associate at the museums and private curator to George Abrams. Together, Seidenstein and Anderson have curated an illuminating exhibition that, through the landscape genre, tells the story of how citizens of the newly independent Dutch Republic related to their environment. The story is given further treatment in this volume, where contributors delve into the objects to expand upon their materiality, imagery, and the contexts of their making and display.

Conceived and well underway before the COVID-19 pandemic upended lives and laid bare persistent social injustices, this publication and the exhibition it accompanies nevertheless resonate with the present moment in unexpected ways. Who among us has not reflected on the meaning of home and community during the periods of isolation and lockdown, or wished to escape to the beauty and solace of nature? Thanks in no small part to the collective work of scholars, organizers, and activists, we are also increasingly conscious of the land we occupy as a vestige and product of colonialism and of the exploitation of Indigenous and enslaved lives. So, too, have we been forced in recent years to reckon with the vulnerability of our planet and the uncertain future of the earth. The great economic, political, and ecological changes that enabled the artistic boom of the early Dutch Republic, many of whose patrons accumulated their wealth on the backs of people of color, find meaningful comparison in our own society. Tranquil yet intrinsically political, landscape is a topic that offers a poignant lens on both past and present.

For helping us hold up this lens, we are grateful to our supporters. This catalogue was made possible by the Andrew W. Mellon Publication Funds, including the Henry P. McIlhenny Fund, and by the WOLFGANG RATJEN FOUNDATION, Liechtenstein. Funding for the exhibition and related programming was provided by the Stanley H. Durwood Foundation Support Fund and the M. Victor Leventritt Lecture Series Endowment Fund. This support has allowed us to open many portals into the world of the early modern Netherlands, whether through programs or the publication you hold in your hands. Like the motif of the road leading into the picture plane—a hallmark of Dutch landscape artists that draws viewers into the scene—we welcome you to get lost in its pages.

*Martha Tedeschi*
Elizabeth and John Moors Cabot Director
Harvard Art Museums

# PREFACE AND ACKNOWLEDGMENTS



When we launched this project in the fall of 2018, the word *crossroads* – suggestive of choice, change, a reckoning with the past, and an eye toward the future – seemed appropriate for an investigation focused on a watershed in the history of landscape, especially one undertaken amid a shift in priorities in the field of Dutch art studies. The events that unfolded in 2020, during the completion of this manuscript, added significant weight to our decision to use that term. Art museums find themselves at a crossroads, called upon more ardently than ever to abandon claims of neutrality, to promote anti-racism, and to dismantle the power structures embedded within these institutions. This has pushed us as individuals to reflect more deeply on our own work and its impact. As specialists in European art, we have dedicated years to material that we long believed had the capacity to speak to viewers across time, place, and lived experience. In recent years, our field has taken initial steps to shift art historical narratives toward more complete histories. The term "Golden Age" has been reassessed and largely abandoned, and the innumerable men, women, and children who were enslaved or otherwise exploited during this era are increasingly visible and acknowledged on museum walls and in scholarship. We understand, however, that this is just the beginning of the work we need to do to make our field and our institutions inclusive and equitable.

Aligning our longstanding affection for the period with these realities remains an ongoing and challenging process. We must continually question how we approach and conduct our work as scholars and as museum professionals – particularly within the sphere of Old Master drawings, where the profusion of unsigned sheets and mimetic artistic practices have demanded that connoisseurship and other traditional methods remain at the core. By combining these with more contextual approaches to the intrinsically political subject of landscape, we hope this project can invite and include all people and points of view. As representations of land – for some viewers visions of respite and beauty, but for many unavoidably associated with environmental degradation, socioeconomic disparity, and the legacies of colonialism – the works in this publication and the exhibition it accompanies may provoke a wide range of responses. We welcome and aspire to learn from them all.

The drawings in the exhibition, selected from the combined holdings of the Harvard Art Museums and the Maida and George Abrams Collection, together reveal the pictorial conventions through which the idea of the Dutch landscape was, in a sense, constructed over the course of a century and a half. Sheets by Pieter Bruegel the Elder and an artist dubbed the Master of the Small Landscapes, progenitors of the landscape tradition as it would develop in the Northern Netherlands, show the divergent ways in which artists belonging to the same moment and milieu could conceptualize the genre. Works by figures such as Abraham Bloemaert, Claes Jansz. Visscher, Cornelis Vroom, Esaias van de Velde, and Jan van Goyen trace the development of what would become quintessentially Dutch landscape idioms and motifs, from cottages and farmhouses to ice skating scenes. A selection of drawings by Rembrandt and members of his circle reveal the ongoing fascination with the rustic, while works by Jan Lievens, Jacob van Ruisdael, and Anthonie Waterloo demonstrate the evolving appeal of woodland and forest imagery. Works by early eighteenth-century practitioners, such as Isaac de Moucheron and Dirk Dalens III, extend the chronological scope of the narrative of Dutch landscape typically presented in American museums. Representations of locales in other parts of Europe and of the Dutch colonies in Brazil and Indonesia provide an illuminating context for the numerous drawings of identifiable sites within the Netherlands, permitting a reexamination of the Dutch predilection for the "local" against the backdrop of the Republic's colonization of territories around the world. Together, these works make clear that the story of the Dutch landscape, with its origins in Antwerp, has important chapters in places far beyond the Republic's domestic borders.

These drawings form the basis of the essays presented here. Each of the texts addresses the theme of crossroads or intersections through a particular lens. Altogether, the volume is additive in intent, aiming to expand, rather than limit, the possibilities for understanding drawings and the subject of landscape. Yvonne Bleyerveld looks at the practice of drawing outdoors and engaging with one's local surroundings as a meaningful interaction between artist and environment. With a focus on works depicting identifiable sites or those more generally indicative of the Dutch countryside (and certain urban areas), she explores the relationship between sketches made outdoors and finished drawings made in the studio – and the sometimes indiscernible line between the two. William W. Robinson addresses the invention and reinvention of motifs through an exploration of architectural structures – rustic, grand, and ruinous – across media, foregrounding the role played by drawing in driving innovation and artistic exchange. Anne Driesse presents five case studies that demonstrate the complex ways in which different drawing materials, particularly combinations of wet and dry media, interact with one another. Her analyses reveal the planning and foresight behind the pursuit of atmosphere, movement, and light. Joseph Koerner considers the relationship between object and beholder, with an in-depth exploration of how this dynamic influenced artistic choices within three intact period albums. George Abrams, past and present owner of many of these objects, shares his personal motivations for wanting to possess them – and to ensure that future generations will have the same opportunity to enjoy their beauty and magic. Our own respective contributions include an essay on landscape drawings as meditations on humankind's often fraught relationship with the land and, interspersed throughout the book, a suite of "touchstones" – masterful drawings that offer a chronological sweep of particularly cogent themes, accompanied by discussions that expand on the introduction to the volume and serve as a framework for the deeper reflections in the essays.

This project benefits from numerous exhibitions and publications on the subject of Dutch landscape drawings that came before. In particular, we acknowledge *Seventeenth-Century Dutch Landscape Drawings and Selected Prints*, organized by Curtis O. Baer and Susan D. Kuretsky at the Vassar College Art Gallery in 1976, and *Landscape in Perspective: Drawings by Rembrandt and His Contemporaries*, organized by Frederik J. Duparc at the Montreal Museum of Fine Arts in partnership with the Harvard University Art Museums (as they were then called) in 1988. Both of these exhibitions included a generous selection of works from the Harvard and Abrams collections and constitute highly important treatments of the theme. We owe a particular debt of gratitude to the extraordinary work and mentorship of William W. Robinson, whose publications dedicated to the Abrams Collection form the foundation of the present study. These include *Seventeenth-Century Dutch Drawings: A Selection from the Maida and George Abrams Collection* (1991), *Bruegel to Rembrandt: Dutch and Flemish Drawings from the Maida and George Abrams Collection* (2002), and *Drawings from the Age of Bruegel, Rubens, and Rembrandt: Highlights from the Collection of the Harvard Art Museums* (2016 and online at harvardartmuseums.org).

We have many others to thank. First and foremost, George Abrams and his late wife, Maida, are of course the founders of our feast. To work on and learn from the collection they fashioned through true love of drawings has been a tremendous privilege. George's enthusiasm for this project from its inception has been in lockstep with his staunch advocacy of the Harvard Art Museums. His passion and commitment are awe-inspiring, and we thank him for the many ways he has supported our work. Edouard Kopp, the 2015–18 Maida and George Abrams Curator of Drawings, encouraged us from the outset to develop and propose this idea, which director Martha Tedeschi, deputy director Maureen Donovan, and chief curator Soyoung Lee embraced wholeheartedly and which Joachim Homann, the current Abrams Curator of Drawings, has continued to buoy in meaningful ways.

To Joachim and to Miriam Stewart, we express special thanks for their review of the manuscript and invaluable feedback, and for their key support at every stage. We warmly thank our editors, Micah Buis, Sarah Kuschner, and Cheryl Pappas, and designers Zak Jensen, Angela Lorenzo, and Adam Sherkanowski for their brilliant work on this publication and for their camaraderie throughout its production. And to the essay authors, Yvonne Bleyerveld, Anne Driesse, Joseph Koerner, and Bill Robinson, we offer our deepest gratitude and admiration. This volume represents a collaboration of the most inspiring kind.

For lending works to the exhibition that permitted important exploration of the Dutch colonial project, we owe much gratitude to our colleagues at Houghton Library, in particular Thomas Hyry, John Overholt, and Carie McGinnis, and at the Harvard Map Collection, where David Weimer has been an unflagging and generous source of support and advice and Scott Walker has spent countless hours designing the map graphics included here and on the walls of the exhibition. For making available prints from the Harvard Art Museums' outstanding holdings, including a generous selection from the Light-Outerbridge Collection, formed by print dealer Robert M. Light and Donald Outerbridge and acquired for the institution by Marjorie B. Cohn, we thank our cherished colleague Elizabeth Rudy.

We could not have realized this project without the exceptional support of curatorial assistant Heather Linton. With extraordinary skill, thoughtfulness, attention to detail, and big-picture thinking, she kept this project on track—even while the museums were closed and staff shifted to remote work during the COVID-19 pandemic—and offered essential contributions throughout. We are also indebted to projects and program manager Jane Braun and registrar Francine Flynn for the invaluable work that they do, and to the innovative thinkers behind our programming initiatives in the Division of Academic and Public Programs, chief among them

David Odo, Tayana Fincher, Jeanne Burke, and former colleague Molly Ryan. The Digital Infrastructure and Emerging Technology and Digital Imaging and Visual Resources teams offered essential advice and are responsible for nearly all of the photography in this book. This project has also benefited immeasurably from the support of our wonderful Communications and Institutional Advancement teams. We are especially indebted to our colleagues in the Paper Lab, most of all Penley Knipe, who has gone above and beyond in offering her time, attention, and expertise to this project, including filling various unexpected needs that arose from the pandemic and museums closure. For the beautiful matting and framing of the works in the show, we thank Adam Baker and Charlotte Karney. We are similarly grateful to our colleagues in Collections Management. It has been a pleasure to work with Elie Glyn, whose elegant exhibition design affords precisely the intimate viewing experience we always hoped to achieve. To Karen Gausch and her exhibition production team, we extend enormous gratitude and our deepest admiration. The Art Study Center team and the staff of Harvard's Fine Arts Library deserve special thanks for kindly and generously fulfilling our many requests to access works and research materials. It was a pleasure to work with curatorial interns George Cozens and Natalie Gale, and we thank them for their research and assistance with this project. And of course, we greatly appreciate the support and goodwill of all our fellow members of the Division of European and American Art.

In addition to those already mentioned, we wish to thank the following individuals for their instrumental advice and efforts on various fronts: Cassandra Albinson, Christopher Atkins, Jennifer Aubin, Francesca Bewer, Pepijn Brandon, Ian Callahan, Liz Cartland, Marjorie B. Cohn, John Connolly, Charles Dumas, Kara Howgate-Mello, Narayan Khandekar, Ethan Lasser, Erica Lawton, Mary Lister, Sophie Lynford, Austėja Mackelaitė, Sarah Mallory, Daron Manoogian, Arthur McClelland, Tara Metal, Katherine Mintie, Casey Monahan, Leonie Müller, Nadine Orenstein, Jessie Park, Georgina Rayner, Robert-Jan te Rijdt, Matt Roza, Peter Schatborn, Laurens Schoemaker, Melanie Sheffield, Jeff Steward, Christina Taylor, Bridget Thompson, Rebecca Torres, Jane Turner, Stephanie Vecellio, Natalia Ángeles Vieyra, Julie Wertz, and Oliver Wunsch. Finally, we extend our thanks to the museums' Security and Visitor Services staff—especially the frontline workers whose jobs have been so complicated by the pandemic—for their invaluable contributions to this and all exhibitions. We hope this project does justice to the immense labor, both visible and invisible, that made it all possible.

*Joanna Sheers Seidenstein*
Assistant Curator, Department of Drawings and Prints,
The Metropolitan Museum of Art, New York
2018–22 Stanley H. Durwood Foundation Curatorial Fellow in the
Division of European and American Art, Harvard Art Museums

*Susan Anderson*
Curatorial Research Associate for Dutch and Flemish Drawings in
the Division of European and American Art, Harvard Art Museums
Private Curator, Maida and George Abrams Collection

# INTRODUCTION
*Susan Anderson*

Fig. 1 The Dutch Republic, Southern Netherlands, and surrounding lands, c. 1648.



Our current moment calls for careful attention to the complex intersections between land and humanity. We struggle, more urgently than ever, to balance our consumption of the earth's resources with its preservation. Participation in the digital realm has dramatically shifted perceptions of distance, as information becomes available and people come together at speeds previously unimaginable. And for many, the COVID-19 pandemic has inspired renewed reflection on the importance of nature in our communities and daily lives, even resulting in migration toward thinly populated areas as city dwellers seek space and escape. The rural landscape—both the actual terrain and its image—has become particularly charged in this era of change and uncertainty.

Four centuries ago, the new country known as the Dutch Republic experienced a similarly intricate shift in the way citizens conceived of the land they inhabited. The Republic's protracted struggle for independence and concurrent global ambitions brought about increasing prosperity for some and remarkable technological and scientific advances that indelibly changed both the land itself and perceptions of it. These developments coincided with the highly innovative explosion of the local Dutch landscape as an artistic subject, in which drawing played a fundamental role. The landscape imagery produced across media in this period constituted a distinctly modern genre that has informed many subsequent artistic landscape practices and our understanding—even today—of the natural and built environment as interpreted through visual art. The combined holdings of Dutch landscape drawings in the Harvard Art Museums and the Maida and George Abrams Collection offer an extraordinary opportunity to consider, through the lens of our present moment and varied scholarly discourses, the multiple ways these works navigate intersections, or crossroads—the places where notions of local identity meet in a world of immigration, emigration, and global expansion; where human engineering and nature collide; where traditions evolve through artistic exchange and technical innovations; and where object confronts beholder.

I offer a few words here to further situate these themes in time and place. In the mid-sixteenth century, the Low Countries comprised an area that includes roughly the contemporary unified borders of the Netherlands, Belgium, and Luxembourg. Its economic and cultural heart was Antwerp, located along the Scheldt River in what was then the duchy of Brabant (now the province of Antwerp, in the historically broader Flemish region of Belgium). Tensions with the ruling Hapsburg king Philip II of

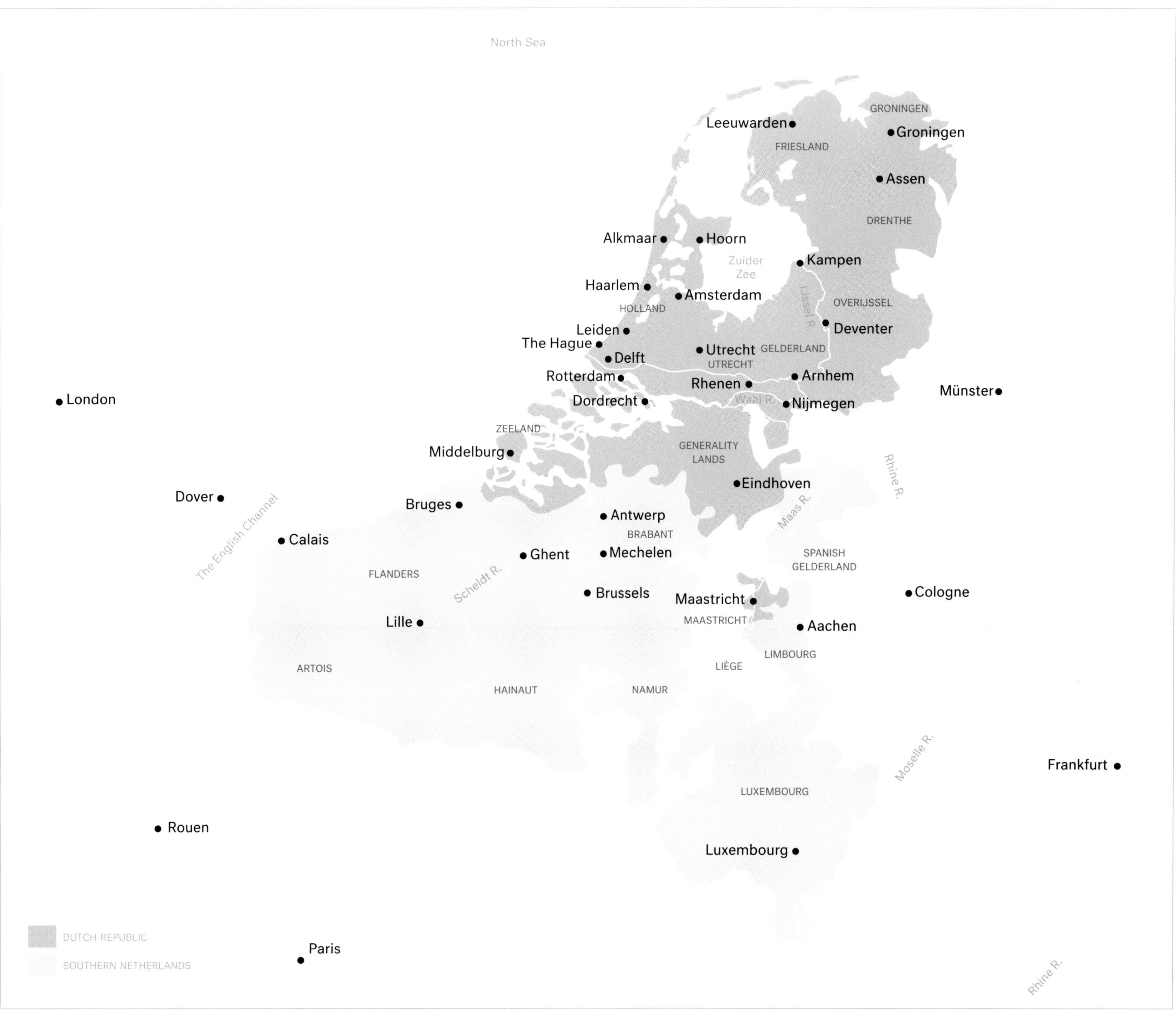

North Sea
GRONINGEN
Leeuwarden
Groningen
FRIESLAND
Assen
DRENTHE
Alkmaar
Hoorn
Zuider Zee
Kampen
Haarlem
Amsterdam
IJssel R.
OVERIJSSEL
HOLLAND
Leiden
Deventer
The Hague
Utrecht
GELDERLAND
Delft
UTRECHT
Rotterdam
Arnhem
Rhenen
Münster
London
Dordrecht
Waal R.
Nijmegen
ZEELAND
GENERALITY LANDS
Middelburg
Rhine R.
Eindhoven
Dover
Bruges
The English Channel
Antwerp
Maas R.
BRABANT
Calais
SPANISH GELDERLAND
Ghent
Mechelen
FLANDERS
Scheldt R.
Cologne
Brussels
Maastricht
MAASTRICHT
Lille
Aachen
LIMBOURG
ARTOIS
LIÈGE
HAINAUT
NAMUR
Moselle R.
Frankfurt
LUXEMBOURG
Rouen
Luxembourg
DUTCH REPUBLIC
SOUTHERN NETHERLANDS
Paris
Rhine R.

Fig. 2 World map (Natural Earth II projection) showing overseas colonies and trading posts held by the Dutch at various points in history. Most were established in the 17th century; in some cases, Dutch control was brief in duration, while in others it extended well into the modern era.



Spain over a host of issues, including taxation, the centralization of power, and the presence of military troops along the French border – as well as the rising Protestant population – eventually incited the Dutch Revolt, also known as the Eighty Years' War (1568–1648). This period of conflict, paused during the Twelve Years' Truce (1609–21), led to the Northern Netherlands' independence, declared through the Act of Abjuration in 1581, recognized by the Spanish in 1609, and made official by the Treaty of Münster in 1648. The United Provinces, as the Dutch Republic was also known, organized an early form of independent federal government, with each province sending representation to a governing body called the States General, which shared power with a succession of stadtholders, an elected (but in practice inherited) position of noble provincial and ultimately national leadership. In addition to the seven represented provinces – Gelderland, Holland, Zeeland, Utrecht, Friesland, Overijssel, and Groningen – the Dutch Republic also encompassed Drenthe and the Generality Lands, which were governed directly by the States General. The combined landmass is approximate to the present-day Netherlands (Fig. 1).

After the northern provinces seceded, the Catholic Spanish crown tightened its grip on the remaining southern provinces. The city of Antwerp, under siege for just over a year in 1584–85, ultimately surrendered, and its Protestant citizens were given four years to leave. The Northern Netherlands, predominantly Protestant, was the natural destination for this immense wave of immigration. Together with the Dutch blockade of the Scheldt, the massive population loss left Antwerp crippled, making way for Amsterdam to become the dominant international center for commerce and culture for decades to come. This era ended only in 1672, the Rampjaar (Disaster Year) of Louis XIV's devastating invasion. During this century, especially in the early years of independence and war, Dutch identity was a fluid and complex concept: by turns it could include or exclude those who permanently entered the Republic's borders from elsewhere, in addition to those who were born there and either stayed, traveled, or immigrated to other parts of the world.

At its height, the Republic's dominion spanned the globe (Fig. 2). Its longstanding participation in international trade, sometimes in hostile competition with the Portuguese, Spanish, and English, was at once a manifestation and enabler of Dutch power. In 1602, the States General granted a charter to the Dutch East India Company (*Verenigde Oost-Indische Compagnie*, or VOC), a trade conglomerate with governmental authority, including the ability to establish colonies and to use military force. The VOC pervaded

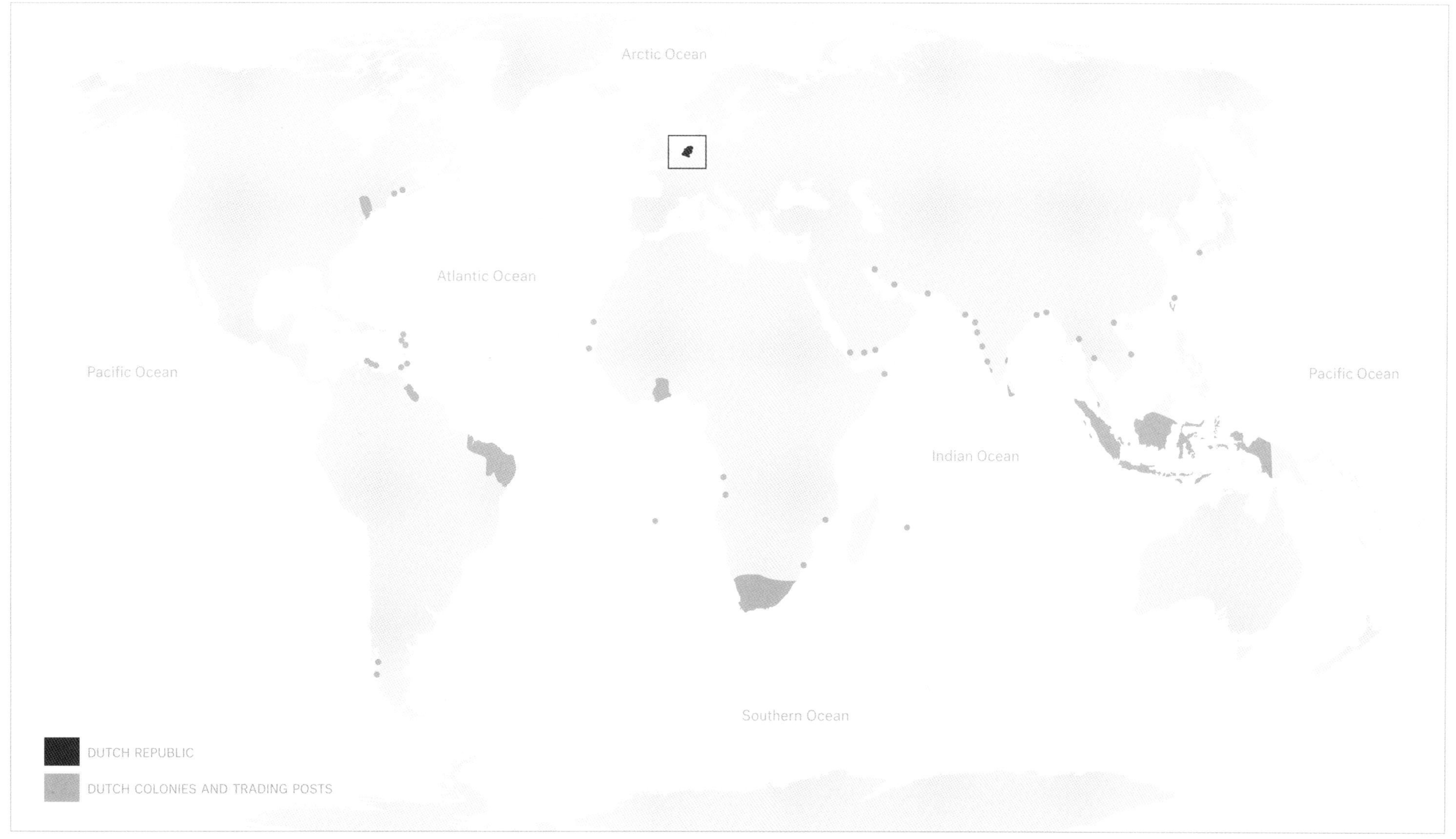


merchant maritime activity across India, the Asia-Pacific region, and southern Africa. In 1621, a charter was granted to the Dutch West India Company (*West-Indische Compagnie*, or WIC), which ran trade routes and conducted military actions throughout the Caribbean, North and South America, parts of the Pacific, and West Africa, where it played a major role in the trade of enslaved people. Combined, the two entities traded in numerous goods, including sugar, spices, coffee, tea, silk, cotton, precious metals, and porcelain, through an immense network of colonial ports, fortresses, and plantations that relied on slavery for its financial success. The resulting knowledge and goods brought back by their ships contributed greatly to the newfound worldliness and wealth in the Republic. The means were condemned by some even in the seventeenth century, but ultimately were accepted as economically and even morally justified amid lasting notions of European superiority.

These developments and frictions provided context for the groundswell of Dutch landscape representations, especially in light of the frequent travel inherent in colonial, European, and domestic politics and commerce and the often dissonant juxtaposition of unfamiliar places and home. Although few in number, artists accompanied their fellow countrymen on voyages throughout the colonized world, from South America to India. Landscape drawings of these far-off places rarely survive, but depictions of the colonies, often based on narrative accounts, circulated in print, intermingling with those of the local scenery in their conception and dissemination. Through the global reach of the Republic, advances in cartography, both technical and aesthetic, progressed concurrently with developments in pictorial landscape, suggesting a broader desire to understand terrain in both a physical and visual sense. Also of great significance to the development of landscape were the legions of Dutch artists who traveled elsewhere on the European continent, such as the Southern Netherlands, France, Germany, Bohemia, England, Scandinavia, and across the Alps to the Italian peninsula. Contact with other European lands and artists, especially, resulted in a continuing exchange of ideas that shaped the ways in which Dutch artists represented landscape, domestic and foreign.

More regularly, Dutch artists traveled within their own country. On the whole, the "local" Dutch landscape can be loosely defined as the Republic's topographically varied regions, each reflecting differing levels of cultivation, and the frequently recognizable structures and features that, taken together, encapsulated the country. Although some individual sites surely evoked a sense of national pride—the ruins of Brederode Castle, for example, as a reminder of victory over Spanish oppression—the landscape subjects specified in any one work gesture much more pointedly to provincial or civic regions and to their own formation of distinct and more narrowly defined local identity. Even generic scenes of dunes or the linen industry resonate with the area around Haarlem, for instance, and topographical cityscapes, each with its own unique architectural structures and skyline, primarily speak to the depicted municipality.

Although artists were active throughout the Republic, the artistic hub lay in a very specific locale today called the Randstad, a densely populated and economically powerful region consisting of major cities (most notably Amsterdam, Haarlem, Leiden, The Hague, Rotterdam, Delft, Dordrecht, and Utrecht) and the surrounding areas, largely in the historical province of Holland, which together form a ring around an agricultural center. The region's countryside provided ample inspiration to its artists as they traveled throughout it with relative ease, and the works that ultimately resulted from these wanderings form the majority of landscape production representing vernacular subjects. To be sure, many artists traversed the country to capture its beauty and distinctive regional character, such as the varied terrain and cities of the Lower Rhine river valley. But the lands around the Randstad's cities provided the most powerful examples of positive and negative change embodied by this new country, to which its artists responded with vigorous interest. By the late sixteenth and early seventeenth centuries, increasing wealth and population density were taking hold in this cultural bulwark, and with that came a dramatic expansion of cities, extensive poldering (reclamation of land from water), and the rapid conversion of much of the countryside to fuel urban needs, whether through tenant farmers who cultivated their land to provide foodstuffs to city dwellers, or at the hands of more ecologically devastating industries, such as timber production. The explosion of interest in the quotidian views of one's own country, often aligned with political independence or civic pride as captured in contemporary written accounts of Dutch cities, largely took place here. Although the local landscape can refer broadly to a comprehensive and collective view of the lands of the Dutch Republic, or more specifically to a small but recognizable site anywhere within its borders, in the surviving artistic output, the Dutch local landscape is mostly represented by depictions of this region's countryside.

Drawing played a key generative and creative role throughout the development of the Dutch landscape as a genre and served as the primary means through which early modern Dutch artists, inspired by their physical environment and by each other, established new conventions for landscape representations that resonated with their increasingly worldly audience. The portability of its varied media allowed artists to engage directly with their outdoor surroundings through observed sketches made en plein air – not a new practice, but one that was brought to new heights.

As the surviving visual record suggests, finished drawings made for sale blossomed into their own category of collectibles. Like prints, they were typically housed by their owners in *kunstboeken* (albums or portfolios). When consisting of landscape drawings, these assemblages could often at once form a record of the Dutch countryside and lands beyond through documentary or topographical sheets, inspire armchair travel or mixed reflections on local achievements, identity, and events, and be admired as stunning examples of draftsmanship and artistry. Professional and amateur draftsmen alike rewarded their buyers with highly detailed, varied, and innovative technical accomplishments not reproducible in other media. The preservation of drawings as one-of-a-kind objects to be viewed purposefully by their owner and invited guests fostered an intimate experience of close looking, conversation, and kinship, as it does today. This sense of unique discovery unfolds on the following pages, where contributors to this volume offer fresh reflections on the phenomenon that was landscape drawing in the Dutch Republic.

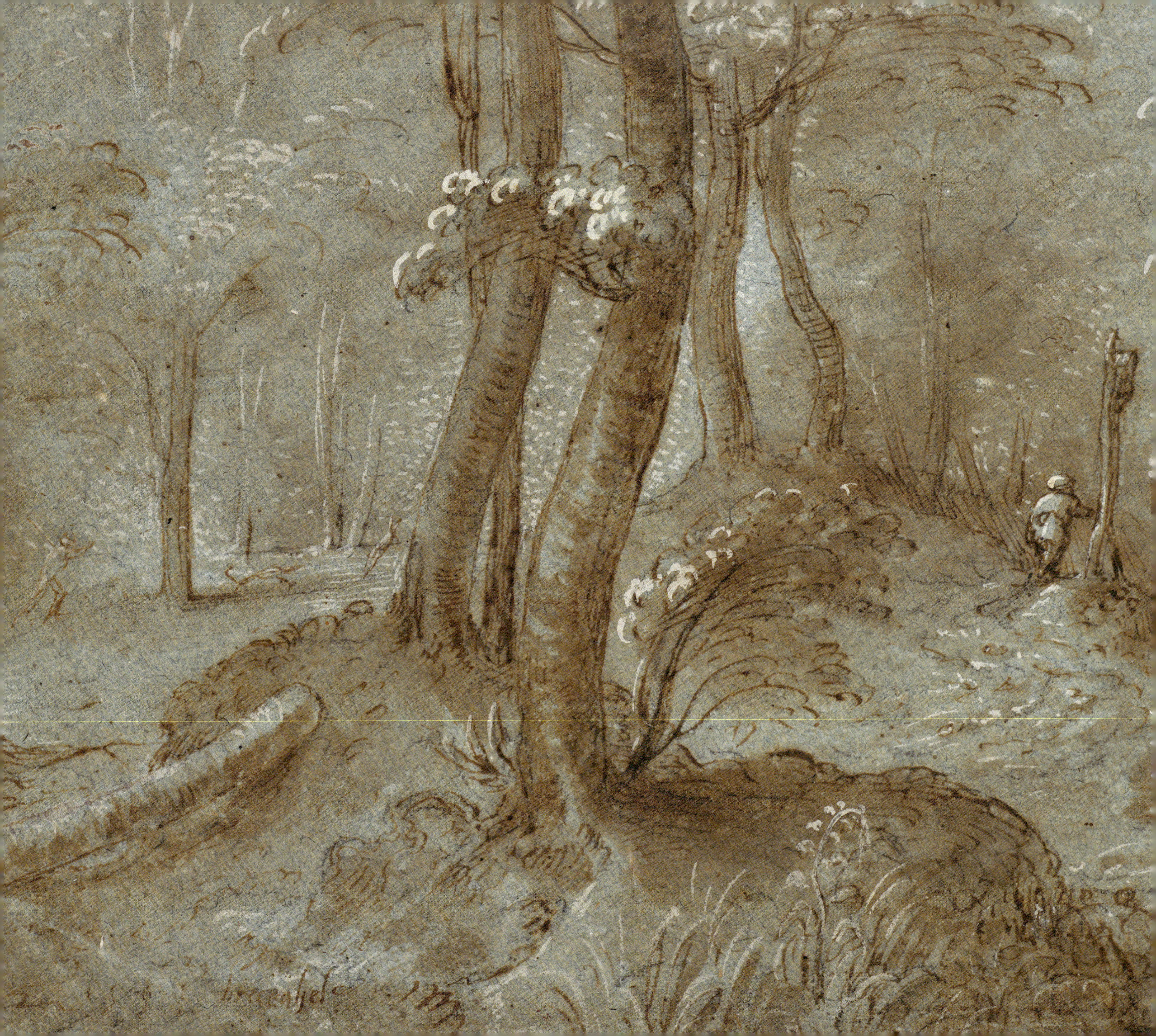

# Pieter Bruegel the Elder
# *Wooded Landscape with a Distant View toward the Sea*, 1554

*On his travels he drew many views from life so that it is said that when he was in the Alps he swallowed all those mountains and rocks which, upon returning home, he spat out again onto canvases and panels, so faithfully was he able, in this respect and others, to follow Nature.*

—Karel van Mander, *Lives of the Illustrious Netherlandish and German Painters* (1604)

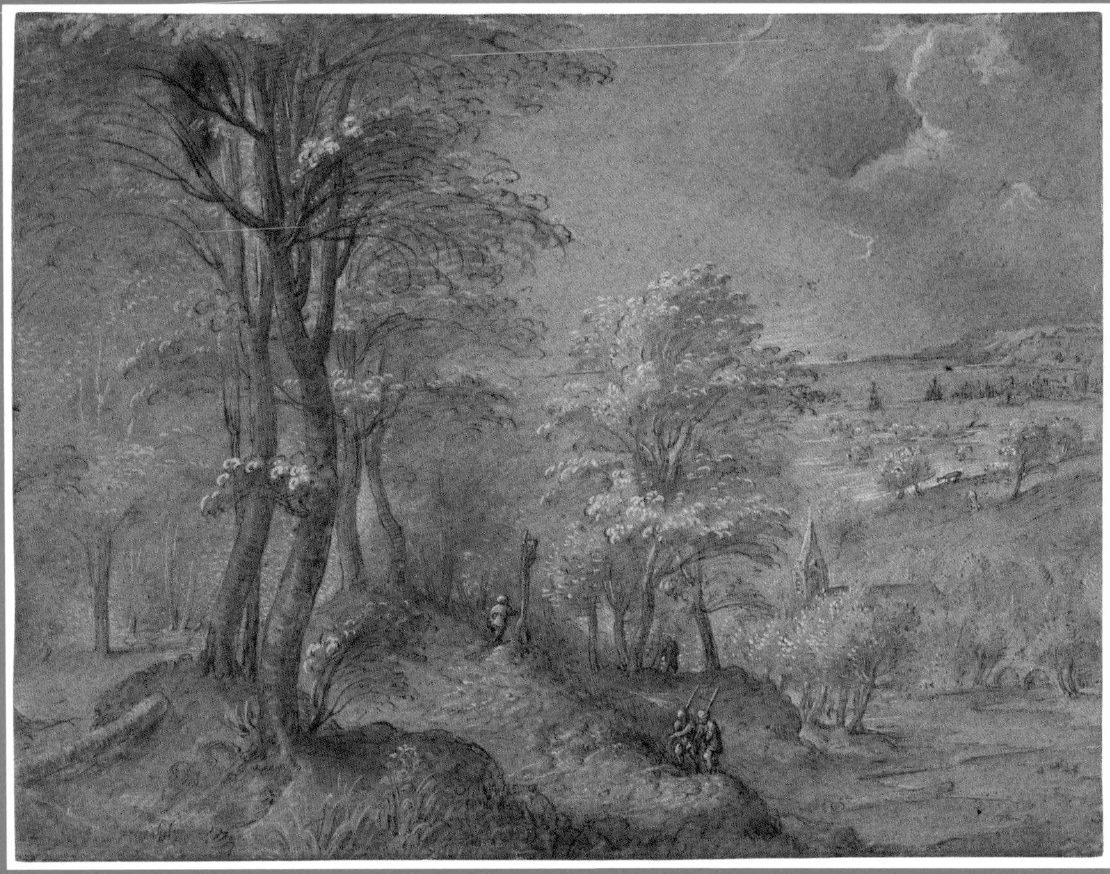

Fig. A Pieter Bruegel the Elder, *Wooded Landscape with a Distant View toward the Sea*, 1554. See p. 229 for full information.

This sheet is by one of the Netherlandish progenitors of the Dutch landscape tradition: Pieter Bruegel the Elder (1526/30–1569). Drawn during the artist's sojourn to Italy in 1552–54, it captures the edge of a rolling woodland, where the forest yields to reveal a church, fields, and a distant harbor below the high vantage point that the viewer shares with the travelers in the foreground. Arguably the most important Netherlandish artist of the sixteenth century, Bruegel – and his encounters with the Italian countryside, especially as relayed in drawings – would have an enduring impact upon his return home to Antwerp, as artist-biographer Karel van Mander (1548–1606) so eloquently observed.

Informing Bruegel's representations of his direct experiences with nature were pictorial techniques from the earlier Flemish landscape tradition (here in the form of the expansive depiction of space receding to a high horizon) and drawings and prints by contemporary Venetian artists, including Titian (c. 1488–1576) and Domenico Campagnola (c. 1500–1564), whose bending, fluidly executed trees and extensive foliage Bruegel incorporated into this sheet. Common to both traditions is the use of blue paper, prepared or dyed, to form a striking mid-tone for the brown ink and white opaque watercolor. Although no print is known to have been made after this drawing, others were published after similarly expansive views by Bruegel and proliferated his version of landscape based on observation – though often, as in this sheet, reimagined.

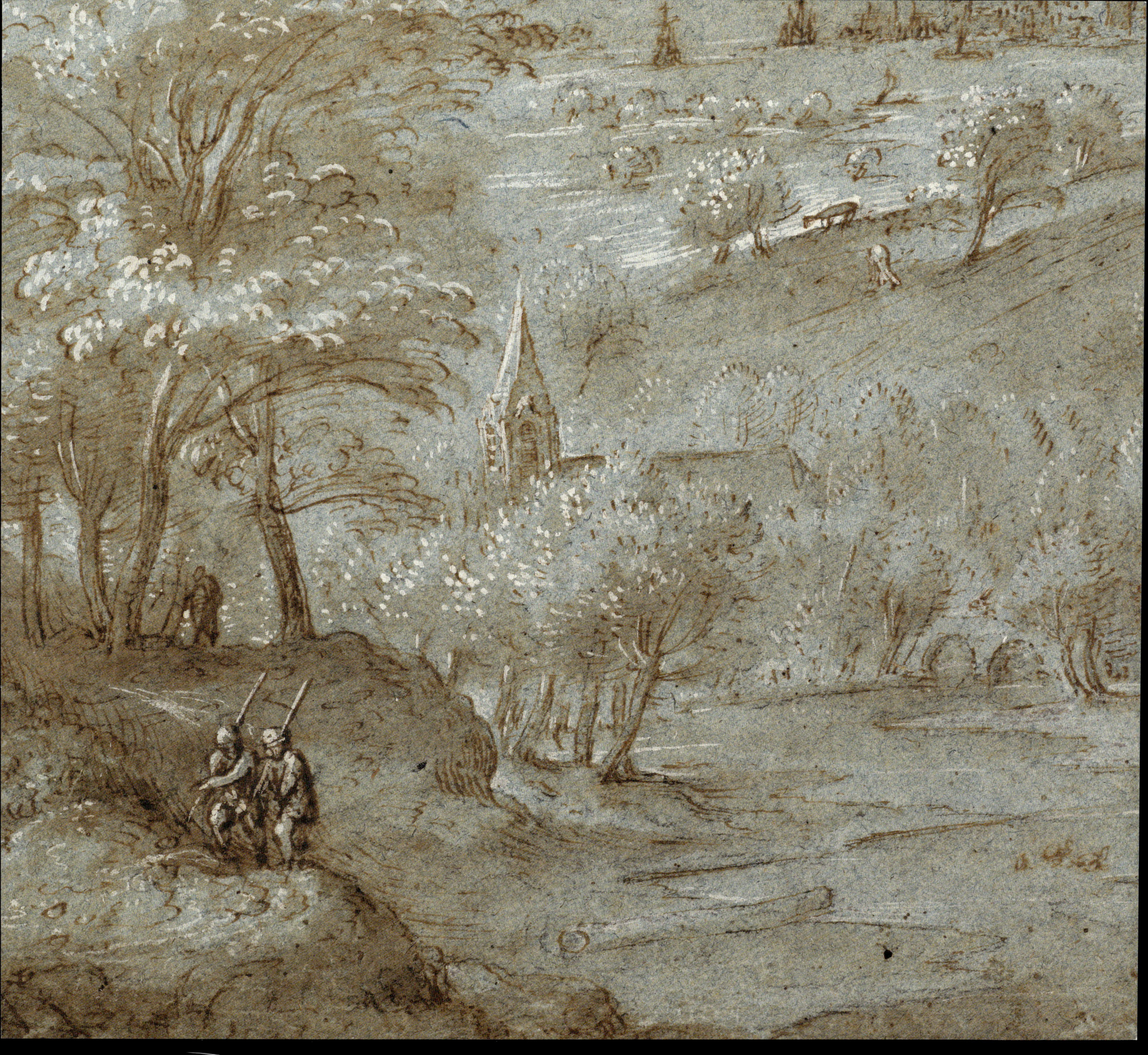

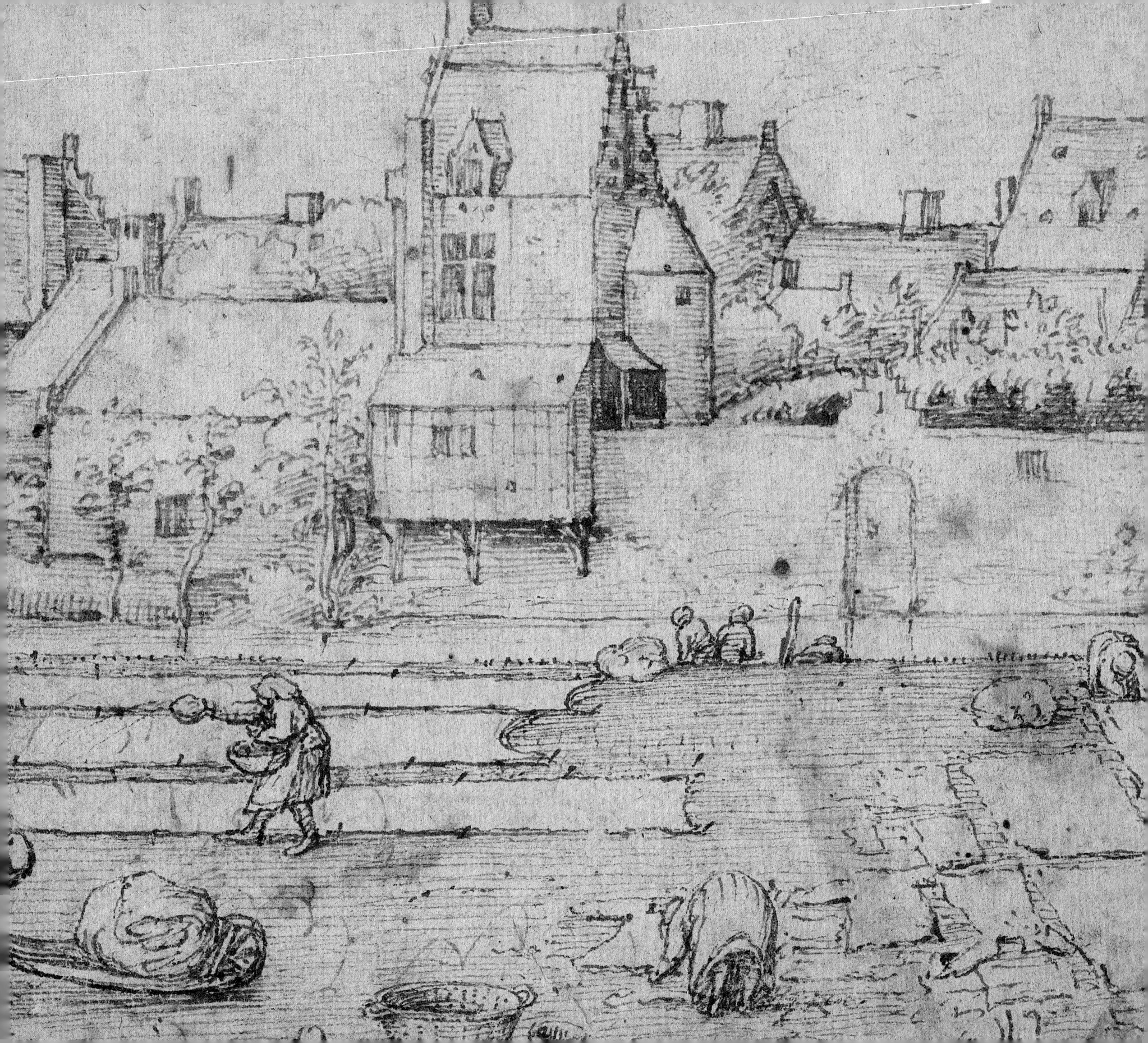

Master of the Small Landscapes
*Women Bleaching Linen near a Walled Town*, c. 1560

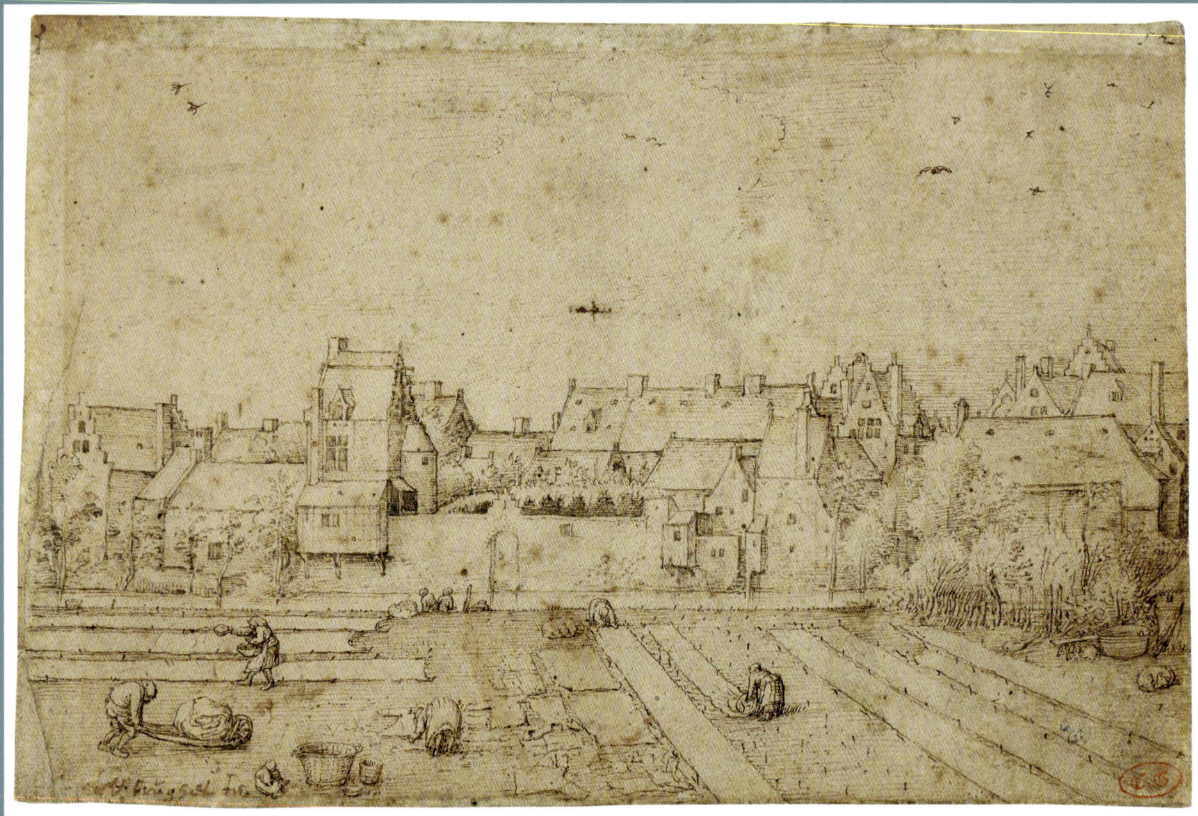

Fig. B Master of the Small Landscapes, *Women Bleaching Linen near a Walled Town*, c. 1560. See p. 230 for full information.

This scene of manual labor belongs to a group of drawings, similar in handling and size, that definitively mark the artistic turn away from imaginary landscapes to the prevailing and persistent taste for the distinctly Flemish countryside. Given to the anonymous artist known as the Master of the Small Landscapes, this group of works relates to a series of forty-four influential prints published by Hieronymus Cock (1510–1570) in Antwerp in two suites, one in 1559 and the other in 1561. The title page of the series describes them as mostly drawn from life in the environs of Antwerp.

Although *Women Bleaching* is not a direct model for any of the prints, as twelve of the drawings are, its two different inks are common throughout the group. The upper portion, rendered in a light-brown ink, depicts vernacular, albeit unidentified, architecture placed close to the viewer on a flat, low horizon, whereas the more generic scene of linen bleaching – a popular local industry – in the lower portion appears in a darker brown ink. The presence of two inks suggests two different campaigns, likely done at two different times. Given the inscription on the print series' title page, the detailed upper portion of the drawing may have been drawn from observation, and the lower portion, less specific in its rendering, in the studio. After the Dutch Republic was formed and Antwerp ceased to be the dominant artistic center in the late sixteenth century, Dutch artists would adapt these rustic depictions by drawing observed motifs in their own surroundings, many of which were transformed into print series, to widely popular effect.

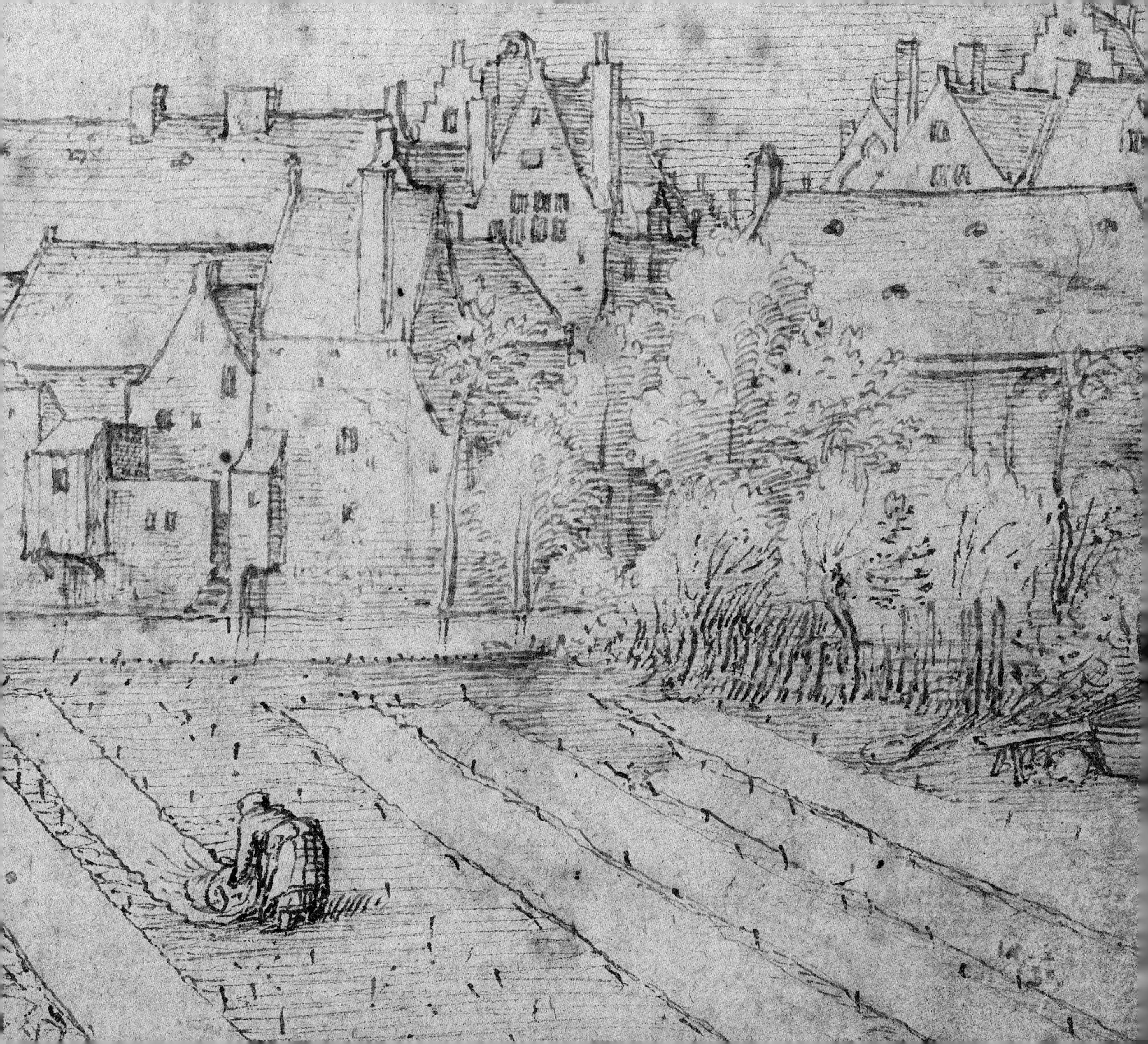

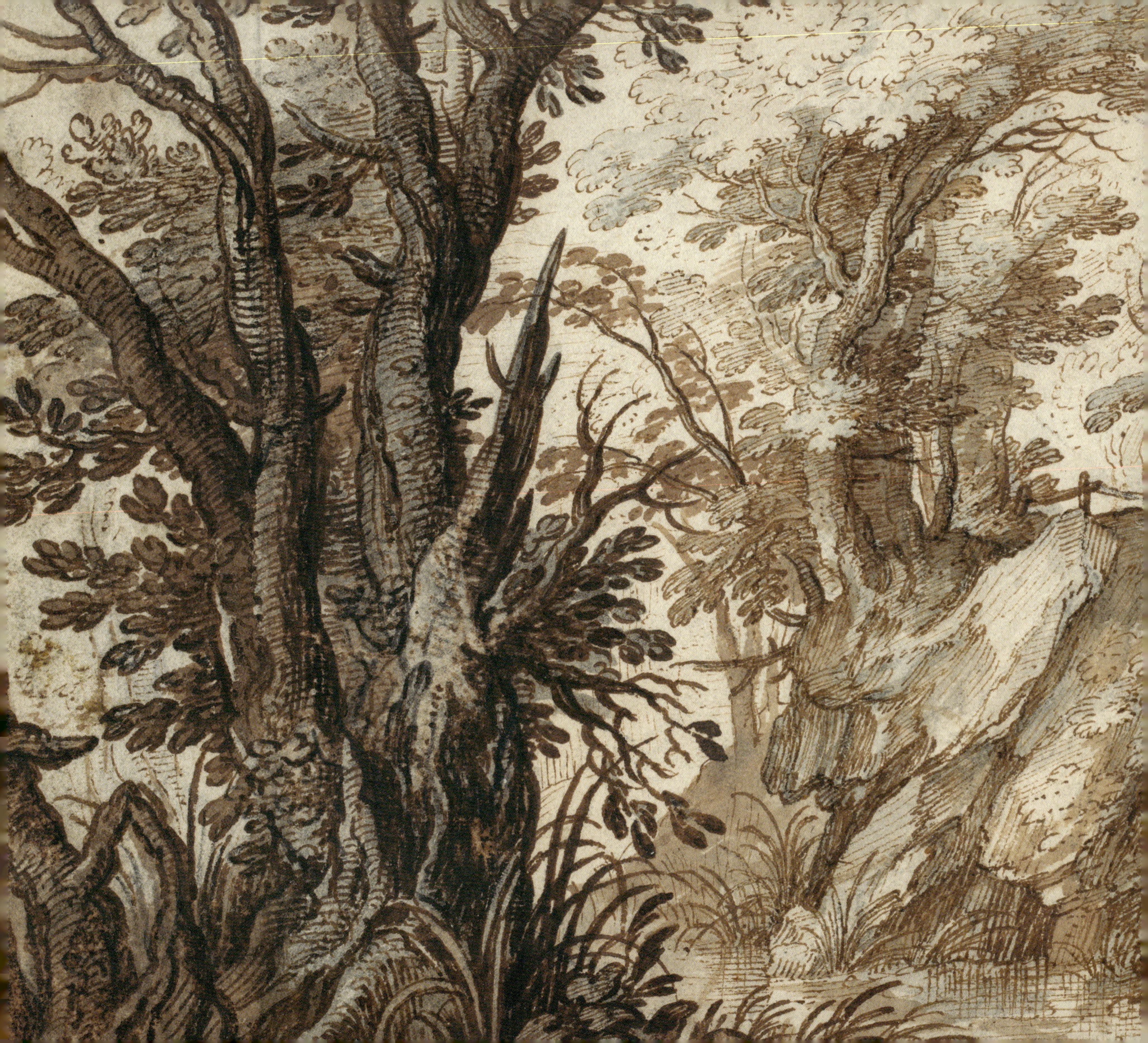

Paul Bril
*Wooded Landscape with Travelers,*
1600

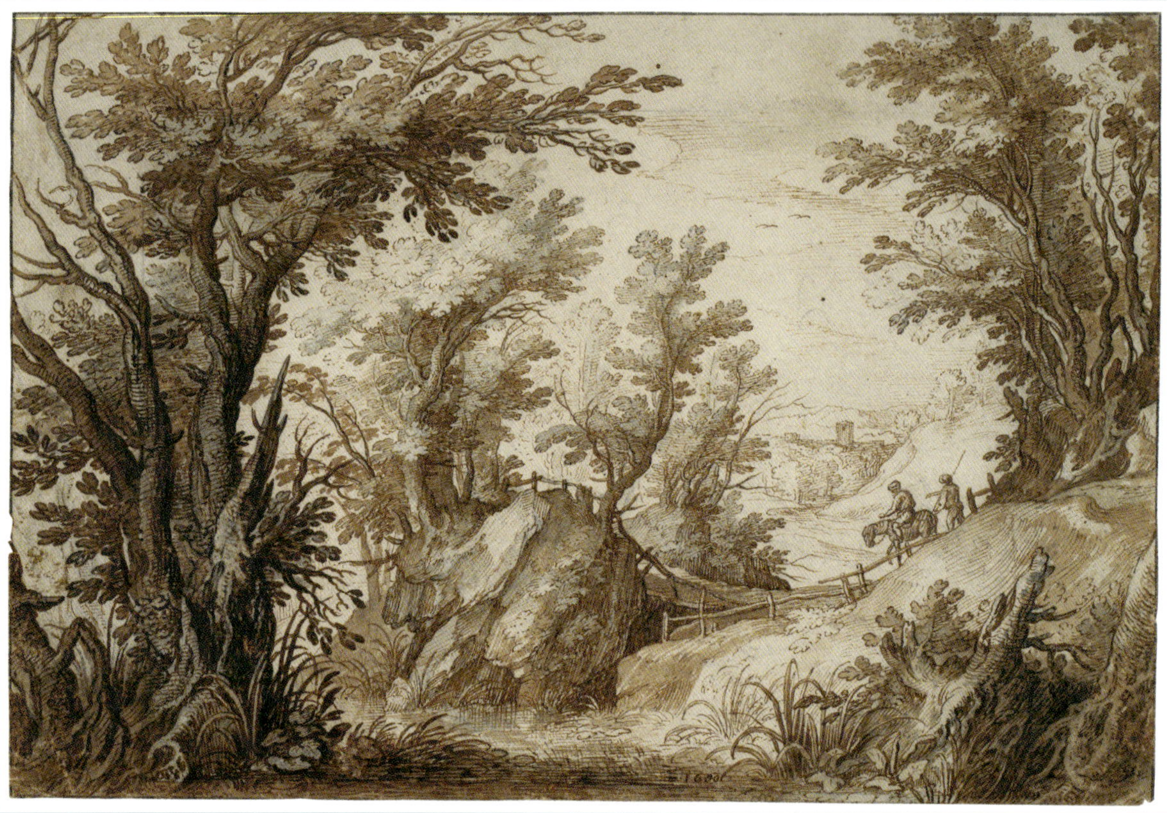

Fig. C Paul Bril, *Wooded Landscape with Travelers*, 1600. See p. 229 for full information.

In this autonomous drawing of an imagined wooded landscape, Paul Bril (1553/54–1626) depicts an encounter between humankind and nature: two figures traverse a fenced road that leads them through established stands of trees. Bril devised a distinctive means to create spatial recession by incorporating alternating passages of light and dark. The tree in the left foreground is the darkest, most brooding element, backlit by a beam of sunlight that illuminates the uppermost branches of a separate cluster of trees, an embankment, and a stone outcrop, which in turn cast a shadow on the lower arboreal and rocky elements and trail—and so on to an opening that reveals a village and, even farther in the distance, mountains.

Born and trained in Antwerp, Bril spent the majority of his highly successful career in Rome. Visits from many of his fellow northerners situated him at the heart of multiple artistic exchanges over the years, most notably with Cornelis van Poelenburch (c. 1586–1667) and Bartholomeus Breenbergh (see p. 125), who are often credited as the founders of the Dutch Italianate movement. Jan Brueghel the Elder (1568–1625), son of Pieter Bruegel the Elder (1526/30–1569), spent time with Bril in the early 1590s and shared with him the woodland scenes drawn by his father. *Wooded Landscape with Travelers* demonstrates Bril's admiration for these works as well as for the landscapes by his Italian contemporaries, particularly in its subject matter and sinuous, towering trees. Although Bril's woodland drawings are intimately entwined with the Italian *campagna*, we find echoes of his compositional strategies and approach to nature in later representations of the distinctly Dutch countryside.

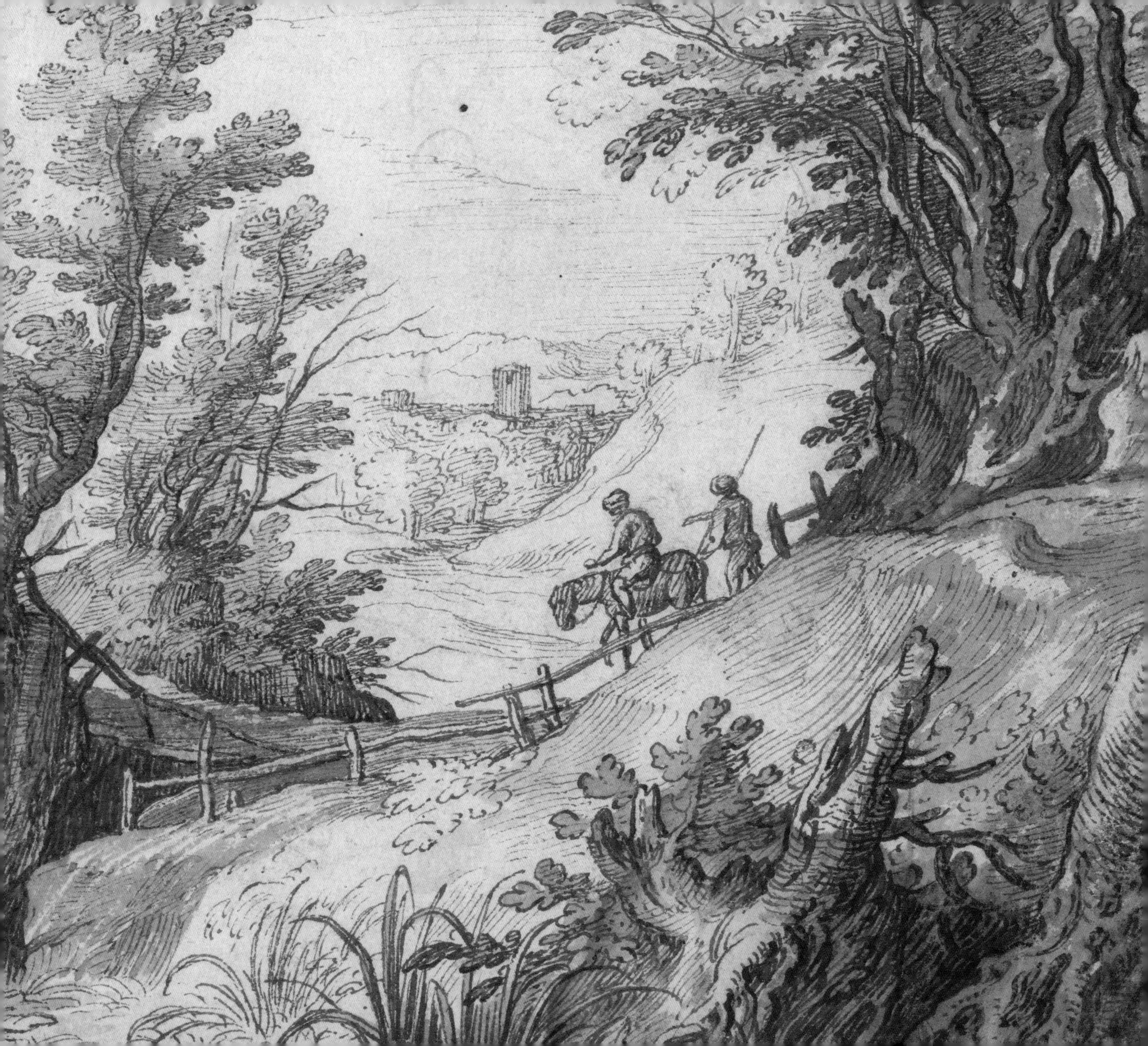

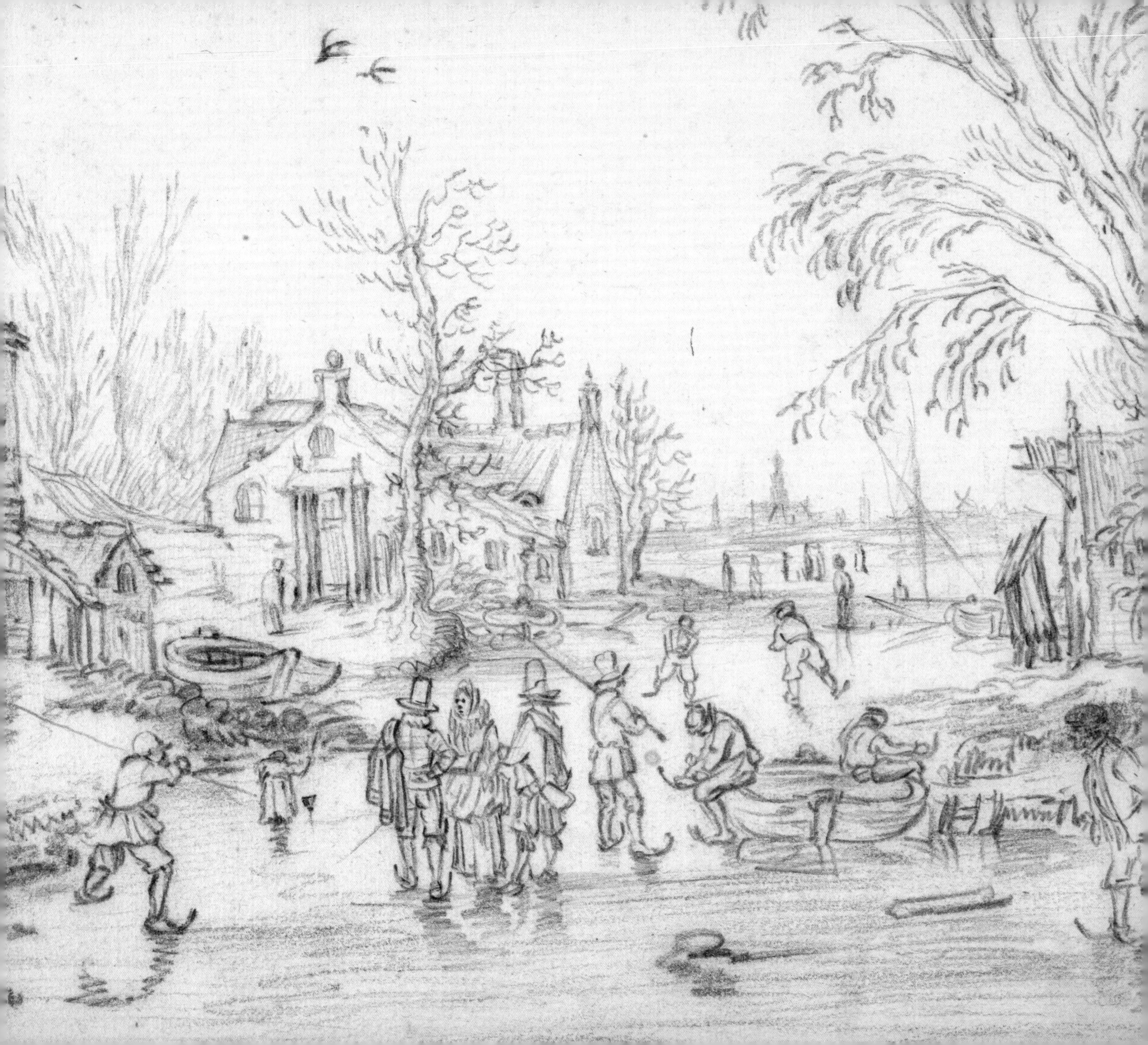

ON THE SPOT

# THE APPEAL OF THE LOCAL

*Yvonne Bleyerveld*

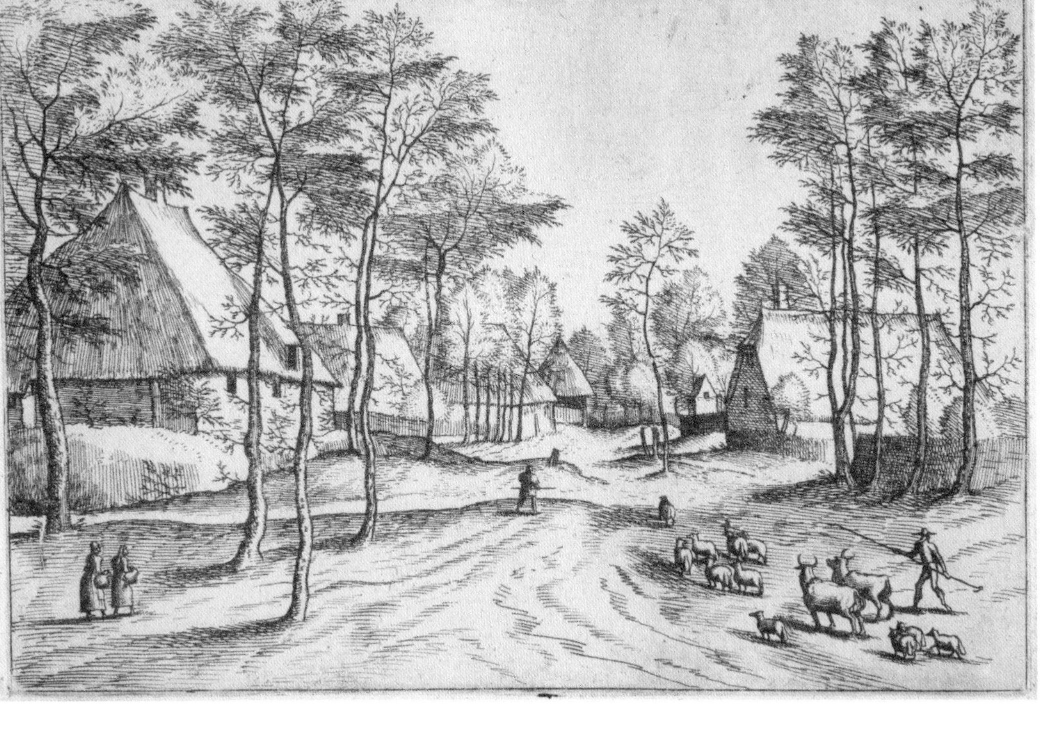



The early decades of the seventeenth century saw fast-growing interest in the depiction of one's own country, particularly in the Northern Netherlands. Dunes and beaches, rivers and dikes, forests and fields, villages and towns—all appealed to the artists of this period, who went outdoors to draw their hometowns, the local countryside, and sites around the region. They made studies from life (*naer het leven*) as an artistic exercise, but also to gather motifs or to devise whole compositions for paintings, prints, and finished drawings intended for sale.[1] Drawings of naturalistic Dutch landscapes, sometimes even with identifiable villages and cities in the background, became popular collector's items.[2] Such landscapes and city profiles were also popular in prints and as decorations in the margins of topographical maps.[3] The image of the characteristic Dutch landscape became increasingly popular in painting as well, especially among artists from Haarlem and Amsterdam.

This appetite for the local environment meant, in large part, a break with sixteenth-century tradition. Earlier artists mainly depicted imaginary and idealized landscapes with panoramic views, capricious rock formations, winding rivers, and gnarled trees. After 1600, these overtly fictional landscapes—which often served as settings for stories from the Bible or classical mythology—became largely a thing of the past.

Sketching on paper en plein air was no doubt a common activity in the seventeenth century. Art theorists encouraged draftsmen to include it in their professional practice, to improve skills in depicting landscape while enjoying the change of scenery afforded by outdoor excursions. Painter and theorist Karel van Mander (1548–1606), for one, advised young artists to go outside on a regular basis: when physically and mentally tired of working in the studio, leave early at dawn, he urged, to observe natural phenomena and draw in nature for relaxation. After all, he wrote, the bow cannot always be tense.[4] Roughly sixty years later, Middelburg bookseller and author Willem Goeree (1635–1711) likewise encouraged artists to draw outdoors. In his 1668 publication *Inleydinge tot de Al-ghemeene Teycken-Konst*—the most important treatise on drawing of its time—he advised artists to visit the countryside for a few days at least two or three times a year in order to record nature in different seasons, to study in a more enjoyable setting, and again, to recharge.[5]

In this essay, I trace the footsteps of seventeenth-century draftsmen of the Dutch landscape, focusing on the practice and tradition

Fig. 1 Joannes van Doetecum or Lucas van Doetecum, after the Master of the Small Landscapes, *Village Street, Cattle, Sheep, and Herdsman in the Foreground*, 1559–61. Etching, 13.4 × 19.7 cm. Royal Library of Belgium, Brussels, S.IV 2147.

Fig. 2 Hans Bol, *View from a Bridge near Delfgauw* (verso, right half), c. 1583–84. Silverpoint on two conjoined sheets of ivory-colored prepared paper, overall: 12.8 × 40.6 cm. The British Museum, London, 1895,0915.983.

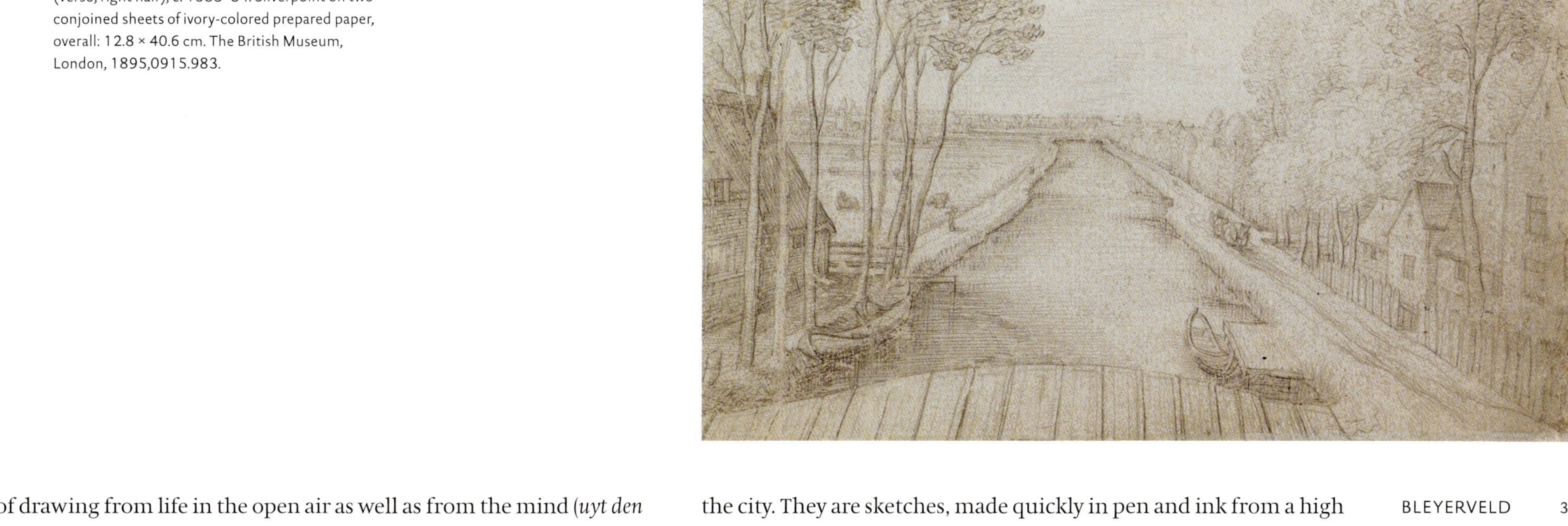



of drawing from life in the open air as well as from the mind (*uyt den gheest*) in the studio. I also examine the often blurry line between the two categories, and the function of seventeenth-century landscape drawings in general, from working sketches to collectors' items.

## DRAWING OUTDOORS IN THE SIXTEENTH CENTURY

By the sixteenth century, Netherlandish artists were recording their observations on paper in the open air. Some traveled to Italy to collect study material, such as Maarten van Heemskerck (1498–1574), who produced many drawings of ancient ruins and sculptures during his four-year stay in Rome.[6] On his journey to the south, Pieter Bruegel the Elder (1526/30–1569) made drawings of landscapes in the Alps and Italy (see p. 24, Fig. A).[7] Yet artists back home in the Netherlands were also drawing outdoors. In his *Schilder-Boeck* (1604), Van Mander tells us that Jan van Scorel (1495–1562) would go to the forest outside his hometown of Haarlem on Sundays and public holidays to copy the trees in color.[8] The Amsterdam painter and printmaker Cornelis Anthonisz. (c. 1505–1553) left a sketchbook with drawings of, among other things, buildings, mills, and gates in the city. They are sketches, made quickly in pen and ink from a high vantage point, possibly a church tower or the roof of a house. These on-the-spot observations were intended as an exercise, but also as a means of collecting motifs that Anthonisz. would later apply to his 1538 painted map of Amsterdam from a bird's-eye view.[9]

Just as likely to work outside was the unidentified artist known as the Master of the Small Landscapes, active in Antwerp around 1555–60. A group of Flemish townscapes attributed to him gives the impression that they were drawn on the spot (see p. 28, Fig. B).[10] He was also designer of a series of prints of forty-four landscapes etched by brothers Joannes (1528/32–1605) and Lucas (active 1554–1579/89) van Doetecum and published by Hieronymus Cock in two sets, one in 1559, the other in 1561.[11] These etchings, like the Master's drawings, show naturalistic views of villages and farms surrounded by trees and hedgerows and fields with farmers, shepherds, and cattle (Fig. 1). According to the title page, the series was based on drawings from life of places close to Antwerp.[12] Long in demand, it was reprinted three times in the seventeenth century.[13] The wide distribution of these prints no doubt inspired later artists to depict Dutch landscapes and village views.[14]

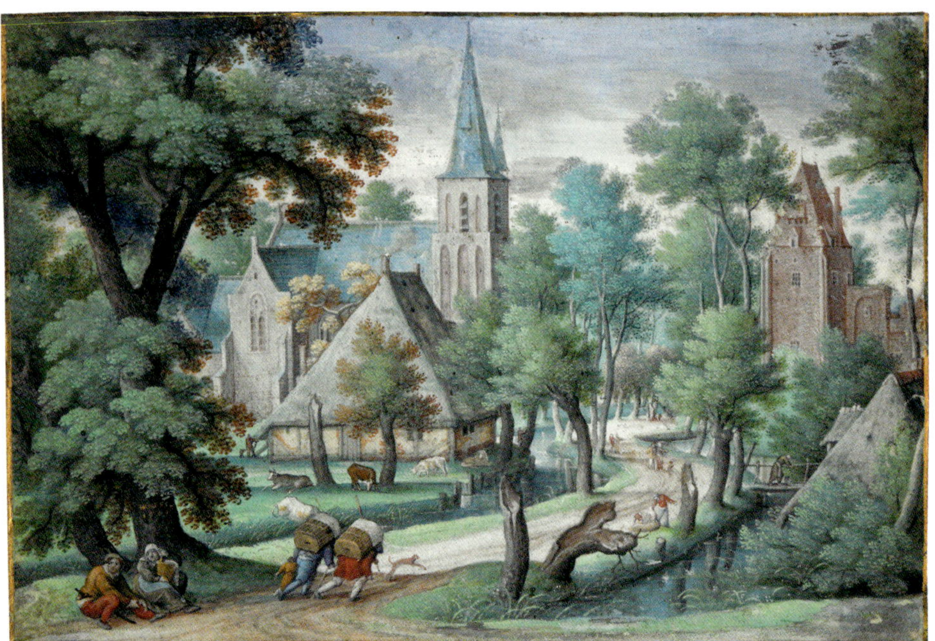

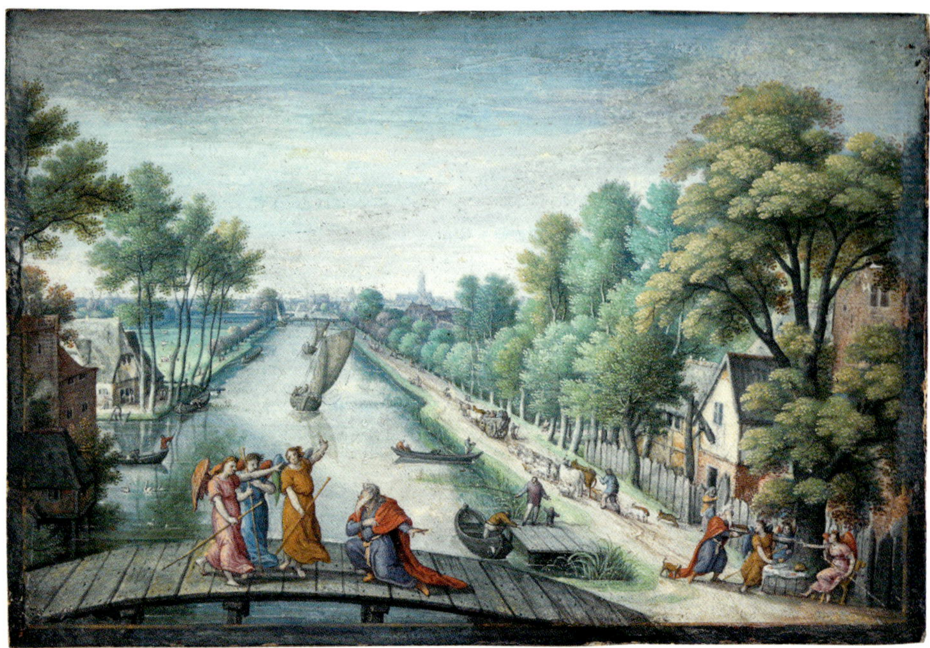



Hans Bol (1534–1593), too, brought his drawing materials outside. He was born in Mechelen and moved to Antwerp in 1572, where he specialized in landscapes meticulously painted in opaque watercolor on paper or parchment.[15] In 1584, with the threat of war looming, Bol fled to the Northern Netherlands as part of a large wave of Flemish immigration. After spending time in Bergen op Zoom, Dordrecht, and Delft, he settled in Amsterdam.[16] In and around the places he stayed, he made precise topographical drawings from life intended as working material or as independent creations.[17] For example, a sketch Bol made on the spot, now in the British Museum, depicts the Pijnacker canal in the hamlet of Delfgauw (Fig. 2). This drawing served as the basis for a watercolor that he made in 1589 and that was subsequently divided into two halves, now reunited in the collection of the Harvard Art Museums (Figs. 3–4). In the right half, the Pijnacker canal serves as the backdrop for Abraham's meeting with the three angels who prophesy the birth of Isaac (Genesis 18:1–19).[18] The left half, meanwhile, depicts an imaginary village with a road winding through it. That the two watercolors were originally one was revealed in 2014, upon the discovery of a large pen and ink drawing that presents the two landscapes – the Pijnacker canal and the imaginary townscape – as one continuous composition.[19] Bol thus combined the sixteenth-century tradition of including biblical scenes with the budding interest in naturalistic landscapes.

## SEVENTEENTH-CENTURY PIONEERS

The first native Dutch artist from whom drawings from life of the local landscape are known is the Haarlem draftsman, printmaker, and painter Hendrick Goltzius (1558–1617). Three of his dune landscapes have been identified; two are dated 1603, and all are drawn from atop a high dune somewhere in the vicinity of his hometown (Fig. 5).[20] Goltzius depicted a vast landscape in finely drawn pen lines, with farms, haystacks, and groves here and there and an almost flat horizon. This marked a turn from the imaginary landscapes the artist had drawn in the 1590s. A potential explanation for this shift can be found in a passage from Goltzius's biography by close colleague Karel van Mander. Evidently, the artist went for a long walk each day to combat his poor health.[21] Perhaps during these walks Goltzius was inspired by the beauty of the Dutch landscape.

Van Mander also tells us that Goltzius's contemporary Abraham Bloemaert (1566–1651) ventured outside to draw the

Fig. 3 Hans Bol, *The Outskirts of a Village with Peasants,* 1589. See p. 228 for full information.

Fig. 4 Hans Bol, *Abraham and the Angels,* 1589. See p. 228 for full information.



farms, fields, and trees in and around his hometown of Utrecht.[22] Indeed, we know of many drawings by Bloemaert with farms, barns, haystacks, locks, and trees that were created either on the spot or on the basis of plein air sketches (see p. 128). He used them to develop a stock of motifs for his paintings and later had them reproduced in print as well.[23]

Groundbreaking for the time was the work of Amsterdam draftsman, printmaker, and publisher Claes Jansz. Visscher (1587–1652), one of the first to specialize in views of the towns, villages, and rural scenery of the Northern Netherlands. He made, for example, a group of drawings of places near Haarlem and Amsterdam, which can sometimes be identified by inscriptions.[24] Visscher also inscribed some of these drawings with the year 1607 or 1608, a time frame that can be applied to the entire group, including a view of Houtewael, on the eastern outskirts of Amsterdam and a popular place for residents of the city to get their milk and cream (see p. 58, Fig. D).[25] In fast zigzags and parallel vertical lines, he recorded the farmhouses there along the Diemerdijk; the inn at the middle of the scene can be recognized by its sign.[26] Later in the century, other artists would also make drawings of the village before it was swallowed up by the expansion of Amsterdam in the 1660s.[27]

Some of these drawings were used by Visscher as designs for his printed series *Plaisante Plaetsen* (Pleasant Places), comprising a title page and eleven views of sites around Haarlem. This series was enormously influential in the formulation of a "realistic" vision of the Dutch landscape.[28] The artist issued the series shortly after he had established himself as an independent publisher in 1611, with a specialty in topographical prints.[29] Interestingly, according to the title page, the primary audience was art lovers who did not have time to travel far (*Liefhebbers die geen tijt en hebt om veer te reijsen*). As Visscher put it, the landscapes offered simple amusement without having to leave one's armchair.[30] He must have found an appealing example in the work of the Master of the Small Landscapes, having copied and published a series of twenty-three prints after that artist in 1612.[31]

Other pioneers of the Dutch landscape included Visscher's contemporaries Esaias van de Velde (1587–1630), his cousin Jan van de Velde II (1593–1641), and the Rotterdam-based Willem Buytewech (1591–1624), each of whom worked in Haarlem in the 1610s. They made etchings of the Dutch countryside featuring villages and farms, agricultural flatlands, dunes, isolated stands of trees, and frozen waterways. These works stimulated the development of

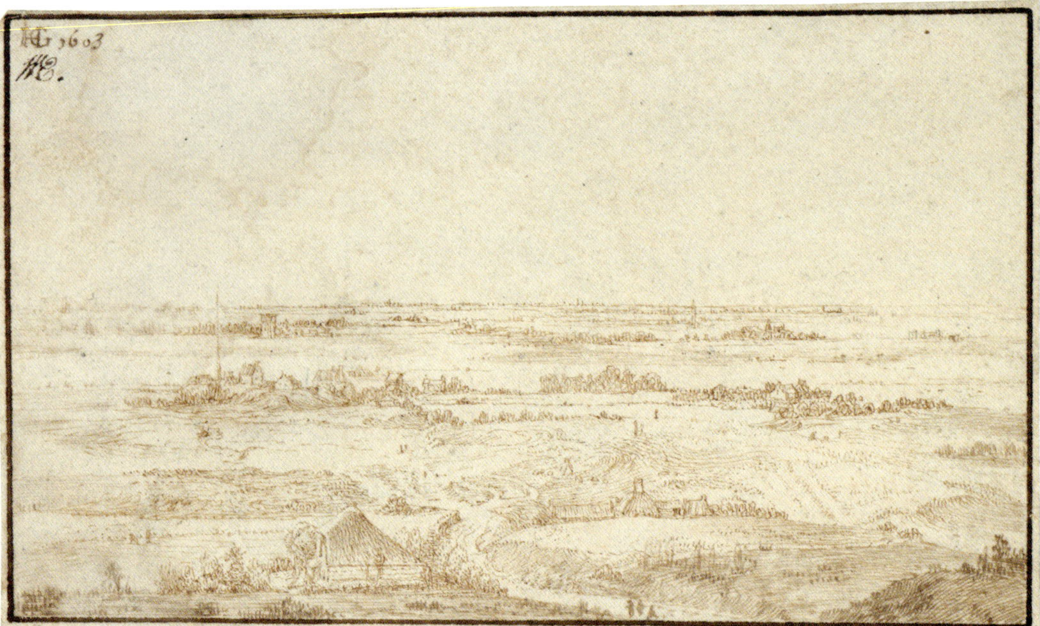

Fig. 5 Hendrick Goltzius, *Dune Landscape near Haarlem*, 1603. Pen and brown ink, framing lines in brown ink, 9.1 × 15.4 cm. Museum Boijmans Van Beuningen (former collection Koenigs), Rotterdam, H 253 (PK).



the genre in all media, helping codify pictorial conventions and shaping longstanding notions of what constitutes a typically Dutch landscape. Jan van de Velde II etched hundreds of them, mostly published in series by Visscher. The prints were often explicitly labeled "from life"—a selling point—even though Van de Velde usually composed variations on his landscapes from the basis of sketches.[32] From Esaias van de Velde about fifty etchings are known, almost all of which picture the surroundings of Haarlem.[33] In his drawings, Esaias also tended to depict characteristic Dutch scenes, such as in *Farms and a Dovecote by a Frozen River*, in which ice skaters drawn in black chalk enjoy the wintertime pursuit (Fig. 6). The motif had been around since Bruegel, but would become particularly popular beginning in the early seventeenth century.[34] In the background is the city of Haarlem, where the artist lived between 1609 and 1618 and which is recognizable by its most prominent feature, the church of Saint Bavo. Esaias van de Velde was also innovative for his use of black chalk in his landscape drawings. He inspired artists such as Pieter de Molijn (1595–1661), Jan van Goyen (1596–1656), and Jacob van Ruisdael (1628/29–1682).[35] His winter landscape drawing, likely an imaginative studio creation owing to its fanciful inclusion of two farms on either side of a frozen river, formed the basis for a second, more elaborate version in pen and gray washes, now in Berlin.[36] It is remarkable that both versions have been preserved; unfortunately, it is not known whether Van de Velde always preceded his more elaborate drawings with a sketch in black chalk.

The growing interest in local surroundings was not restricted to the visual arts. From the early seventeenth century onward, written accounts of Dutch cities also entered the market. They often included information about the history, inhabitants, culture, or economy of these cities and the neighboring countryside. The first of these accounts explored Amsterdam (1611), followed by Leiden (1614) and Haarlem (1628).[37] This was the very time that the Republic was becoming an economic and colonial world power; Dutch merchants sailed to the far reaches of the globe, establishing trading posts, settlements, and colonies in both hemispheres and playing a significant role in the slave trade. People and goods from around the world became a highly visible presence in Dutch cities. No doubt these developments triggered a growing demand for representations and texts that articulated Dutch identity and expressed self-awareness of the new bourgeois elite.[38]

Fig. 6 Esaias van de Velde, *Farms and a Dovecote by a Frozen River*, c. 1617–18. See p. 232 for full information; see also the detail on p. 34.

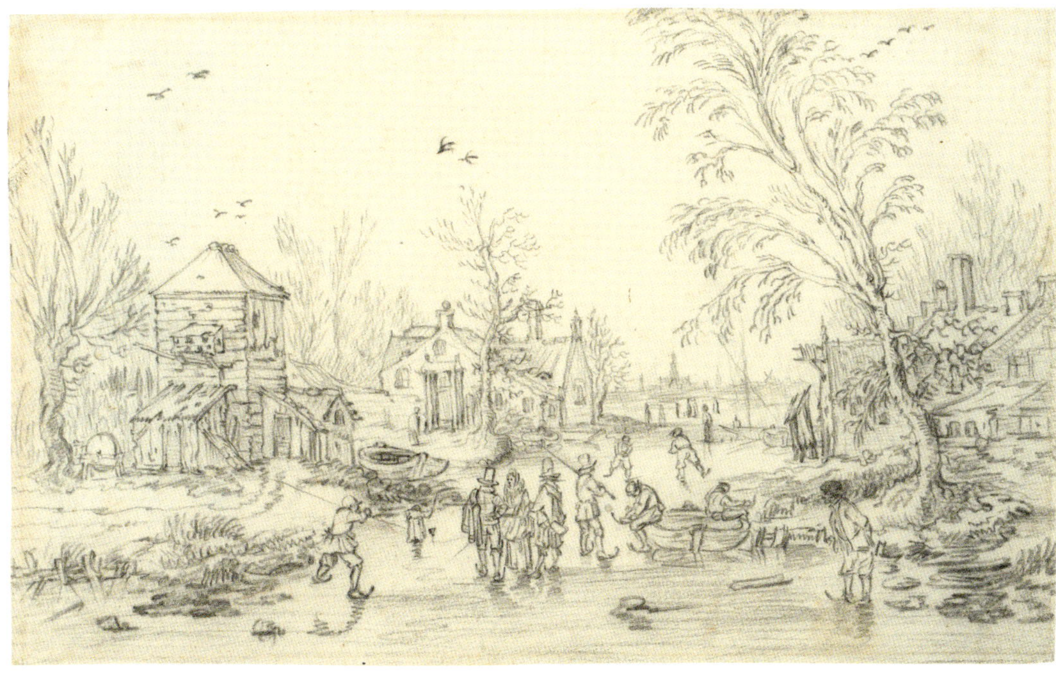

DRAWING IN THE OPEN AIR

Evidence of the widespread practice of drawing en plein air can be found in the multitude of seventeenth-century landscape drawings and prints that include an artist at work with a sketchbook or loose sheet of paper on a drawing board on his lap.[39] A striking example is *Forest Interior with Draftsman* by Jan Lievens (1607–1674), in which an artist depicted in a deep forest leans against a tree, recording his impressions (Fig. 7). There is a second version of the drawing, on Asian paper, in Dresden.[40] Most likely, both images were based on a lost sketch made on the spot.[41] In the aforementioned treatise, Goeree advised artists to go outside with company; perhaps Lievens took this advice, drawing his fellow traveling artist here.[42] But as the drawing was finished in the studio, Lievens may have just as easily added the figure later, as a more poetic way to reference relaxation in the forest.

In his treatise *De Teecken-Const* (1636), poet Cornelis Pietersz. Biens (1590/95–1645) urged young artists to go outside and draw landscapes on "tablets or otherwise" (*tafelette of andersints*).[43] A *tafelette* (or *tafelet*) was a thick, prepared piece of parchment or paper drawn upon with a stylus to produce a metalpoint. They were sometimes bound together into a booklet, also called a *tafelet*.[44] Notably, no seventeenth-century *tafeletten* with landscape drawings survive. This lacuna in the visual record has spurred an interesting hypothesis: their ability to be wiped clean and reused might have made *tafeletten* the ultimate study material.[45]

In addition to drawing boards and *tafeletten*, artists employed small, handy sketchbooks. These were easy to carry and could contain hundreds of sheets of paper.[46] Of the numerous sketchbooks in use in the seventeenth century, however, only a few have survived. Over time, many were taken apart, sometimes by the artist himself in order to use or sell the drawings separately.[47] From the highly productive landscape painter and draftsman Jan van Goyen, we know of a number of sketchbooks and hundreds of loose sketchbook pages.[48] On his travels through the Republic, Southern Netherlands, and the Rhineland, he recorded his impressions of landscapes and cities in quick sketches. He did so in black chalk, like his Haarlem teacher Esaias van de Velde. The material is well suited for working outdoors because it is easy to handle and to carry.[49] Van Goyen's *Landscape with Cottages and Figures* (Fig. 8) can be recognized as a sketchbook page because of its small size and rounded corners; the gray washes in the drawing may have been applied later. It was taken from the so-called Lilienfeld sketchbook, which Van Goyen

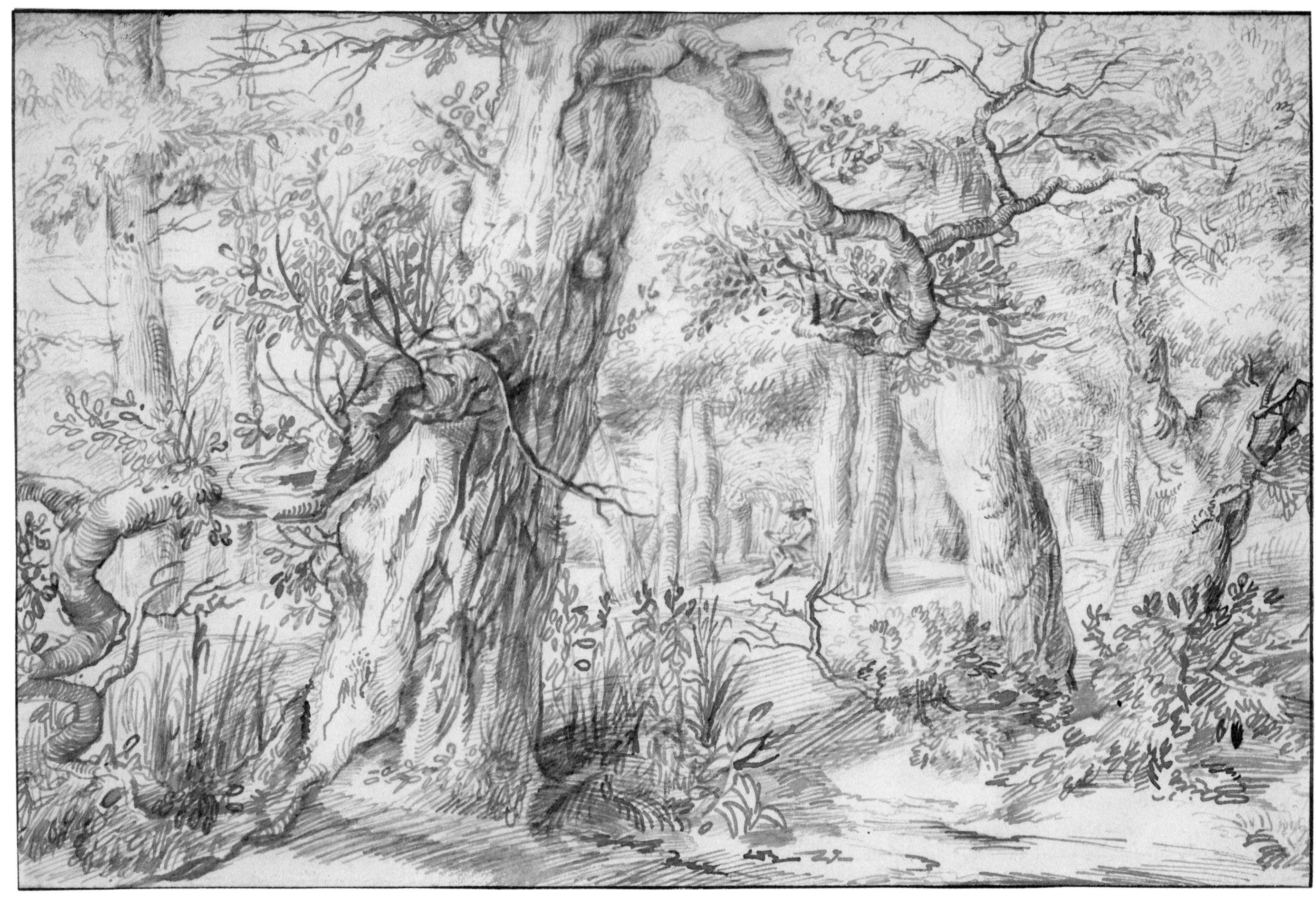

Fig. 7 Jan Lievens, *Forest Interior with Draftsman*, 1664–65.
See p. 230 for full information.

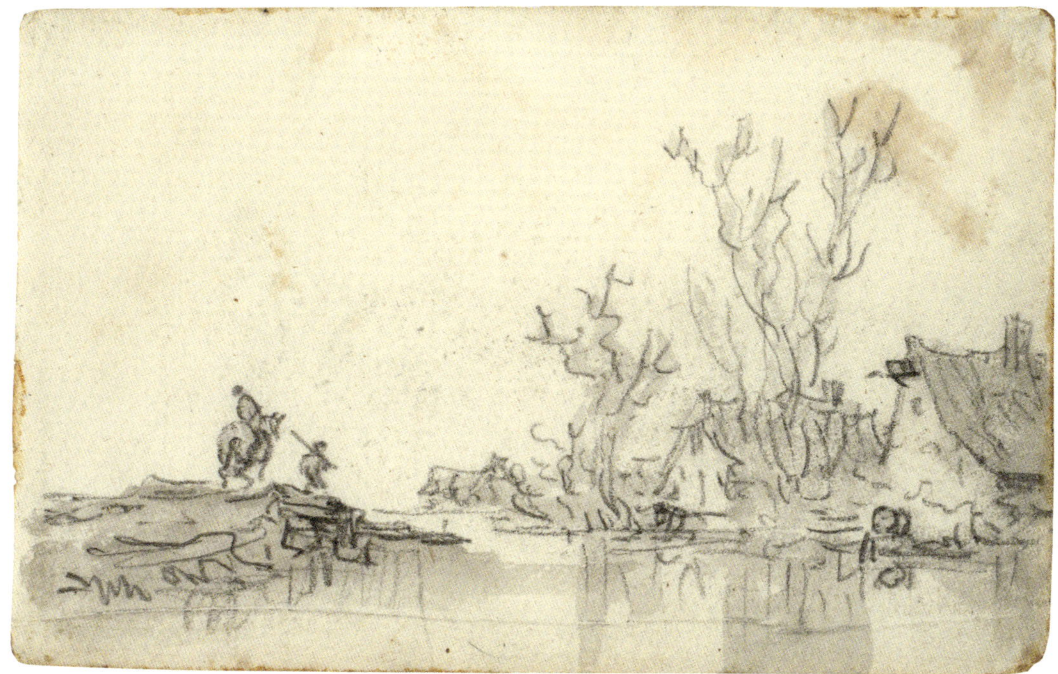

Fig. 8 Jan van Goyen, *Landscape with Cottages and Figures*, c. 1650. See p. 230 for full information.

brought with him on a trip to the Rhineland around 1650–51 and was eventually disassembled in the twentieth century. The original order and page numbers can no longer be deciphered; the current numbering of the pages was implemented later.[50] The spontaneous character of *Landscape with Cottages and Figures*, with its scratchy lines, is remarkable – it is as if Van Goyen hastily took out his sketchbook to record the scene during a short stop.

Besides chalk, pen and ink – indelible and much less forgiving – were also used to draw outside, as attested by the works of Goltzius. For Rembrandt and his pupils, this was the most popular technique for studies from life, of figures as well as landscapes (see the drawing by Lievens below and the essay by William Robinson in this volume). In his *Inleyding tot de Hooge Schoole der Schilderkonst* (1678), Samuel van Hoogstraten (1627–1678), a pupil of Rembrandt, thus advised fellow artists to regularly seek the woods or hills to record nature in a drawing book with chalk, but also with pen.[51]

## FAVORITE LOCATIONS

Artists who went outside to draw in the seventeenth-century Dutch Republic discovered a variety of landscapes. In coastal regions, the land had already been largely cultivated, in part due to the constant struggle against the water, which required embankment, dune management, and drainage of polders. On the sandy soil of the east and south, in regions such as Overijssel, Gelderland, and Brabant, development was less rapid, and many parts of the country were still hardly accessible. Large forested areas had been felled in the sixteenth century for fuel and construction. As a result, the land was wide open, making it possible to enjoy distant views of the landscape.

Hilly dunes were situated at the coast. The moraine landscape in the east, around Rhenen, Nijmegen, and Arnhem, was hilly as well. Cities had grown explosively from the late sixteenth century onward, especially in the core region of the province of Holland, and were well connected to each other. Over land, there existed a network of country roads, often situated on the dikes. On the water, citizens traveled by barge, which operated on a fixed timetable. Bridges contributed to this infrastructure, and inns made the journey more comfortable along the way. In rural areas, economic activity often ultimately benefited urban regions, including agriculture and horticulture, peat-cutting, and the exploitation of unspoiled nature. The villages housed not only farmers, but also many craftsmen operating independently or in small-scale workshops.[52]

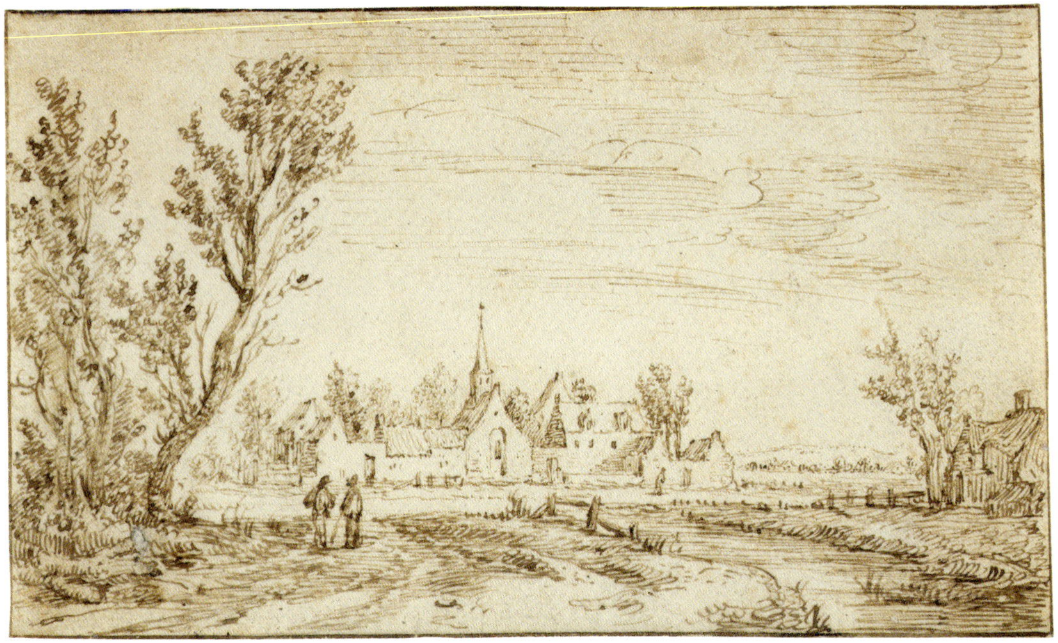

In his treatise on drawing, Goeree made suggestions for where to find suitable places to practice: areas with hills, dunes, trees, shrubs, and water that were easily accessible on foot. These were namely in the vicinity of Cleves, Liège, and Aachen, along the Rhine in Germany, but also included some sites in the Netherlands.[53] Indeed, artists had their favorite locations to draw outside. Areas in and around Haarlem and Amsterdam, such as the ruins of Brederode Castle and the Abbey of Egmond, both near the Dutch coast, were regularly depicted. Another iconic building was the Haarlem leprosy hospital, an institution established outside the city in the fifteenth century. Van Goyen depicted the building in a picturesque manner, with two figures walking in the foreground (Fig. 9). The group of trees at left and the farm at right give the impression that Van Goyen invented this composition, but he undoubtedly studied the hospital in person. He was perhaps inspired by Visscher, who included a print of the same building in his *Pleasant Places*, albeit from a different point of view.[54] Allart van Everdingen (1621–1675), who lived in Haarlem for some time in the early 1640s, also depicted the hospital in an etching.[55]

Many artists traveled eastward to the hilly Rhine region, often via Utrecht, Rhenen, Arnhem, and Nijmegen to the German city of Cleves. After the Treaty of Münster ended the Dutch Revolt against Spain in 1648, the journey became easier. These artists made numerous studies from life during their trips, as drawings by Van Goyen, Rembrandt, Jacob Esselens, Lambert Doomer, and Albert Cuyp attest (see p. 116, Fig. J).

In Utrecht, the Romanesque church of St. Mary (Mariakerk) garnered interest, probably because the twelfth-century building with Italian allure was already considered of "respectable" age. Architectural painter Pieter Saenredam drew (and painted) the church many times, as did Van Goyen, Doomer, and Herman Saftleven.[56] Notably, Rembrandt—who made many landscape drawings of identifiable locations near Amsterdam (see the essay by William Robinson)—depicted the Mariakerk as well (Fig. 10). While Saenredam drew the building up close, Rembrandt opted for a viewpoint farther away. Standing on the city wall of Utrecht, he studied the church from behind the roofs of houses. On the left side of his composition, behind the trees, is the church's southwest tower; the northwest tower had been destroyed by Spanish troops in 1576.[57]

Fig. 9 Jan van Goyen, *Landscape with the Hospital for Lepers outside Haarlem*, c. 1628–30. See p. 229 for full information.

Fig. 10 Rembrandt van Rijn, *View of Mariakerk in Utrecht from the South*, c. 1652. See p. 231 for full information.

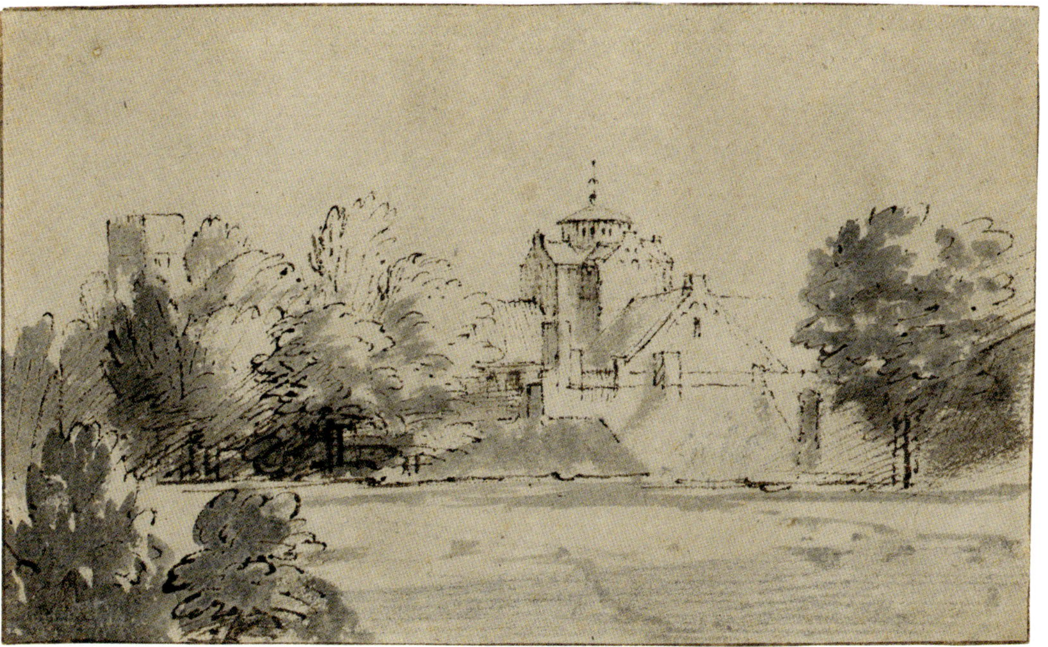



## FROM LIFE OR FROM THE MIND?

In addition to drawing from life (*naer het leven*), it was important for artists to learn to draw from memory (*van onthout*) and the mind (*uyt den gheest*).[58] Van Mander saw this as an essential aspect of an artist's training, for anyone who is able to create from memory or their imagination can combine all previous observations into one complete composition.[59] Van Hoogstraten, too, stated the importance of recalling nature from drawing outdoors in order to depict it without a visual aid.[60] Following this principle, many of the thousands of extant seventeenth-century drawings of Dutch landscapes, towns, and villages must have been made in the studio, on the basis of sketches made in the open air or from memory. It explains in part the relatively low survival rate of the surely innumerable drawings made outdoors, most of which were thrown away after being used for training purposes or as working material in the studio. It is also highly likely that many landscape drawings began outdoors and were further refined inside. In the studio, an artist could use his imagination and incorporate or even surpass what he had seen outside. This synthesis resulted in carefully composed and finished drawings intended for sale.

Spontaneity in perception and execution is thought to be characteristic of drawing from life, but this is not always the case.[61] Did Van Ruisdael, for example, draw his *Trees and a Cottage at the Edge of a Road*, with two figures walking along a forested path, in the open air or in his studio (Fig. 11)? The loose style in black chalk suggests the former, as if he captured the moment in the blink of an eye. On the other hand, an experienced landscape specialist like Van Ruisdael certainly could have drawn such a view by heart.[62] In any case, we can assume that drawings of identifiable locations with accurate and carefully documented topographical details were made from life. Van Ruisdael's body of work includes panoramas of Amsterdam, Haarlem, and Naarden, as well as drawings of notable places in Amsterdam, which bear witness to careful observation and were undoubtedly made on the spot.[63] The artist must have also wandered through Harderwijk with his drawing materials,[64] and his depiction of a drawbridge and city gates was recently identified as a view of the Kamperbuitenpoort in Amersfoort (Fig. 12).[65] The scene is rendered in such detail, including the house by the front gate, the drawbridge, and crane, that it is inconceivable it was not drawn on-site. As a result, we now know that Van Ruisdael also stayed and worked in Amersfoort.

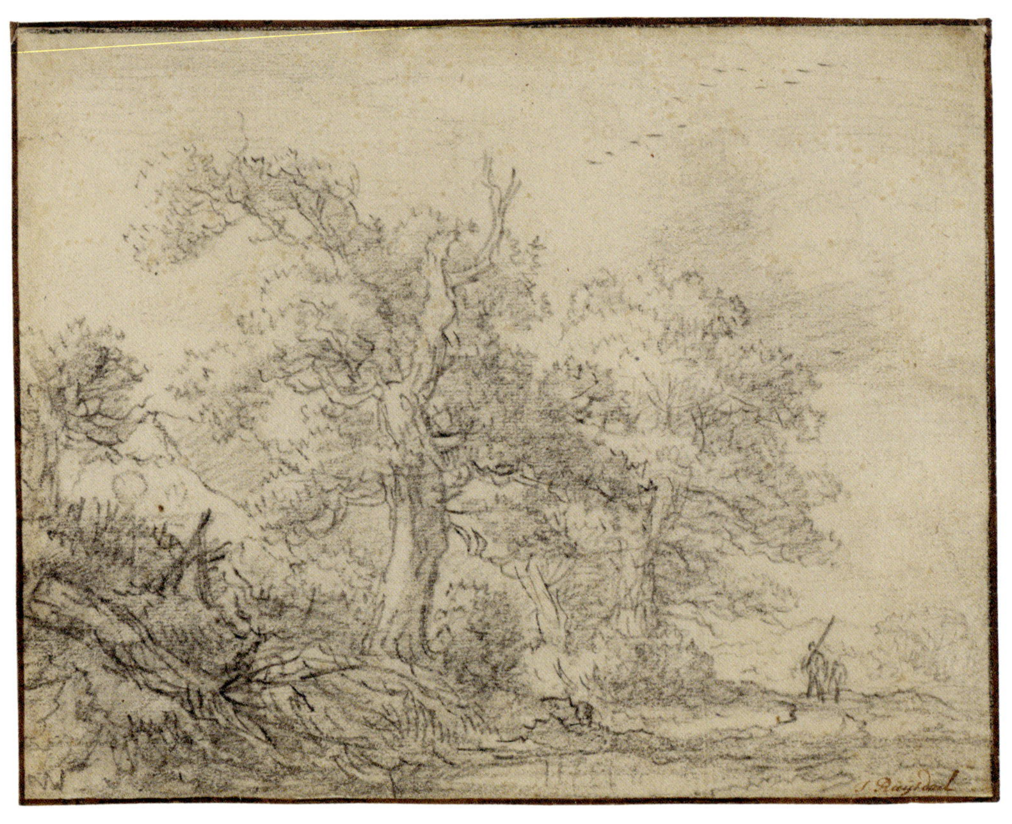
J. Ruysdael

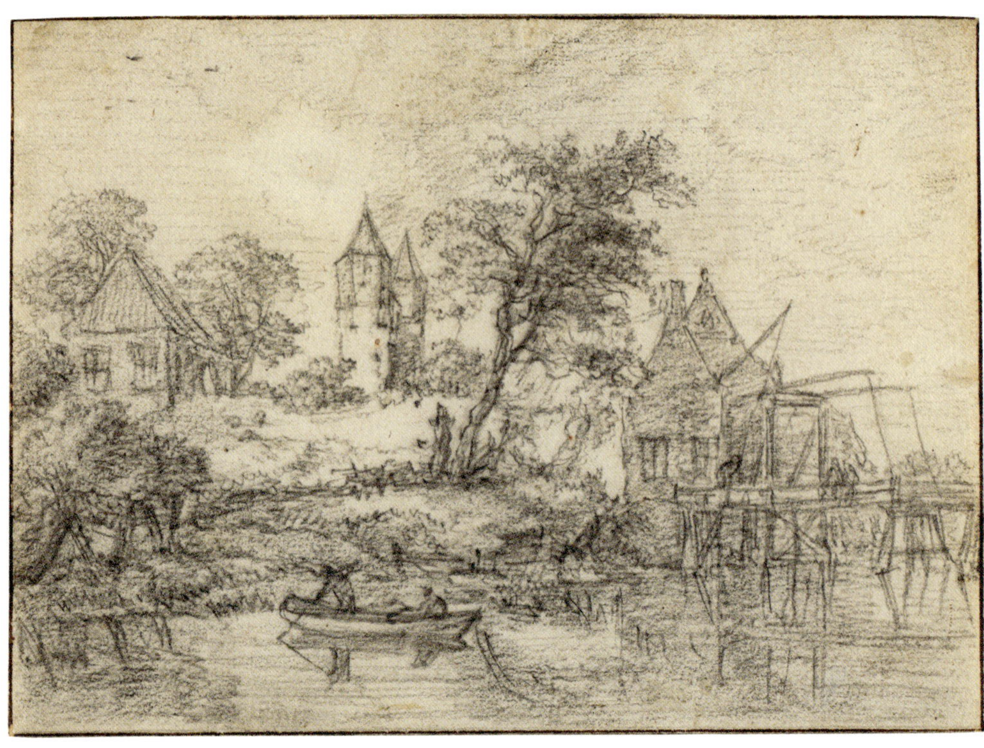

Fig. 11 Jacob van Ruisdael, *Trees and a Cottage at the Edge of a Road*, c. 1648–55. See p. 231 for full information.

Fig. 12 Jacob van Ruisdael, *The Kamperbuitenpoort in Amersfoort*, c. 1650. See p. 232 for full information.

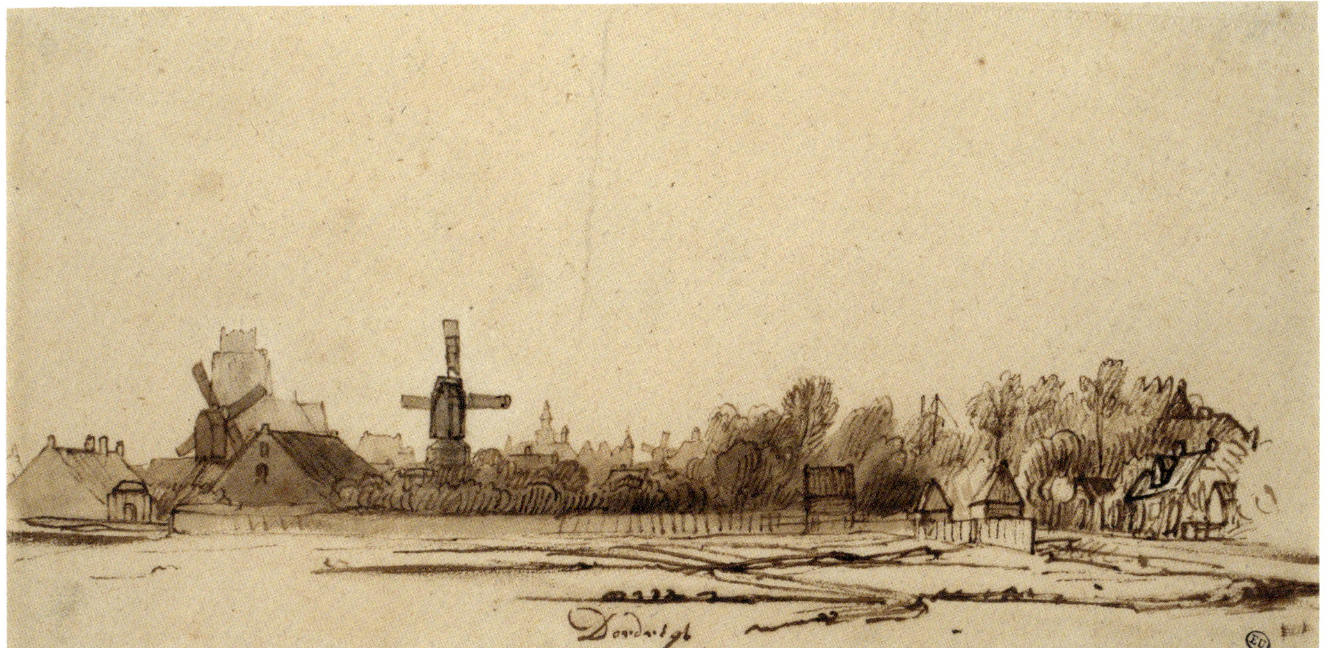

Fig. 13 Nicolaes Maes, *View of Dordrecht*, 1653–60. See p. 230 for full information.

Nicolaes Maes (1634–1693), too, traveled around with his pen, brush, and ink, following the example of his teacher, Rembrandt. The topographical accuracy of his *View of Dordrecht*, made from a point outside the city, guarantees it was drawn on location (Fig. 13). Maes drew the city from the east, with a view of the back of the Grote Kerk behind the windmill Het Raephout. To the right, the mill called De Hoogmoet and the tower of town hall can be recognized, and behind the trees one can make out the high roof of the Vriesepoort.[66] In a second drawing by Maes, made from a slightly different angle, the city gate is more central.[67] Both drawings are believed to have been made in the years 1653–60, after the artist had returned to his hometown of Dordrecht.

A meticulously observed landscape by Lievens, with the contours of Haarlem on the horizon, also gives the strong impression that it was, for the most part, made outside (Fig. 14). Many landscape drawings by the artist are known, most executed in pen and brown ink. They can be divided by theme into imaginary forest scenes (see Fig. 7), which are in keeping with the sixteenth-century tradition of the Flemish landscape, and panoramic landscapes with sometimes recognizable locations, as in this case.[68] Lievens's sketchbooks have been lost, but it is known that in Antwerp in 1686, Johannes Philippus Happart owned a small book with landscape drawings by the artist.[69] *Landscape with a Distant View of Haarlem* was made atop a high dune. Lievens first composed the design in black chalk (perhaps partly) on the spot, then worked it into a highly refined drawing with short pen strokes and parallel hatching, reminiscent of Goltzius's dune landscapes (see Fig. 5). Haarlem is seen from the northwest, primarily recognizable by the outline of St. Bavo's church in the middle. To the left, the towers of the Bakenesserkerk, the church of St. John, and the obtuse tower of the Klokhuis are visible; at right, the high roof of the town hall peeks out.[70] Within the strongholds of the city walls sit a large number of mills. The drawing is so precise that, in any case, Lievens must have observed the city profile on location, even if he later added details in his studio.[71]

Drawing from life was first and foremost an artistic exercise and a method of collecting motifs. Did the practice also give rise to a new aesthetic, related to or distinct from the period's broader interest in spontaneity in works of art? Put another way: did artists make drawings in the studio that purposefully simulated the appearance of works made outside, on-site? Unfortunately, we may never know for sure; but if this was indeed the case, it might help explain why

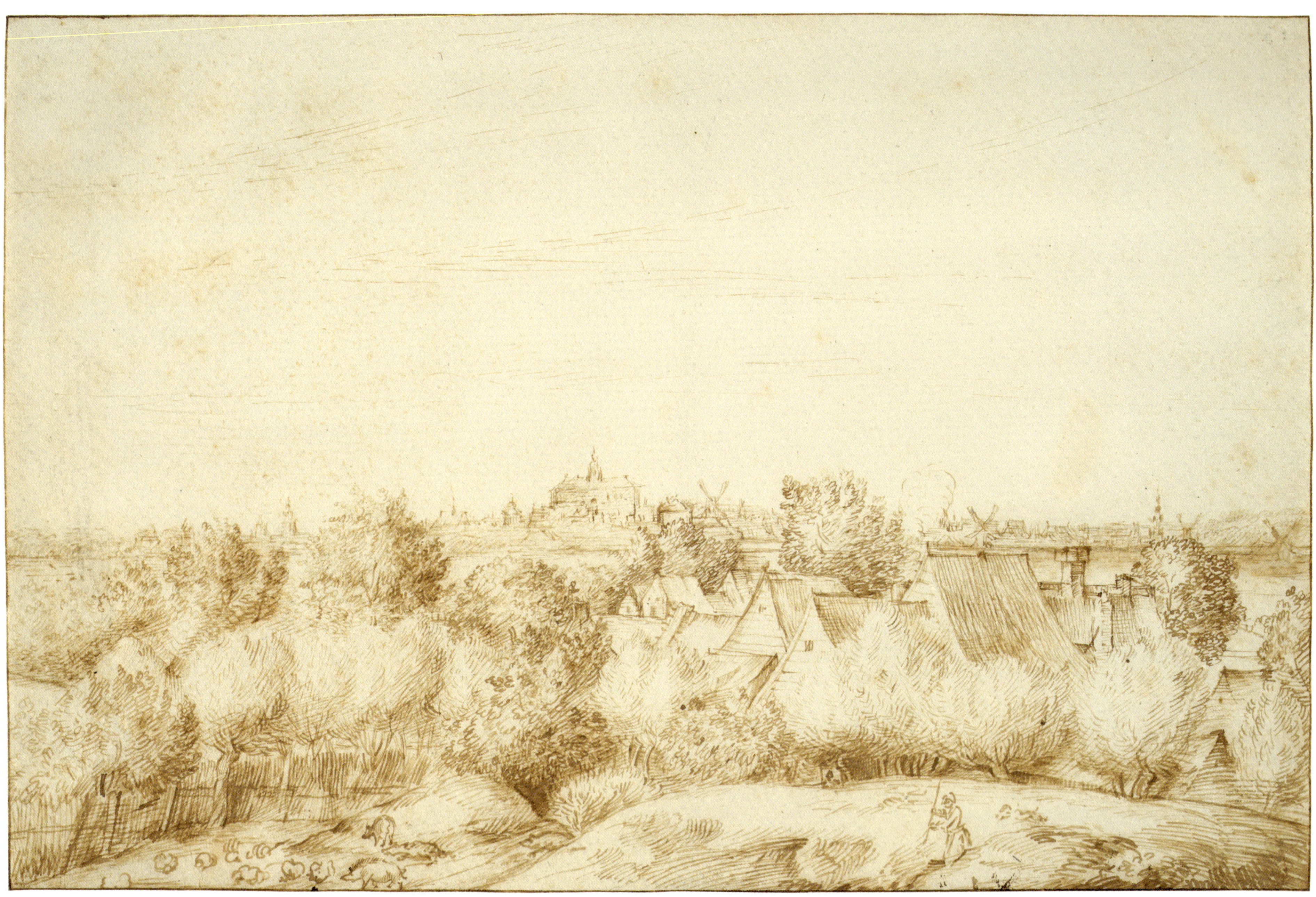

Fig. 14 Jan Lievens, *Landscape with a Distant View of Haarlem*, 1664–65. See p. 230 for full information.

Fig. 15 Jan van Goyen, *On the Seashore*, 1652. See p. 230 for full information.

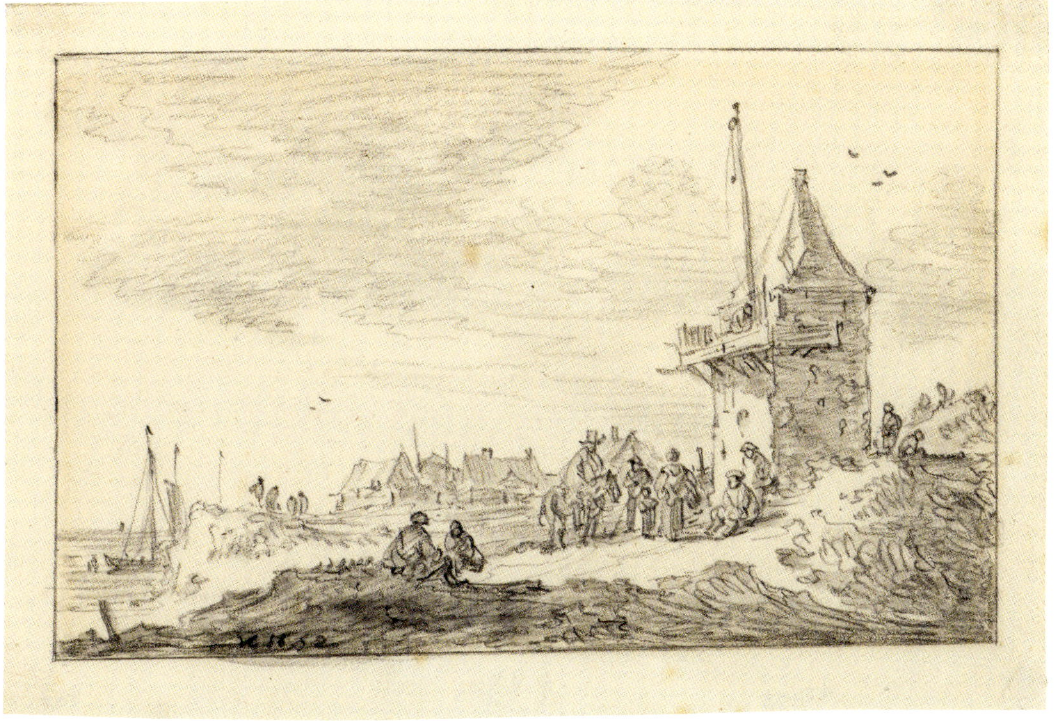



the visual distinction between drawings from life (*naer het leven*) and those from the mind (*uyt den gheest*) is often ambiguous.

## LANDSCAPE DRAWINGS FOR THE MARKET

While little is known about the seventeenth-century market for Dutch landscape drawings, there are indications that demand existed from the beginning of the century. Van Mander tells us, for example, that Bloemaert's drawings of the rural areas around Utrecht were popular among art lovers.[72] The large number of preserved watercolors of landscapes and townscapes by Hans Bol also point toward a vibrant market.[73] One of the earliest documented Dutch collections of drawings was that of Amsterdam merchant and painter Jan van de Cappelle (1626–1679). Among the 7,000 drawings that he owned were significant numbers of sheets by landscape specialists: 880 by and after Hendrick Avercamp (1585–1634), 417 by Van Goyen, 88 by Esaias van de Velde (plus two of his sketchbooks), and 57 by Pieter de Molijn; he also owned 277 landscape drawings by Rembrandt (see p. 134).[74]

The many thousands of landscape drawings made especially for the art market are also an indication of the genre's popularity.[75] In some periods, Van Goyen concentrated on drawing instead of painting; between 1651 and 1653, he turned out some 350 finished drawings but relatively few paintings.[76] *On the Seashore* (1652), which depicts a meeting between a wealthy gentleman on horseback and a group of villagers at a sea beacon just outside a coastal town, is characteristic of Van Goyen's work from this period (Fig. 15). Sea beacons served as landmarks for passing ships—an iron basket with flammable material would be hoisted inside the structure to signal the shoreline. One such burning beacon had previously appeared in Visscher's *Pleasant Places*.[77] This reference to the economic activity along the Dutch coast together with the chattering bystanders undoubtedly appealed to the imagination of many collectors.

Van Goyen's contemporary De Molijn, who worked as a painter, draftsman, and etcher in Haarlem, also produced hundreds of drawings specifically for the market in the 1650s. Most are of desolate dune landscapes around Haarlem, such as his *Panoramic Landscape* from around 1659 (see p. 164, Fig. O). The vista is clearly a product of the mind. The composition is carefully balanced, with alternating light and dark strips executed in chalk and gray washes. The diagonal line from the tall, overgrown dune at left to the distant view at right is emphasized by figures who cross the

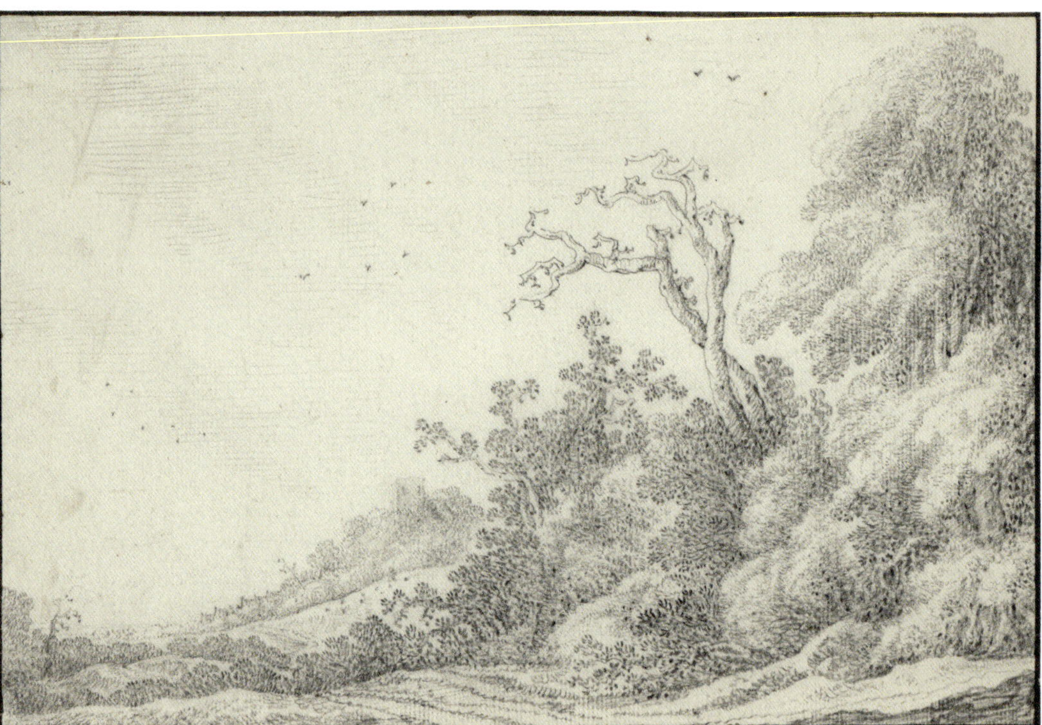

Fig. 16 Franchoys Ryckhals, *Landscape with Trees and a View to the Distance*, c. 1632. See p. 232 for full information.

Fig. 17 Simon de Vlieger, *View of Weesp*, c. 1649–53. See p. 233 for full information.



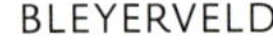

landscape – travelers or merchants and their packed donkeys. Unlike Van Goyen, no sketches made in the open air are known from De Molijn, although he almost certainly drew outside.

The landscape drawings by Middelburg artist Franchoys Ryckhals (1609–1647) were also intended for the market.[78] He preferred to work in black chalk, building up his landscapes in fine lines and dots (Fig. 16). Some are decorated with shepherds and cattle, others contain stylized forests with clearly contoured and erratically shaped trees. The landscape from the Abrams Collection, with its meticulous detail and successful contrasts between light and dark, is a charming example. The view at left draws the eye to a series of farmhouse roofs and a tower on a hill. Ryckhals also proves himself to be an able observer who undoubtedly memorized the terrain or made sketches outside before composing this landscape in his studio.

Perhaps the most impressive topographical drawing of the seventeenth century is the *View of Weesp* by Simon de Vlieger (Fig. 17). The exceptionally large and elaborate cityscape must have been realized between January 1649, when De Vlieger (1600/1601–1653) bought a house in Weesp, and the artist's death in 1653. Weesp is situated southeast of Amsterdam near the river Vecht, which plays a prominent role in the drawing. On the right riverbank, the backs of the buildings on the Hoogstraat, one of the town's busiest streets, can be seen. The jetties with cranes on the water, where a few ships are docked and beer barrels are piled high, testify to the many breweries in Weesp. The Vecht lent itself perfectly to the beer industry, supplying a key ingredient (water) as well as a means of transporting the barrels. De Vlieger drew the city from the road along the river that leads to the drawbridge and the Muiderpoort (Muiden Gate). He chose a vantage point along a sharp bend that offered him a wide view of the water, the long row of houses, and the mills in the distance.

Despite the large format, the artist must have completed at least the first draft of this drawing on-site, observing and sketching with a particularly sharp eye for detail to capture the atmosphere of the waterfront. Was the artist perhaps commissioned by a well-to-do resident of Weesp to make this impressive cityscape? Whatever the case may be, the composition kept De Vlieger busy: he made two smaller drawings from the same point of view, each showing more or less half of the scene in the Abrams work. Most likely intended as pendants, the two sheets remained together until they were separated at auction in 1775.[79]

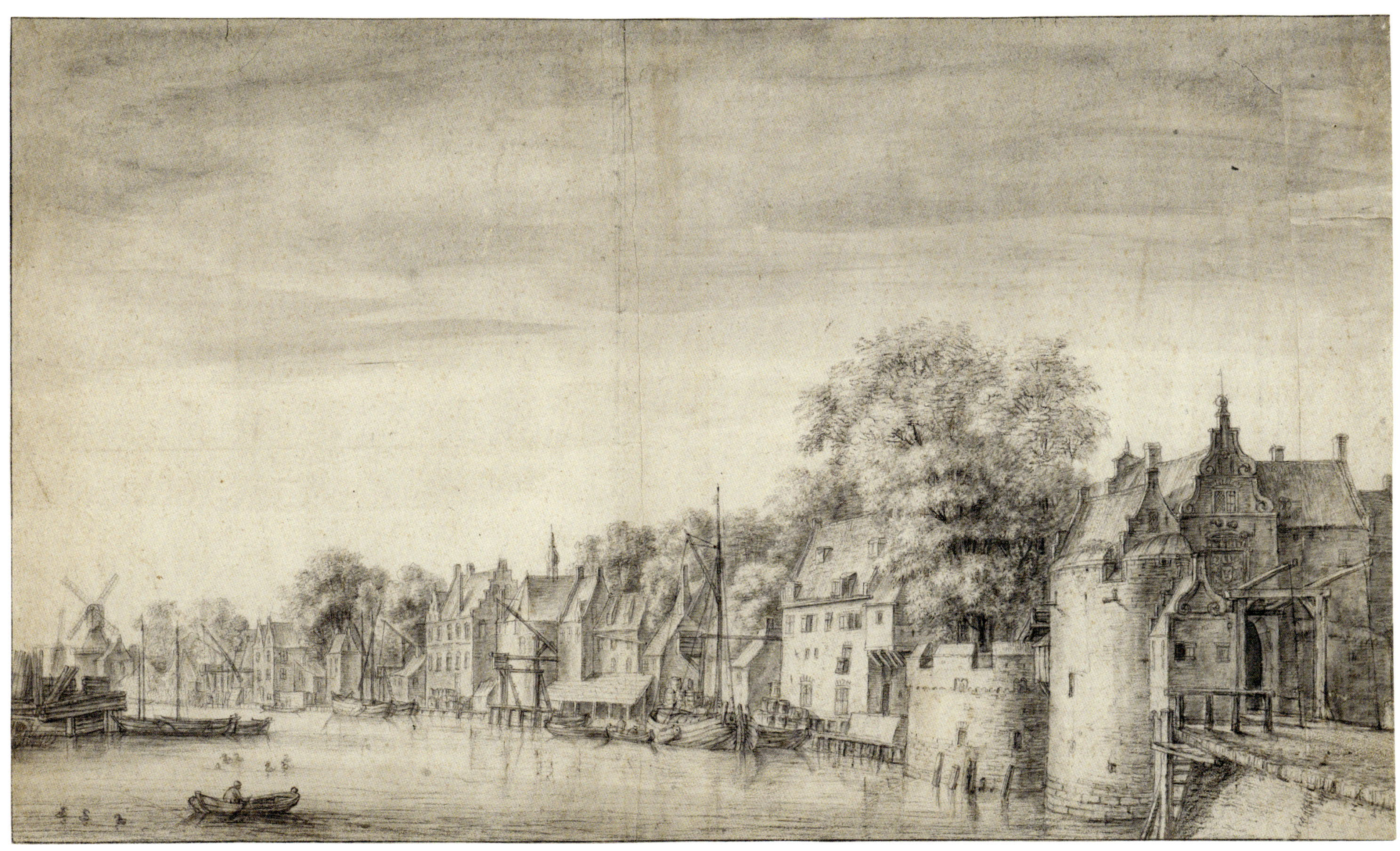

## AN APPEALING THEME

Drawing outside was a useful exercise, one also espoused for its restorative possibilities by seventeenth-century art theorists. As early as the sixteenth century, artists came to see that one need not roam far to make interesting observations in the open air: the local environment offered attractive rural landscapes, city profiles, iconic buildings, and picturesque places to be captured. Sketches drawn outside were used as the basis for drawings, prints, and paintings or sold directly to collectors, potentially after having been worked out in the studio.

We know from the large number of seventeenth-century drawings of Dutch landscapes that have been preserved that they were in demand. Thanks to the Republic's rapidly growing economy, wealthy governors and merchants sought works of art that were accessible and immediately recognizable.[80] New genres such as marine paintings, scenes from everyday life, and still lifes entered the scene, but domestic landscapes also answered the call.

Unfortunately, there are no records or accounts about the period perception of Dutch landscapes and cityscapes. Likely, these drawings elicited pride, self-confidence, and a sense of recognition. At a time when many turned their gaze toward the outside world, artists and their clients looked inward, to the local landscape. It was a world within reach; anyone could follow in the footsteps of landscape artists – whether literally on foot, by carriage or barge, or simply in one's mind.

Yvonne Bleyerveld is Senior Curator of Prints and Drawings at the RKD – Netherlands Institute for Art History in The Hague and Professor by Special Appointment of Art on Paper in the Faculty of Humanities at Leiden University.

## NOTES

Essay translated from Dutch by Bartholomew & Jonker. Thanks to Susan Anderson, Angela Bartholomew, Sabine Craft-Giepmans, Henk van de Graaf, Menno Jonker, Christi Klinkert, Laurens M. Schoemaker, Joanna S. Seidenstein, and Frans Smeding for their help and comments.

1. Painting en plein air wouldn't become common practice until the nineteenth century. For the concept of *naer het leven*, see Peter Schatborn, "The Importance of Drawing from Life – Some Preliminary Notes," in *Seventeenth-Century Dutch Drawings: A Selection from the Maida and George Abrams Collection*, by William W. Robinson (Cambridge, Mass.: Harvard University Art Museums; Amsterdam: Rijksmuseum; Vienna: Graphische Sammlung Albertina; New York: Pierpont Morgan Library; Lynn, Mass.: H. O. Zimman, 1991), 7–12.
2. In this context, "naturalistic" can be defined as the aim to render the native Dutch landscape observed by the artist as faithfully as possible.
3. For topographical prints, see Boudewijn Bakker and Huigen Leeflang, *Nederland naar 't leven: Landschapsprenten uit de Gouden Eeuw* (Amsterdam: Museum het Rembrandthuis, 1993).
4. Karel van Mander, *Den grondt der edel vry schilder-const*, ed. Hessel Miedema (Utrecht: Haentjens Dekker & Gumbert, [Haarlem: 1604] 1973), fols. 34r–35r.
5. Willem Goeree, *Inleydinge tot de Al-ghemeene Teycken-Konst* (Middelburg: 1668), 38–39; annotated by Michael Kwakkelstein in Willem Goeree, *Willem Goeree: Inleydinge tot de Al-ghemeene Teycken-Konst: Een Kritische Geannoteerde Editie*, ed. Michael W. Kwakkelstein (Leiden: Primavera Press, 1998), 120–21.
6. See, most recently, Tatjana Bartsch, *Maarten van Heemskerck: Römische Studien zwischen Sachlichkeit und Imagination* (Munich: Hirmer, 2019).
7. Nadine M. Orenstein, ed., *Pieter Bruegel the Elder: Drawings and Prints* (New York: Metropolitan Museum of Art; Rotterdam: Museum Boijmans van Beuningen, 2001), 6, and cats. 1, 8, 24, 85.
8. Karel van Mander, *Het Schilder-Boeck* (Haarlem: Paschier van Wesbvach, 1604), fol. 234v.
9. Daantje Meuwissen, "Attributing the Berlin Sketchbook to Cornelis Anthonisz," *Simiolus* 39 (2017): 15–43, esp. 34–40.
10. For the Master of the Small Landscapes and his drawings and prints, see Orenstein, *Pieter Bruegel the Elder*, 289–99. The oeuvre attributed to him was likely the work of several Antwerp artists; see, most recently, Alexandra Onuf, *The Small Landscape Prints in Early Modern Netherlands* (New York: Routledge, Taylor & Francis Group, 2018), 3.
11. *The New Hollstein Dutch and Flemish Etchings, Engravings and Woodcuts, 1450–1700*, vol. 5, *The Van Doetecum Family*, part 1, compiled by Henk J. Nalis (Rotterdam: Koninklijke van Poll, 1998), nos. 118–61.
12. Ibid., 94 (under no. 1). See also Erik P. Löffler, "A Subject of the Small Landscapes Series Identified," *Print Quarterly* 28 (2011): 46–49.
13. *The New Hollstein Dutch and Flemish Etchings, Engravings and Woodcuts, 1450–1700*, vol. 5, *The Van Doetecum Family*, part 1, 94–95. The series was reprinted in 1601, 1633, and 1676.
14. On the influence of the Master of the Small Landscapes, see Walter S. Gibson, *Pleasant Places: The Rustic Landscape from Bruegel to Ruisdael* (Berkeley: University of California Press, 2000), 1–49.
15. Bol apparently chose this specialty after first practicing large-scale watercolors on canvas, which have not survived due to their fragility. See Stefaan Hautekeete, "New Insights into the Working Methods of Hans Bol," *Master Drawings* 50 (3) (2012): 329–56.
16. Van Mander, *Het Schilder-Boeck*, fol. 260v.
17. See Hautekeete, "New Insights into the Working Methods of Hans Bol."
18. The tower of the New Church (Nieuwe Kerk) in Delft, which can be seen on the horizon in the gouache, is missing in the British Museum drawing. In reality, the tower is not visible from this point; the city center of Delft is farther right.
19. William W. Robinson and Susan Anderson, *Drawings from the Age of Bruegel, Rubens, and Rembrandt: Highlights from the Collection of the Harvard Art Museums* (Cambridge, Mass.: Harvard Art Museums, 2016), cat. 10a–b.
20. On these, see, most recently, Yvonne Bleyerveld, Albert J. Elen, and Judith Niessen, *Bosch to Bloemaert: Early Netherlandish Drawings in Museum Boijmans Van Beuningen, Rotterdam* (Paris: Fondation Custodia; Bussum: Toth, 2014), cats. 78–79.
21. Van Mander, *Het Schilder-Boeck*, fol. 284r.
22. Ibid., fol. 298r.
23. For the drawings by Bloemaert, see Jaap Bolten, *Abraham Bloemaert, c. 1565–1651: The Drawings*, 2 vols. (Leiden: J. Bolten, 2007). Bolten dates a group of landscape drawings in the Staatliche Museen zu Berlin to between 1585 and 1590/91, putting the drawings, as studies from life, earlier than Goltzius's drawn dune landscapes. See vol. 1, nos. 1336–1400.
24. William W. Robinson, *Bruegel to Rembrandt: Dutch and Flemish Drawings from the Maida and George Abrams Collection* (Cambridge, Mass.: Harvard University Art Museums; London: British Museum; Paris: Institut Néerlandais; New Haven, Conn.: Yale University Press, 2002), cat. 5. See also Ger Luijten et al., eds., *Dawn of the Golden Age: Northern Netherlandish Art, 1580–1620* (Amsterdam: Rijksmuseum, 1993), cat. 324.
25. Frits Lugt, *Wandelingen met Rembrandt in en om Amsterdam* (Amsterdam: P. N. van Kampen, 1915), 136.
26. The verso shows another scene taken from life: a tree stump near a water hole, with the annotation *Elsen stamm* (alder trunk).
27. For drawings of the village by Rembrandt (in the Museum Boijmans Van Beuningen, Rotterdam, and the National Gallery of Art, Washington, D.C.), see Peter Schatborn and Erik Hinterding, *Rembrandt: The Complete Drawings and Etchings* (Cologne: Taschen, 2019), nos. D559–60.
28. Friedrich W.H. Hollstein, *Dutch and Flemish Etchings, Engravings and Woodcuts, ca. 1450–1700*, vol. 38 (Amsterdam: M. Hertzberger, 1949–2010), nos. 149–60; and Luijten et al., *Dawn of the Golden Age*, cat. 327.
29. Bakker and Leeflang, *Nederland naar 't leven*, 54. For Visscher as a publisher of topographical prints, see Gibson, *Pleasant Places*, 27–49.
30. See also Huigen Leeflang in Bakker and Leeflang, *Nederland naar 't leven*, 29.

31. Hollstein, *Dutch and Flemish Etchings, Engravings and Woodcuts, ca. 1450–1700*, vol. 38, nos. 292–317.
32. Bakker and Leeflang, *Nederland naar 't leven*, 70.
33. Ibid., 64.
34. For works by Bruegel, see Orenstein, *Pieter Bruegel the Elder*, cats. 62–63.
35. George Keyes, "Esaias van de Velde and the Chalk Sketch," *Nederlands Kunsthistorisch Jaarboek* 38 (1987): 136–45.
36. Staatliche Museen Preussischer Kulturbesitz, Kupferstichkabinett, Berlin, 3846. See George Keyes, *Esaias van de Velde, 1587–1630* (Doornspijk: Davaco Publishers, 1984), cat. D 69.
37. See Eco O.G. Haitsma Mulier, "De eerste Hollandse stadsbeschrijvingen uit de zeventiende eeuw (dl. 2)," *De zeventiende eeuw* 9 (1993): 97–111.
38. Bakker and Leeflang, *Nederland naar 't leven*, 9, 18.
39. For instance, see Joris Abrahamsz. van der Haagen's *View in the Vicinity of Doorwerth* (1650) in the Rijksmuseum in Amsterdam (RP-T-1884-A-342). For other examples, see Bob van den Boogert, ed., *Buiten tekenen in Rembrandts tijd* (Amsterdam: Museum Het Rembrandthuis, 1998).
40. Kupferstich-Kabinett, Dresden, C 1436. See Werner Sumowski, *Drawings of the Rembrandt School*, vol. 7 (New York: Abaris Books, 1979), no. 1667x.
41. Peter Schatborn in Ger Luijten et al., *Drawings for Paintings in the Age of Rembrandt* (Washington, D.C.: National Gallery of Art, 2016), 56–57, cat. 2.
42. Goeree does this in the second, extended edition of his publication (Middelburg: 1670), at p. 74.
43. E. A. de Klerk, "*De Teecken-Const*, een 17de eeuws Nederlands Traktaatje," *Oud Holland* 96 (1982): 16–56, esp. 51. Also mentioned in Goeree, *Willem Goeree*, 120n92.
44. Marijn Schapelhouman, *Rembrandt and the Art of Drawing* (Amsterdam: Rijksmuseum, 2006), 8.
45. Ernst van de Wetering, "Verdwenen tekeningen en het gebruik van afwisbare tekenplankjes en *tafeletten*," *Oud Holland* 105 (1991): 210–27.
46. This aspect is made visible, for example, in a drawing by Paulus van Vianen now in the Kupferstichkabinett, Berlin (13612); see Teréz Gerszi, *Paulus van Vianen: Handzeichnungen* (Hanau: Verlag Werner Dausien, 1982), no. 10.
47. Edwin Buijsen, *Between Fantasy and Reality: 17th-Century Dutch Landscape Painting* (Baarn: De Prom, 1993), 49–50.
48. See Edwin Buijsen, "De schetsboeken van Jan van Goyen," in *Jan van Goyen*, ed. Christiaan Vogelaar (Leiden: Stedelijk Museum De Lakenhal, 1996), 22–37. Only Van Goyen's sketchbook from the Bredius-Kronig collection stayed completely intact. For other seventeenth-century sketchbooks, see Schatborn, "The Importance of Drawing from Life," 9–10; Jeroen Giltaij, "A Newly Discovered Seventeenth-Century Sketchbook," *Simiolus* 31 (2007): 81–93 (on Jan van Kessel); and Abraham Bredius, "Het schetsboek van Jacob de Wet," *Oud Holland* 37 (1919): 215–22.
49. In the seventeenth century, black chalk (in addition to red chalk) was also a popular medium for figure studies from life, for instance by Jacques de Gheyn; see Yvonne Bleyerveld and Ilja M. Veldman, *The Netherlandish Drawings of the 16th Century in Teylers Museum* (Haarlem: Teylers Museum; Leiden: Primavera Press, 2016), 63, cat. 46.
50. Buijsen, "De schetsboeken van Jan van Goyen," 28, 130–34.
51. Samuel van Hoogstraten, *Inleyding tot de Hooge Schoole der Schilderkonst* (Rotterdam: Fransois van Hoogstraeten, 1678), 139.
52. For more, see Jan Bieleman, *Five Centuries of Farming: A Short History of Dutch Agriculture, 1500–2000* (Wageningen: Wageningen Academic Publishers, 2010), 35–76; Willem Frijhoff and Marijke Spies, *1650: Bevochten Eendracht* (The Hague: Sdu Uitgevers, 1999), 55, 169–72; Boudewijn Bakker in Bakker and Leeflang, *Nederland naar 't leven*, 8–9; and Jan de Vries, "The Dutch Rural Economy and the Landscape," in *Dutch Landscape: The Early Years, Haarlem and Amsterdam 1590–1650*, ed. Christopher Brown (London: The National Gallery, 1986), 79–86. I am very grateful to Laurens Schoemaker, Sabine Craft-Giepmans, and landscape ecologist Frans Smeding for sharing their knowledge.
53. Goeree made these suggestions in the second, extended edition of his publication (Middelburg: 1670), at pp. 72–73.
54. Hollstein, *Dutch and Flemish Etchings, Engravings and Woodcuts, ca. 1450–1700*, vol. 38, no. 157; and Luijten et al., *Dawn of the Golden Age*, cat. 327.9.
55. Hollstein, *Dutch and Flemish Etchings, Engravings and Woodcuts, ca. 1450–1700*, vol. 6, 171, Dut. 43. With thanks to Laurens Schoemaker for the identification of the hospital.
56. See Catharina C.S. Wilmers, *De getekende stad: Utrecht in oude tekeningen, 1550–1900* (Utrecht: Matrijs, 2005), 249–62; and Liesbeth Helmus, ed., *Pieter Saenredam, het Utrechtse werk* (Utrecht: Centraal Museum, 2000), 95–182.
57. The washes in this drawing are not by Rembrandt's hand and were probably added later.
58. Schapelhouman, *Rembrandt and the Art of Drawing*, 48.
59. Hessel Miedema in Van Mander, *Den Grondt der edel vry schilder-const*, 437–38.
60. Van Hoogstraten, *Inleyding tot de Hooge Schoole der Schilderkonst*, 139.
61. See, for instance, Werner Sumowski, "Observations on Jan Lievens' Landscape Drawings," *Master Drawings* 18 (4) (1980): 370–73, esp. 370.
62. See also Seymour Slive, *Jacob van Ruisdael: A Complete Catalogue of His Paintings, Drawings, and Etchings* (New Haven, Conn.: Yale University Press, 2001), 492.
63. See, for instance, ibid., cats. D1–2, D37–38, D67–69, D71, D77, D96–97. For a topographical index, see ibid., 763.
64. Laurens M. Schoemaker, "A Little Street in Harderwijk by Jacob van Ruisdael," *RKD Bulletin* 1 (2016): 3–10.
65. Laurens M. Schoemaker, "Jacob van Ruisdael tekent de Kamperbuitenpoort in Amersfoort," in *Connoisseurship: Essays in Honour of Fred G. Meijer*, ed. Charles Dumas (Leiden: Primavera Press, 2020), 269–74.
66. I am very grateful to Henk van de Graaf for the identification of the buildings and the viewpoint of the artist.
67. For the second view of Dordrecht, see Hans Buijs and Ger Luijten, eds., *Goltzius to Van Gogh: Drawings and Paintings from the P. & N. de*

*Boer Foundation* (Paris: Fondation Custodia; Bussum: Uitgeverij Thoth, 2014), cat. 82 (by Peter Schatborn). For landscape drawings by Maes, see William W. Robinson, "Landscape Drawings by Nicolaes Maes," *Kroniek van het Rembrandthuis* (2011): 42–47.

68. Peter Schatborn, introduction to *Jan Lievens, 1607–1674: Prenten & Tekeningen*, by Peter Schatborn and E. Ornstein-Van Slooten (Amsterdam: Het Museum, 1988), 16–20, esp. 18.
69. The book appeared in an inventory from February 27, 1686. See Hans Schneider, with a supplement by Rudi E.O. Ekkart, *Jan Lievens: Sein Leben und seine Werke* (Amsterdam: Israël, 1973), 393, no. SZ. 444.
70. Compare Ariane van Suchtelen and Arthur W. Wheelock, *Dutch Cityscapes of the Golden Age* (The Hague: Royal Picture Gallery Mauritshuis; Washington, D.C.: National Gallery of Art, 2008), cat. 35.
71. A drawing by Lievens in the British Museum, London (1876,1209.628) shows the same scenery as the work in the Abrams Collection, although from a slightly different viewpoint.
72. Van Mander, *Het Schilder-Boeck*, fol. 298r.
73. For examples, see Hautekeete, "New Insights into the Working Methods of Hans Bol."
74. Abraham Bredius, "De schilder Johannes van de Cappelle," *Oud Holland* 10 (3) (1892): 26–40, esp. 37–39. For an English translation of the inventory of Van de Cappelle's estate, see Margarita Russell, *Jan van de Cappelle 1624/6–1679* (Leigh-on-Sea, U.K.: F. Lewis, 1975), 48–57.
75. Very little is known about the prices these works fetched in the seventeenth century. A notebook belonging to collector Sybrand I Feitama (1620–1701) offers some insight, but his reports on the purchase of drawings begin only in 1685. Most of Feitama's drawings (including landscapes) were estimated at around 10 guilders, while the most expensive drawings would have cost between 100 and 275 guilders. See B. P. J. Broos, "'Notitie der Teekeningen van Sybrand Feitama': De boekhouding van drie generaties verzamelaars van oude Nederlandse tekenkunst," *Oud Holland* 98 (1984): 13–39, esp. 26–28. For context, the annual income of an unskilled worker in Holland in this period was only 300 guilders (for full-time, year-round work), while a doctor could earn as much as 4,000 guilders a year; wealthy merchants and patricians amassed or inherited fortunes of hundreds of thousands of guilders. Henk van Nierop, "The Anatomy of Society," in *Class Distinctions: Dutch Painting in the Age of Rembrandt and Vermeer*, ed. Ronni Baer (Boston: Museum of Fine Arts, 2015), 31. See also "Value of the Guilder versus the Euro," International Institute of Social History, February 15, 2019, https://iisg.amsterdam/en/research/projects/hpw/calculate.php.
76. Robinson and Anderson, *Drawings from the Age of Bruegel, Rubens, and Rembrandt*, cat. 45.
77. Hollstein, *Dutch and Flemish Etchings, Engravings and Woodcuts, ca. 1450–1700*, vol. 38, no. 150. Van Goyen also included the motif in one of his sketchbook drawings; see ibid.
78. Fred G. Meijer, *Franchoys Ryckhals: Een Zeeuwse meester uit de Gouden Eeuw* (Zieriksee: Stadhuismuseum; Zwolle: WBOOKS, 2019), 31.
79. They are now in the Amsterdam Museum and the Fondation Custodia, Collection Frits Lugt, Paris. See B. P. J. Broos and Marijn Schapelhouman, *Nederlandse Tekenaars geboren tussen 1600 en 1660* (Amsterdam: Amsterdams Historisch Museum, 1993), cat. 170.
80. Ilja M. Veldman, "From Allegory to Genre," in *Images for the Eye and Soul: Function and Meaning in Netherlandish Prints (1450–1650)*, by Ilja M. Veldman (Leiden: Primavera Press, 2006), 193–222, esp. 222.

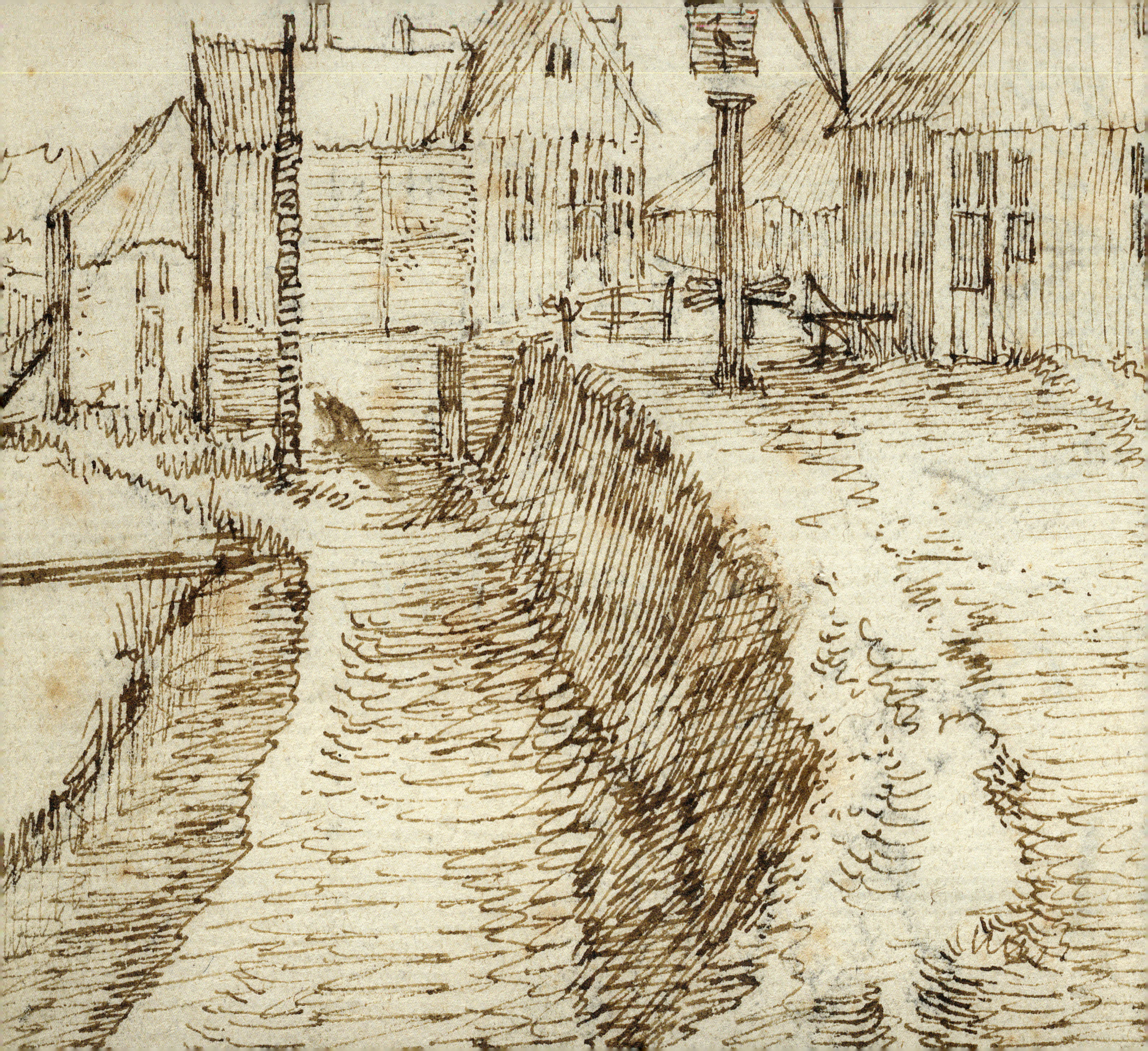

Claes Jansz. Visscher

*View of Houtewael*, c. 1607–8

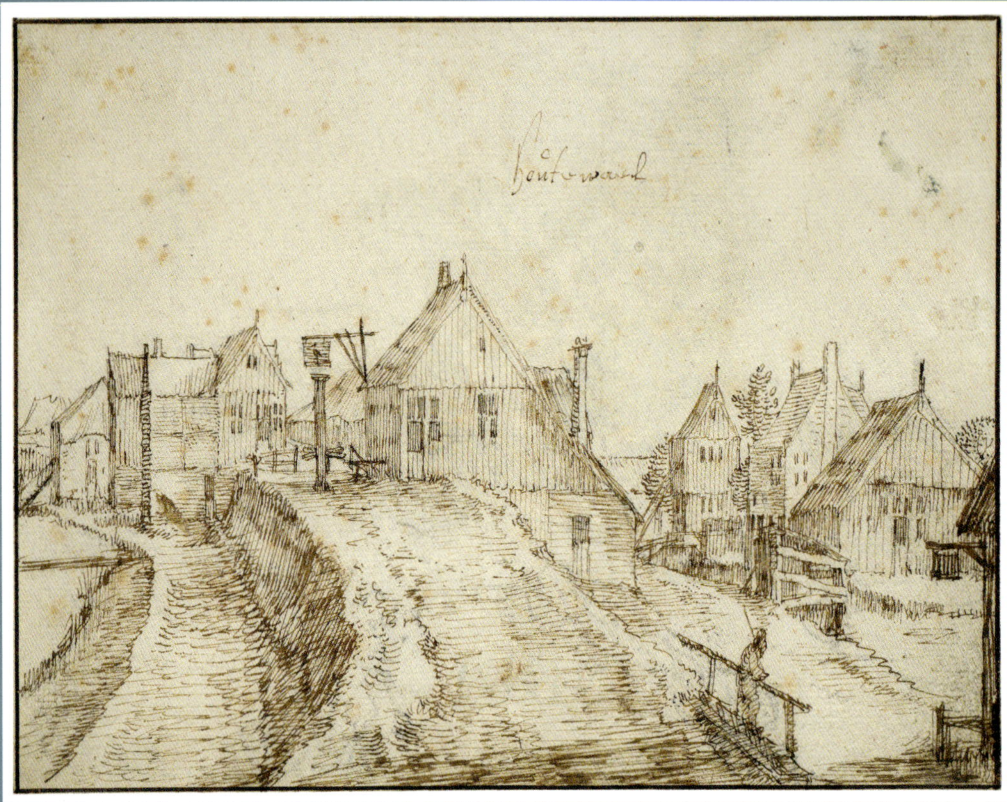

Fig. D Claes Jansz. Visscher, *View of Houtewael*, c. 1607–8. See p. 232 for full information.

This small cluster of wooden and thatched structures along a dike captured the attention of pivotal Dutch artist Claes Jansz. Visscher (1587–1652), whose energetic and spontaneous pen lines evocatively render the various textures of each visual component. Identified as Houtewael by Visscher at upper center, this village outside Amsterdam is recognizable in other artists' drawings of the locale, including those made several decades later by Rembrandt (1606–1669) and his school. Undoubtedly drawn on the dike leading up to the structures, *View of Houtewael* is one of a suite of drawings, similar in subject matter, that Visscher drew in and around Amsterdam and Haarlem. He used many from this project, although not this sheet, as the basis for etchings depicting scenes from Haarlem and its environs in his enormously influential series of twelve prints *Plaisante Plaetsen* (Pleasant Places; 1611–12), which were inspired by Flemish print series from decades prior.

Elements such as a low horizon, humble structures, and a road or path leading into the composition became common means to represent the Dutch countryside and implied interactions between urban and rural inhabitants. Draftsmen who followed close on the heels of Visscher would adopt his quick and deft use of the pen – evocative of the fleeting nature of observation – in their own landscape sheets.

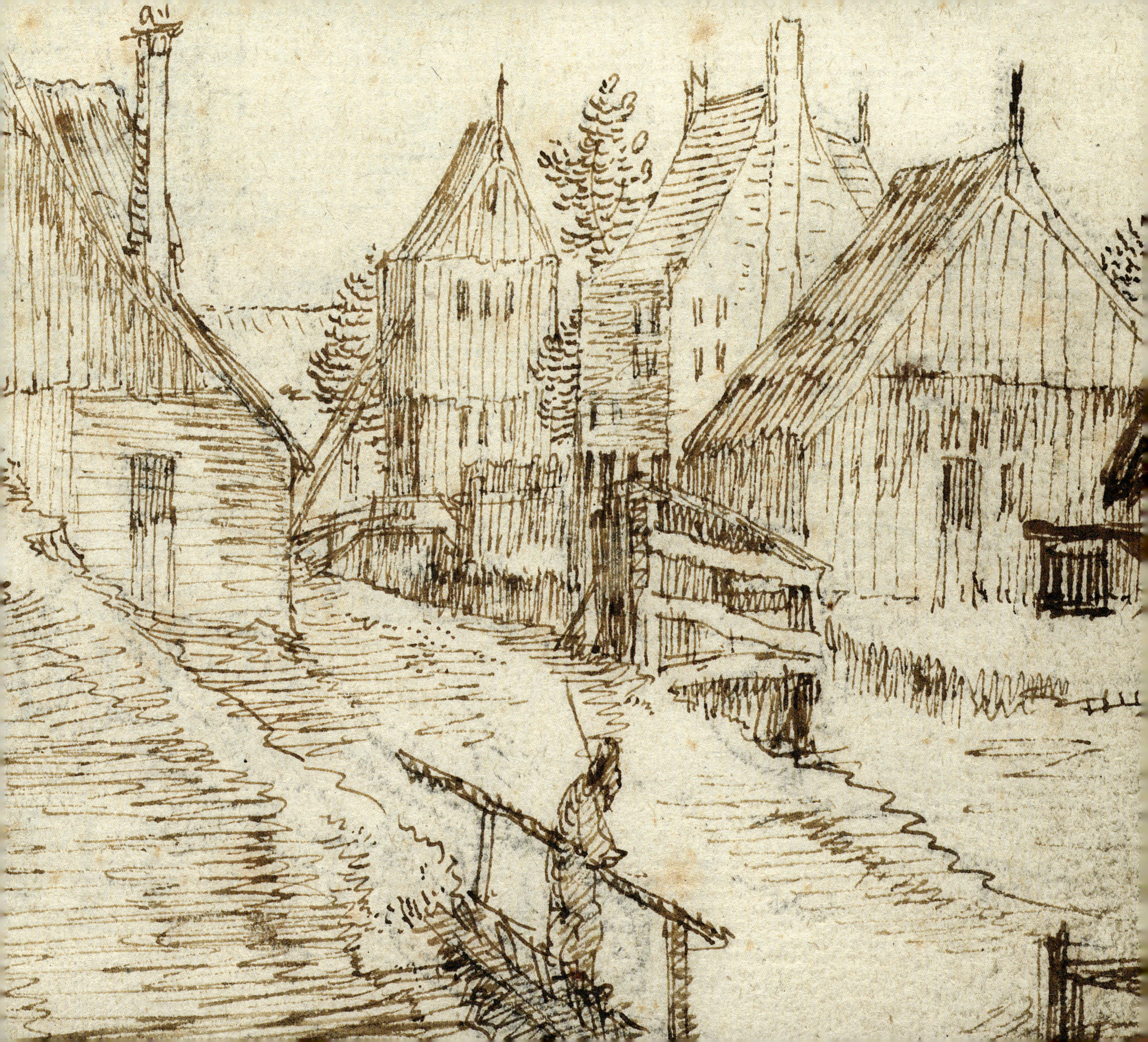

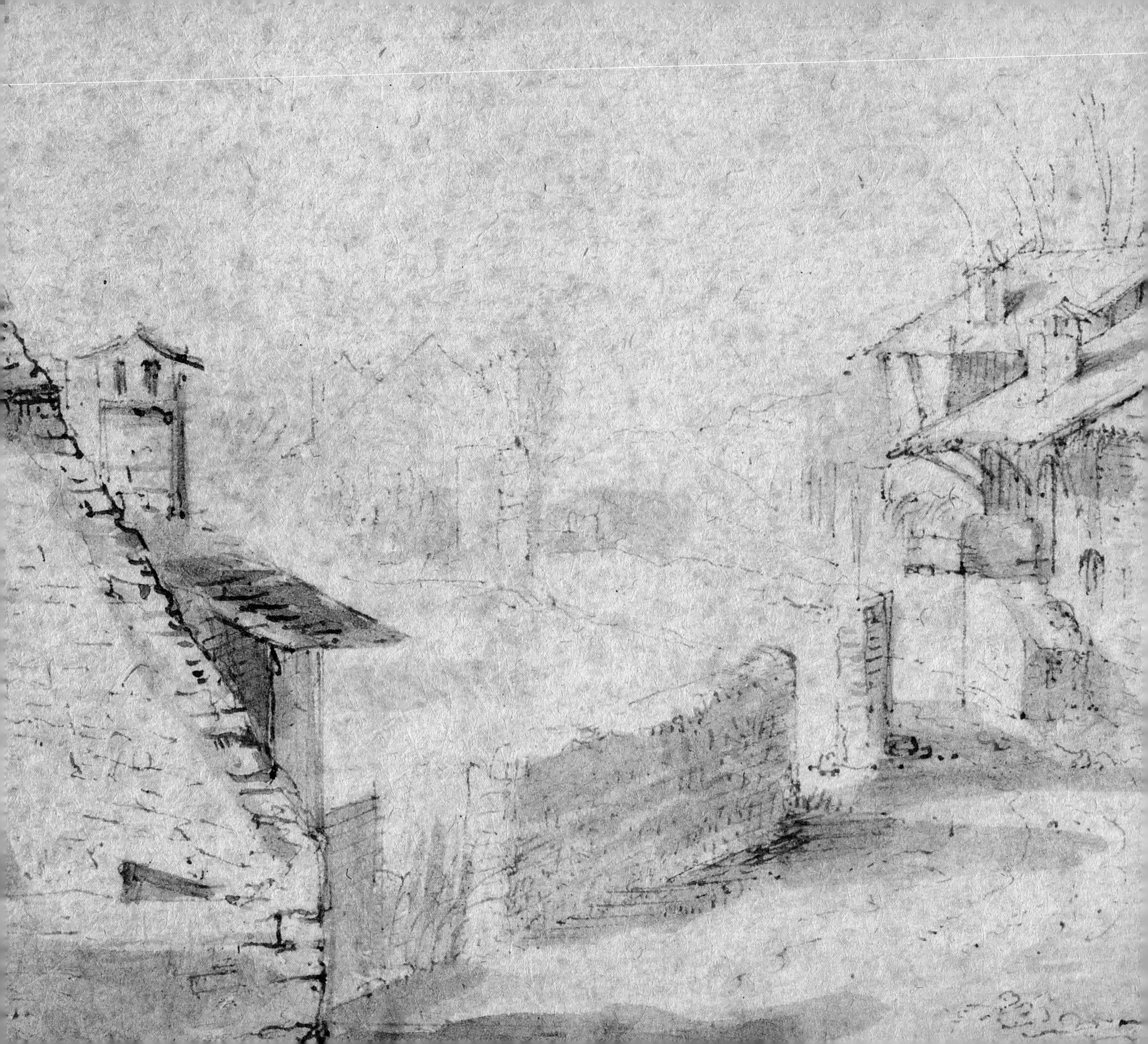

Paulus van Vianen
*A Village Street in Primolano*,
1607

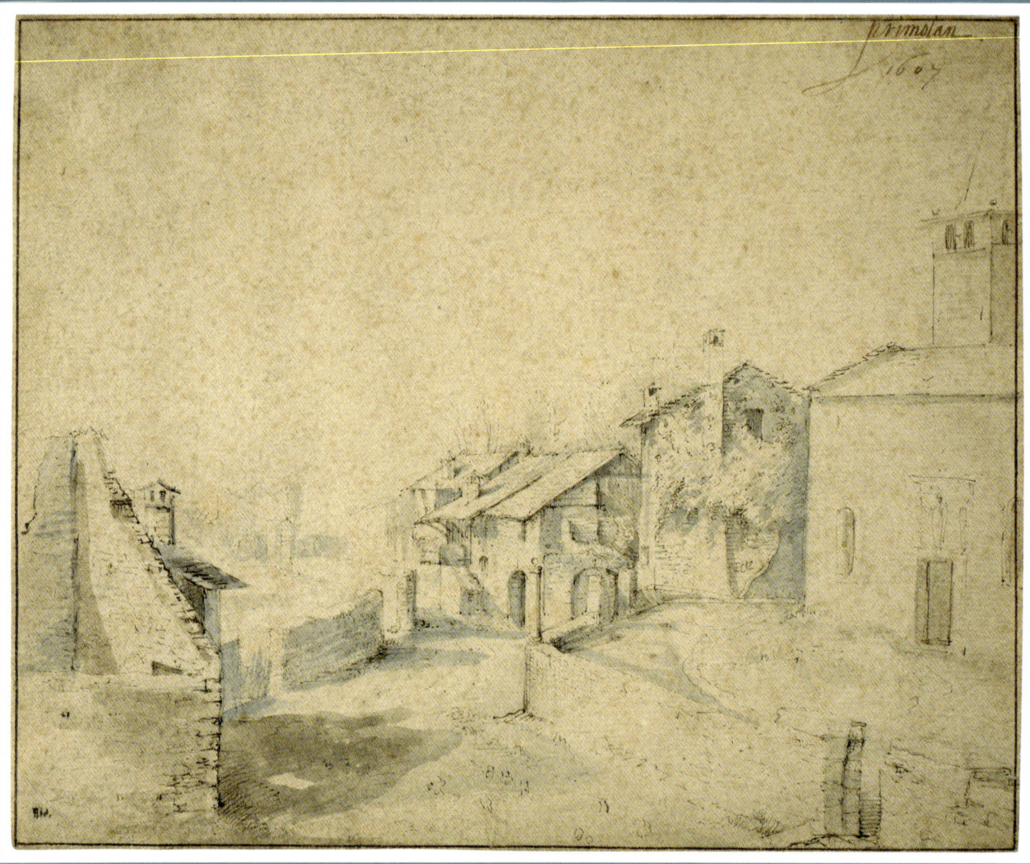


Fig. E Paulus van Vianen, *A Village Street in Primolano,* 1607. See p. 232 for full information.

Utrecht-born silversmith Paulus van Vianen's (1570–1613) view of Primolano, an alpine town located in what is now the far northern Dolomites area of Italy's Vicenza province, is inscribed *Primolan / 1607* at upper right. Opinions differ as to whether the inscription is in the artist's hand, casting a modicum of doubt on its topographical accuracy and presumed rendering from life. Nonetheless, the cluster of small structures must have been recognizable, and the delicate use of pen applied to the painstakingly rendered architecture suggests that the artist was working from observation. His use of increasingly fainter lines as the buildings recede, together with the application of pale blue wash – a tonal element also used in Flanders and by Flemish émigrés to the Dutch Republic – imbues this sheet with a magical sense of atmosphere.

Although Van Vianen's artistic roots and apprenticeship were in the Northern Netherlands, his career took him on an international path throughout Europe, which included positions in Munich and Salzburg before he ultimately earned a lifetime appointment as *Kammergoldschmeid* to Holy Roman Emperor Rudolf II in Prague (1603–13). Van Vianen's metalwork was his crowning achievement, in particular his stunning developments in the bold and flamboyant auricular style. His delicate landscape drawings, including this one, offer a window into his quiet interpretations of locations encountered on his travels.

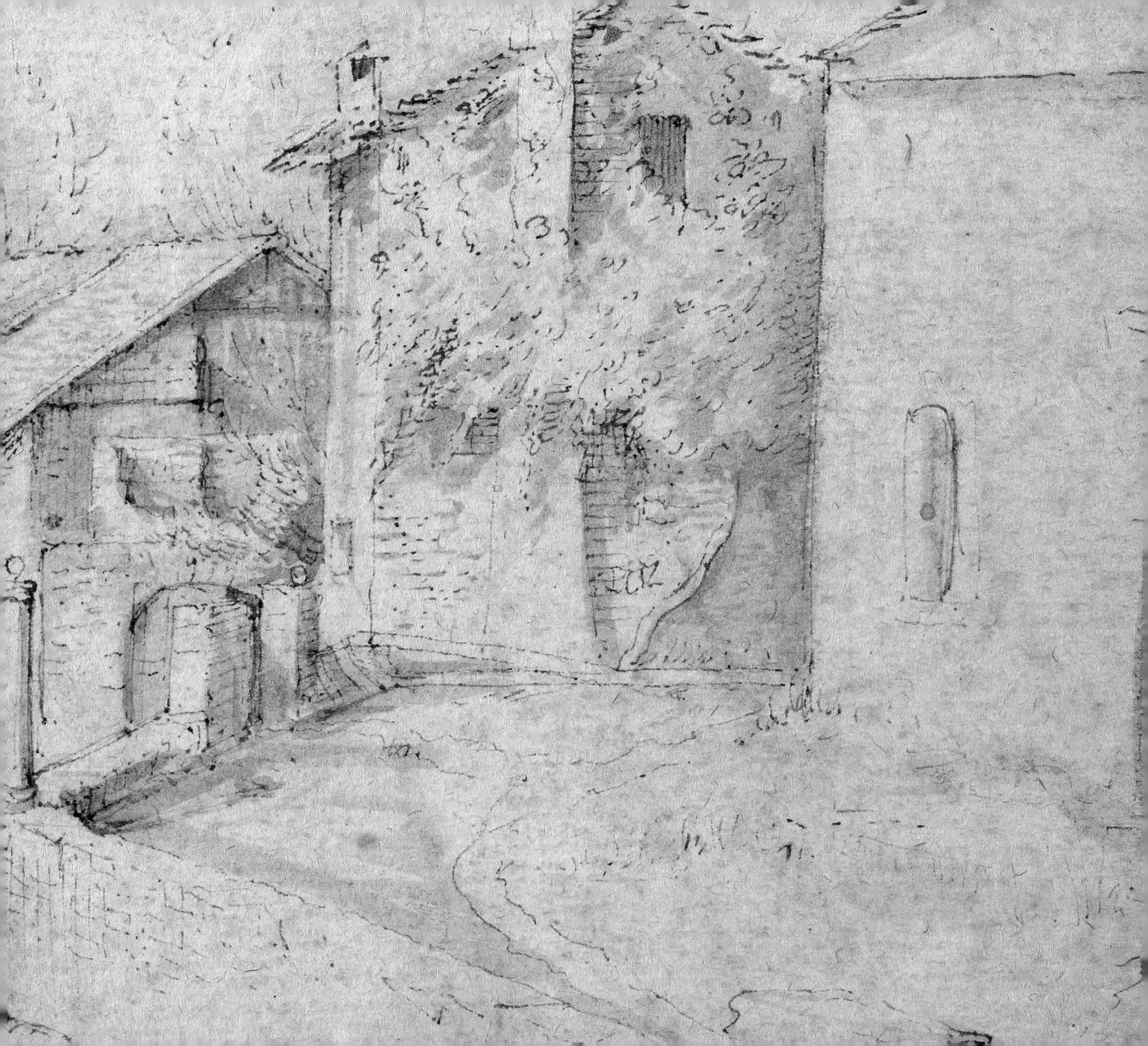

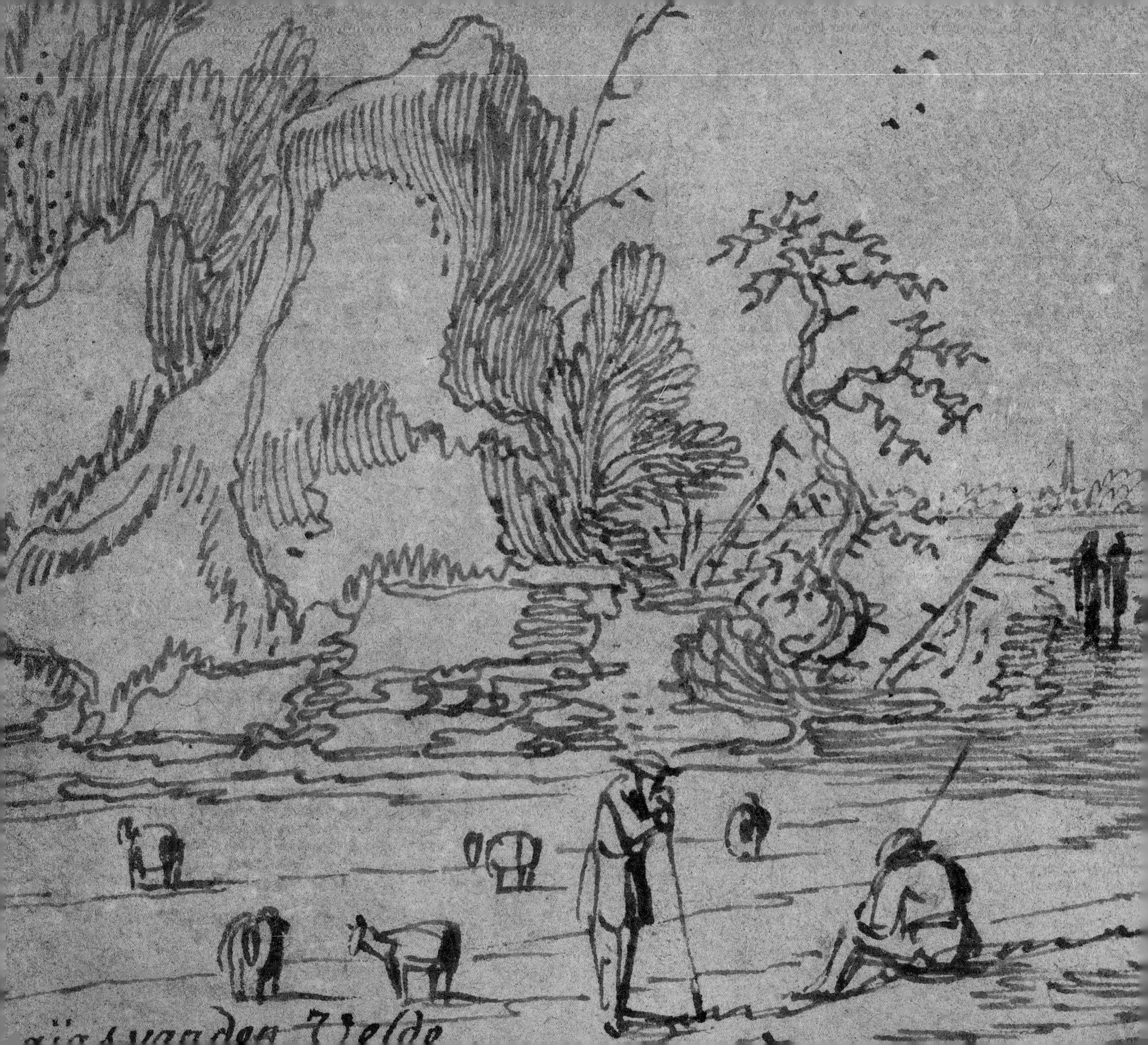
vanden Velde

Esaias van de Velde
*Shepherds and Sheep before a Rock*, c. 1615–16

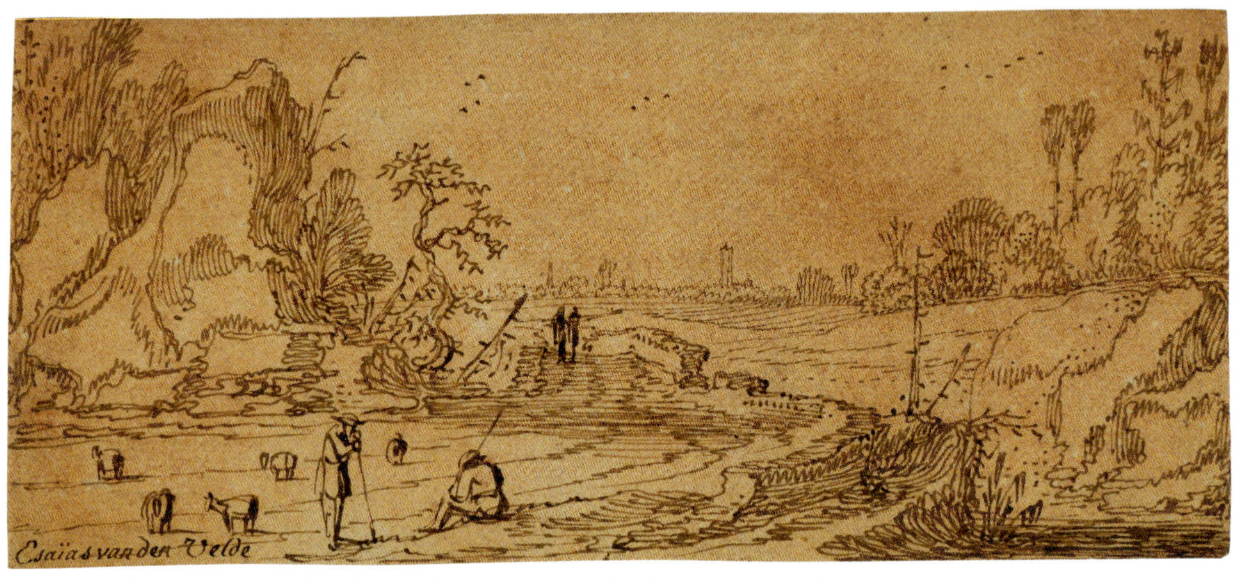


Fig. F Esaias van de Velde, *Shepherds and Sheep before a Rock*, c. 1615–16. See p. 232 for full information.

In this small but powerful drawing, Esaias van de Velde (1587–1630) portrays a bending road in front of fields that open up to a town in the distance. Rock formations in the left and right foreground and a cluster of trees in the right middle ground enclose the scene. Two nondescript travelers walk across a bridge toward the center of the sheet, at the visual waypoint between the distant buildings and the immediate rural environs.

This drawing, executed in brown ink, is one of at least twenty-five landscapes on similarly sized oblong paper toned with red chalk wash—twelve attributable to Esaias and thirteen to his equally innovative and noteworthy cousin, Jan van de Velde II (1593–1641). Apart from this group, neither artist used red tone in their works, in contrast to the monochrome drawings in black chalk with or without gray wash that were common in Esaias's oeuvre and widely adopted by later generations. The use of paper prepared in this way was also unusual in the art of the period more generally and speaks to the Van de Veldes' interest in the exploration of media. Of this suite, three drawings, including this one, were reproduced in a group of six landscape etchings published by Claes Jansz. Visscher (1587–1652), who credited Esaias as the designer on the title page. The claim that they were drawn from life is not expressly stated via inscription, as with earlier print series of the regional countryside, but rather alluded to through plausibly local subjects such as this.

Like many of his fellow artists, Esaias, native to Amsterdam and active in Haarlem and The Hague, would have known the characteristic features of the lands surrounding the country's most prosperous cities—and would have also been familiar with the growing extant works already depicting rustic imagery. Here, through a controlled use of the pen, he offers a vision, masterfully composed, of what could be found in the countryside around the province of Holland.

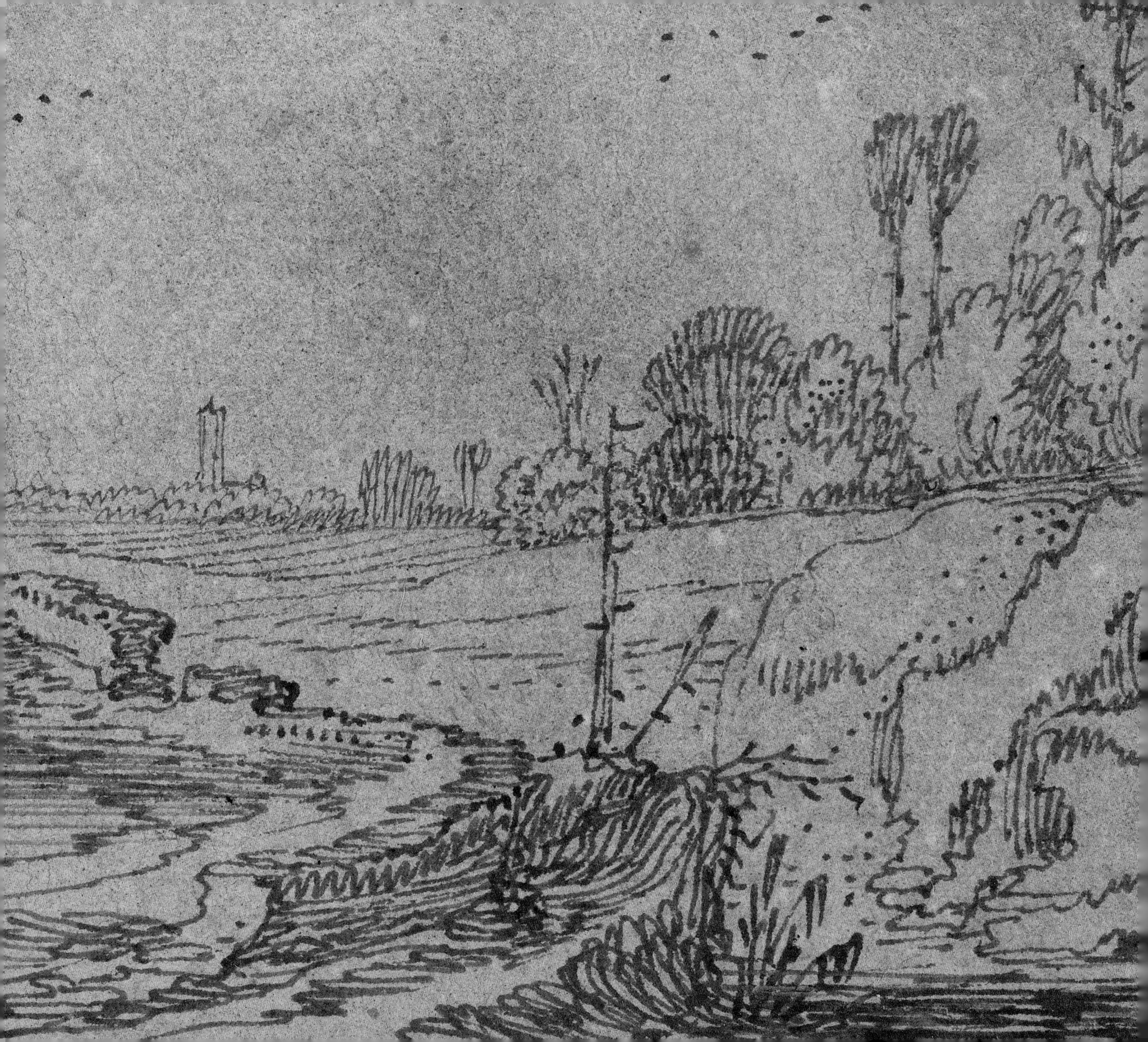

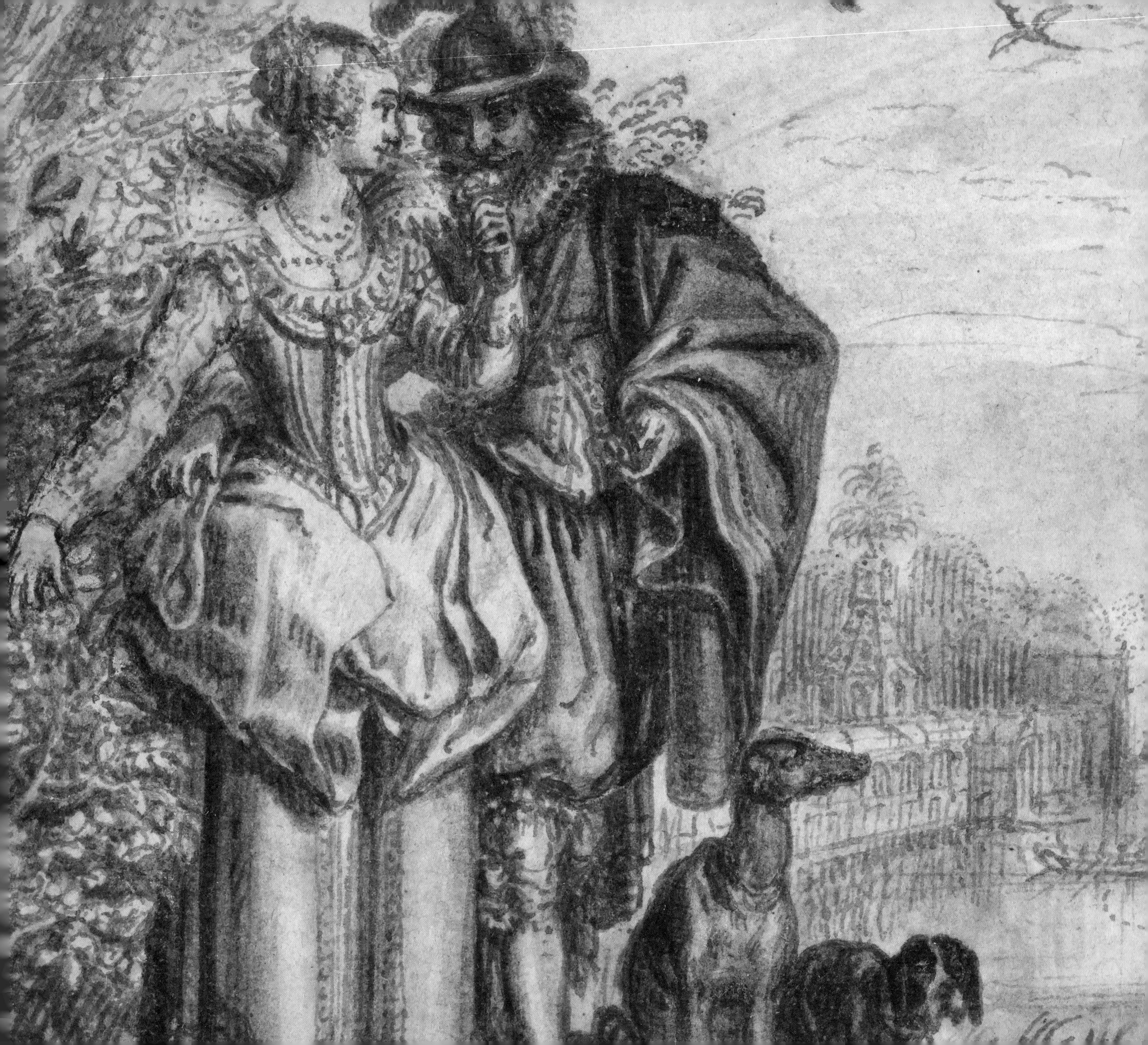

Adriaen van de Venne
*Spring*, 1622

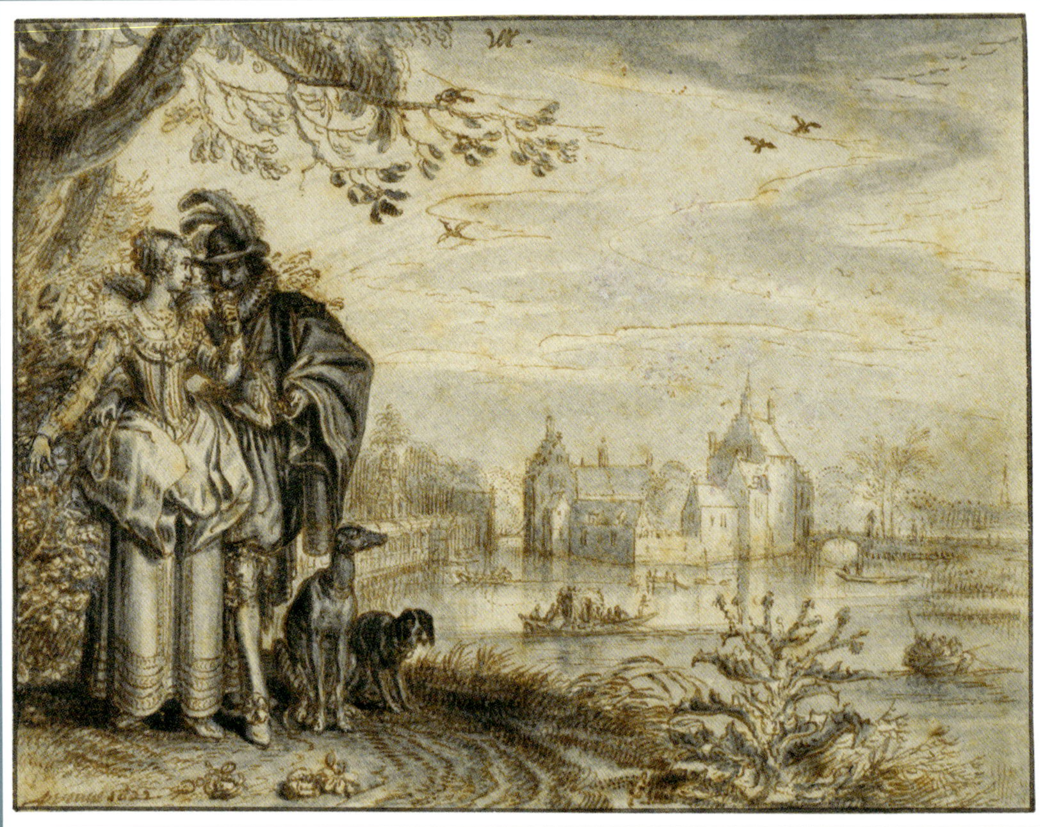

Fig. G Adriaen van de Venne, *Spring*, 1622. See p. 232 for full information.

Well-established iconographic series such as the Four Seasons and the Twelve Months persisted into the seventeenth century as attractive themes in both drawings and prints, either as models for complete sets or as inspiration for an independent work. Active in Middelburg and The Hague, Adriaen van de Venne (1589–1662) drew *Spring* as the first of four drawings of the seasons that served as preparatory designs for prints illustrating Jacob Cats's *Houwelick* (Marriage) of 1625, a behavioral code scripted in verse for women in various phases of life. Accompanying the portion of Cats's poem dedicated to the Bride, *Spring*, inscribed *Ver*, depicts a fashionably dressed young couple in courtship in front of a handsome, well-kept castle and a waterway enjoyed by several boating parties. In *Summer* (Wife) and *Autumn* (Mother), the couples labor and then harvest, and in *Winter* (Widow), an elderly couple appears in a similar setting to *Spring*, but with the waterway now frozen and populated by carriages and figures on foot, the castle crumbling behind.

Despite the presence of incising—a common artifact of the transfer process from drawing to printing plate—Van de Venne's signature and date of 1622 on all four drawings imply that he was aware of the ultimately salable nature of these print designs. Like many drawings that prepared prints, *Spring* functioned as both a utilitarian and collectible object.

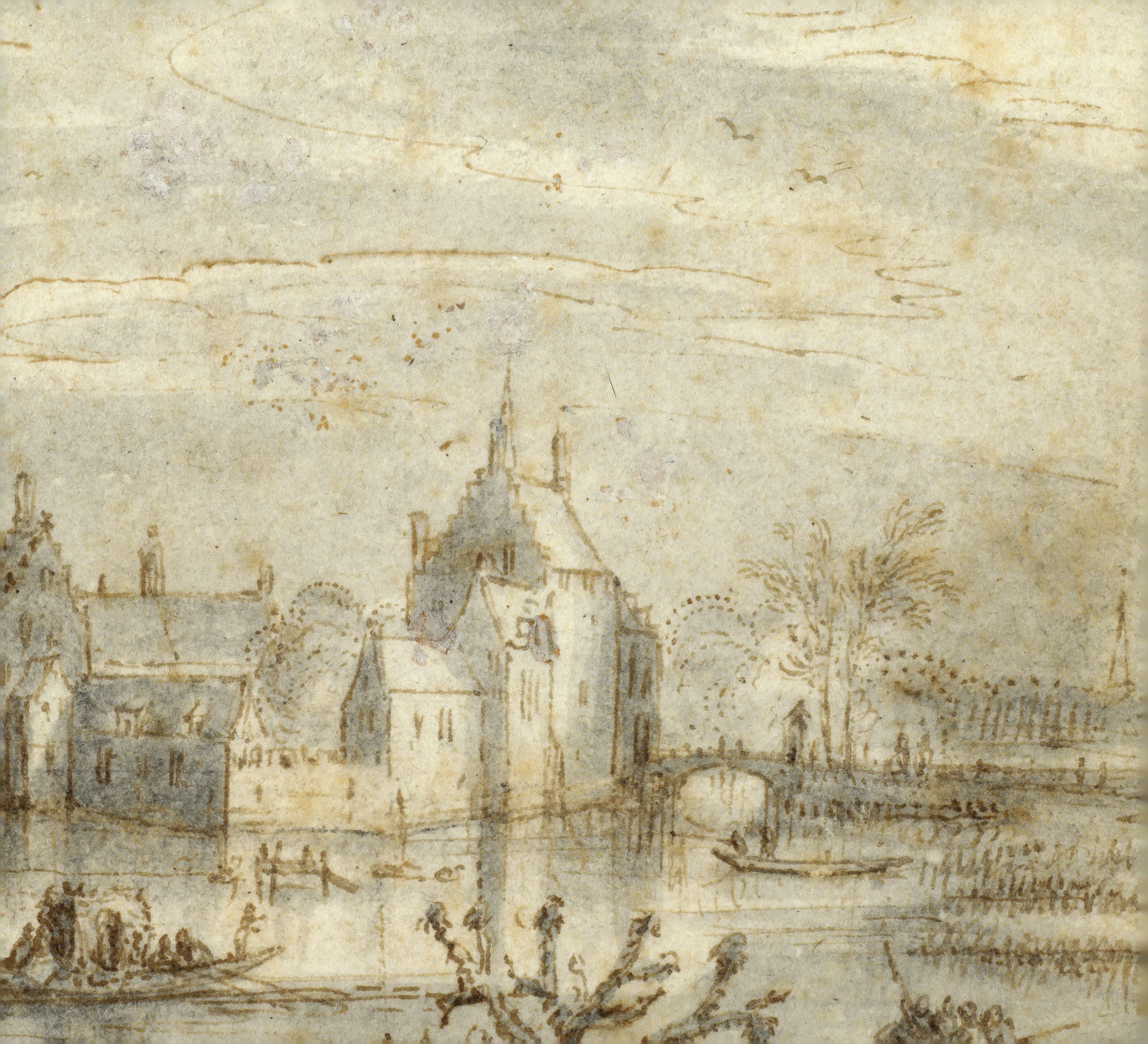

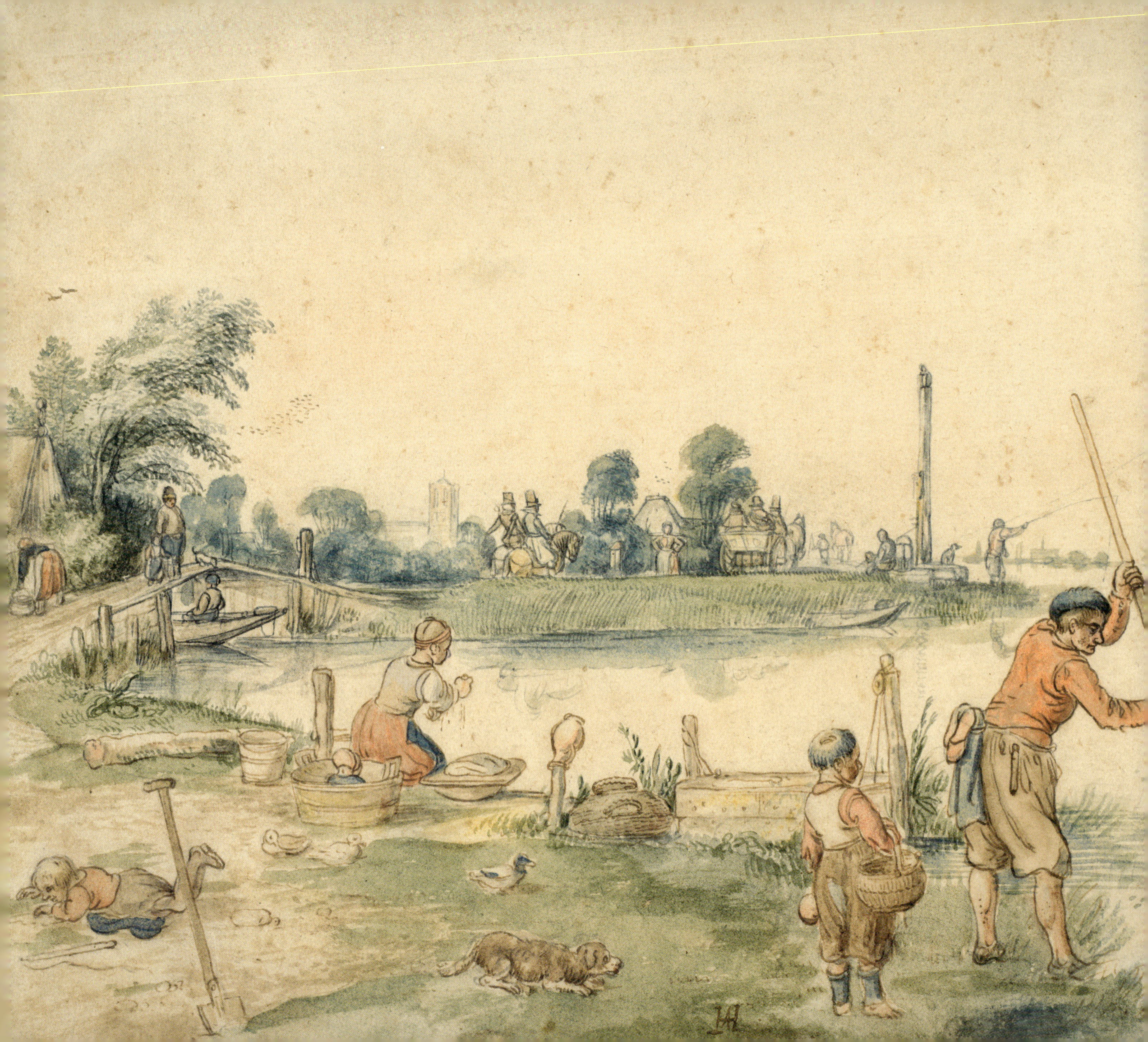

# SHIFTING TERRAIN

## ENVIRONMENTAL CHANGE, GLOBAL EXPANSION, AND THE DRAWN LANDSCAPE

*Joanna Sheers Seidenstein*

Fig. 1 Cornelis Vroom, *Landscape with a Road and a Fence*, 1631. See p. 233 for full information.



We stand on a path between field and forest, a wooden fence separating us from the dense, dark trees. The dry, sandy ground, pebbles, and tufts of grass absorb our attention as we follow the rutted path with our eyes until it slopes out of view and leaves us looking out over a sun-drenched meadow. Here, the hyper-specific detail and varied penwork of the foreground give way to a slice of paper that is untouched save for two tiny circular strokes: a pair of sheep sleeping in the sun. Only after some time do our eyes adjust and allow us to discern, beyond the strip of trees and farm buildings, a tiny cityscape rising between a river and rolling dunes in the distance.

This drawing, Cornelis Vroom's (1590/92–1661) *Landscape with a Road and a Fence* of 1631 (Fig. 1), emphatically situates the viewer *away* from city, river, and coast – signifiers of the developed maritime region in which the majority of the Dutch population lived in the seventeenth century. There, large urban centers, commercial farms, and scheduled barges assigned pronounced values to both space and time.[1] In contrast, the so-called inland zone, with its higher elevation and sandy soil, remained largely untouched by these developments; here, subsistence living continued to prevail as the population decreased.[2] Carefully composed with extensive graphite underdrawing, Vroom's sheet defines this pastoral landscape through its distance, and difference, from the mercantile world. It is, however, hardly an unequivocal image of the pleasant respite scholars have often attributed to such imagery.[3] For seventeenth-century viewers, the sheep dotting the landscape might have evoked classical notions of *otium* (idleness), but they may as well have brought to mind uncultivated, and uncultivable, land. So remarked an artist by the name of Vincent Laurensz. van der Vinne (1628–1702) as he traveled from his native Haarlem eastward into Germany in the early 1650s: "The closer you come to Cologne the less buckwheat there is, and more sheep put out to grass in large flocks can be seen. We also passed . . . many villages, most of which had been laid to waste."[4] The war with Spain, compounded with centuries of land use, including the extensive logging and grazing that spread sand over once grassy fields, had yielded many such impoverished landscapes.[5] As the second half of the century unfolded, ongoing military conflict, occupation by foreign powers, and the continual risks and failings of the Republic's colonial enterprise overseas made evident the vulnerability of Dutch territory as both physical and political entity.

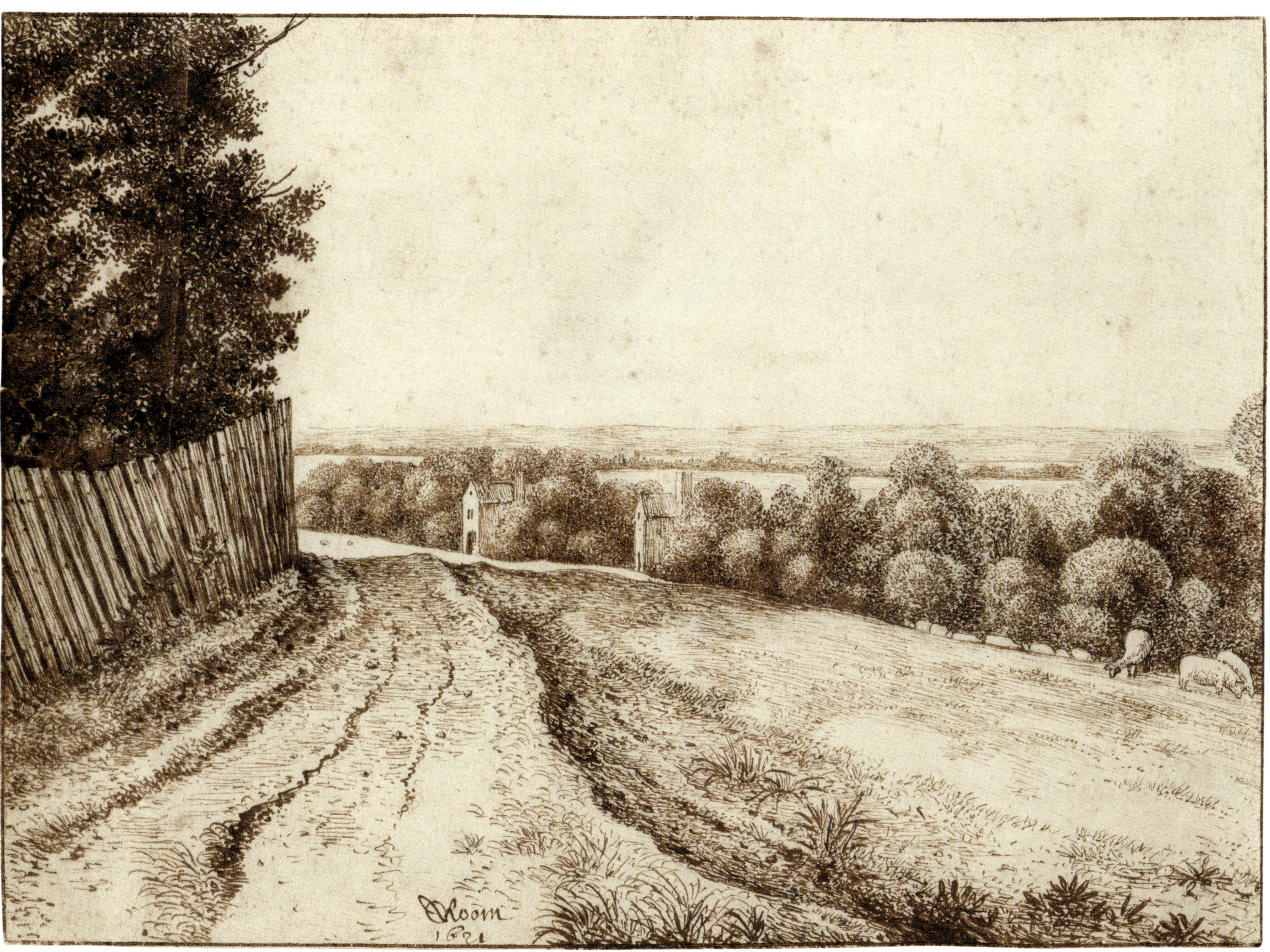
CVroom
1621

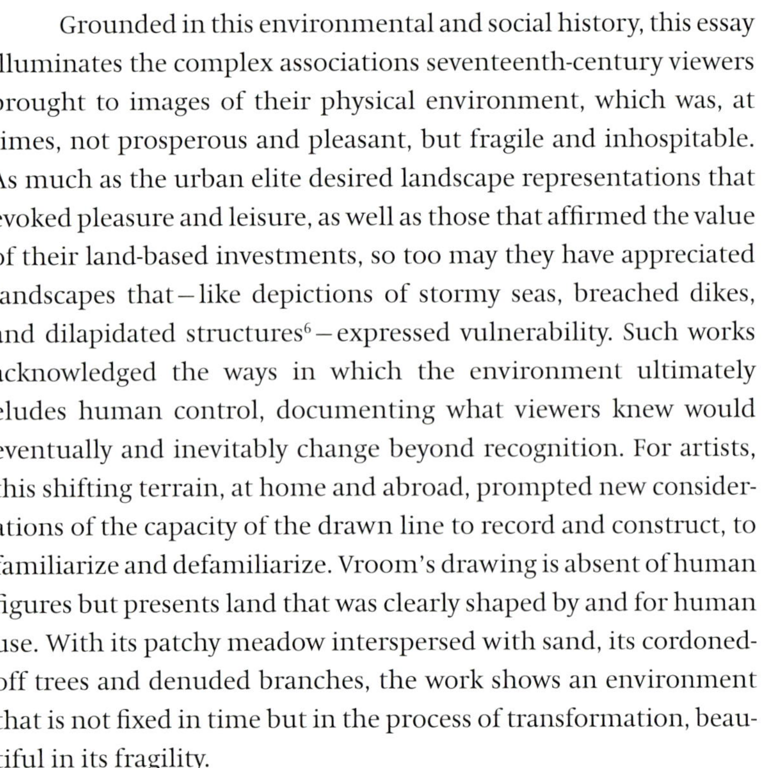

Fig. 2 Claes Jansz. Visscher, *Bleaching Fields near the Haarlemmer Hout*, 1611–12. Etching, 10.4 × 15.9 cm. Harvard Art Museums/Fogg Museum, Light-Outerbridge Collection, Gift of Robert M. Light, M24417.56.

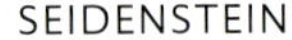


Grounded in this environmental and social history, this essay illuminates the complex associations seventeenth-century viewers brought to images of their physical environment, which was, at times, not prosperous and pleasant, but fragile and inhospitable. As much as the urban elite desired landscape representations that evoked pleasure and leisure, as well as those that affirmed the value of their land-based investments, so too may they have appreciated landscapes that—like depictions of stormy seas, breached dikes, and dilapidated structures[6]—expressed vulnerability. Such works acknowledged the ways in which the environment ultimately eludes human control, documenting what viewers knew would eventually and inevitably change beyond recognition. For artists, this shifting terrain, at home and abroad, prompted new considerations of the capacity of the drawn line to record and construct, to familiarize and defamiliarize. Vroom's drawing is absent of human figures but presents land that was clearly shaped by and for human use. With its patchy meadow interspersed with sand, its cordoned-off trees and denuded branches, the work shows an environment that is not fixed in time but in the process of transformation, beautiful in its fragility.

## PLEASANT PLACES?

The idea of the countryside as a place of mental and physical refreshment is an enduring one. It was expressed by various ancient writers, most famously by Virgil, whose *Eclogues* was translated into Dutch at the beginning of the seventeenth century.[7] This topos, in combination with the urbanization of the Dutch Republic and the real desire for respite from work and from the heat, noise, and smells of the city, informed the frequent invocation of pleasure and pleasantness in reference to the outdoors and its representation in seventeenth-century art and literature. The countryside was indeed a place *away*—outside the city, but typically not far from it and often directly connected to the mercantile world, as much of the farmland in the maritime region was owned by urban investors. Unlike Vroom's *Landscape with a Road and a Fence*, most landscapes produced in the period are peopled, and many show sites of human labor. Claes Jansz. Visscher's (1587–1652) suite of Haarlem views from 1611–12, which he described on the series' title page as *Plaisante Plaetsen* (Pleasant Places) for "those who do not have the time to travel" (see p. 39), includes multiple scenes in which farm workers toil, effectively creating the landscape to be consumed, visually and economically, by these armchair travelers (Fig. 2).

Such celebration of rural labor, also grounded in ancient topoi, had long appealed to the urban elite. As Larry Silver has discussed, the laborers in Pieter Bruegel the Elder's (1526/30–1569) *Months*, painted for the suburban villa of Antwerp merchant Nicholas de Jonghelink, appear as "natural extensions of agriculture itself."[8] This assertion of a "natural order" explains the preponderance, famously noted by John Barrell with regard to eighteenth-century British landscape, of images of the rural poor in homes in which such individuals, in life, never would have been welcome.[9]

Hendrick Avercamp's (1585–1634) *Landscape with a Fisherman* of the 1620s (Fig. 3), one of many finished ink and watercolor drawings by the artist, presumably made for well-to-do buyers,[10] presents such a scene of supposed social and ecological harmony. In the foreground, a man with a fishing net, a woman washing linens, and barefoot children experience land and water in a very direct, physical manner. In contrast, in the midground, a group of finely attired figures on horseback and in a coach move through, rather than inhabit, the landscape. Avercamp frequently juxtaposed members of different classes in his work. His many winter landscapes articulate vividly the realities of economic disparity: although the wealthy figures enjoying themselves on the ice and the poor struggling to warm and feed themselves occupy the same space, they have very different experiences of the cold.[11] In the present drawing, as in the winter scenes, the artist renders his laborers with simple contours and minimal modeling, a figural style undoubtedly informed by Bruegel's celebrated peasant scenes. The level of detail with which Avercamp renders the fishing activity, however, suggests that the drawing may also register more specific, contemporary realities.

By the end of the 1620s, land reclamation campaigns, enabled by innovative windmill technology and the construction of extensive networks of dikes and canals, had transformed many of the country's lakes into tracts of highly fertile land called polders. This feat of engineering substantially increased the country's farmland and connected much of its waterways to the sea, to the great profit of those who had invested in this land. The concomitant reduction of bodies of freshwater, however, took a significant toll on the rural poor, already largely divested of their own landholdings and often reliant on freshwater fishing as a source of sustenance and income.[12] Read as a depiction of a landscape—and a community—at risk of disappearing, Avercamp's drawing might have functioned for seventeenth-century viewers as a nostalgic depiction of a traditional way of life and an intimation of the economic and ecological

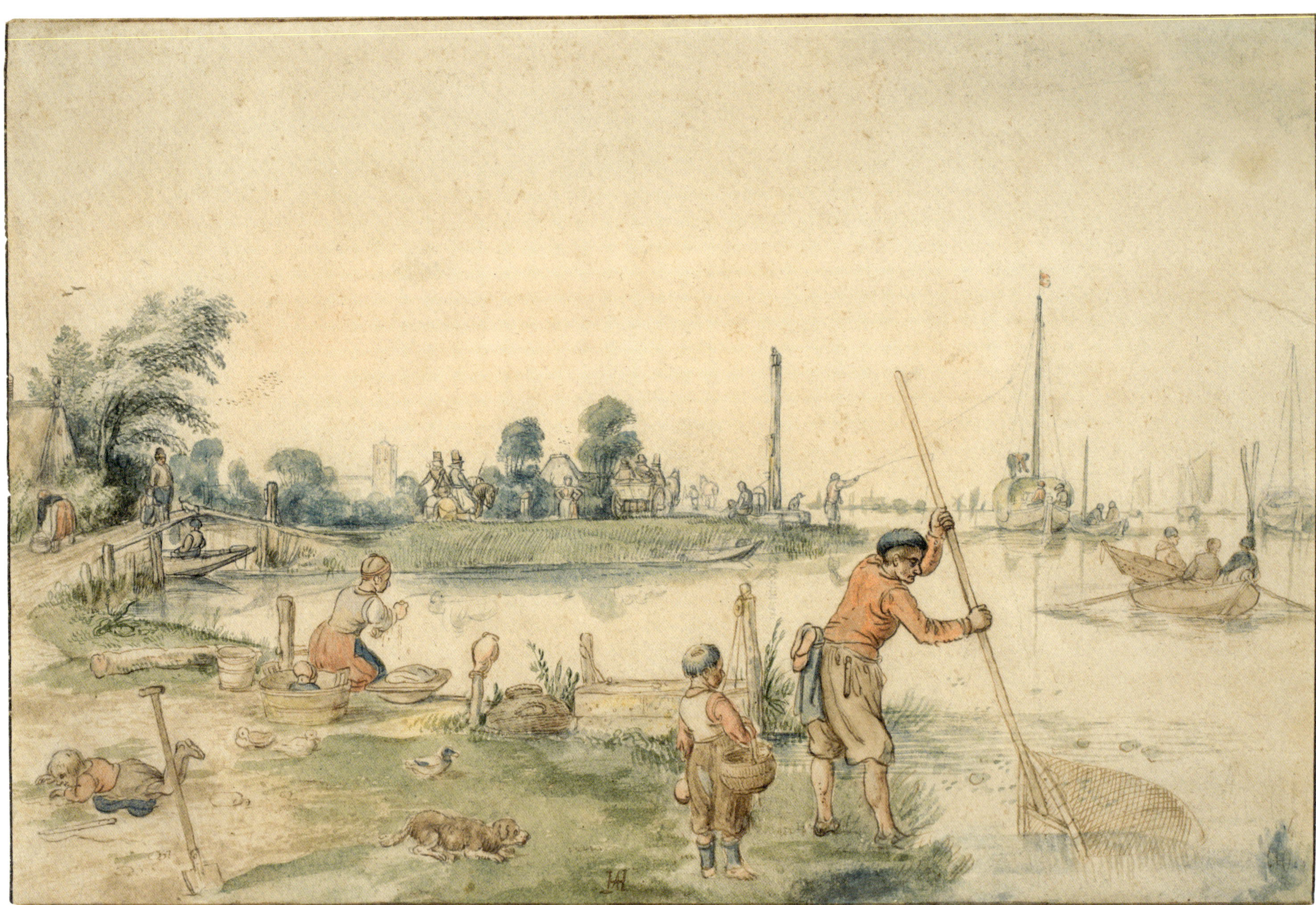

Fig. 3 Hendrick Avercamp, *Landscape with a Fisherman*, 1620s. See p. 228 for full information; see also the detail on p. 72.

Fig. 4 Abraham Rutgers, *Dike on a River*, 1686–87. See p. 232 for full information.

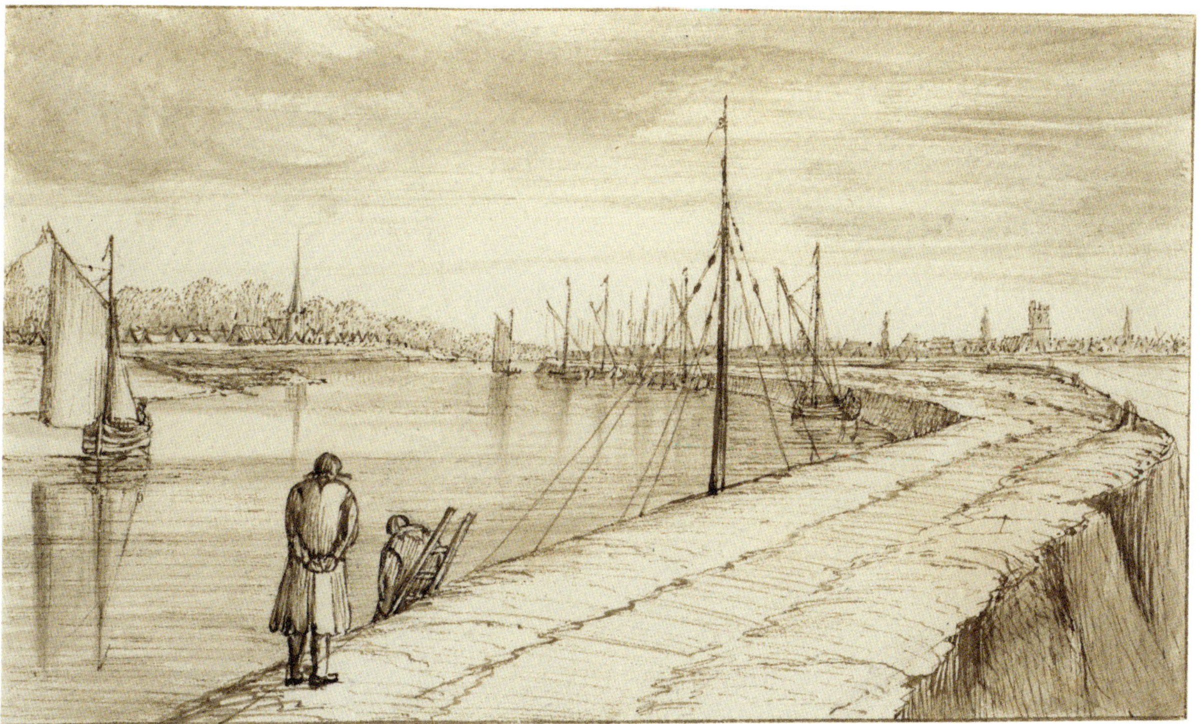



change in progress. From this vantage, it emerges as a counterpoint to works like Abraham Rutgers's (1632–1699) later *Dike on a River* (Fig. 4), which, even as a depiction of an older river embankment, celebrates human engineering: this dike protects the wedge of farmland at right from flooding, while simultaneously serving as a lookout for the mercantile and leisure activity taking place on the river. That Avercamp's drawing was identified, in the eighteenth century if not earlier, as a view of Ouderkerk aan den Amstel, just south of Amsterdam, suggests that for some early viewers it brought to mind a specific location and situation, perhaps the transformative poldering of North Holland in the 1620s.[13] The man with the fishing net—whose haul is as yet uncertain—bears a belabored expression, while the boy standing next to him learns a profession that may no longer be viable. The younger child at left has laid down his (toy?) fishing rod altogether to dig or draw in the dirt.

## UNCERTAIN SPACES

While laborers were an expected and essential part of the countryside, the beggars and wayfarers whom the urban day-tripper might also encounter were perceived as threats to "the natural order."[14] Such figures, traveling on foot, often with walking sticks and heavy packs, can be seen in many seventeenth-century landscapes, including some of Visscher's *Pleasant Places* (see Fig. 2). While more subtle than the scenes of ambush that figure into the landscape prints of the period and that challenged the expectations of viewers accustomed to evocations of calm and safe peregrinations, the motif of the itinerant poor also called into question the pleasantness and security of the countryside.[15]

A drawing of a river landscape by Vroom is suggestive of this tension (see p. 108, Fig. H). A pleasure boat, identified by the canopy under which its passengers sit, glides across calm water, lulling us into what would seem to be an emphatically pleasant scene. But while Vroom's passengers enjoy themselves, other figures experience the landscape differently: namely, the two rowers and, more ambiguously, the wayfarer at the edge of the spit of land in the midground, whose spindly trees are a quotation of Willem Buytewech's (1591–1624) famous print series of 1616 (see pp. 196–99).[16] Vroom's wayfarer perfectly bridges one of the trees and its reflection in the water, forming a long vertical line perpendicular to the horizontal axis of the pleasure boat and the water's

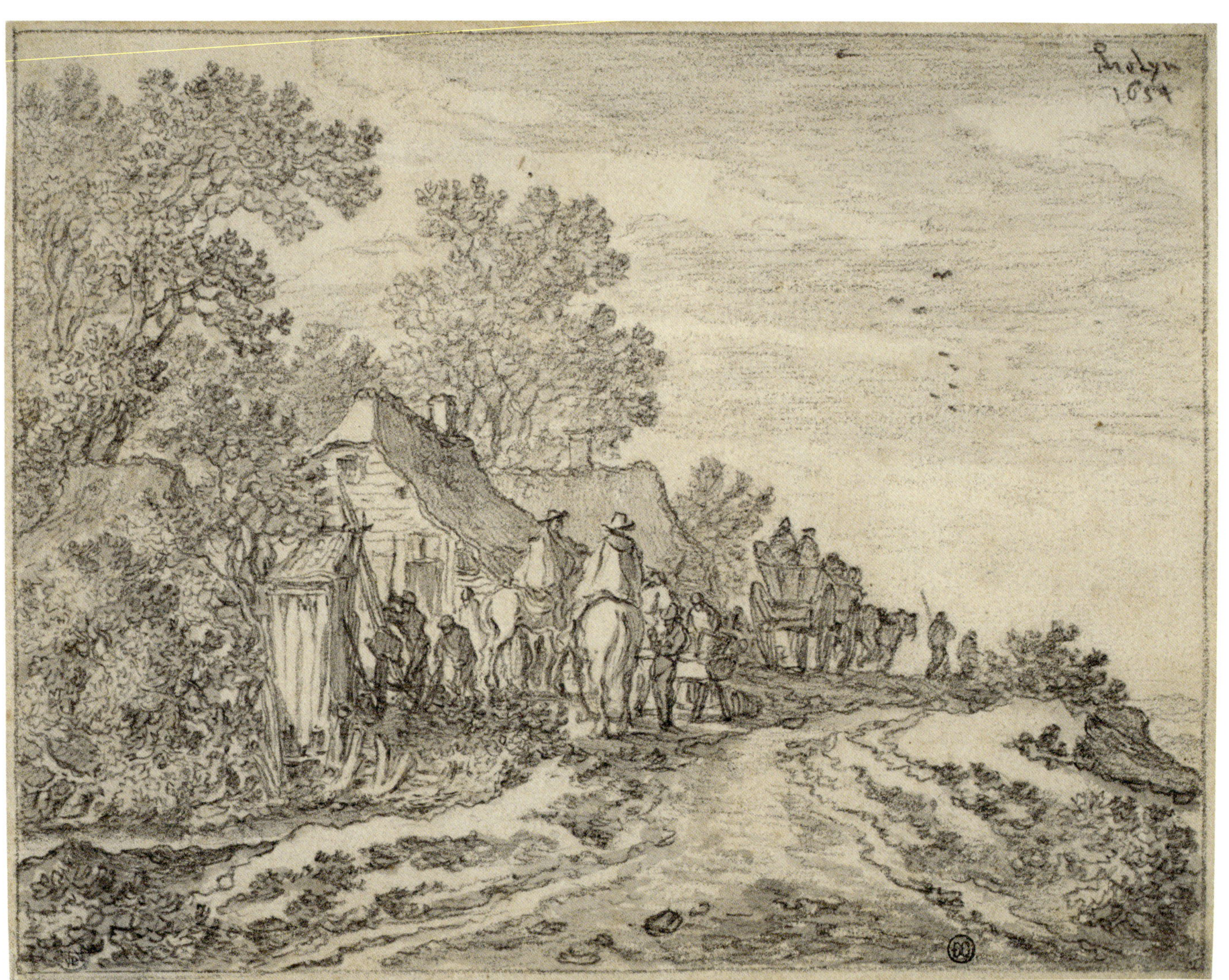

Fig. 5 Pieter de Molijn, *Travelers on a Country Road*, 1654. See p. 230 for full information.

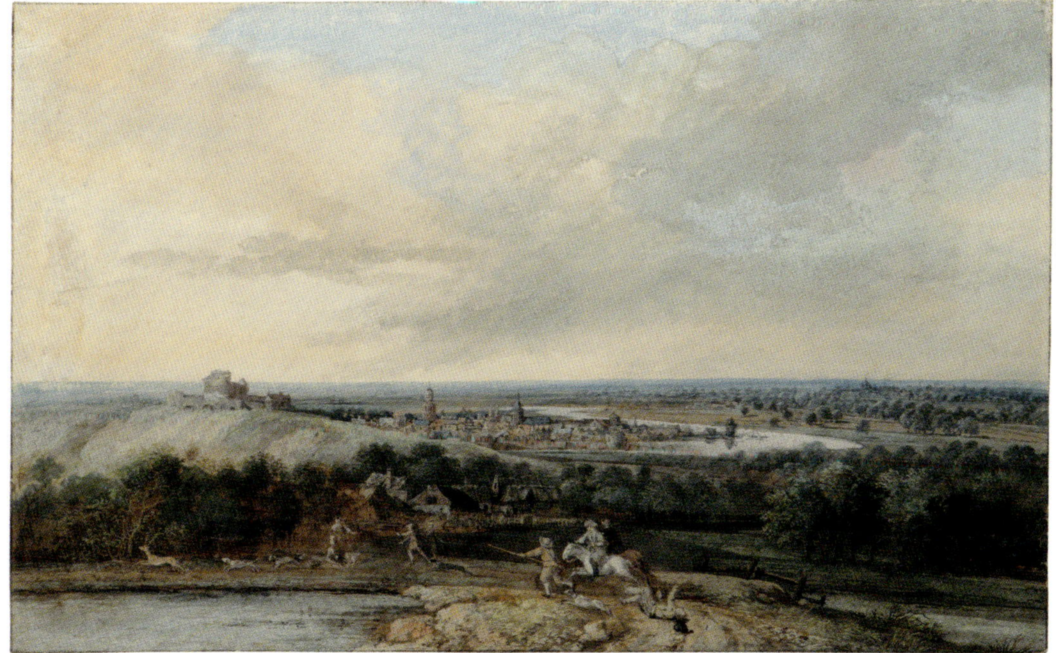

Fig. 6 Gerrit Battem, *Landscape with Hunters*, c. 1665–84. See p. 228 for full information.



surface. This carefully placed figure is, in every respect, a stranger: we cannot discern his identity, actions, or expression. In his very ambiguity, the wayfarer's presence undercuts, and perhaps threatens, the idyllic experience of the boating party.

The unknowns that accompanied the act of travel figured prominently in the drawn landscape throughout the century. In a signed and dated work of 1654 (Fig. 5), landscape specialist Pieter de Molijn (1595–1661) conveys uncertainty through the space of the drawing. The sheet retains, together with its autograph black chalk framing line, its original proportions: measuring 149 × 195 millimeters, it corresponds to one of De Molijn's preferred formats.[17] Its constrained width, in combination with the artist's characteristically agitated line, produces a feeling of confinement that is exacerbated by the absence of a vista into the distance. Here, as in many of his drawings, De Molijn composes the scene such that the viewer looks uphill—taking even further the low vantage point so popular in seventeenth-century landscape.[18] He effectively obscures the horizon or vanishing point, an effect amplified by his placement of figures at the very peak of the slope, about to step out of view. The viewer is led to this threshold of visibility and invisibility by the various travelers seen from behind—two riders attended by servants, a group in a horse-drawn wagon, and two figures on foot—and by the road on which they travel. Leading into the composition from the very edge of the picture plane, this path, like the one in Vroom's *Landscape with a Road and a Fence* (see Fig. 1), draws us into the scene but does not take us to a destination. Instead, it leaves us literally in limbo, at a watering hole for those in transit, complete with an outhouse at left.[19] Moreover, unlike Vroom, De Molijn offers no sense of where this space is in relationship to anything else. Only the tiny wedge of vague horizontal strokes at right gives any acknowledgment of what lies beyond.

De Molijn's obscuring of the horizon is all the more striking in consideration of the panoramic landscapes that, beginning in the middle decades of the century, Philips Koninck (1619–1688) and Gerrit Battem (1636–1684) made into a specialty (Fig. 6).[20] With their bird's-eye view, these works, like their sixteenth-century precursors (see p. 24, Fig. A), offered expansive vistas into the distance, but with all the specificity, observed or imagined, called for by seventeenth-century naturalism. The result is a multitude of visual information laid out for the viewer's consumption from picture plane to

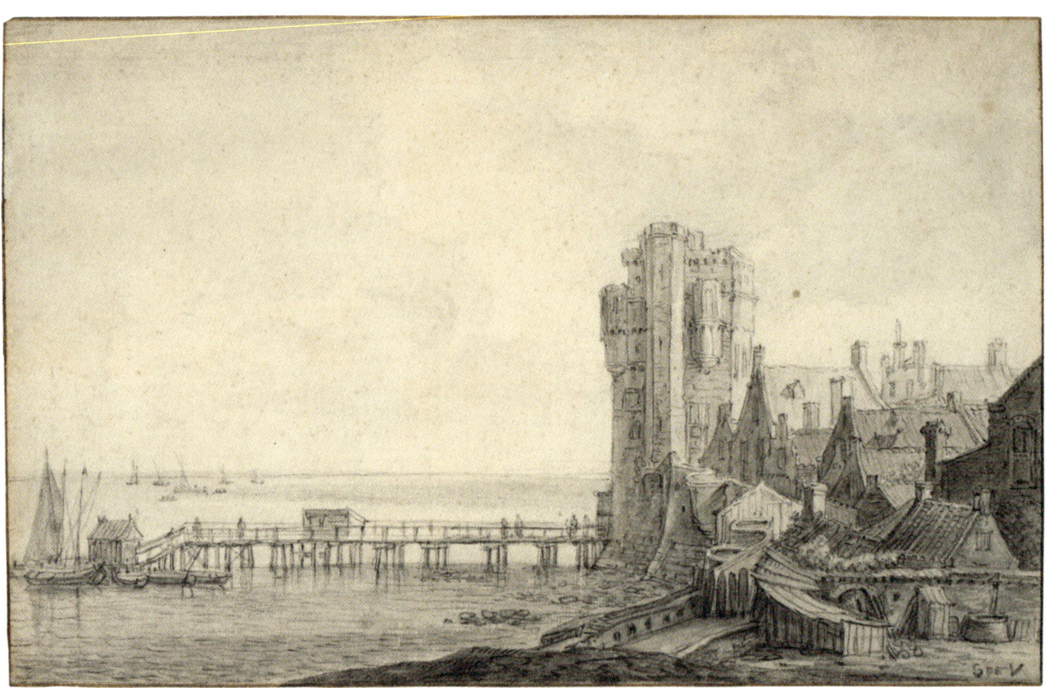

Fig. 7 Simon de Vlieger, *A Port Town*, late 1630s. See p. 233 for full information.

Fig. 8 Cornelis Claesz. van Wieringen, *Coastal View with Ships, Crag with Castle, and Bridge*, 1600–1610. See p. 233 for full information.



horizon – in other words, to the extent permitted by human vision. This is precisely what De Molijn withholds from us. Instead of visibility and clarity, his spatial manipulations yield limitation and uncertainty.

## EXPANSION

De Molijn's and Battem's disparate approaches to depicting distance coincided with the expanding horizons of the Dutch world. While merchants in the Northern Netherlands had long participated in international trade, in the last decade of the sixteenth century the newly established Republic took it on as a national project. The two *Schipvaarten* (journeys) to the east in the 1590s and the chartering of the East India Company (VOC) in 1602 and the West India Company (WIC) in 1621 ushered in an era of expansive global commerce and colonization. The Dutch were ever conscious of the successes and failures of these efforts, which the press reported on regularly.[21] By the 1630s, works such as Simon de Vlieger's (1600/1601–1653) drawing of a port surrounded by calm water were unavoidably embedded with associations with maritime trade (Fig. 7).[22] Here, unlike in De Molijn's drawing, the viewer is invited to gaze, along with the tiny figures on the pier, toward the horizon dividing the shimmering water from the great expanse of sky. Contrasting with the soft, airy strokes in this area of the sheet is the intricate linework of the dense buildings on the shore at right. While we see neither the city within nor the world beyond, this depiction of their intersection brings both to mind, underscoring the commercial ties that link them together.

Importantly, the VOC's and WIC's far-flung trading posts and settlements were all the more pronounced in the minds of the Dutch at home because they existed not just as ideas or news stories, but in images. Representations of these places circulated widely and in various forms. From Frankfurt, the De Bry family published numerous illustrated accounts of the global travels of explorers and merchants from all over Europe. These various publications came to form two multivolume series, one dedicated to the eastern hemisphere, the other to the New World.[23] Illustrations played a significant role within these volumes, and they depicted places of direct significance to the Dutch. As Sarah Mallory has shown, volumes published in 1600 and 1601 included images of the previously unpopulated island of Mauritius, which the Dutch claimed

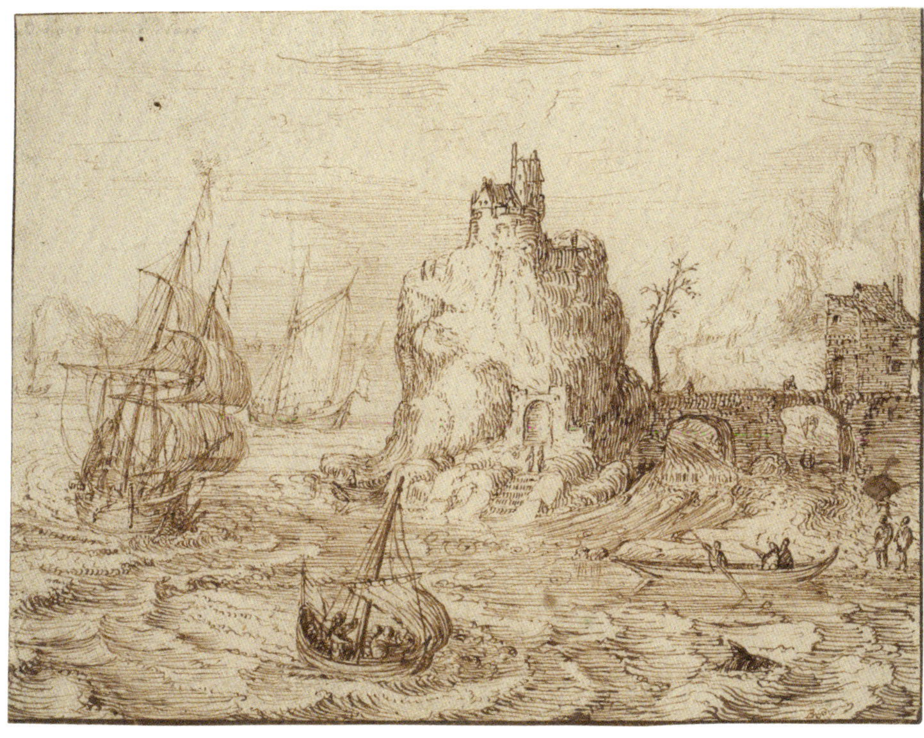

as their own during their celebrated second *Schipvaart* in the late 1590s.[24] This very particular landscape thus entered into the visual record just as the conventions of Dutch landscape were forming. Drawings such as Cornelis Claesz. van Wieringen's (1575/77–1633) *Coastal View* (Fig. 8), with its craggy coast and sea creature evoking a general notion of foreign climes and maritime danger,[25] were supplanted by representations of real overseas sites, increasingly grounded in observation, if still also highly mediated by artistic conventions and Eurocentric expectations.

No overseas colony held as indelible a place in the seventeenth-century European imagination as northeastern Brazil, taken by the Dutch from the Portuguese in 1630 and lost to them again twenty-four years later. Among the retinue accompanying Johan Maurits upon his assumption of the governorship of the colony in 1636 was landscape painter Frans Post (1612–1680). Born and presumably trained in Haarlem,[26] Post represented the Brazilian landscape through the lens of conventions established by artists such as Vroom and De Molijn (Fig. 9). The region's hills, ruins, and palm trees also corresponded to the way European artists had long visualized the biblical east. Jan Pynas's (1581/82–1631) *Mountainous Landscape with an Arched Bridge over a River* (Fig. 10) presents such a landscape, much like those that form the backdrops of the artist's biblical scenes, but here without any figural component. A sense of drama is nevertheless conveyed through the long pen strokes that define the clouds sweeping through the sky, the layers of wash that suggest light, and the impetuous application of wash that evokes the clouds' shadows shifting across the earth. Post's Brazilian landscapes can be understood as an extension of this tradition, of which Pynas was one key exponent. Whether because of their exoticism or their familiarity—or likely the combination of the two—Post's Brazilian views enjoyed a broad European market long after his return to the Netherlands in 1644 and even after the colony fell in 1654. These paintings may have been understood by many of their owners as images not specifically of Brazil but of the New World more generally.[27]

Nevertheless, Post's landscapes, which accompanied a 1647 account of Brazil written by Amsterdam-based scholar Caspar Barlaeus (1584–1648), fulfilled a very specific function within that context: contributing to the book's overarching aim to entice settlers, (re)gain supporters, and counter reports of instability,

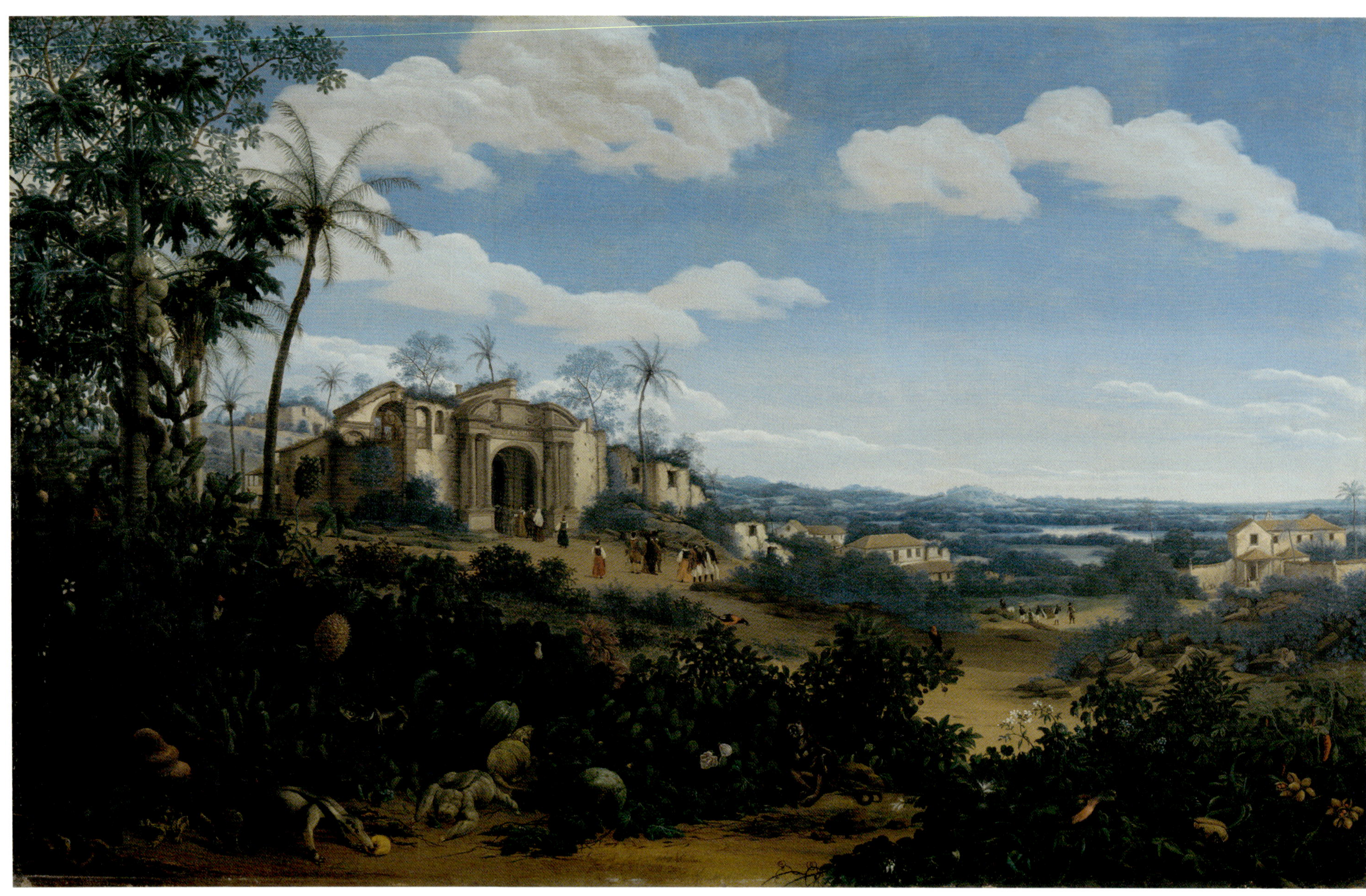

Fig. 9 Frans Post, *View of Olinda, Brazil*, 1662. Oil on canvas, 107.5 × 172.5 cm. Rijksmuseum, Amsterdam, SK-A-742.

Fig. 10 Jan Pynas, *A Mountainous Landscape with an Arched Bridge over a River*, 1605–7. See p. 231 for full information.

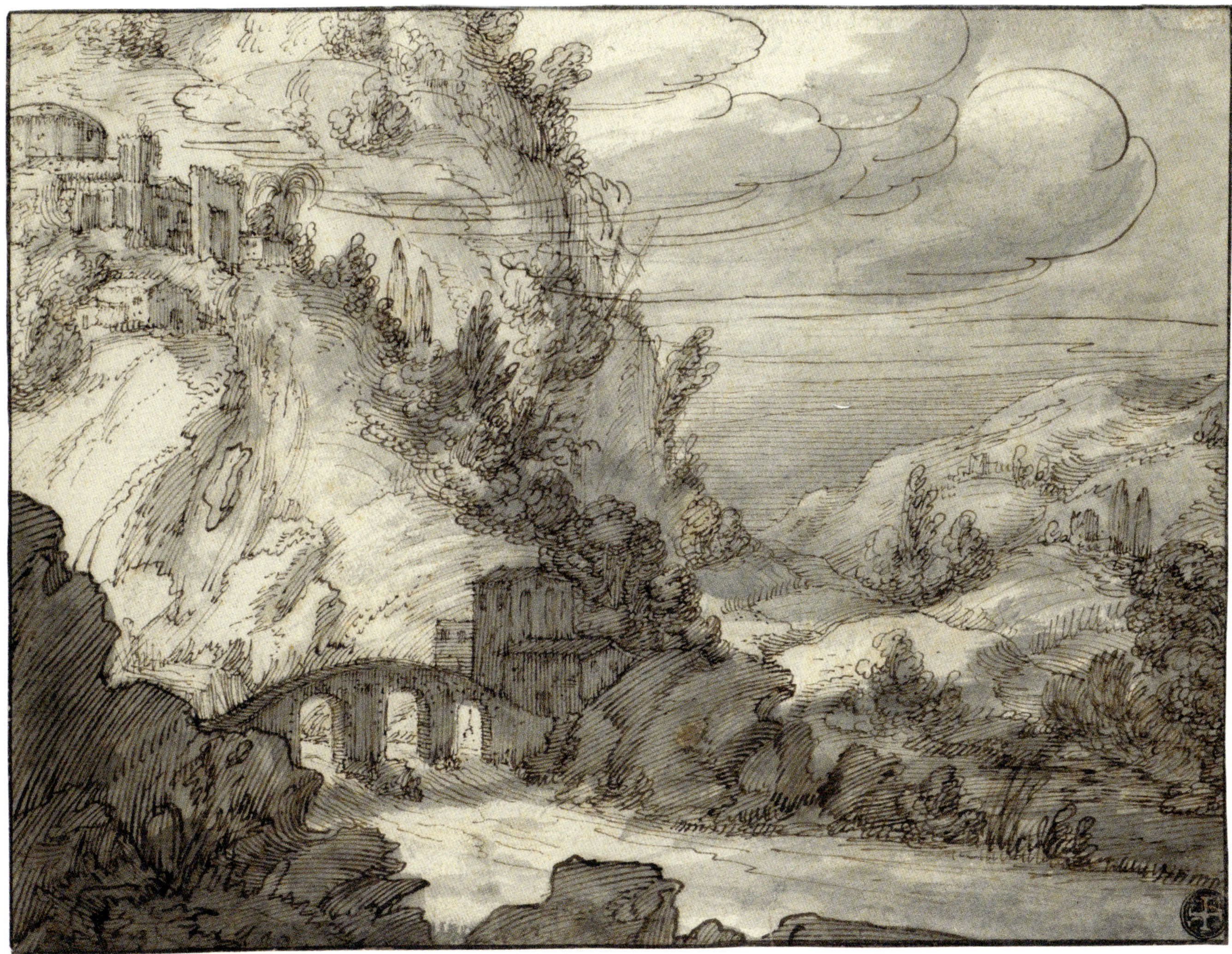

Fig. 11 Jan van Brosterhuysen, after Frans Post, *View of Olinda*, 1647. See p. 234 for full information.



financial loss, and continued military conflict in the region.[28] Undertaken at Maurits's request, *Rerum per octennium in Brasilia* was framed as the official, authoritative, and as the text repeatedly emphasizes, truthful and objective account of his eight-year leadership. It also presented an argument for a shift in Dutch expansionist philosophy, making clear that the Brazilian project was, at least in part, ideologically motivated, not purely mercantile.[29] In the text, Barlaeus writes of "the grandeur of the state . . . [the desire] to spread out across the empty regions and uncultivated lands."[30] By the late seventeenth century, after the fall of the colony, Dutch Brazil is invoked by writers as an example of the kind of "princely" expansion that should be avoided.[31]

Post's illustrations – thirty-three full-page spreads, translated into print from the precise, to-scale drawings he made for this purpose[32] – illuminate the conventions of Dutch landscape as potent tactics, used here to conceal fragility and assert authenticity. In line with the book's emphasis on veracity, Post deploys naturalism and distant viewpoints for the semblance of objectivity; his pictorial methods almost seem to obscure themselves even as they reorder the landscapes for European viewers. His view of Olinda (Fig. 11), for example, presents the capital of the former Portuguese colony, razed by the Dutch in 1630, in a way that masks this violent history and suggests potential and renewal.[33] Tiny ruins appear in the distance, nearly indiscernible. In a similar vein, the figures at work on the beach in the foreground are almost certainly enslaved Africans – representatives of the millions the Dutch and other powers forcibly transported across the Atlantic between the seventeenth and mid-nineteenth centuries. The brutality of their enslavement and forced labor here erased, they are blatantly portrayed as "extensions of agriculture" for the sake of Dutch economic gain. The projection of a "civilized," prosperous (and pleasant?) colony is, as both Ernst van den Boogaart and Elizabeth Sutton have discussed, the leitmotif of Barlaeus's book and an essential piece of Maurits's image as a leader and of his justification for continued Dutch presence in Brazil.[34] The sheer number of landscape images in the book, interspersed with cartographic material, can be read as an assertion of Dutch dominion. It also points to the perceived importance and effectiveness of landscape representation in conveying information – and shaping opinions – about the world.

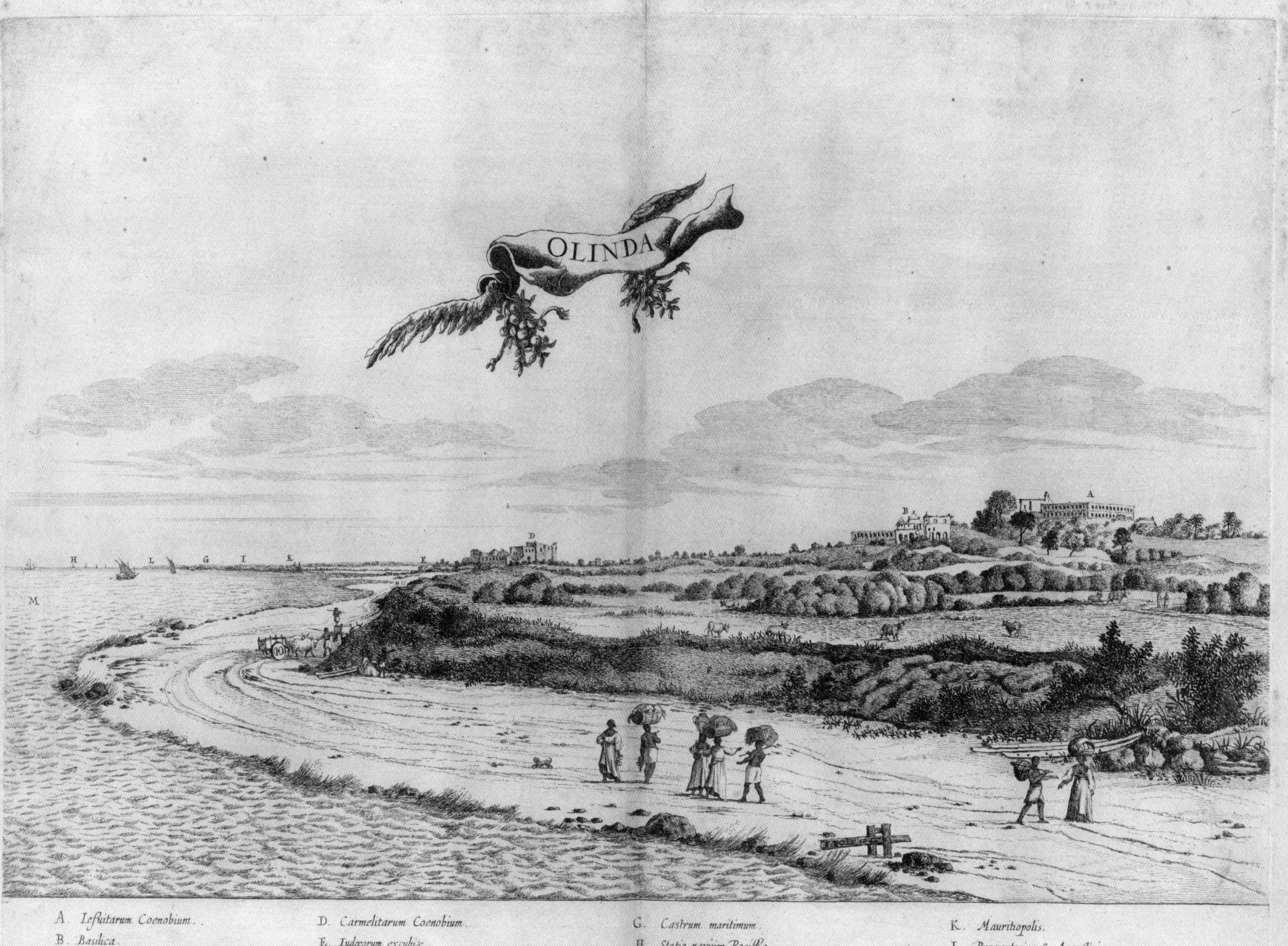
OLINDA
A. Iesuitarum Coenobium.
B. Basilica.
C. Coenobium Franciscanorum.
D. Carmelitarum Coenobium.
E. Iudæorum excubiæ
F. Collapsa urbis moenia.
G. Castrum maritimum.
H. Statio navium Reciffæ.
I. Reciffa.
K. Mauritiopolis.
L. Promontorium S. Augustini.
M. Oceanus.

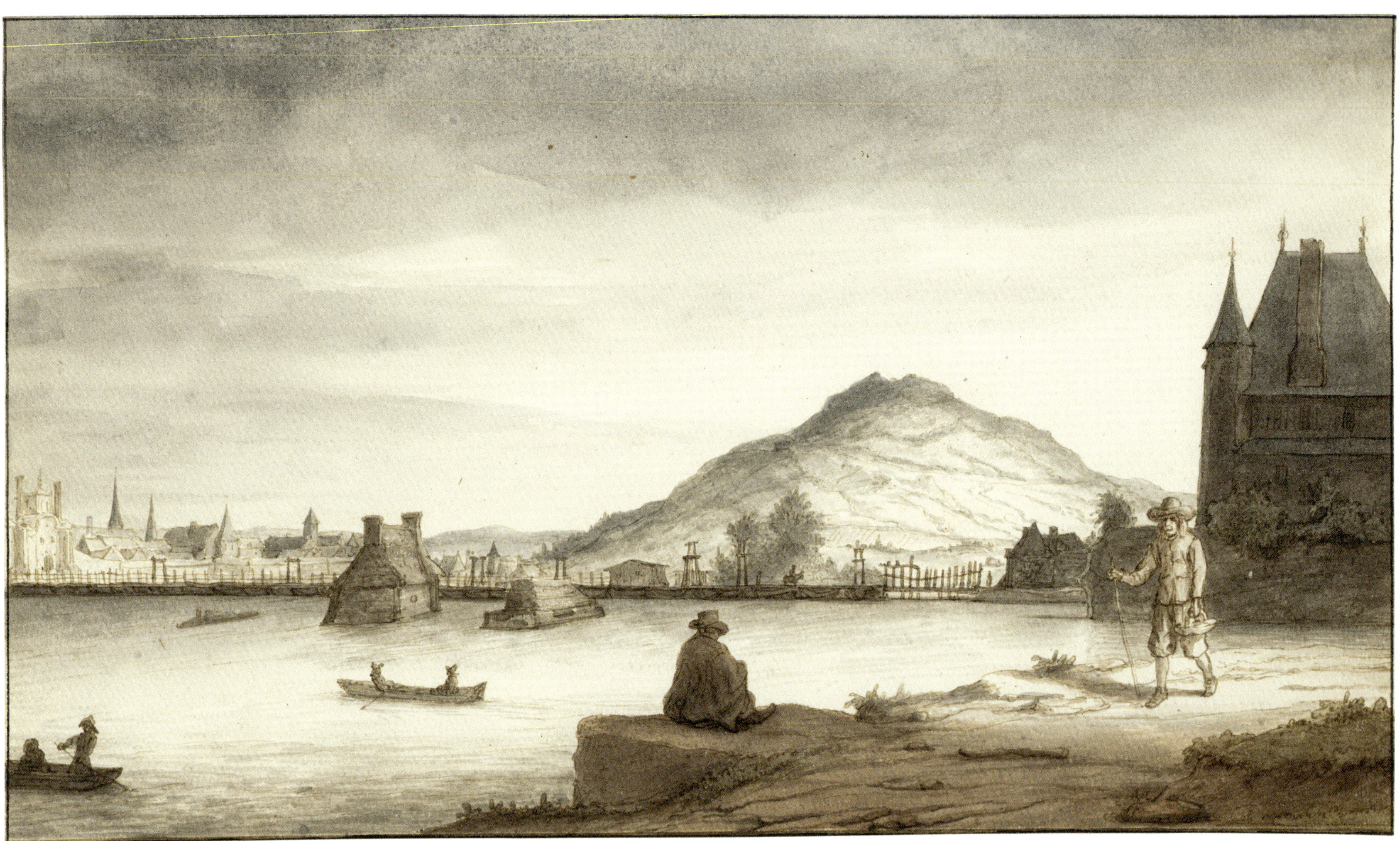

Fig. 12 Lambert Doomer, *View of Rouen with Mont Sainte-Catherine*, early 1670s. See p. 229 for full information.



## AUTHENTICITY AND SUBJECTIVITY

The desire to assemble and possess topographical material found unique expression in the Atlas Blaeu-Van der Hem (now in the Austrian National Library). In the 1660s, Dutch lawyer and collector Laurens van der Hem (1621–1678) began to commission and collect an enormous number of landscape drawings. Taking as his starting point a copy of Joan Blaeu's (1596–1673) eleven-volume *Atlas maior* of 1662, Van der Hem ultimately assembled a total of forty-six volumes comprising more than two thousand prints and drawings, some executed directly on the album leaves.[35] A major contributor to this project was Lambert Doomer (1624–1700), who became known for his drawings of various European locales. It was for a similar, if smaller, project that Doomer produced his view of Rouen in the early 1670s (Fig. 12). One of two autograph repetitions of a lost sketch made during his travels through France in the 1640s, this work belonged to a large series of French, German, and Dutch views almost certainly commissioned by a Dutch patron.[36] In tones of brown and silvery gray, Doomer evokes the cool, damp air of an overcast day in the French city, as seen from the south bank of the Seine looking east. Rather than depict Rouen's city center on the other side of the river, this viewpoint features the outskirts of the city and several remnants of its medieval history, including the ruins of the twelfth-century bridge from which the ashes of Joan of Arc were thrown in 1431. In the foreground of the sheet sits a draftsman at work. As Yvonne Bleyerveld discusses in this volume (see p. 41), draftsmen appear frequently in the landscape imagery of the period, underscoring the repeated encouragement of artists in seventeenth-century theory to draw outside, even if so many finished drawings were ultimately made in the studio.[37] Although Doomer's figure is positioned such that we cannot see his drawing materials, he is the quintessential image of the artist in the act of drawing in the open air – seated, behatted, and seen from behind. This motif was popularized in the sixteenth century by Bruegel and Joris Hoefnagel (1542–1600), specifically in connection with their depictions of far-off places. Bruegel included it in some of his Italian landscapes – those views that, according to painter and theorist Karel van Mander (1548–1606), the artist "swallowed" and so faithfully "spat out again" upon his return home.[38] In the subsequent decades, Hoefnagel incorporated the motif into some of the illustrations he designed for the *Civitates orbis terrarum*, a monumental compilation of city views and maps published in six volumes between 1572 and 1617 – an

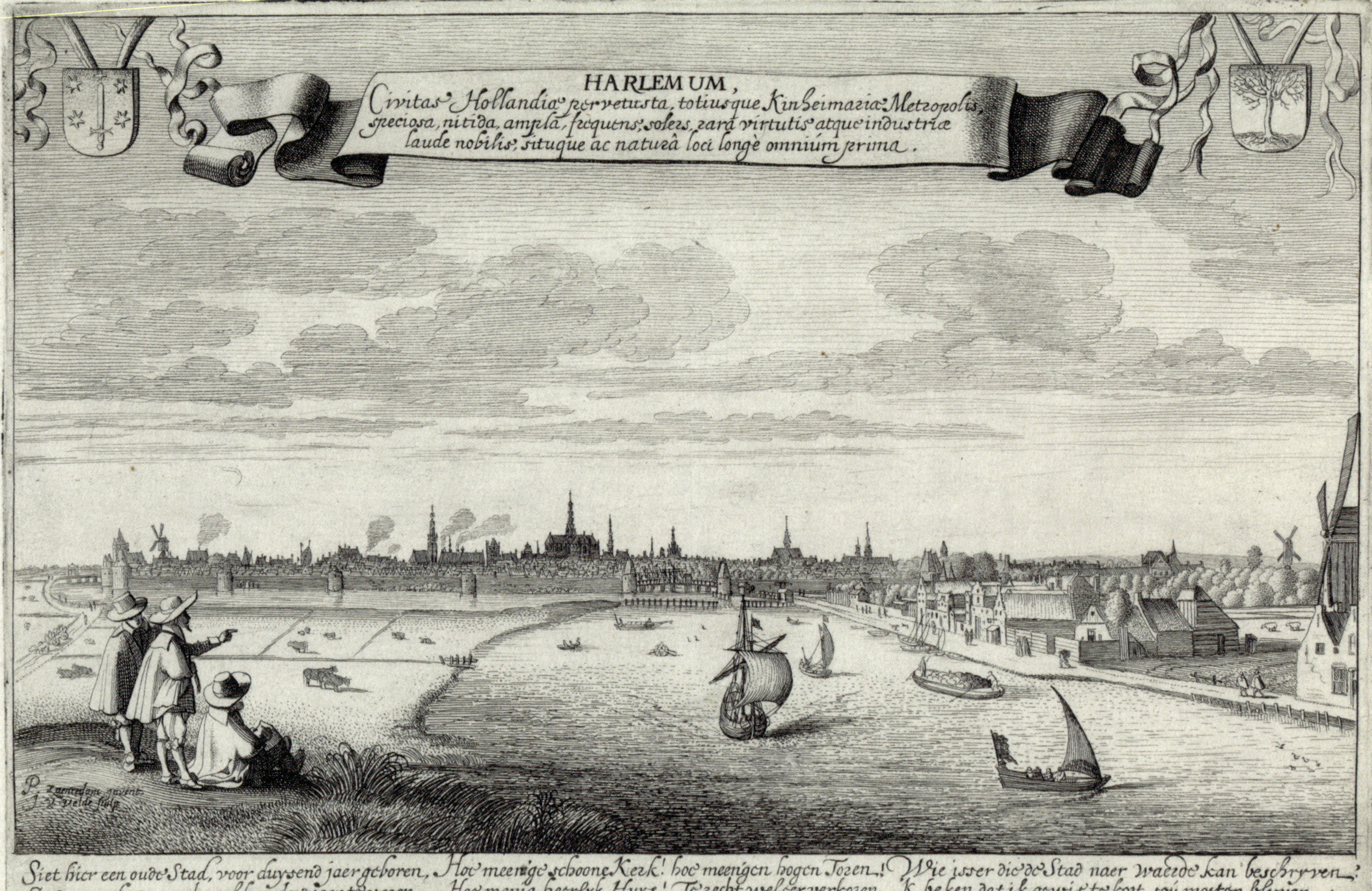
HARLEMUM,
Civitas Hollandiæ pervetusta, totiusque Kinheimariæ Metropolis,
speciosa, nitida, ampla, frequens, solers, rara virtutis atque industriæ
laude nobilis, situque ac naturâ loci longè omnium prima.
Siet hier een oude Stad, voor duysend jaer geboren,
En daer en boven noch wel hondert jaer te voren,
Het sy dat Ridder Lem, gelyk men meest so seyd,
Of liever 't Haerlemsch Huys haer gronden heeft geleyd.
Hoe meenige schoone Kerk! hoe meenigen hogen Toren!
Hoe menig heerlyk Huys! Te recht wel eer verkoren,
Om haer cieraed, en roem, om haere deugd, en lof,
En wel gelegenheyd tot onser Graven Hof!
Wie isser die de Stad naer waerde kan beschryven?
'K beken dat ik gewis te kort sou moeten blyven:
En kon ik so ik wou, so ik genegen ben,
So is de plaetz te kleyn, de plaet houd mijne pen.

Fig. 13 Jan van de Velde II, after Pieter Saenredam, *View of Haarlem and the Spaarne River from the South*, 1628. Etching, 16.1 × 23.7 cm. Rijksmuseum, Amsterdam, RP-P-OB-15.518.



important model for subsequent topographical projects, including the Blaeu-Van der Hem atlas and the Barlaeus-Post volume on Brazil.[39] It was surely the examples of Bruegel and Hoefnagel, and the "faithfulness" attributed to their work, that prompted several seventeenth-century artists to incorporate the motif of the draftsman in their depictions of local and foreign terrain. In most cases, as in Doomer's drawing, the artist appears in the foreground, in the act of producing the view that we see; his presence asserts its authenticity and invites the viewer, the armchair traveler, to follow in his footsteps.[40]

In some instances, the draftsman is accompanied by other figures – model viewers also undoubtedly derived from Hoefnagel's *Civitates* illustrations.[41] Calvinist minister Samuel Ampzing's 1628 *Description and Praise of the City of Haarlem*, a versified account of the Dutch city and its environs, begins with a view designed by Pieter Saenredam (1597–1665) and cut by Jan van de Velde II (1593–1641). Here, a draftsman is joined by two onlookers: one gazes toward the prospect that will be depicted, the other leans over to peer at the image in progress, suggesting a comparison – even competition – between reality and representation (Fig. 13). Such a *paragone* may be at the heart of an enigmatic drawing by Roelant Roghman (1627–1692). In this imagined landscape, a duo right out of Hoefnagel's work appears at left: one figure still mounted on his horse and gesturing forward with his crop, the other seated on a rock in the pose of the draftsman at work (Fig. 14). The contrasting body language of the two and the distance that separates them suggest a tension, whether between maker and viewer or between two travelers deciding how, or if, to continue their journey. With his sensitive application of green, yellow, and gray washes, Roghman conveys the movement of clouds in the sky, breeze in the trees, light and shadow on the ground, and even the sound of the flowing stream, transcending the visual in his evocation of the sensory experience of the outdoors. He thus invites us to join the two figures in making a choice: to proceed or to rest, to enjoy the outdoors or a drawn representation thereof.

As much as the motif of the draftsman in the landscape asserted authenticity, assuring the viewer of the firsthand knowledge and observation in which the representation was (or was not) grounded, it also served as a reminder of artifice. In Visscher's views of Haarlem and its surrounds, such draftsmen occasionally appear alongside the rural laborers (see Fig. 2), performing their own (re-) creation and ordering of the landscape. So pictured, these figures

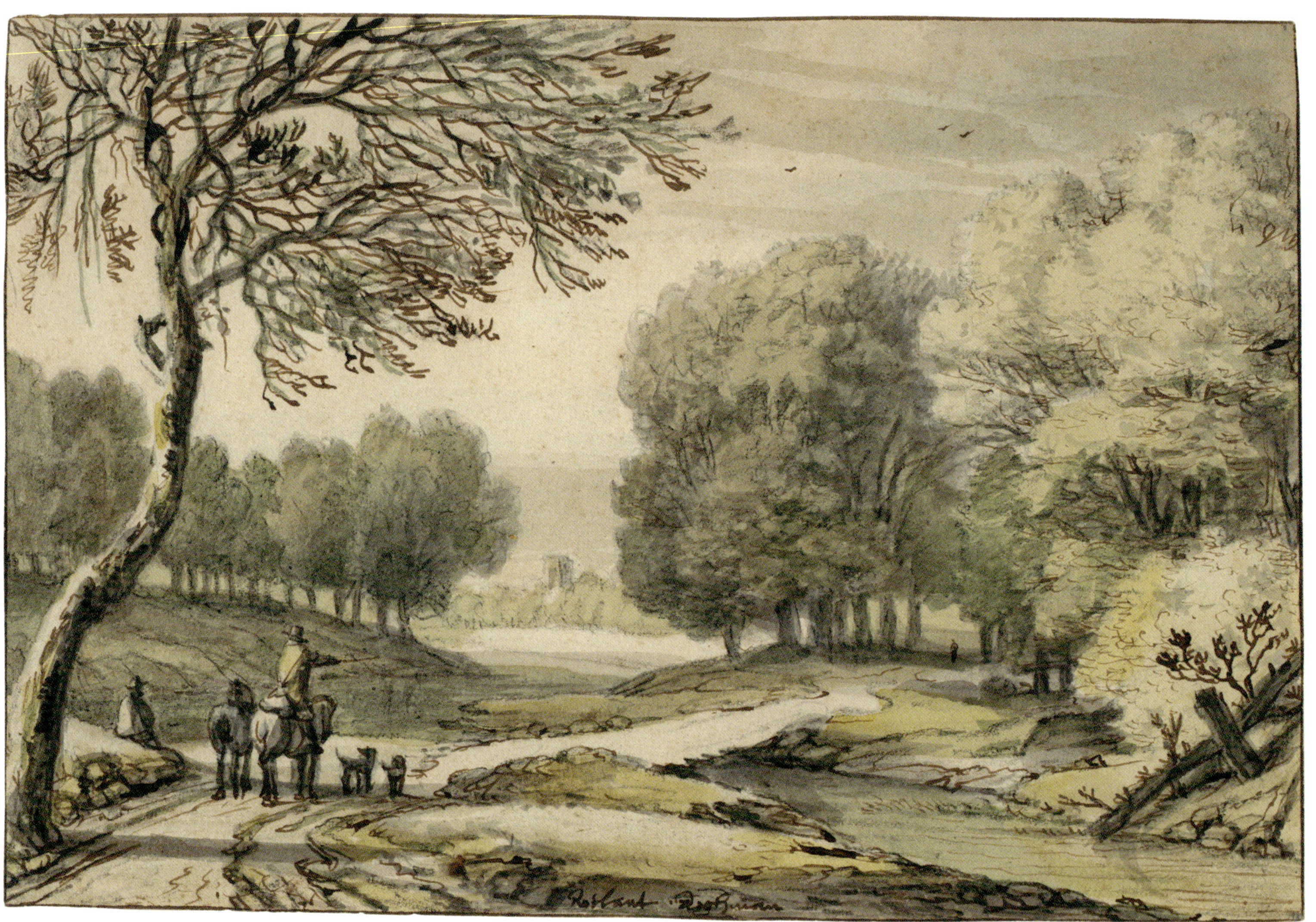
Roelant Roghman

Fig. 14 Roelant Roghman, *Wooded Landscape with Riders and Dogs*, 1660s. See p. 231 for full information.



make clear the particular, individual perspectives from which they observe the environs, an acknowledgment of the subjectivity and pretense at the heart of any landscape representation.

### DISASTER AND DECLINE

In spite of its overseas losses and continued military conflict (particularly with England), the Dutch Republic remained Europe's dominant maritime power through the 1660s. The year 1672—the so-called Rampjaar, or Year of Disaster—was, however, a turning point. In March, a coalition led by French king Louis XIV declared war on the Republic. With the French army invading from the south and the east, the English navy attacking a Dutch fleet in the Channel, and the prince-bishopric of Münster and electorate of Cologne joining the effort on land, the Dutch Republic was effectively surrounded. Towns were swiftly captured and occupied. Amsterdam's stock exchange crashed. The populace, thoroughly demoralized and disillusioned with leadership, protested and rioted throughout the country, most violently on August 20, when a mob brutally murdered former grand pensionary Johan de Witt and his brother, Cornelis. Under the Prince of Orange, William III, who had been elevated to stadtholder that June, the Republic began to see some important advances, aided by an alliance with Spain. But the conflict with France dragged on until 1678, with the Dutch experiencing substantial economic and territorial losses and many in the Republic now living amid wreckage.

A fascinating document of this period are the drawings of Valentijn Klotz (c. 1650–1721), a military engineer and amateur artist who, along with Constantijn Huygens (1596–1687) and Josua de Grave (1643–1712), accompanied the Dutch army on its campaign into the Southern Netherlands between 1672 and 1676. Klotz sketched the various towns and villages through which the company traveled. Precisely inscribed by the artist with their dates of execution and the names of the sites depicted, these works are thought possibly to have served as reference material for the military.[42] Klotz's view of Mechelen's Katelijnepoort (Fig. 15) seems to hover between the documentary and the anecdotal. A fortified gate located at the northern edge of the Flemish city, the Katelijnepoort served in the seventeenth century as the entry and exit point for all traffic to and from Antwerp. Klotz's detailed rendering thus depicts a site of enormous potential importance for the war, though Mechelen ultimately remained safe from invasion. The looming threat over the site would not have escaped the artist's

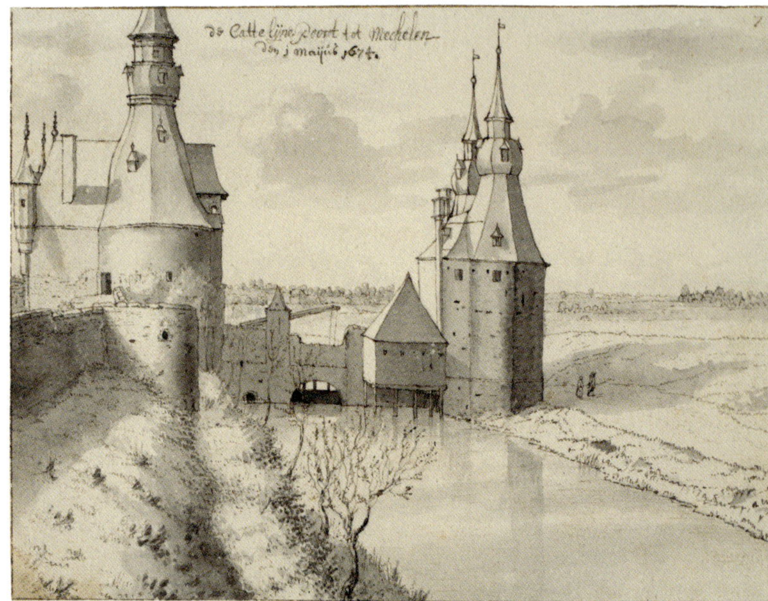



consciousness as he drew. The drawing's pleasing composition, inclusion of figures, and use of wash to render the fall of light on the medieval structure's weathered surfaces, as well as the reflections in the water, point to an ultimately artistic, rather than military, intent. However, for Dutch and Flemish viewers, the inscribed date – May 1, 1674 – would have carried enduring associations with a tremendously vulnerable period in their history.

In 1679, the end of the Franco-Dutch War was marked with a gift from Johan Maurits, by then long retired from his overseas service, to Louis XIV in the form of a suite of Brazilian landscapes painted by Post during his tenure in South America.[43] The fallen colony, preserved in paint, now served as diplomatic offering. In spite of this gesture, tensions between the two countries continued, with long-lasting consequences for the Republic, which entered a period of economic decline. Some sectors – agriculture and the art market among them – never fully recovered.[44] In the decades that followed, amid the Dutch stadtholder's assumption of the English throne and the subsequent transfer of his court to London, the Republic unequivocally lost to England its standing as Europe's preeminent maritime power. As early as 1634, sailor-poet Elias Herckmans (1596–1644) wrote in his *Praise of Seafaring* of the "laudable victories" of the Dutch efforts overseas, and almost in the same breath, of the inevitable way empires "follow one after the other."[45] Echoing Dutch scholars who had already pointed to the risks of imperial ambition in their discussions of fallen ancient empires like Rome and Carthage, Herckmans also made a direct analogy between the expanding Dutch Republic and Rome.[46] When the Republic nearly collapsed in 1672 – less than a century after its establishment – its fragility could no longer be ignored.

Around 1700, Isaac de Moucheron (1667–1744) produced a set of four drawings that likely meditate on the theme of rise and decline. These works invoke the ancient poet Ovid's characterization of the Four Ages, an account of the successive stages of human existence from an age of innocence and bounty to those marked by human engineering and violence (Figs. 16–19).[47] Accordingly, the drawings appear to progress from an arcadian idyll, to a palace garden, to a stormy landscape with ruins, and finally to a wood with travelers. In the depiction of bathers enjoying the outdoors (Fig. 16), whose discarded clothing identifies this as a scene from contemporary life, the man pulling on the tree branch alludes directly to a well-established visual tradition for the Age of Gold, suggesting humankind's harmony with nature. Yet the denuded

Fig. 15 Valentijn Klotz, *View of the Katelijnepoort in Mechelen*, 1674. See p. 230 for full information.



branch implies that this relationship is already a fragile and fleeting one. The motif anticipates the drawing of the palace (Fig. 17), whose manicured grounds refer to the cultivation and architectural developments that marked the Age of Silver. The statue and urn that together portray the tale of Ceres and Proserpina (the mythological origins of the four seasons) further align this scene with the Silver Age, characterized by Ovid as the period in which the eternal spring of the Age of Gold was reduced and divided into different, less hospitable seasons. The inclusion of the figure kneeling before the statue of Ceres—an allusion to another iconographic tradition in which farmers beseech this goddess for a good harvest—points to humankind's dependence on nature and vulnerability to its vicissitudes. The potted plant held by the figure appears in the next drawing of a shepherd bracing against the wind (Fig. 18), no longer gracing a grand palace but instead standing amid crumbling ruins—a clear indication of decline, with nature playing the role of antagonist. Finally, in the wooded landscape (Fig. 19), all signs of cultivation and construction have vanished, signaling a return to wilderness.

De Moucheron's drawings anticipate, by about 150 years, Thomas Cole's (1801–1848) *The Course of Empire* (1834–36). Itself probably grounded in the Four Ages tradition, Cole's cycle of five paintings progresses from what the artist called the "savage state," to the arcadian, to the consummation of empire, to its destruction, and finally to desolation, depicting nature as the ultimate witness to the failures of human engineering and ambition. While Cole's work spoke to nineteenth-century anxieties surrounding the waning of the British empire and the promise of American expansion,[48] these concerns, as we have seen, were not new. The rise and decline of civilization was already an established literary topos, expressed at times with emphatic implications for the present day. In the wake of the fall of Dutch Brazil and the Year of Disaster, such warnings had never felt more prescient. De Moucheron's series, with its contemporary bathers and travelers, seems to trace this progression, or perhaps to show that in any age, at any moment, prosperity and peace may swiftly be followed by destruction and decline. The last drawing in the suite, in which travelers journey beneath an unsettled sky through a landscape that appears to be on the cusp of winter and spring, is, of the four, most closely aligned in terms of imagery and composition with the longer Netherlandish landscape tradition (see p. 32, Fig. C). In its design, it evinces the notion of retreat or return and, perhaps, renewal.

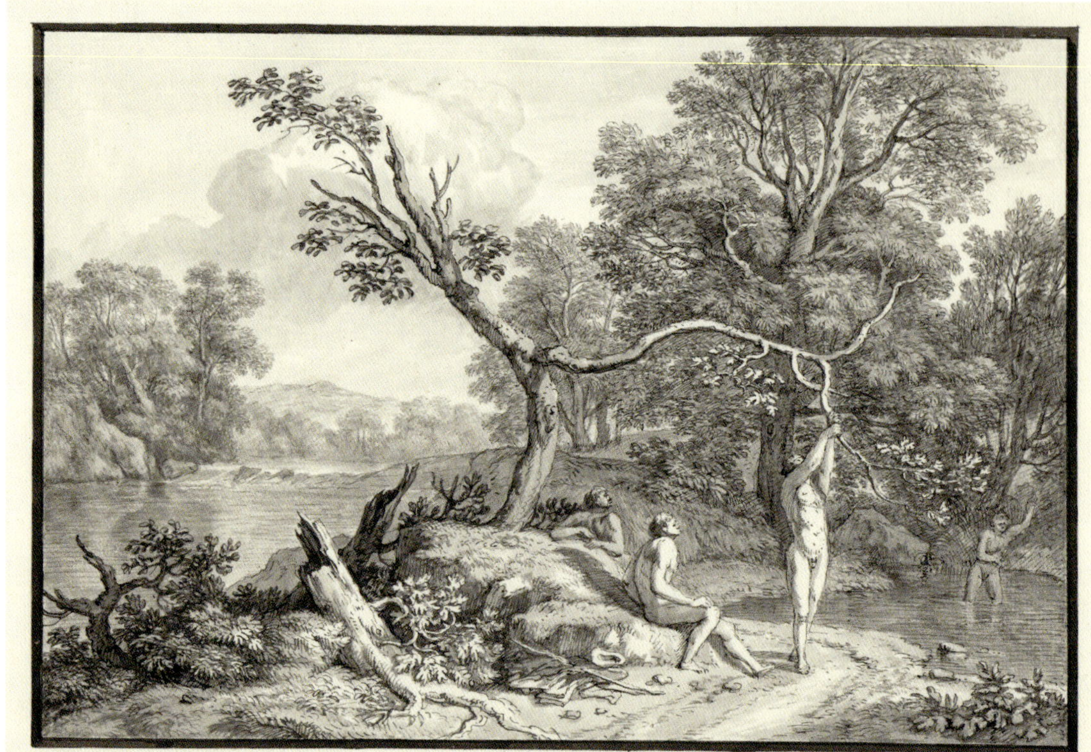
I. Moucheron . fecit

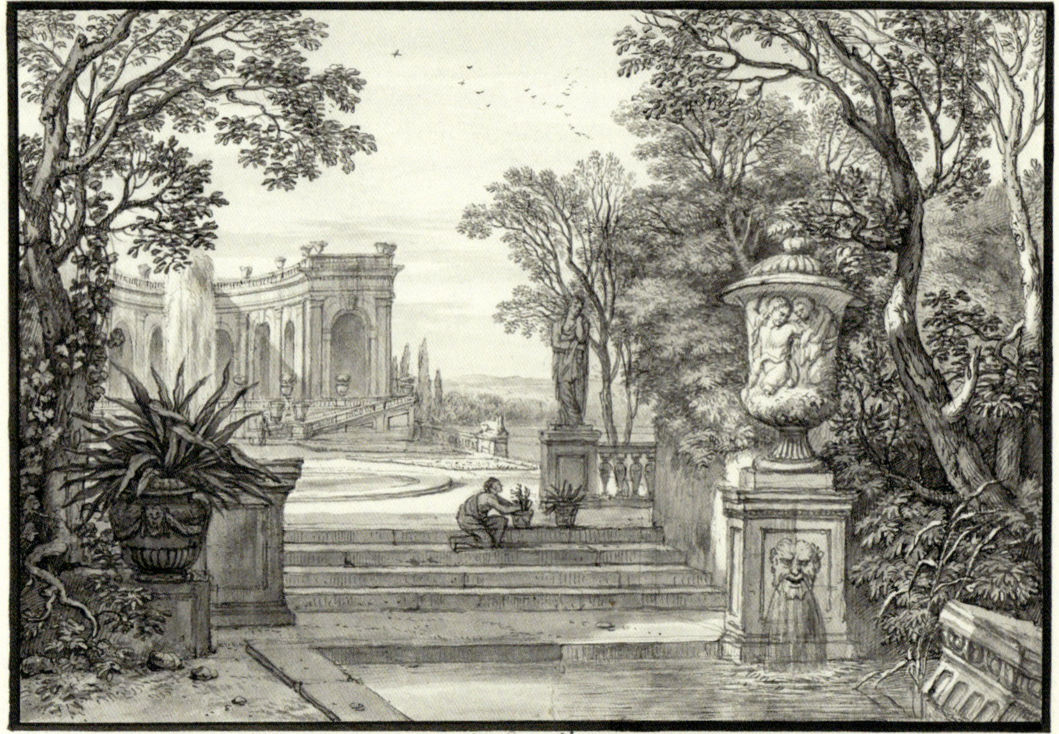
I. Moucheron . fecit

Figs. 16–19 Isaac de Moucheron, *Wooded Landscape with Bathers* (top left); *Landscape with a Formal Garden* (bottom left); *A Shepherd with His Flock Sheltering from a Storm among Antique Ruins* (top right); *Man Leading a Horse by a Pond in a Stormy, Wooded Landscape* (bottom right), c. 1700. See p. 231 for full information.

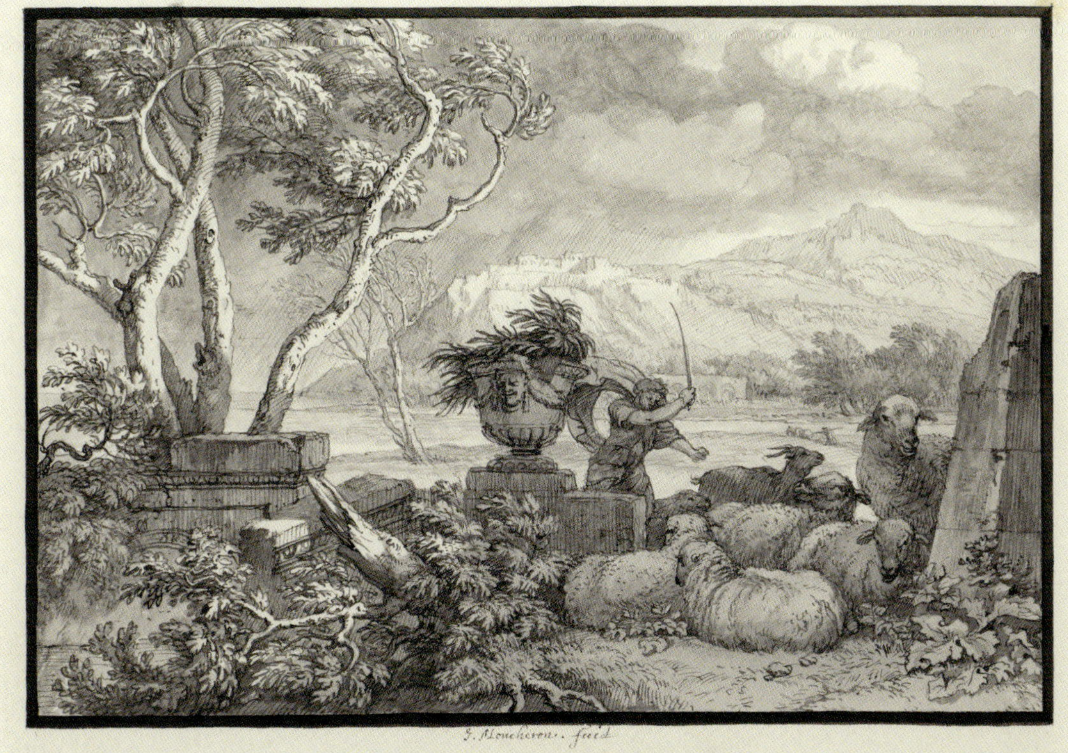

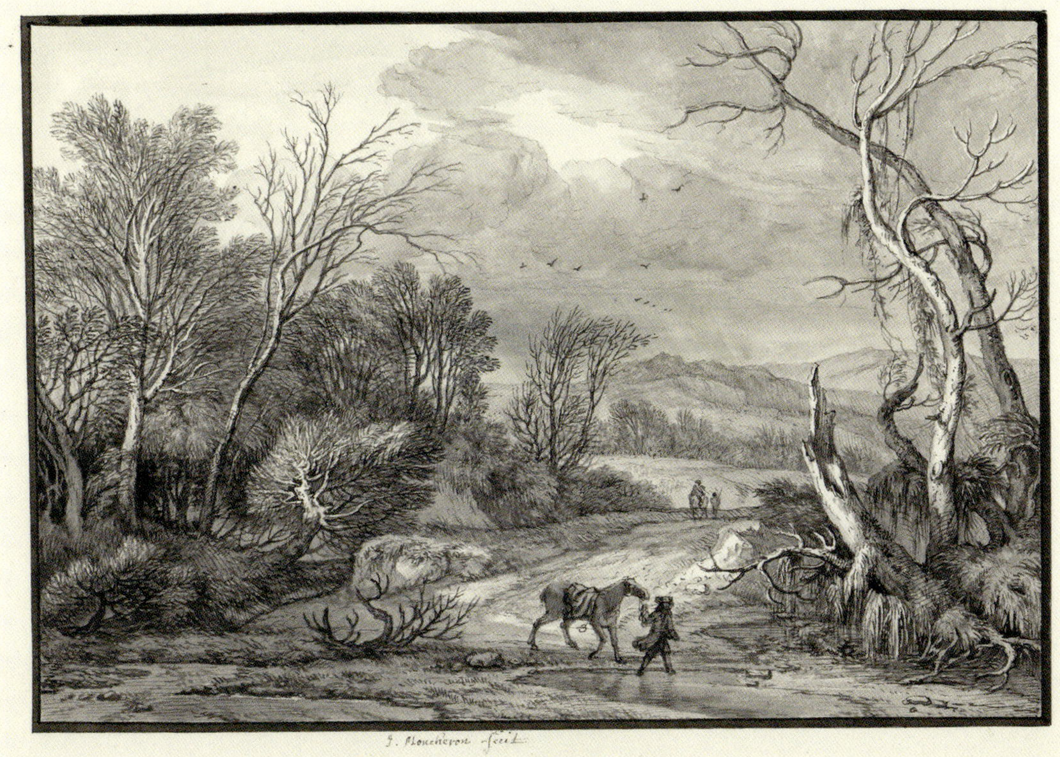

Fig. 20 Anthonie Waterloo, *A Forest at Twilight*, c. 1675–85. See p. 233 for full information.



## RETURN TO WILDERNESS

As De Moucheron's series shows, nature—long regarded as separate from rather than encompassing human activity—could be by turns respite, resource, challenge, and witness. It is also often victim. In the seventeenth century, the landscape that the Dutch were most conscious of victimizing was the forest. Woodland in the Netherlands, already long under threat, was rapidly disappearing.[49] The country's shrinking forests were recognized as early as 1605, when Dutch scholar Paullus Merula (1558–1607) wrote a treatise on the importance of hunting laws as a means of preservation.[50] In the 1612 Dutch edition of Lodovico Guicciardini's (1521–1589) account of the Netherlands, the translator notes that hardly any forests remained in the province of Holland.[51] It is clear from the literary and visual record that the woodlands that had been preserved were prized. Traditionally hunting domains for nobles, the forested areas that remained in the Northern Netherlands in the seventeenth century—generally located on the outskirts of major cities—became spaces for leisurely walks. In his *Description and Praise of the City of Haarlem*, Ampzing writes about a wood south of Haarlem, describing it as "a pleasure garden . . . [a] quiet retreat and secret pleasure, free from city noise and worries."[52]

In the early modern period, "wilderness" was not understood as a space untouched by humans, but rather as a resource for the kind of recreation evoked by Ampzing. Many artists depicted these woods in prints, showing figures enjoying nature that had been protected for that very purpose. Yet, in the later decades of the century, forest imagery without human presence abounds. For many artists, woodland offered appealing pictorial challenges, in particular the limitations such spaces place on vision. In a spectacular sheet by Jan Lievens (see p. 186, Fig. Q), probably a study made on the spot, a screen of trees fills the sheet. Light—the reserve of the paper—gleams between the loose pen strokes, but despite this porousness, we cannot see what lies beyond. Moving his pen rapidly and in all directions, Lievens captured the movement and vitality of the trees.

By contrast, Anthonie Waterloo's (1609–1690) many drawings of woods, often featuring chopped branches and logs, take on the feeling of memorials. An example on blue paper, executed in black chalk, charcoal, and wash, with only faint amounts of white chalk, evokes the visual experience of twilight (Fig. 20). Instead of serving as the mid-tone of the drawing, as blue paper usually does, here it becomes the primary light tone, while the combination of

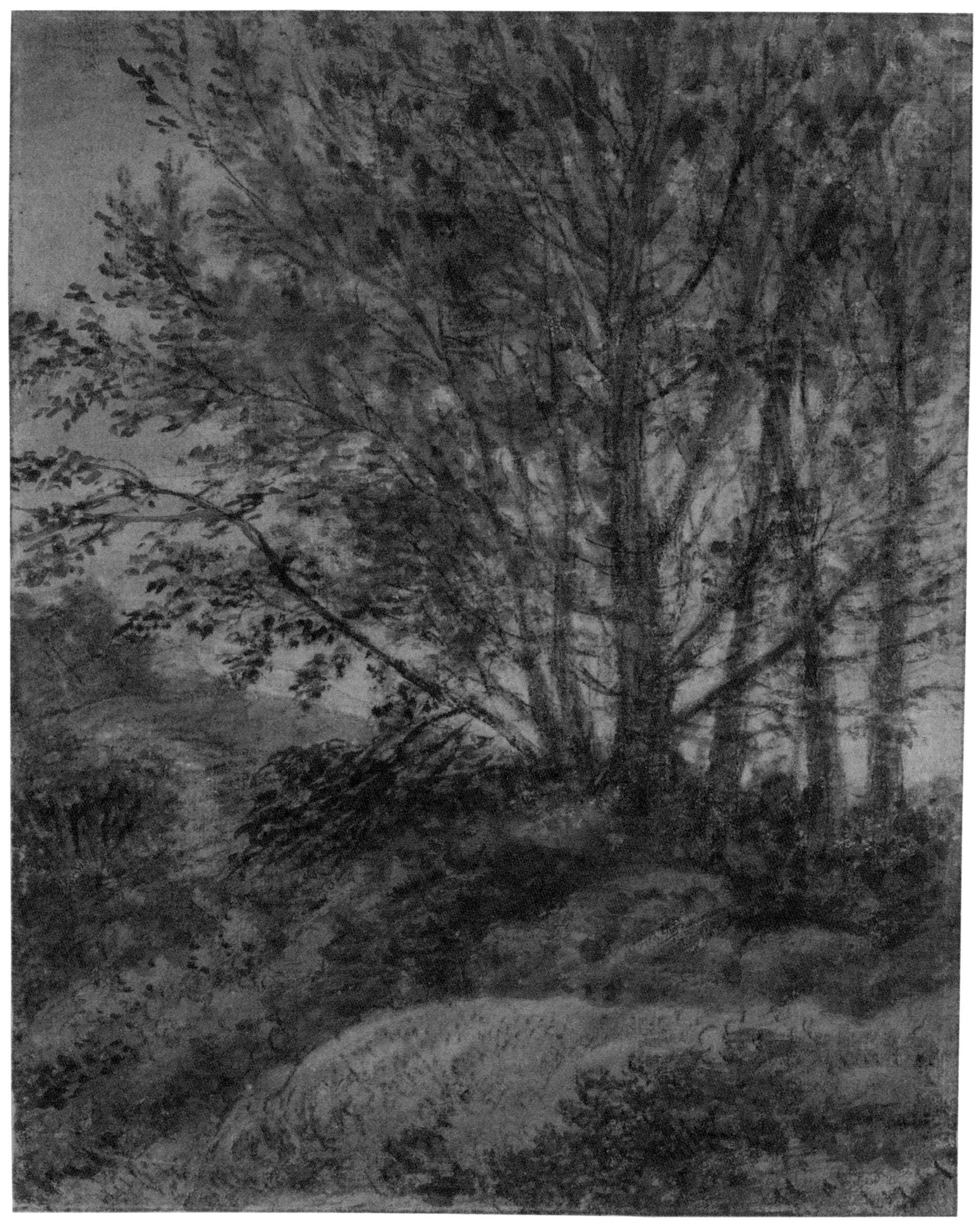

Fig. 21 Dirk Dalens III, *Landscape with Rustic Scene*, c. 1725–35. See p. 229 for full information.



dry and wet media renders the contours of trees and rocks soft and fuzzy. Between day and night, we are at the threshold of visibility—as if in a moment, all will either become dark as dusk falls or come into focus with the dawn. The framing line edging the sheet, likely original to the drawing, indicates that the cropping of the trees was the artist's intention and not the result of later trimming of the sheet. Indeed, several of Waterloo's other drawings and prints feature similar cropping,[53] a tactic that serves to immerse us in the composition, positioning us so close to the woods that we cannot see the tops of the trees and suggesting a sense of solitude. At the drawing's insistence, not just invitation, we commune with nature—a true and fleeting pleasure.

Seventeenth-century draftsmen were masters at devising and deploying tactics like the low vantage point, the path leading into the composition, the precise cropping of a scene, and the evocation of the auditory, olfactory, and tactile sensations of the outdoors—all of which serve to immerse the viewer within the depicted landscape. Growing out of this practice in the late seventeenth and eighteenth centuries was a vogue for large-scale landscape paintings produced as decorative programs for domestic interiors, expressly meant to create the illusion of being surrounded by the outdoors. A specialist of such designs, Dirk Dalens III (1688–1753) employed these tactics in both monumental and small-scale works.[54] In watercolor drawings like his *Landscape with Rustic Scene* (Fig. 21), the suggestion of the rustling leaves, the flowing water, and the calls and barks of the hunters and dogs transport us to a world *away*—in the case of this imagined, vaguely Italian landscape, to nowhere specific. As in Vroom's *Landscape with a Road and a Fence* (see Fig. 1), this is a place defined by its difference from the urban world. But here, the hunting activity, traditionally a pastime of the privileged elite, and the reclining shepherd—a figure hovering between the classical and the quotidian—convey that this "no place" is indeed one of social harmony and leisure, an imaginative realm created precisely for the viewer's pleasure.

Central to the idea of armchair travel is a belief that an image can be an adequate substitute for lived experience, that reality can be encountered virtually. Early modern Dutch artists sought the "reality effect" in all media, whether through illusionistic mimesis or through empathetic portrayals of subjects meant to involve and move the beholder on an emotional level. In such works, the viewer is at once taken in by the representation and delighted by

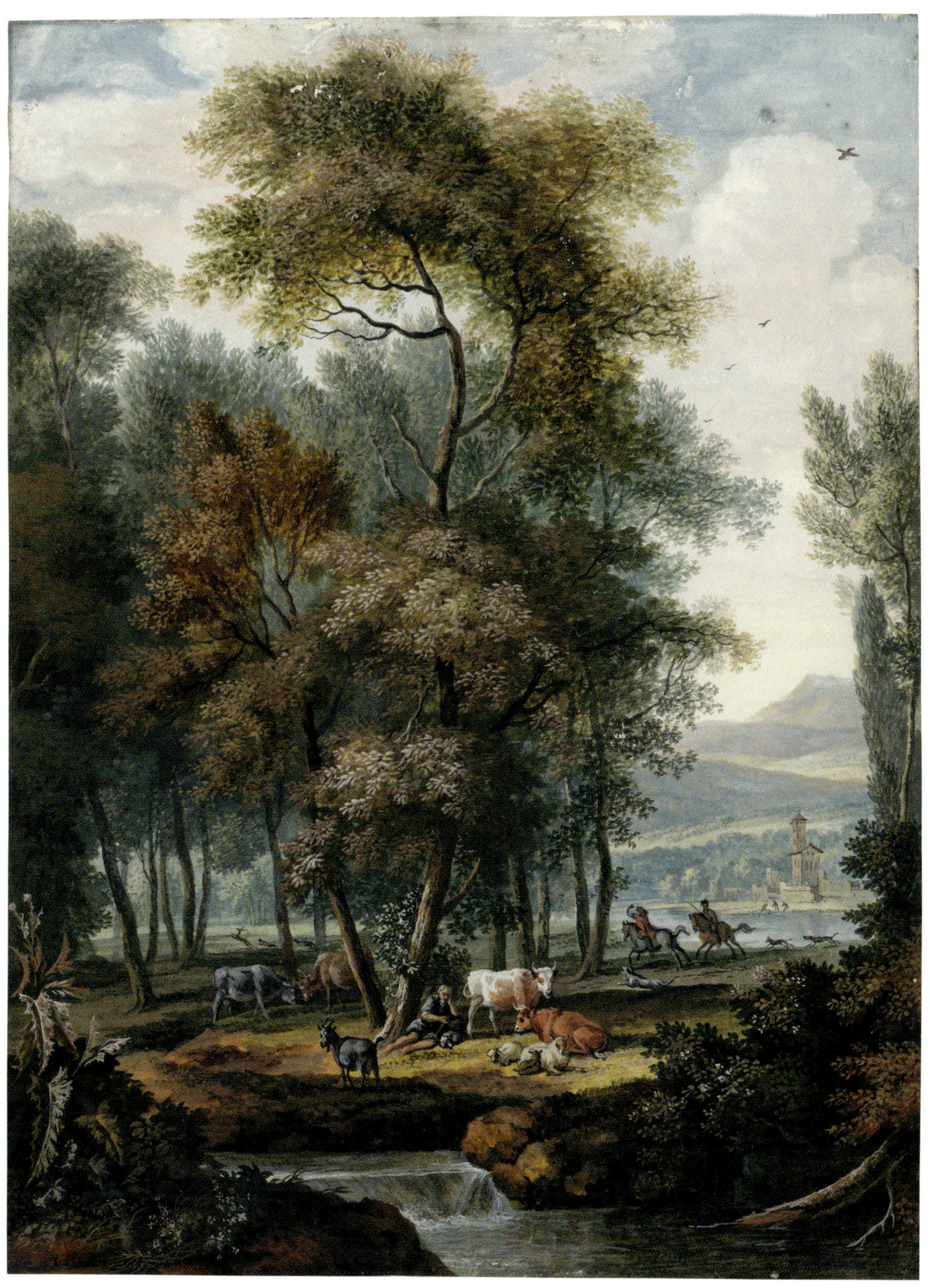

its artifice. Landscape has its own, special capacity to draw in the viewer, often through conventions that nearly efface themselves, such that the viewer can, momentarily, feel truly transported to a place, however near or far, familiar or unfamiliar, real or unreal. Drawing, with its wide-ranging technical possibilities and with the rapidity of execution it permits – famously prized by nineteenth-century artists intent on capturing the ephemerality of the natural and urban worlds – played a vital role in this phenomenon. Small in size, and often meant to be held in one's hands, landscape drawings, like snow globes, allow us to peer – and to virtually step – into tiny worlds that are both unremarkable and enthralling. While they immerse, they also estrange – putting into focus what in life we might pass by, or through, without notice. Like Avercamp's child drawing in the dirt (see Fig. 3), an allusion perhaps to the motif of the artist at work outside, seventeenth-century draftsmen enjoyed a direct, physical connection to the land. Their drawings, whether made outdoors or in the studio, so often seek to simulate that firsthand encounter with the ever-changing natural environment. They also remind us of what can slip away.

## NOTES

1. Jan de Vries, *The Dutch Rural Economy in the Golden Age, 1500–1700* (New Haven, Conn.: Yale University Press, 1974); Jan de Vries, *Barges and Capitalism: Passenger Transportation in the Dutch Economy, 1632–1839* (Utrecht: HES Publishers, 1981); and Jan de Vries, "The Dutch Rural Economy and the Landscape," in *Dutch Landscape: The Early Years, Haarlem and Amsterdam 1590–1650*, ed. Christopher Brown (London: The National Gallery, 1986), 79–86. On Vroom's drawing, see William W. Robinson and Susan Anderson, *Drawings from the Age of Bruegel, Rubens, and Rembrandt: Highlights from the Collection of the Harvard Art Museums* (Cambridge, Mass.: Harvard Art Museums, 2016), 315, where Robinson notes the "disjunction in scale between near and far"; and George Keyes, *Cornelis Vroom: Marine and Landscape Artist*, 2 vols. (Alphen aan den Rijn: Canaletto, 1975), 1:81–83, 2:227–28. See also the classic study on the country and the city by Raymond Williams, *The Country and the City* (New York: Oxford University Press, 1973).
2. De Vries, "The Dutch Rural Economy and the Landscape," 84–85.
3. See ibid., 85–86; and Julie Berger Hochstrasser, "Inroads to Seventeenth-Century Dutch Landscape Painting," *Nederlands Kunsthistorisch Jaarboek* 48 (1997): 192–221.
4. Vincent Laurensz. van der Vinne, "Dagelijckse aentekeninge van't gene ick in mijn reijs onthoudens waerdich gesien ende bewandelt hebbe, etc., bij, mij Vincent Laurensz vanderVinne, anno 1652," printed in Bert Sliggers, Jr., *Dagelijckse aentekeninge van Vincent Laurensz van der Vinne* (Haarlem: Fibula-Van Dishoeck, 1979), 50. Translated and discussed in Marijn Schapelhouman, "A Note on the Pleasures of Traveling in Former Time," in *Home and Abroad: Dutch and Flemish Landscape Drawings from the John and Marine van Vlissingen Art Foundation*, ed. Jane Shoaf Turner and Robert-Jan te Rijdt (Amsterdam: Rijksmuseum; Paris: Fondation Custodia; Curaçao: BCD Group N.V., 2015), 10.
5. On the impact of war on the countryside, see Pepijn Brandon, "The Armed Forces," in *The Cambridge Companion to the Dutch Golden Age*, ed. Helmer J. Helmers and Geert H. Janssen (Cambridge: Cambridge University Press, 2018), 79–80.
6. See especially Susan Donahue Kuretsky, "Dutch Ruins: Time and Transformation," in *Time and Transformation in Seventeenth-Century Dutch Art*, ed. Susan Donahue Kuretsky (Poughkeepsie, N.Y.: Frances Lehman Loeb Art Center, Vassar College; Sarasota, Fla.: John and Mable Ringling Museum of Art; Louisville, Ky.: J. B. Speed Art Museum, 2005).
7. See, for example, Robert Fucci, "Arcadia Unbound: Early Dutch Landscape Prints and the *Amenissimae aliquot regiunculae* of 1616 by Jan van de Velde II," *Art in Print* 4 (5) (January–February 2015): 17–19.
8. Larry Silver, *Peasant Scenes and Landscapes: The Rise of Pictorial Genres in the Antwerp Art Market* (Philadelphia: University of Pennsylvania Press, 2012), 123.
9. John Barrell, *The Dark Side of the Landscape: The Rural Poor in English Painting, 1730–1840* (Cambridge: Cambridge University Press, 1980).
10. On the market for Avercamp's drawings, see Marijn Schapelhouman, "The Drawings, Reflections on an Oeuvre," in *Hendrick Avercamp: Master of the Ice Scene*, ed. Pieter Roelefs (Amsterdam: Rijksmuseum; Washington, D.C.: National Gallery of Art, 2009), 87–88.
11. Pieter Roelofs has noted how rarely members of different classes interact in Avercamp's work. See Roelofs, "The Paintings: The Dutch on Ice," in ibid., 66.
12. I thank Pepijn Brandon for pointing this out to me in connection with the Avercamp drawing during a conversation in February 2020. See Petra van Dam and Mijla van Tielhof, *Waterstaat in stedenland, Het Hoogheemraadschap van Rijnland voor 1857* (Utrecht: Matrijs, 2006); and J. L. Price, "Water and Land," in Helmers and Janssen, *The Cambridge Companion to the Dutch Golden Age*, 32–33.
13. Simon Fokke (1712–1784) produced an engraving after the drawing that identifies the composition as Ouderkerk and dates it to 1622, presumably based on the inscription, written in a seventeenth-century hand on the verso of the drawing: *Ouwerkerk 1622*. See William W. Robinson, *Bruegel to Rembrandt: Dutch and Flemish Drawings from the Maida and George Abrams Collection* (Cambridge, Mass.: Harvard University Art Museums; London: British Museum; Paris: Institut Néerlandais; New Haven, Conn.: Yale University Press, 2002), 40. In addition, Ouwerkerk is the name of a town in the coastal province of Zeeland, where more modest land reclamation was also carried out.
14. On the associations with vagrants in the Dutch countryside, see Henk van Nierop, *Treason in the Northern Quarter: War, Terror, and the Rule of Law in the Dutch Revolt*, trans. J. C. Grayson (Princeton, N.J.: Princeton University Press, 2009), 121–35.
15. See Anuradha Gobin, "Picturing Liminal Spaces and Bodies: Rituals of Punishment and the Limits of Control at the Gallows Field," *RACAR* 43 (1) (2018): 15–18.
16. Curtis O. Baer, ed., *Seventeenth-Century Dutch Landscape Drawings and Selected Prints from American Collections* (Poughkeepsie, N.Y.: Vassar College Art Gallery, 1976); and Robinson, *Bruegel to Rembrandt*, 50.
17. Robinson, *Bruegel to Rembrandt*, 64.
18. Hans-Ulrich Beck, *Pieter Molyn, 1595–1661: Katalog der Handzeichnungen* (Doornspijk: Davaco, 1998), 20.
19. On the motif of the outhouse, or privy, see Walter S. Gibson, "Bloemaert's Privy: The Rustic Ruin in Dutch Art," in Kuretsky, *Time and Transformation in Seventeenth-Century Dutch Art*, 63–72.
20. On Battem and his connection to and emulation of Koninck, see Hans Verbeek, *Travels through Town and Country: Dutch and Flemish Landscape Drawings, 1550–1830* (Haarlem: Teylers Museum, 2000), 128; and with regard to this drawing specifically, William W. Robinson, *Seventeenth-Century Dutch Drawings: A Selection from the Maida and George Abrams Collection* (Cambridge, Mass.: Harvard University Art Museums; Amsterdam: Rijksmuseum; Vienna: Graphische Sammlung Albertina; New York: Pierpont Morgan Library; Lynn, Mass.: H. O. Zimman), 1991, 176.
21. See Michiel van Groesen, *Amsterdam's Atlantic: Print Culture and the Making of Dutch Brazil* (Philadelphia: University of Pennsylvania Press, 2017).

22. On the dating and imagery of this drawing, see Christopher P. van Eeghen, “Simon de Vlieger as a Draftsman, II: Chalk Drawings Other than Pure Landscapes,” *Master Drawings* 49 (2) (Summer 2011): 197.
23. The series were issued under the titles *Indiae orientalis* and *India occidentalis*. See Michiel van Groesen, *The Representations of the Overseas World in the De Bry Collection of Voyages* (Leiden: Brill, 2008).
24. Sarah Mallory, “Memory Spaces and Far Away Places: Mauritius, Golden Age Myths and the Origins of Dutch Landscape,” in *Dutch Golden Age(s): The Shaping of a Cultural Community*, ed. Jan Blanc, Gouden Eeuw: New Perspectives on Dutch Seventeenth-Century Art 1 (Turnhout: Brepols, 2021), 163–86.
25. See Joaneath Spicer, “A Pictorial Vocabulary of Otherness: Roelandt Saverij, Adam Willarts, and the Representation of Foreign Coasts,” *Nederlands Kunsthistorisch Jaarboek* 48 (1997): 22–51; and Robinson, *Bruegel to Rembrandt*, 36–37.
26. Post’s artistic training is not documented, but it is presumed that he trained in his hometown with his father, a lesser known painter, and his brother, painter and architect Pieter Post (1608–1669). It has been proposed that he also apprenticed with De Molijn.
27. Benjamin Schmidt, *Inventing Exoticism: Geography, Globalism, and Europe’s Early Modern World* (Philadelphia: University of Pennsylvania Press, 2015), 279–316.
28. Caspar Barlaeus, *Rerum per octennium in Brasilia et alibi nuper gestarum, sub praefectura illustrissimi comitis I. Mauritii, Nassoviae, &c. comitis, nunc Vesaliae gubernatoris & equitatis foederatorum Belgii Ordd. Sub Avriaco ductoris, historia* (Amsterdam: Blaeu, 1647). For a modern English edition, see Caspar Barlaeus, *The History of Brazil under the Governorship of Count Johan Maurits of Nassau, 1636–1644*, trans. and ed. Blanche T. van Berckel-Ebeling Koning (Gainesville: University Press of Florida, 2011).
29. For the well-known characterization of Dutch global activity as “expansion without empire,” see Pieter C. Emmer and Wim Klooster, “The Dutch Atlantic, 1600–1800: Expansion without Empire,” *Itinerario* 23 (2) (1999): 48–69. For persuasive arguments that this notion does not square with Dutch Brazil, see Arthur Weststeijn, “Republican Empire: Colonialism, Commerce and Corruption in the Dutch Golden Age,” *Renaissance Studies* 26 (4) (September 2012): 491–509; and Groesen, *Amsterdam’s Atlantic*, esp. 10.
30. Barlaeus, *Rerum per octennium in Brasilia*, 124; trans. Berckel-Ebeling Koning, *The History of Brazil under the Governorship of Count Johan Maurits of Nassau*, 122.
31. Weststeijn, “Republican Empire,” 508.
32. While the majority of Post’s illustrations are landscape views of the Brazilian colony, they also include depictions of key sites on the west coast of Africa and of Maurits’s birthplace in Germany, along with several naval battles and other marine scenes. The book features a number of cartographic illustrations designed by Georg Marcgraf (1610–c. 1644) and Cornelis Golijath (1617–1668) as well. Post’s original drawings, believed to have been reproduced for the publication by Jan van Brosterhuysen (c. 1596–1650), are preserved in the British Museum. Some of Post’s illustrations also appear in Franciscus Plante’s (1613–1690) epic poem on the Dutch conquest of Brazil, *Mauritiados* (1647), and in subsequent editions of Barlaeus’s text.
33. On silence in Post’s Brazilian views, see Michael Gaudio, *Sound, Image, Silence: Art and Aural Imagination in the Atlantic World* (Minneapolis: University of Minnesota Press, 2019), 33–62.
34. Ernst van den Boogaart, “A Well-Governed Colony: Frans Post’s Illustrations in Caspar Barlaeus’s History of Dutch Brazil,” *Rijksmuseum Bulletin* 59 (3) (2011): 236–71; and Elizabeth Sutton, “Possessing Brazil in Print, 1630–54,” *Journal of Historians of Netherlandish Art* 5 (1) (Winter 2013), DOI: 10.5092/jhna.2013.5.1.3. See also ibid.
35. For a facsimile, see Erlend de Groot and Peter van der Krogt, eds., *The Atlas Blaeu-Van der Hem of the Austrian National Library*, 7 vols. (’t Goy-Houten: HES & DE GRAAF Publishers, 1996–2008). See also Stijn Alsteens, “The Atlas Blaeu-Van der Hem of the Austrian National Library,” *Master Drawings* 48 (1) (Spring 2010): 105–20.
36. The series remained intact through the mid-eighteenth century, appearing in the 1754 sale of Jeronimus Tonneman in Amsterdam. Stijn Alsteens and Hans Buijs, *Paysages de France: Dessinés par Lambert Doomer et les artistes hollandais et flamands des XVIe et XVIIe siècles* (Paris: Fondation Custodia, 2008), 34–36; and Robinson and Anderson, *Drawings from the Age of Bruegel, Rubens, and Rembrandt*, 101–3.
37. Bob van den Boogert et al., *Buiten tekenen in Rembrandts tijd* (Amsterdam: Museum Het Rembrandthuis, 1998), 19–25.
38. Karel van Mander, *The Lives of the Illustrious Netherlandish and German Painters, from the First Edition of the Schilder-Boeck (1603–1604)*, vol. 1, ed. and trans. Hessel Miedema (Doornspijk: Davaco, 1994–99), 190. See also p. 24, Fig. A in the present volume.
39. On Hoefnagel’s employment of this motif, see Marisa Anne Bass, *Insect Artifice: Nature and Art in the Dutch Revolt* (Princeton, N.J.: Princeton University Press, 2019), 61–64.
40. On the *Rückenfigur* (figure seen from behind) and belatedness of the viewer, see Joseph Leo Koerner, *Caspar David Friedrich and the Subject of Landscape*, 2nd ed. (London: Reaktion Books, 2009).
41. On “model viewers” in Hoefnagel’s illustrations, see Bass, *Insect Artifice*, 76–78; and Harald Hendrix, “The Rise of a Proto-Tourist Infrastructure in Late Sixteenth-Century Rome and Naples,” in *Artes Apodemicae and Early Modern Travel Culture, 1550–1700*, ed. Karl A.E. Enenkel and Jan L. de Jong (Leiden: Brill, 2019), 221–23.
42. On Klotz’s work, see M. H. Breitbarth-van der Stok, “Josua de Grave, Valentinus Klotz en Barnardus Klotz,” *Bulletin van de Koninklijke Nederlandse Oudheidkundige Bond* 68 (1969): 93–115; and Egbert Haverkamp-Begemann, *Fifteenth- to Eighteenth-Century European Drawings: Central Europe, The Netherlands, France, England*, The Robert Lehman Collection 7 (New York: Metropolitan Museum of Art, 1999), 286.
43. See Pedro Corrêa do Lago and Blaise Ducos, *Frans Post: Le Brésil à la cour de Louis XIV* (Paris: Musée du Louvre; Milan: 5 Continents Editions, 2005). On the cult of heroes centered on admirals who played a role in Dutch

Brazil that emerged in this very period, see Michiel van Groesen, "Heroic Memories: Admirals of Dutch Brazil in the Rise of Dutch National Consciousness," in *The Legacy of Dutch Brazil*, ed. Michiel van Groesen (New York: Cambridge University Press, 2014).

44. Jonathan I. Israel, *The Dutch Republic: Its Rise, Greatness, and Fall, 1477–1806*, rev. ed. (Oxford: Clarendon Press, 1995), 843; and David Onnekink and Gijs Rommelse, *The Dutch in the Early Modern World: A History of a Global Power* (Cambridge: Cambridge University Press, 2019), 138–82.
45. Elias Herckmans, foreword to *Der Zee-vaert lof* (Amsterdam: Jacob Wachter, 1634), n.p. Translated and discussed in Arthur Weststeijn, "Republican Empire: Colonialism, Commerce and Corruption in the Dutch Golden Age," *Renaissance Studies* 26 (4): 499.
46. Ibid.
47. William W. Robinson identified this group of drawings as a series. All once in the early eighteenth-century collection of Johan Pieter van den Brande (1707–1758), possibly having been inherited from his father, Pieter van den Brande (167?–1718), these sheets remained together until dispersed in the 1972 Van Pallandt collection sale. Between 2004 and 2019, they were acquired by the Harvard Art Museums. On their provenance and the likelihood that they form a cohesive program, see Robinson, *Bruegel to Rembrandt*, 178; and Robinson and Anderson, *Drawings from the Age of Bruegel, Rubens, and Rembrandt*, 207–9.
48. See Tim Barringer and Elizabeth Kornhauser, *Thomas Cole's Journey: Atlantic Crossings* (New York: Metropolitan Museum of Art, 2018), 33–43; and Angela Miller, *The Empire of the Eye: Landscape Representation and American Cultural Politics, 1825–1875* (Ithaca, N.Y.: Cornell University Press, 1993), 137–65.
49. On the history of forests in the Netherlands, see Jaap Buis, *Historia forestis: Nederlandse bosgeschiedenis*, 2 vols. (Utrecht: H & S, 1985). On the broader pictorial tradition of the forest landscape in northern art, see Christopher S. Wood, *Albrecht Altdorfer and the Origins of Landscape*, rev. ed. (London: Reaktion Books, 2014); Ulrike Handschke, *Die flämische Waldlandschaft: Anfänge und Entwicklungen im 16. und 17. Jahrhundert* (Worms: Wernersche Verlagsgesellschaft, 1988); and Martin Papenbrock, *Landschaften des Exils: Gillis van Coninxloo und die Frankenthaler Maler* (Cologne: Böhlau, 2001).
50. Paullus Merula, *Placaten ende ordonnancien op 't stuck van de wildernissen* (The Hague: Beuckel Cornelisz. Nieulant, 1605). See Stefan Bartilla, "Die Wildnis: Visuel Neugier in der Berg- und Waldlandschaften und ihres Naturbegriffs um 1600," Ph.D. diss., Albert-Ludwigs-Universität Freiburg, 2000, 90–91.
51. Bartilla, "Die Wildnis," 90.
52. Samuel Ampzing, *Beschryvinge ende lof der stad Haerlem in Holland. In rijm bearbeyd: ende met veele oude en nieuwe stucken buyten dicht uyt verscheyde kronijken, handvesten, brieven, memorien ofte geheugenissen, ende diergelijke schriften verklaerd, ende bevestigd* (Haarlem: Adriaan Roman, 1628), 91–92.
53. See Haverkamp-Begemann, *Fifteenth- to Eighteenth-Century European Drawings*, 263–66; and Jane Shoaf Turner, *Rembrandt's World: Dutch Drawings from the Clement C. Moore Collection* (New York: Morgan Library & Museum, 2012), 102–5.
54. On Dirk Dalens III, see Vadim Sadkov et al., *Netherlandish, Flemish and Dutch Drawings of the XVI–XVIII Centuries: Belgian and Dutch Drawings of the XIX–XX Centuries* (Amsterdam: Foundation for Cultural Inventory, 2010), 97; Charles Dumas, "Dirk Dalens III en zijn bronnen," *Kunstschrift* 41 (6) (1997): 32–37; and Meta Walraven-Schipper, "De Landschappen van Dirk Dalens III (1688–1753) in de achttiende-eeuwse decoratieve," Ph.D. diss., Rijksuniversiteit Leiden, 1996.

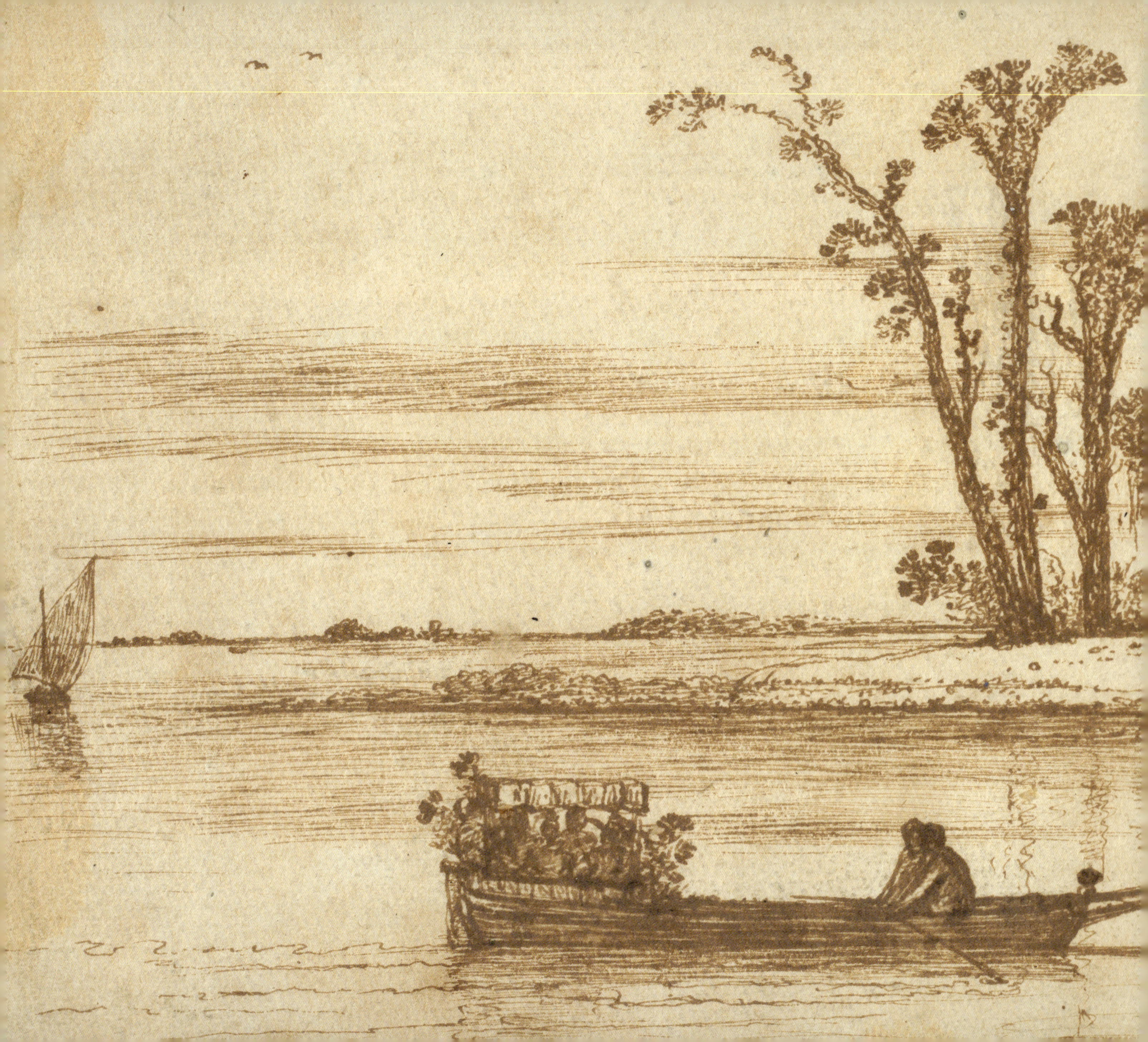

# Cornelis Vroom
## *River Landscape*, c. 1622–23

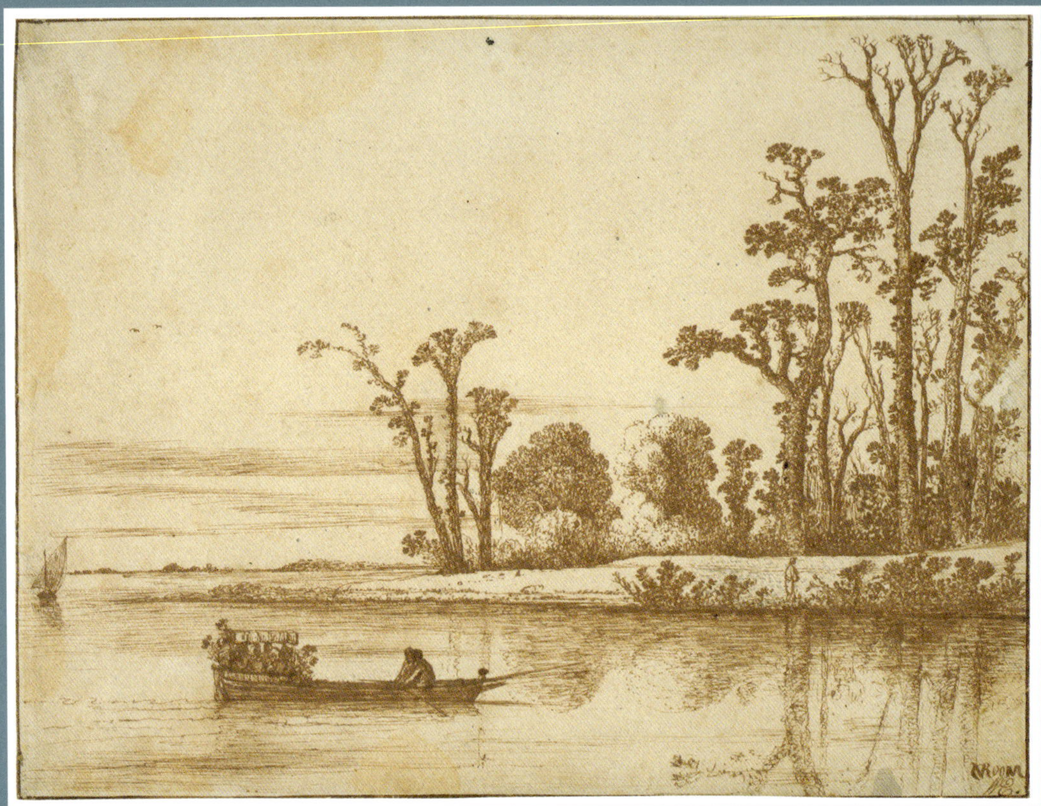

Fig. H Cornelis Vroom, *River Landscape*, c. 1622–23. See p. 233 for full information.

A small sailboat catches a breeze at lower left, its profile contrasting with the long and shallow boat in the foreground, which barely leaves a ripple in its wake as it glides through mirror-like water. The cut boughs under its canopy, together with the tall trees just coming into leaf, evoke the fresh air and smells of spring. Through these elements, Cornelis Vroom (1590/92–1661) captured this riparian moment in a way that references traditional depictions of the seasons or months – spring and May in particular – although this sheet stands as its own work, detached from any known series. The reaching trees strongly recall the prints of Willem Buytewech (see pp. 196–99). Vroom translated his forebear's wiry lines and stippled foliage into tightly packed strokes and loops, which here contrast vividly with the thin horizontal strokes of the sky and water. The strong horizontals and verticals, barely interrupted by the lazy bend of the river, together lend this drawing a cohesive tension. One of very few extant drawings by Vroom, *River Landscape* speaks to his position as both artistic heir to and continuing innovator of Haarlem's early, energetic role in developing Dutch landscape traditions.

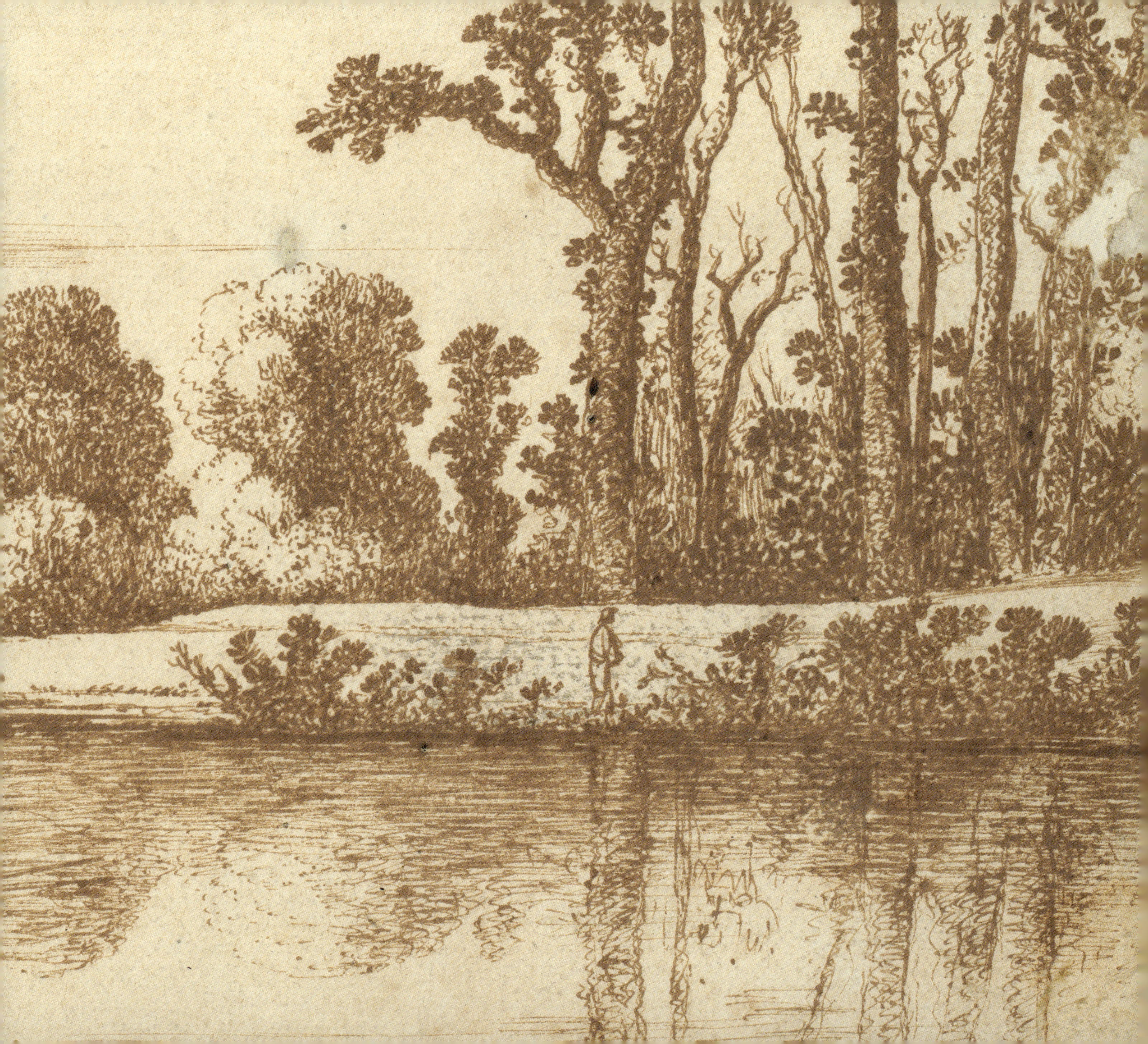

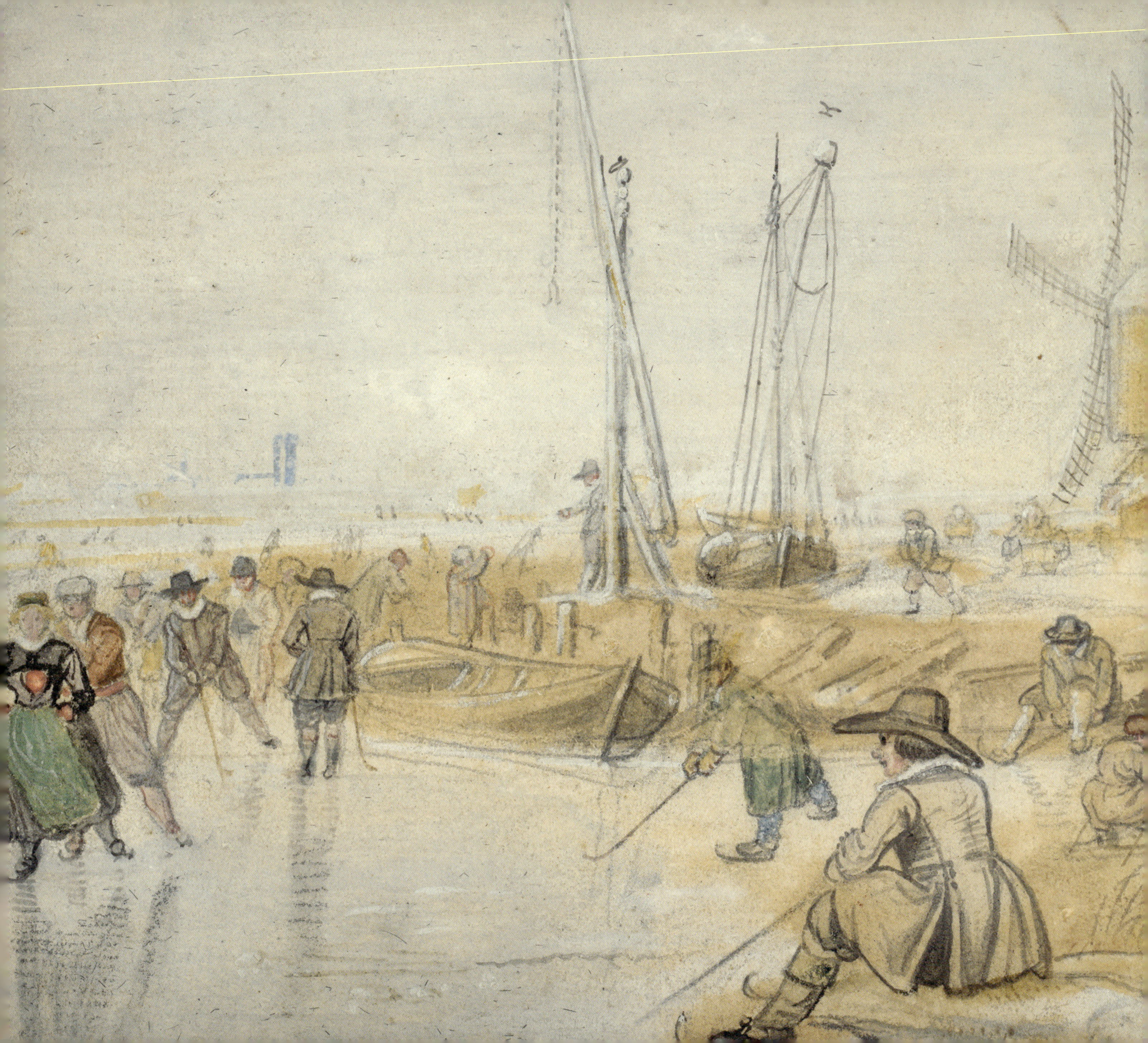

Hendrick Avercamp

*A Winter Landscape*, late 1620s

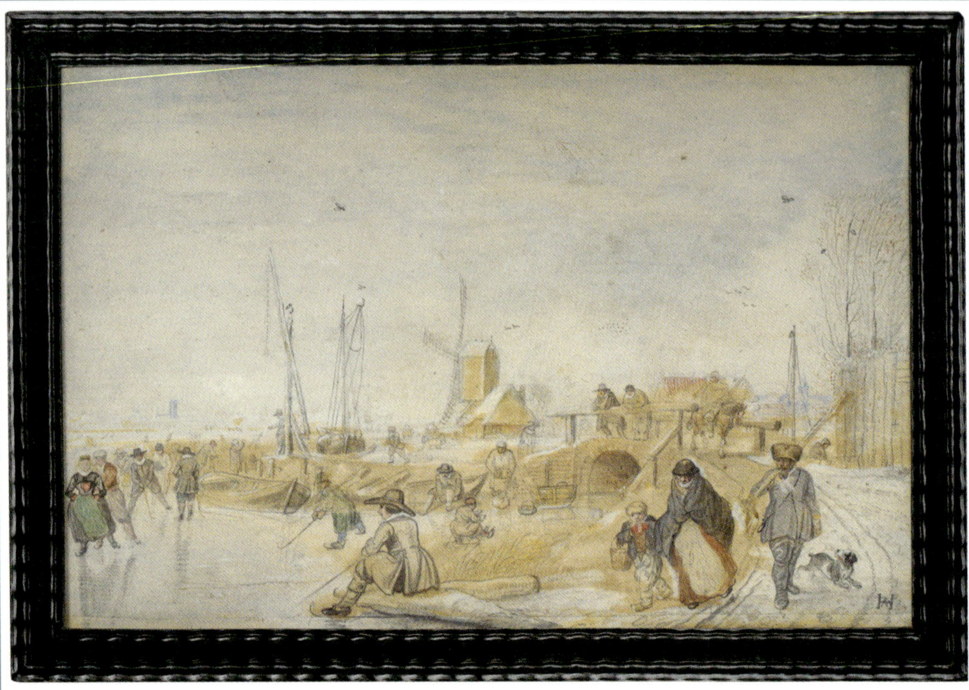

Fig. 1 Hendrick Avercamp, *A Winter Landscape*, late 1620s. See p. 228 for full information.

Hendrick Avercamp (1585–1634), active in the village of Kampen during the first few decades of the seventeenth century, was an early producer of drawings for the market and the first true specialist in the winter scene as an independent subject. Existing at the intersection of drawing and painting, this monogrammed sheet, one of his many surviving works in transparent and opaque watercolor, still bears its original seventeenth-century frame. Because of this rare occurrence, it is among the few drawings from the period known with certainty to have hung on the walls for domestic display; drawings were far more likely to be preserved in albums.

*A Winter Landscape* captures Avercamp's approach to the coldest of seasons in its vast expanse of gray sky punctuated by an empty hoist for fishing nets, moored sailboats, a windmill absent of sails, and bare trees bending in the raw wind. Characteristic of his heavily populated scenes, the people mingling together on and around the frozen waterway – many of whom relate to his surviving figure studies – represent a variety of types, including a sled rider, seen at center, and the hunter who flanks the scene at right.

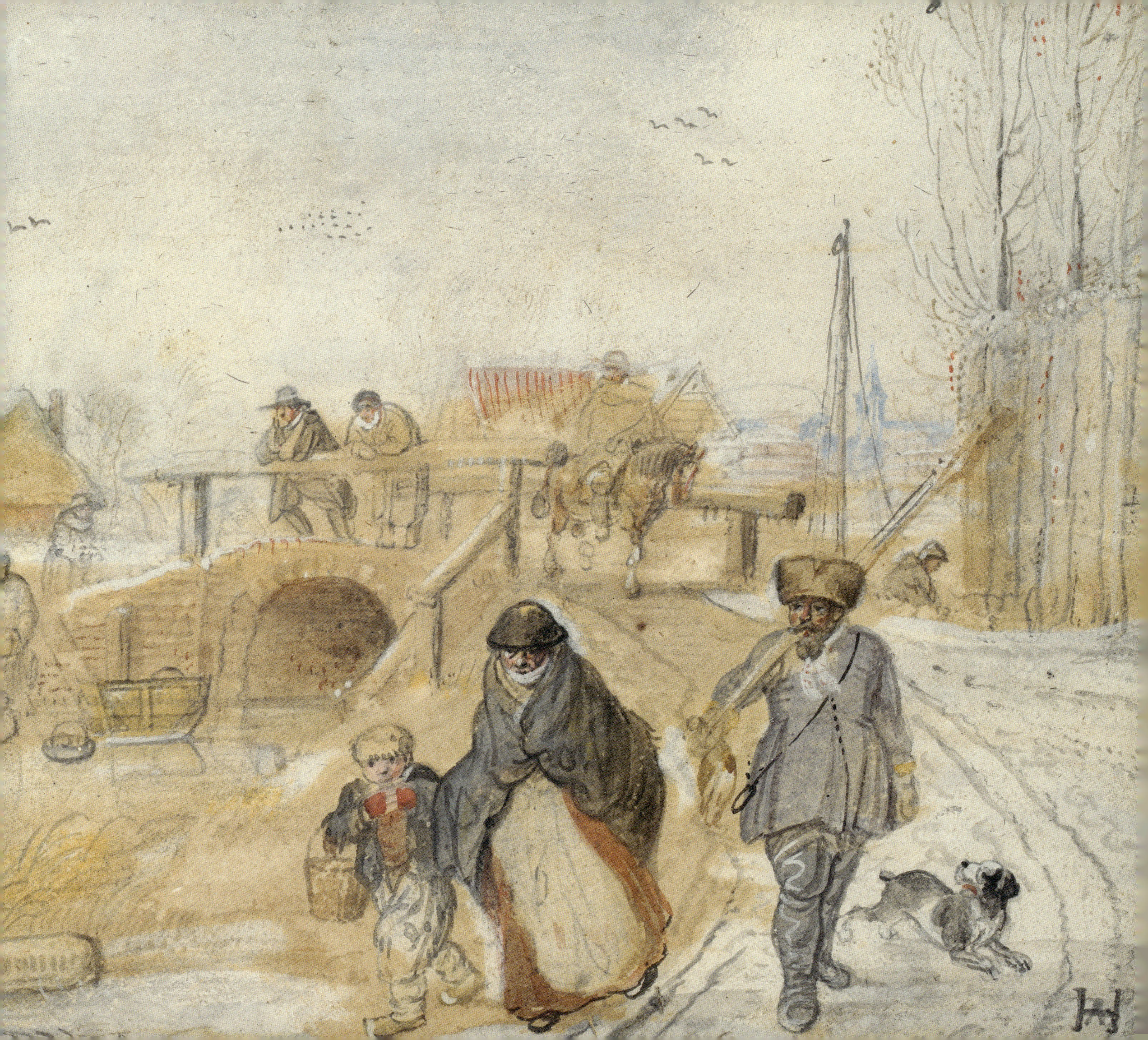

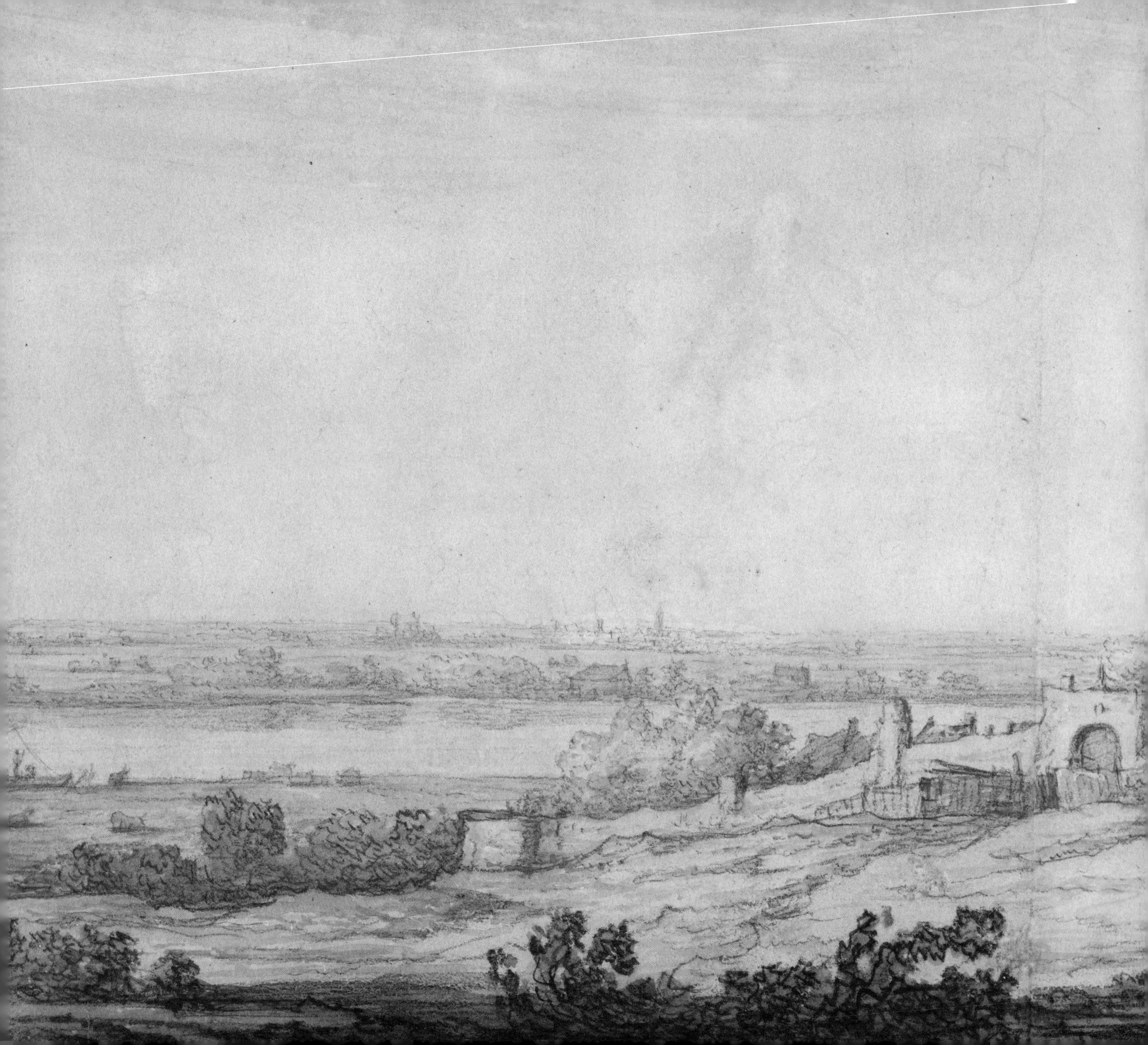

## Albert Cuyp
## *View of Rhenen*, c. 1642–46

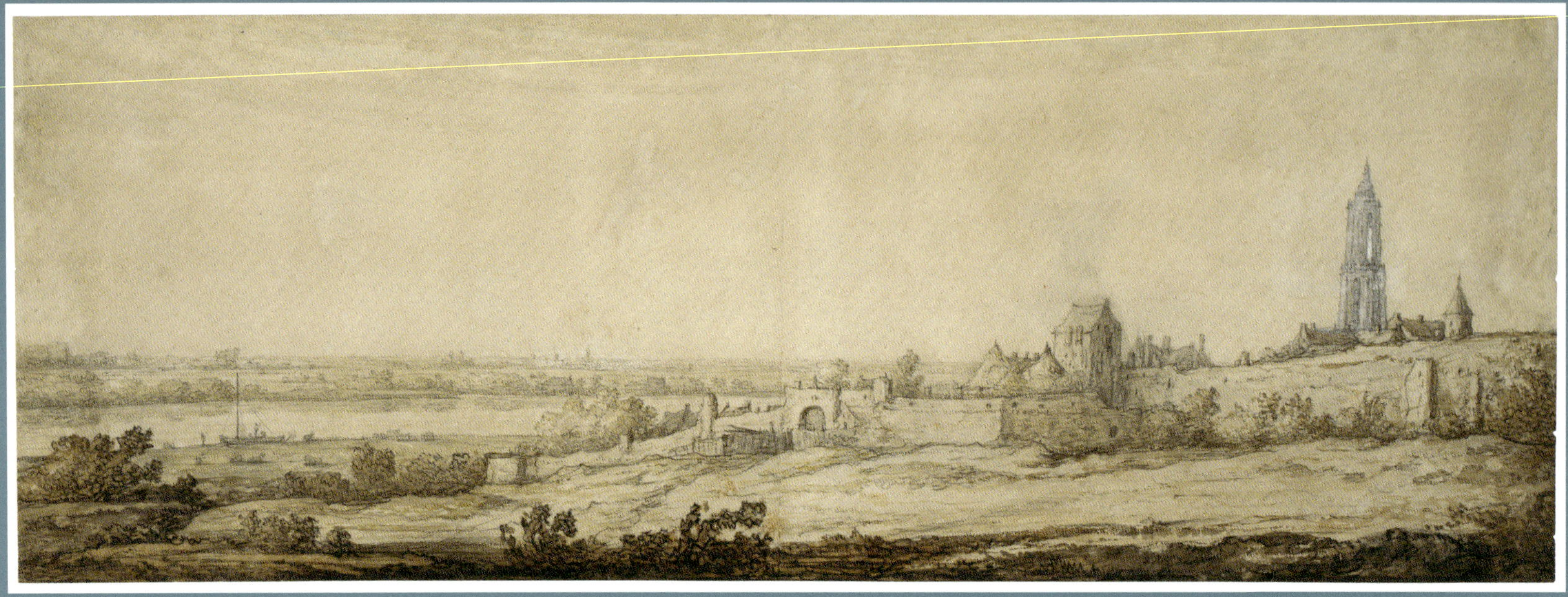

Fig. J Aelbert Cuyp, *View of Rhenen*, c. 1642–46. See p. 229 for full information.

The distinctive Gothic tower of the church of St. Cunera punctuating the sky immediately identifies this locale as Rhenen, a medieval city situated southeast of Utrecht along the Lower Rhine. Drawn by Albert Cuyp (1620–1691) with his innovative combination of black chalk and toned wash with touches of gum arabic (see p. 173), *View of Rhenen* joins his group of about fifteen surviving large panoramas of city views that have long been heralded as masterpieces of artistic topography. By comparing Cuyp's Rhenish view with those of others who captured this popular subject on their journeys (Cuyp traveling from his native Dordrecht), we can situate the artist at a particular spot on the Grebbeberg, a hill to the east of the city overlooking the Lower Rhine and De Betuwe, a region across the river.

Rhenen's walls form an expanse that Cuyp portrayed as nearly integral to the sloping hill on which they sit, interrupted at the center of the drawing by the arch of the Bergpoort that led to the outer gate of the medieval fortifications. Cuyp's panoramas record and celebrate Dutch cities; with Rhenen especially, his placement of the municipality toward the middle of the composition, amid vast stretches of unbuilt land, is also a reminder of urban presence within the broader ecological whole.

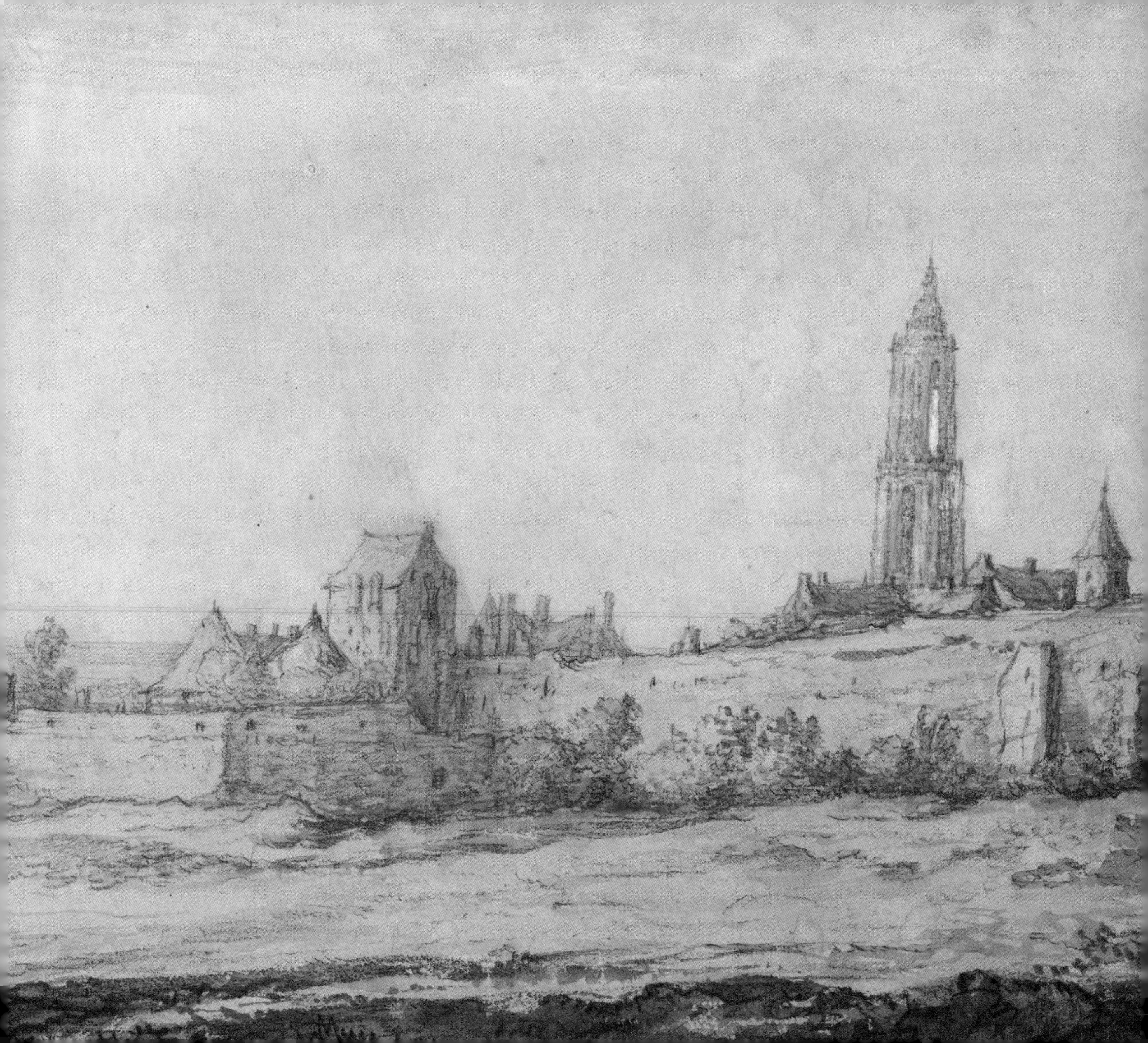

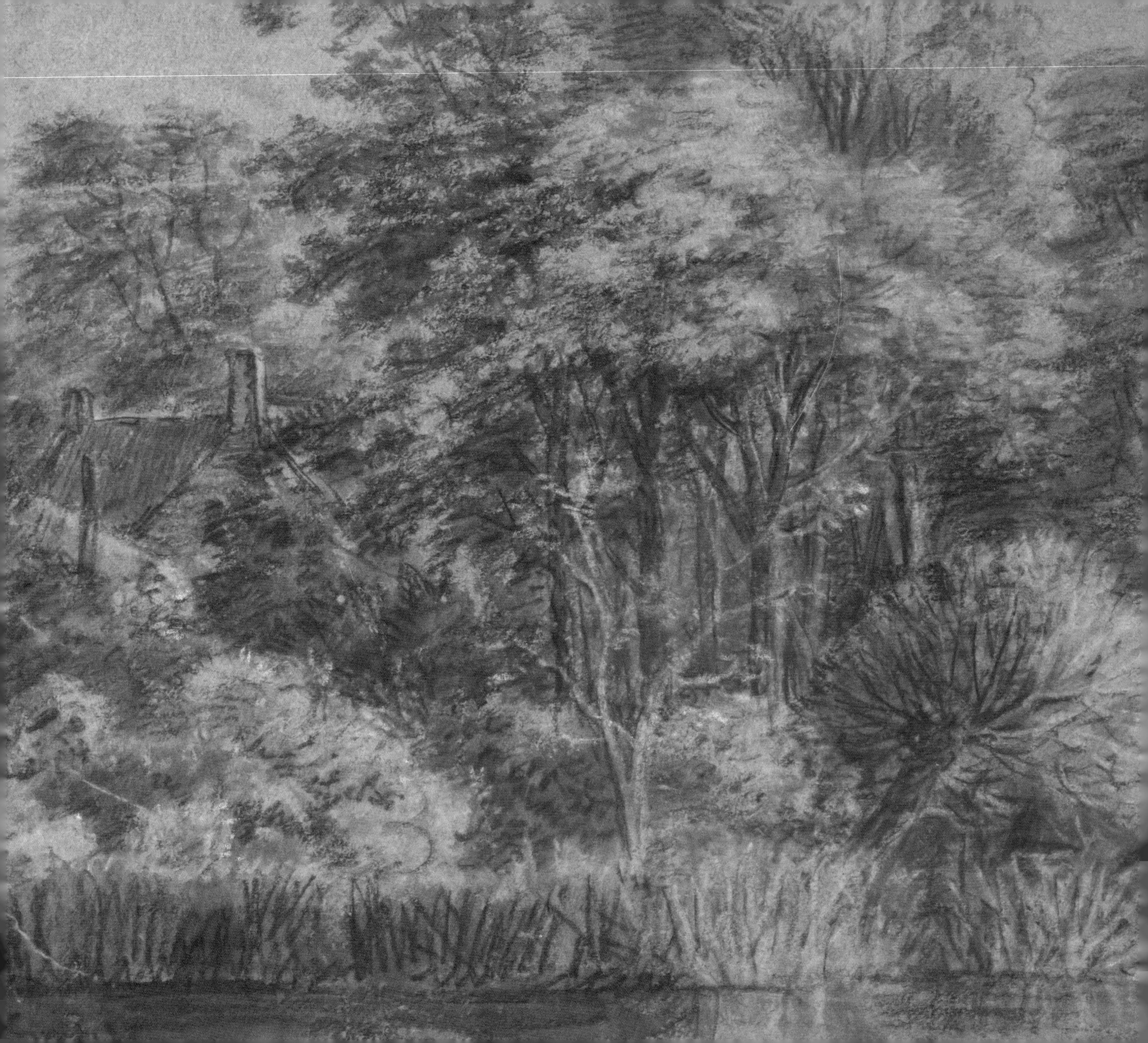

Simon de Vlieger
*Landscape with Trees by a River,*
c. 1645–53

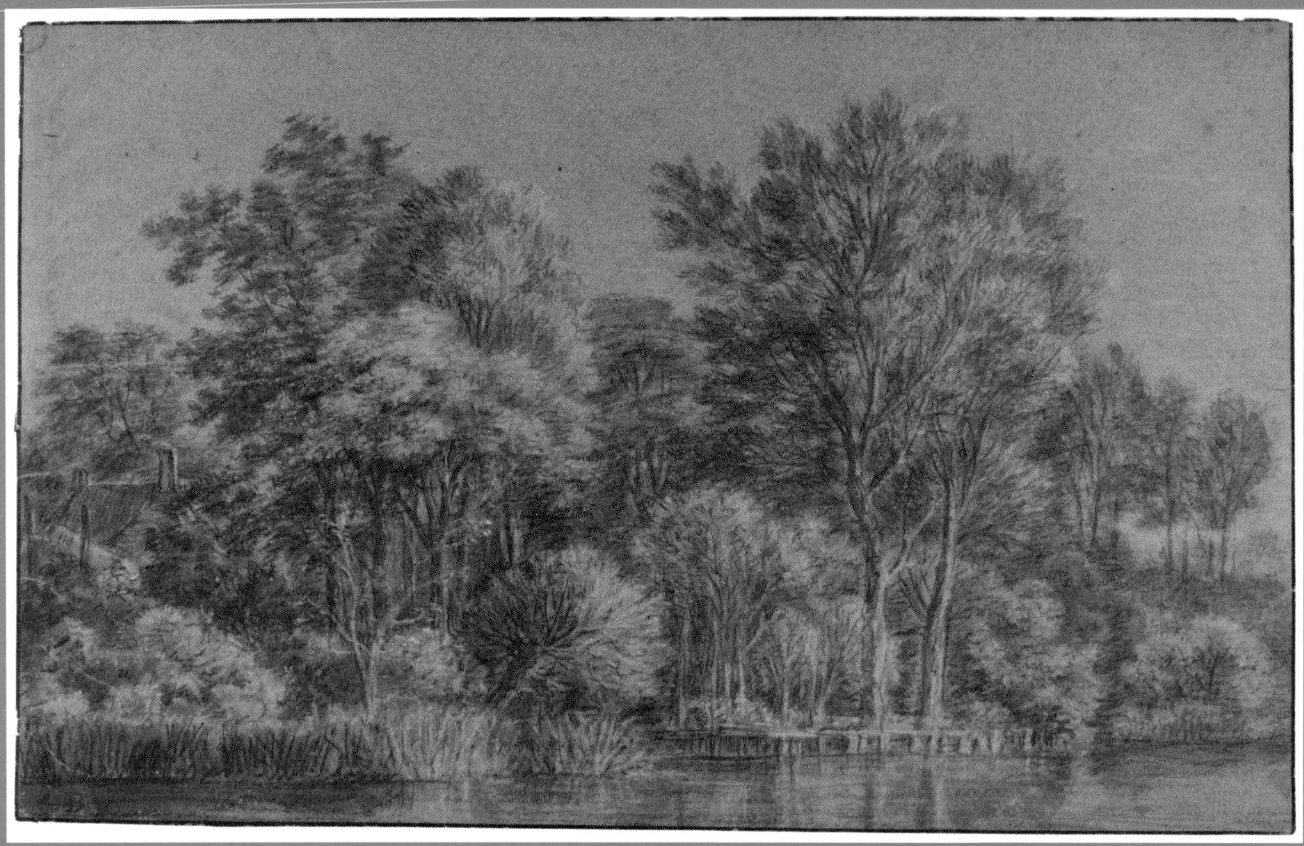

Fig. K Simon de Vlieger, *Landscape with Trees by a River*, c. 1645–53. See p. 233 for full information.

Simon de Vlieger (1600/1601–1653) selected a sheet of blue paper for this lush and technically impressive drawing. Its tone unifies the sky, water, and monumental trees, which he rendered with a combination of black and white chalk and gray wash. The rapidly drawn leaves seem to rustle in a light breeze. Aside from the implied presence of the artist himself, humanity plays a minimal role here, with only hints of architecture visible through the foliage at left and a small dock, sans boat, at water's edge.

De Vlieger's prolific and multifaceted drawn corpus includes works in various genres. Among his landscapes are views of beaches, rivers, forests, townscapes, villages, and farms, sometimes on sheets that, like this one, are quite large. His approaches to subject and media resonate with similar drawings by his longer-lived contemporary Anthonie Waterloo (1609–1690). After completing this drawing, likely during his later years in Amsterdam or thereafter in Weesp, De Vlieger added a finishing touch: his monogram, S. D. V., at lower left.

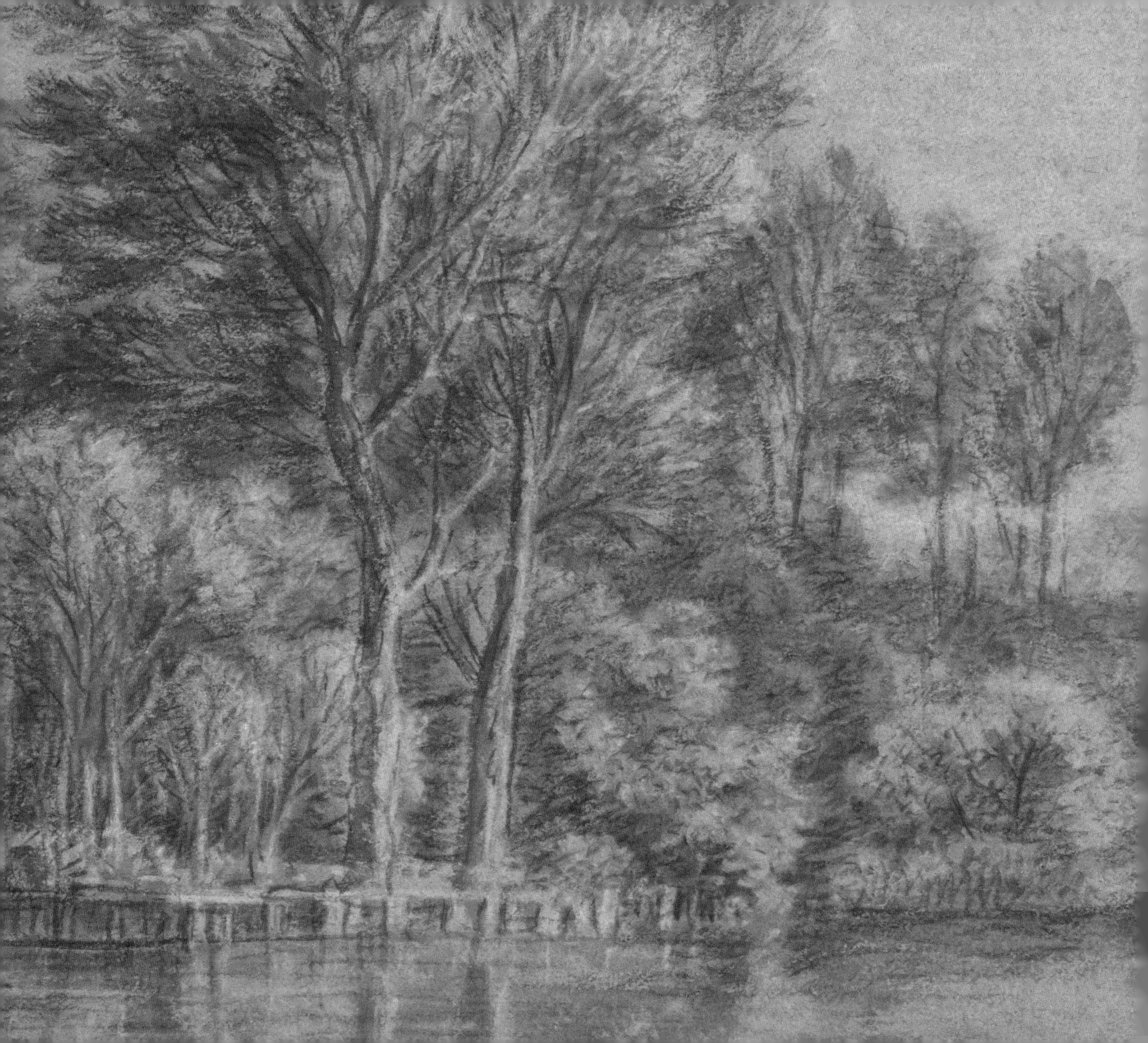

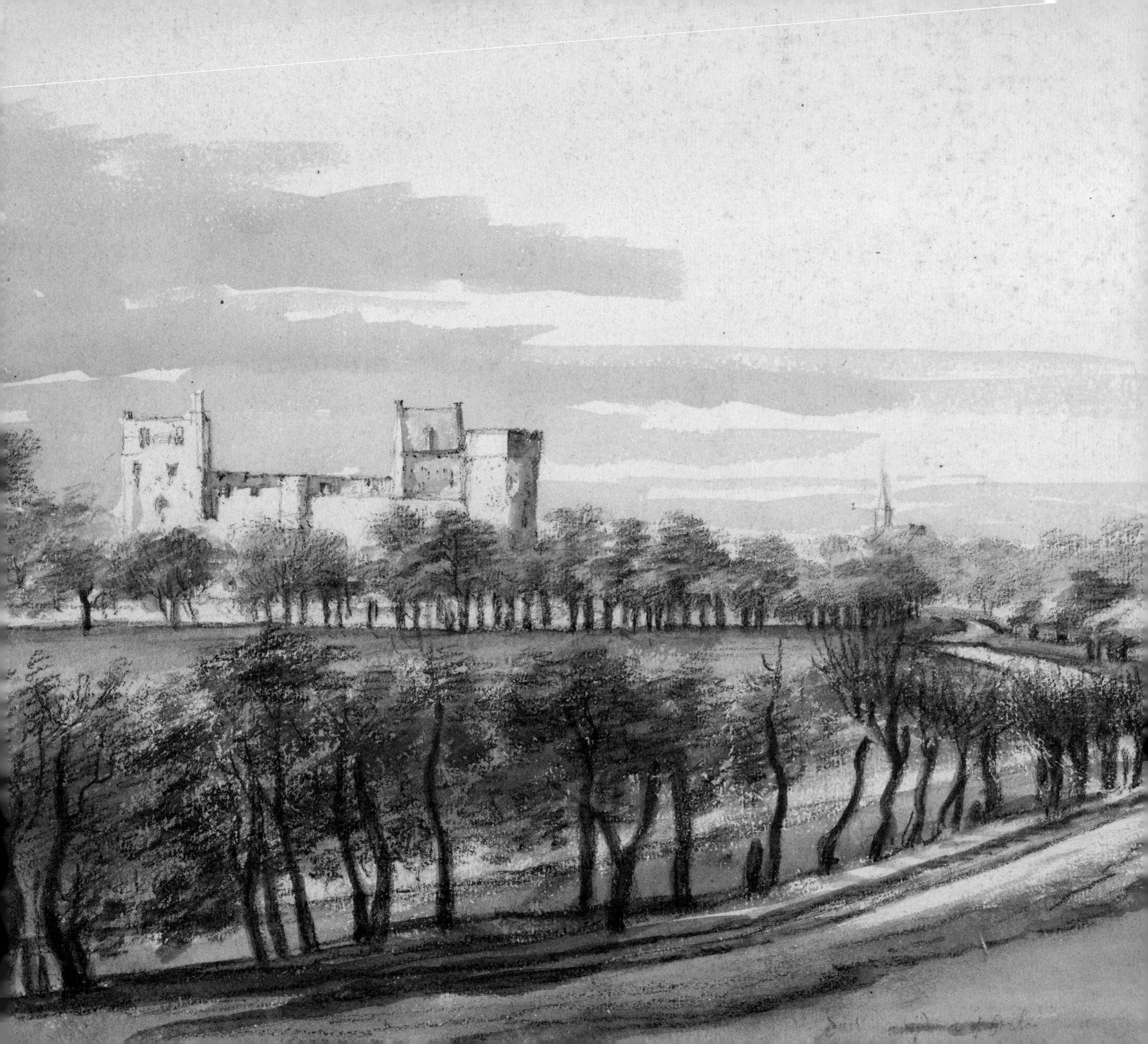

# FARMSTEADS, CASTLES, RUINS

## THE RUSTIC LANDSCAPE AND THE PRESENCE OF THE PAST

*William W. Robinson*

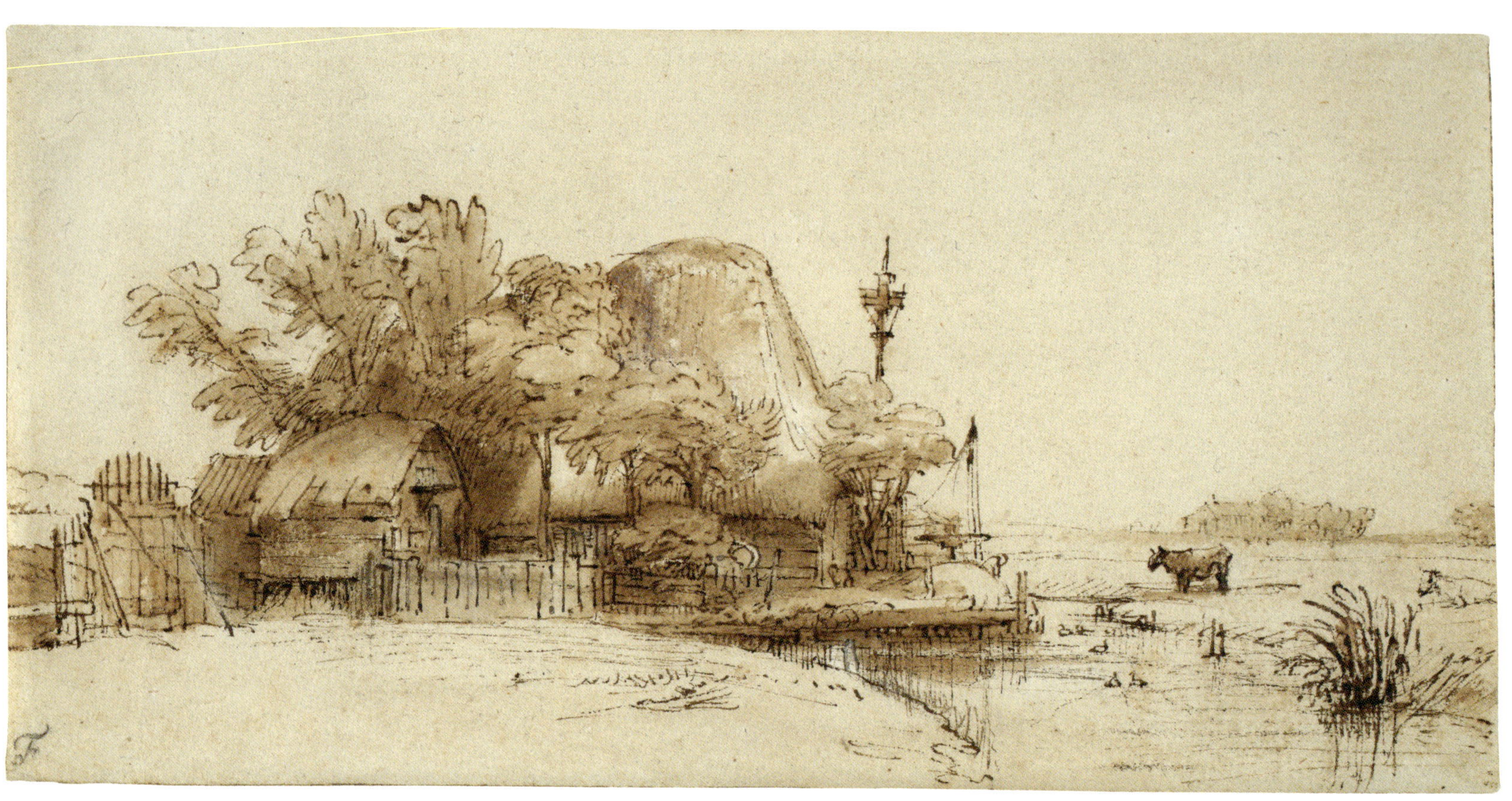

Fig. 1 Rembrandt van Rijn, *A Farm on the Amsteldijk(?)*, c. 1648–50. See p. 231 for full information.

Fig. 2 Bartholomeus Breenbergh, *Ruins in a Landscape*, 1620s. See p. 229 for full information.

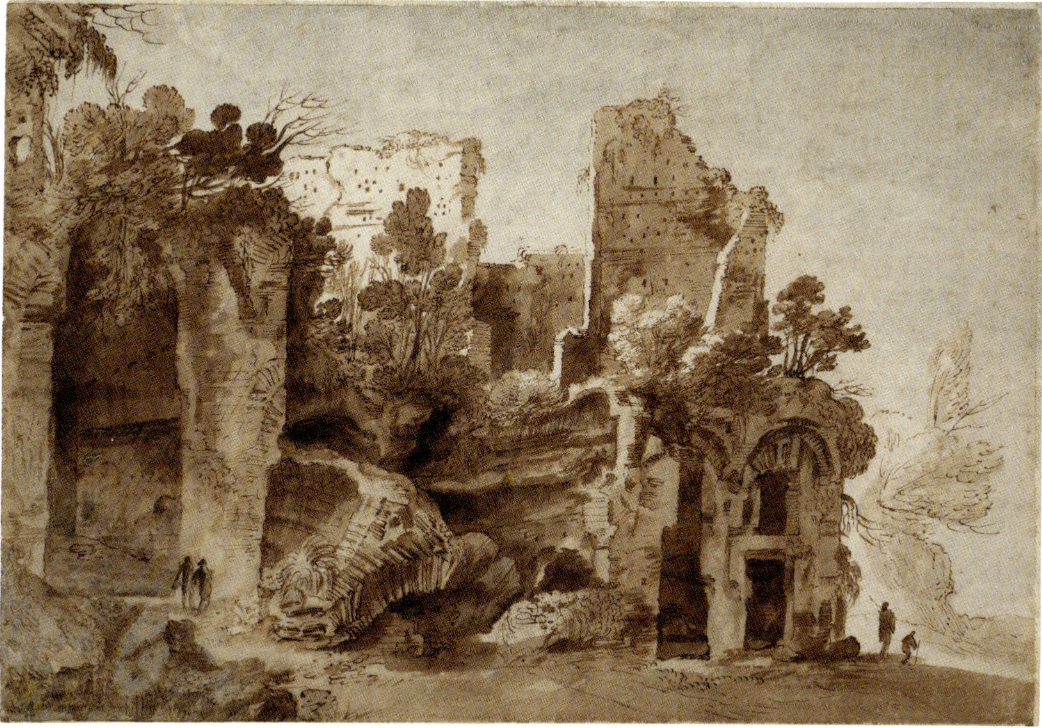



In Rembrandt's (1606–1669) drawing *A Farm on the Amsteldijk(?)* (Fig. 1), the hump of a thatched barn and a patchwork of outbuildings, shaded by a few trees, rise impressively over flat, watery meadows. The artist stood or sat near the homestead as he sketched, so that it occupies most of the view. He summoned his remarkable skills with pen and brush to describe details of the structures and evoke the restless passage of light and shade over their weathered surfaces, imparting a compelling naturalism and monumentality to the humble motif.[1]

Rembrandt's many drawings of country scenery belong to an essential tradition within Netherlandish art on paper of views of farmsteads and cottages located in the suburbs and exurbs of large cities such as Antwerp, Brussels, Utrecht, Haarlem, Leiden, and Amsterdam. As Walter S. Gibson showed in a major study of the rustic landscape, the novel premise of this imagery, from its origins in the *Small Landscapes* published in the mid-sixteenth century (see p. 37), was its insistence on the aesthetic pleasure viewers would derive from contemplation of vernacular structures of the countryside.[2] An early reference to the *Small Landscapes* as "books of village houses" (*dorpshuysboecken*) and "books of farms" (*livres de fermes*) attests that, from the outset, these agrarian buildings were regarded as the defining element of the prints.[3] Print series produced in the last third of the sixteenth century and the first decades of the seventeenth by Hans Collaert I (1525/30–1580), Claes Jansz. Visscher (1587–1652), Willem Buytewech (1591/92–1624), and Jan van de Velde II (1593–1641) further propagated the taste for views of cottages and farms, while also introducing portrait-like representations of castles and the ruins of country houses, walls, towers, city gates, and churches set within the landscape. These man-made structures carried wide-ranging political and economic associations for seventeenth-century viewers. For the artists, they presented distinct pictorial and technical challenges, from deciding on the optimal vantage point to rendering architectural detail and the fall of shifting light on variegated surfaces. The artistic choices they made over the course of the century constituted true innovations and subtle permutations on established practice.

At the turn of the seventeenth century, the architectural motif that loomed largest in the contemporary imagination was the ancient ruin. By 1600, Netherlandish artists' study of the architectural legacy of Rome was well established, dating to the early decades of the previous century. Dutch Italianate artists integrated their studies of ancient ruins and the living Italian countryside into a modern arcadian landscape peopled by herders, mule drivers, and travelers, and they developed new techniques to simulate the effects of Mediterranean sunlight. Bartholomeus Breenbergh (1598–1657), a pivotal figure in this development, spent ten years in Rome (1619–29) working alongside Paul Bril (see p. 32, Fig. C) and other Northern European artists and producing dozens of drawings from life of ancient ruins, the Roman Campagna, and the dramatic landscape north of the city. In his study of an overgrown, partially collapsed ancient building (Fig. 2), reserves of white paper represent walls and foliage struck by the brilliant sunlight, while varied tones of brown wash convey differences in the depth of the shadows. The sketchy, loose penwork describes details of the masonry, trees, and shrubs encroaching on the crumbling walls and contours fractured by the light. After he returned to the Netherlands, Breenbergh consulted many of his Roman drawings to compose the ruins that loom in the background of his paintings of religious, mythological, and pastoral scenes, whose human figures appear diminutive in comparison. A number of Dutch artists would continue to incorporate Italian and Italianate motifs in their work even as local, vernacular architecture—occasionally also represented as ruin—assumed a more prominent place within the landscape tradition.

A central figure in the introduction of native architectural imagery in the seventeenth century was the prolific Haarlem draftsman and printmaker Jan van de Velde II. Between 1615 and his death in 1641, Van de Velde designed and etched several suites of landscapes, some published by Visscher, that served, along with Visscher's own *Plaisante Plaetsen* (Pleasant Places) and Buytewech's *Verscheyden Lantschapjes* (Various Landscapes; see pp. 196–99), as touchstones for his fellow Dutch artists.[4] Van de Velde's etchings are distinguished by their broad range of scenery—which includes both the rustic and the arcadian—and do not confine themselves to a single region or the surroundings of a specific city. Many prominently feature ruins, castles, or cottages, motifs that also populate the artist's drawings. Of these three loosely defined, ultimately fluid categories, the cottage, or farmstead, descending directly from the *Small Landscapes*, would become the most vibrant and distinctive development within seventeenth-century Dutch landscape art.[5]

Van de Velde did not adapt his drawing *A Farmhouse in the Trees* (Fig. 3) for print, but it features the sort of rural imagery found in some of his etchings.[6] It probably dates from around 1620.[7] Above the farmstead, puffy clouds and a darkening sky drift into view from the right, perhaps heralding a shower. Van de Velde's

Fig. 3 Jan van de Velde II, *A Farmhouse in the Trees*, c. 1620.
See p. 232 for full information

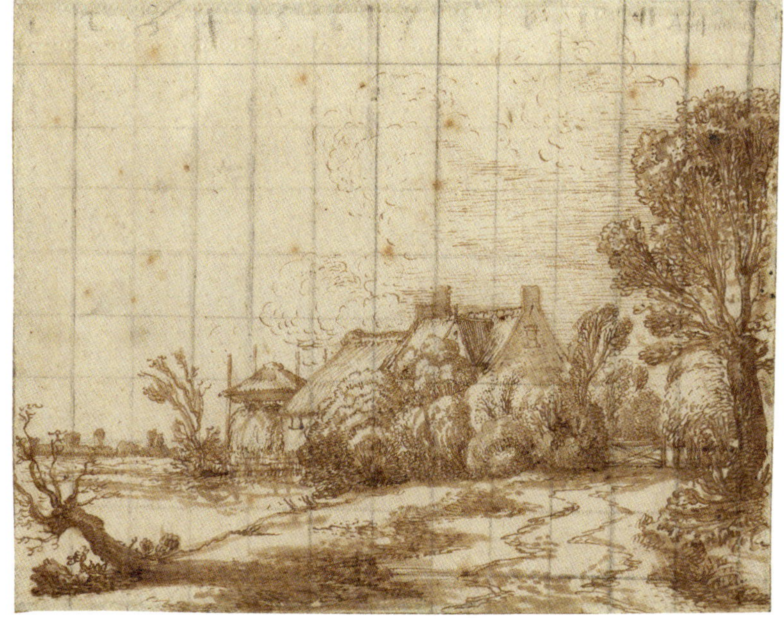

lively technique – the dots and zigzags that describe the foliage, free handling of the wash, jagged marks of the tracks in the road, and wavy parallel strokes that evoke the bulge in the barn roof – animates the view with a pulsing energy that even he could not replicate in etching. The sheet has been squared in black chalk, the cells of the grid numbered one to twelve, and *Autumnus* inscribed at upper right. We do not know whether Van de Velde or a later hand applied the grid, but this was not his usual practice: only one other squared landscape by him has come to light, and the grids on the two works use different numbering systems.[8] Perhaps the squaring and inscription were added by a later artist who intended to transfer the composition for a print or painting in a series of Seasons, although no other version is known. The intimation of windy, changing weather would be appropriate for autumn.[9]

Dutch connoisseurs of the first half of the seventeenth century delighted in such imagery, particularly depictions of weathered, neglected cottages and other rural buildings. Gibson cites Cornelis Pietersz. Biens (1590/95–1645), who published *De Teecken-Const*, an instructional book on drawing, in 1636: when depicting cottages, Biens wrote, "choose the old, curious, broken and half-fallen peasant houses covered with reeds or straw, overgrown with vegetation, with old walls, broken doors and windows, curious haystacks, dovecotes, ploughs, wagons."[10] In *Het Schilder-Boeck*, published in Haarlem in 1604, Karel van Mander (1548–1606), biographer and the Netherlands' leading art theorist, recommended that painters depict humble cottages as *seldtsamer cluchten* (bizarre or grotesque whimsicalities). As Gibson notes, these exhortations express an aesthetic judgment of the pleasure derived from contemplating tumbledown rural dwellings, not a moral rebuke aimed at the inhabitants responsible for their upkeep.[11]

Abraham Bloemaert (1566–1651) almost single-handedly invented and propagated this taste for ramshackle farm buildings. As early as the 1580s, Bloemaert drew studies from life of cottages, sheds, barns, dovecotes, and outhouses in the countryside around Utrecht.[12] These drawings, many of which survive, caught the attention of Van Mander, who wrote that Bloemaert's landscape paintings incorporate "well-observed and quaint peasant houses, peasants' implements, trees, and countryside – things which are to be seen in great variety round about Utrecht and which are drawn by him; for he does a great deal after life and he has a clever manner of drawing and penmanship to which he sometimes adds some watercolors so that it looks particularly good."[13] He could have been

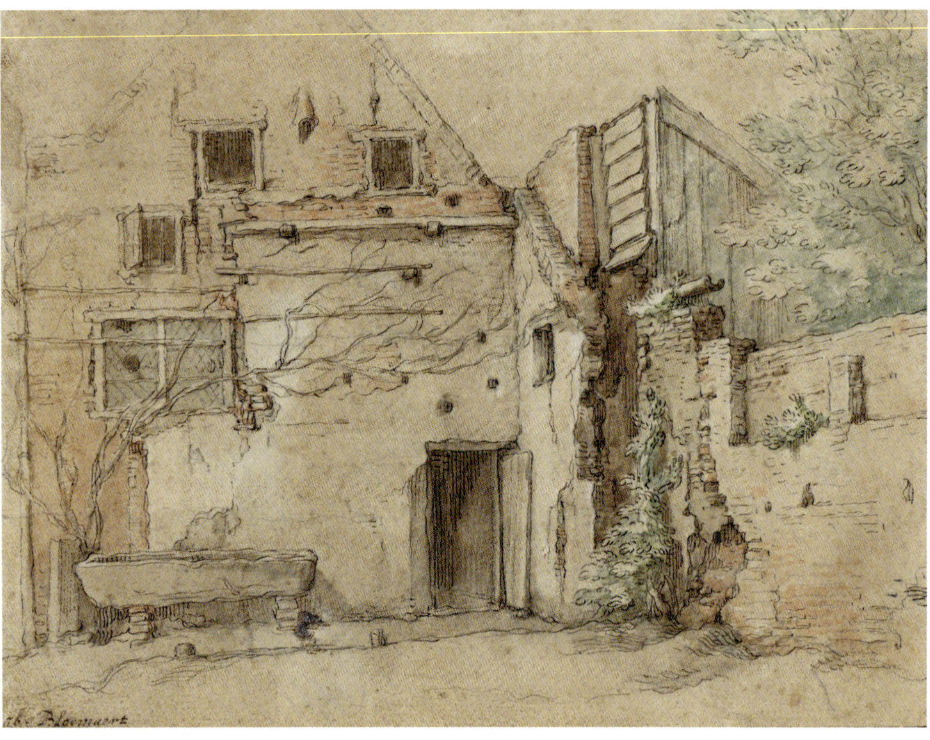

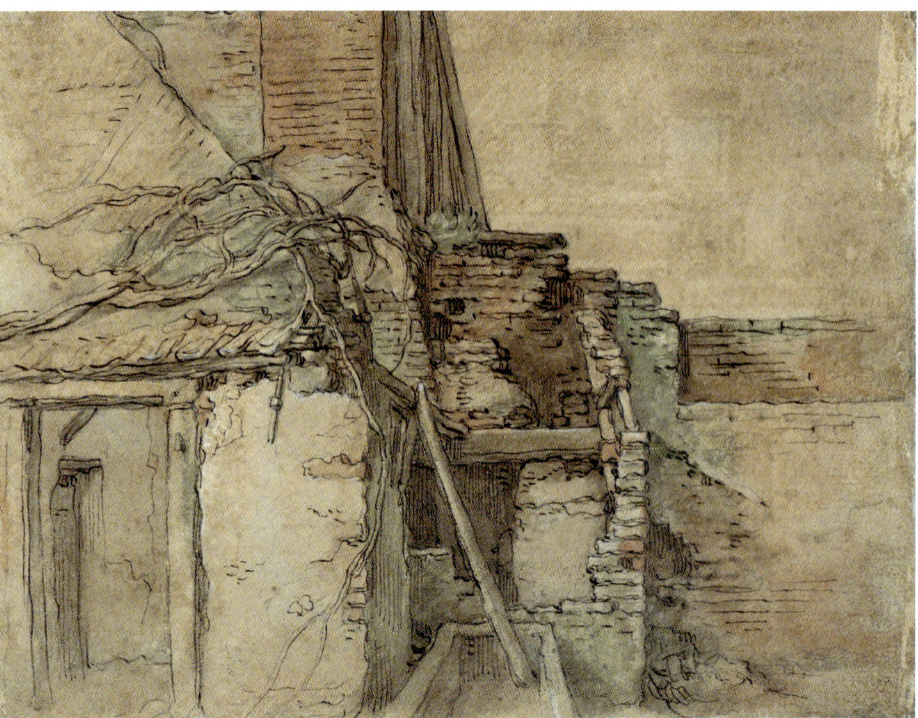

Fig. 4 Abraham Bloemaert, *A Dilapidated Farmhouse* (recto), c. 1595–1605. See p. 228 for full information.

Fig. 5 Abraham Bloemaert, *Walls of a Farmhouse* (verso), c. 1595–1605. See p. 228 for full information.

Fig. 6 Boëtius Adamsz. Bolswert, after Abraham Bloemaert, *Reclining Shepherd in a Landscape*, c. 1613–14. Etching, 15.6 × 24.4 cm. Harvard Art Museums/Fogg Museum, Light-Outerbridge Collection, Purchase through the generosity of Manson Benedict, M24455.

Fig. 7 Salomon van Ruysdael, *Landscape with Farmhouse*, 1628. Oil on panel, 32.9 × 42.5 cm. The Frick Collection, New York, Gift of Kathleen Feldstein in memory of Martin Feldstein, 2020, 2020.1.01.

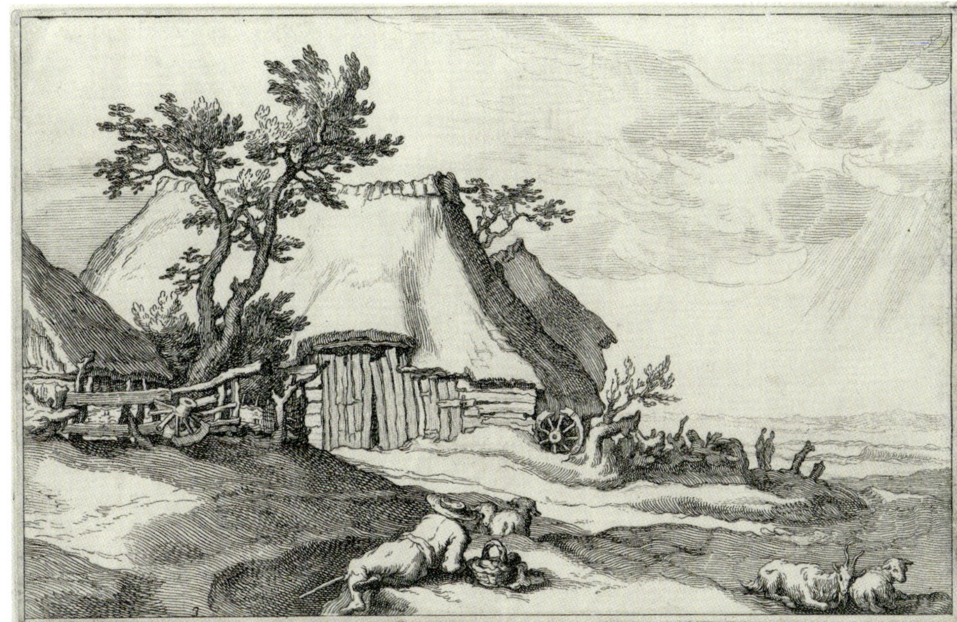

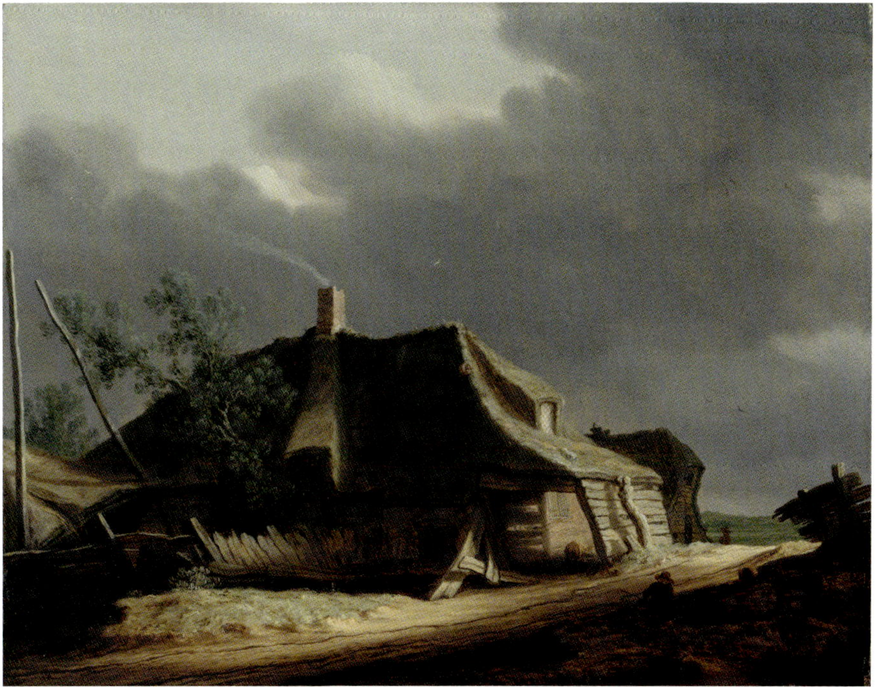



describing *A Dilapidated Farmhouse* (c. 1595–1605), a close view of the facade and adjacent wall of a cottage in an advanced state of decline (Fig. 4). The open door hangs askew, peeling plaster exposes the brick and masonry, and trees sprout from cracks in the wall. On the verso (Fig. 5), a log steadied in an abandoned trough acts as a makeshift support for a sagging beam.[14] In this and many other such drawings by Bloemaert, the structure and its condition are the focus, while the inhabitants and landscape context are secondary or omitted altogether.

Like Van de Velde, Bloemaert was an important model for Dutch landscapists who continually revised the tradition of the "village houses" in the 1620s, 1630s, and beyond. His studies served as designs for two series of etchings with farmhouses produced by Boëtius Adams Bolswert (c. 1580–1633) around 1613–14 (Fig. 6). The prints proved so popular that Visscher copied both series and published them as a set in 1620.[15] The etchings after Bloemaert's designs stimulated interest among landscape painters in close-up views of farm buildings, in many instances focusing on their disrepair or ramshackle character.[16] A 1628 picture by Salomon van Ruysdael (1600/1603–1670) clearly registers the impact of Bloemaert's inventions on the generation of landscapists whose careers began in the 1620s (Fig. 7).[17] Jan van Goyen (1596–1656), Pieter de Molijn (1595–1661), and Jacob van Ruisdael (c. 1628/29–1682) also explored the rustic landscape in their paintings, while Van Goyen, De Molijn, and many others turned out scores of finished drawings with rustic imagery – fully resolved compositions, usually signed and often dated – that were intended for sale to connoisseurs (see p. 80).

Rembrandt's drawings, along with those of his one-time associate Jan Lievens (1607–1674) and pupils Jacob Koninck (c. 1614/15–by 1666), Pieter de With (c. 1635–1689 or later), and Abraham Furnerius (1628–1654), illustrate the persistence and permutations of this imagery in the third quarter of the seventeenth century. *A Farm on the Amsteldijk(?)* (see Fig. 1) is a dazzling example. The sheet features a type of dwelling typical of the region to the north and south of Amsterdam.[18] Scholars have tentatively located the property on the well-traveled dike road that followed the course of the Amstel River southeast of the city.[19] Rembrandt and his pupils must have frequently walked this route, judging from the number of their drawings and etchings that represent sites on the ten-kilometer stretch of the Amstel between Amsterdam and the village of Ouderkerk.[20]

The property depicted in the Harvard sheet was uniquely alluring. Rembrandt produced multiple drawings of the site, each from a different vantage point.[21] Drawings attributed to De With also feature this farm, and together these views offer a composite portrait of the place and the agricultural pursuits of its residents.[22] Nestled beside the tall barn in the Harvard drawing, next to a small shed or outhouse, we see a dovecote with a thatched roof; the tower to the right of the barn probably served as a landing stage for the birds. To the right of the dovecote is the low plank wall of a boathouse. From a drawing by Rembrandt (now in Chicago) that shows the back of the property, with two figures seated on a bench outside the house, we may infer that the canal in which ducks swim in the Harvard work is not a mere ditch but leads to a more substantial waterway.[23] That the farmer engaged in fishing in addition to keeping cattle and pigeons is confirmed by the two tall poles to the right of the building: in other sketches of the site, nets have been hoisted here to dry.[24]

Farms situated near large cities in the province of Holland were generally small holdings owned by urban investors whose tenants produced food for the city's populace. The family that leased this land presumably milked the cows to make butter and cheese and sold their pigeons and fish locally or at an Amsterdam market.[25] Two adjacent buildings visible in the Chicago drawing provide additional information about the neighborhood. A neglected cottage a few steps from the farmhouse had probably proved too small and was replaced by the building featured in the Harvard view.[26] On the other side of this dilapidated cottage stood a substantial dwelling, with two chimneys and a separate kitchen. In a drawing by De With of the front of the property along the road, a small banner hangs over the door of this house, advertising the premises as a tavern.[27] It is possible that our farmer's fish, pigeons, butter, and cheese were served at this inn.[28]

On another occasion, Rembrandt left Amsterdam via the Heiligewegspoort, a gate on the site of the present-day Koningsplein, and followed the Heiligeweg (Holy Way) two and a half kilometers to the Schinkel River. At the Overtoom, a busy junction where a rolling bridge moved small craft from the Schinkel to another waterway, he turned south onto the Schinkelweg, the road along the riverbank. He passed a cluster of three houses, then turned around, facing back toward the Overtoom and the city, and drew what he saw (Fig. 8).[29] Small farmers, artisans, and innkeepers occupied the cottages in this area, and the signs hung on two of the lodges

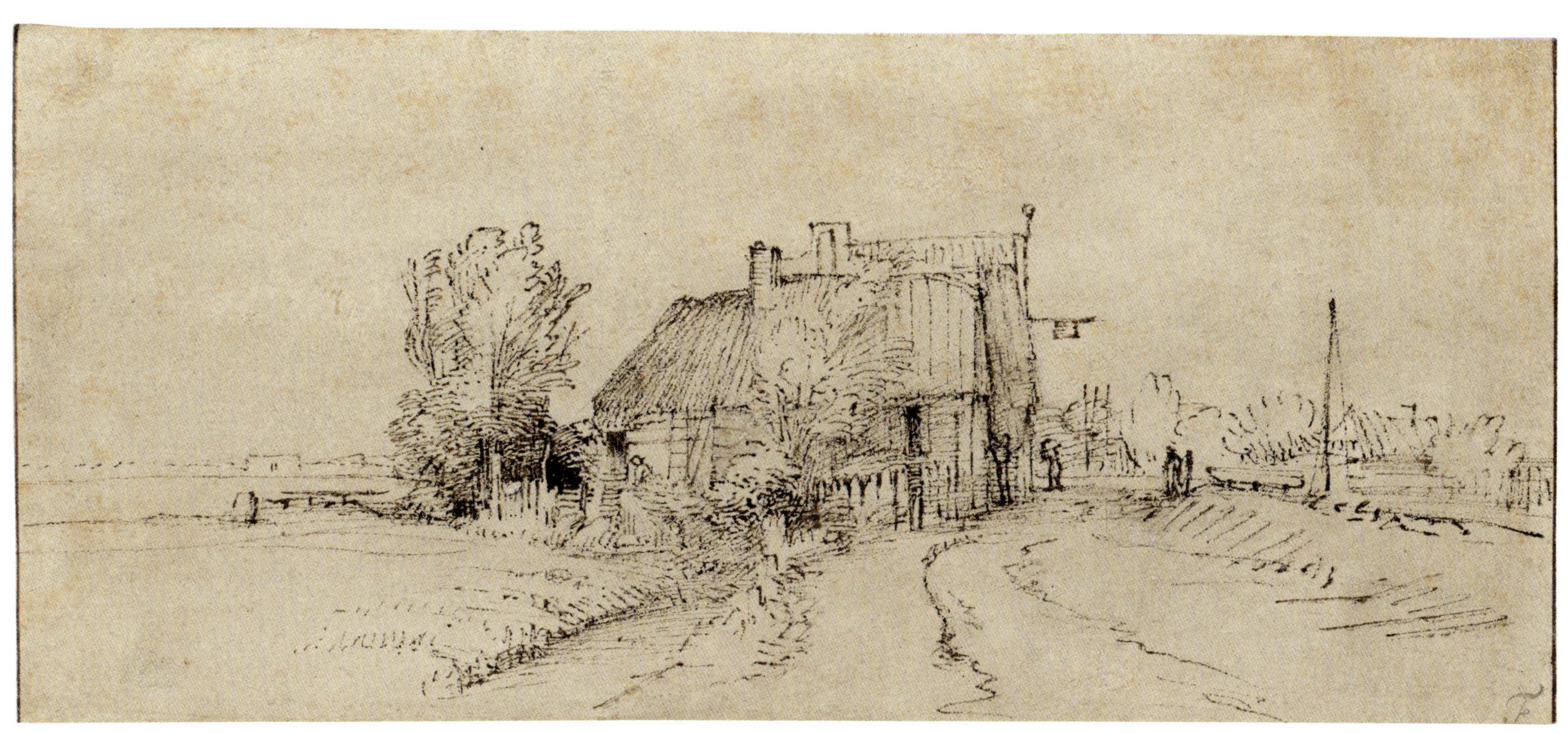

Fig. 8 Rembrandt van Rijn, *Houses on the Schinkelweg*, c. 1650–52. See p. 231 for full information.

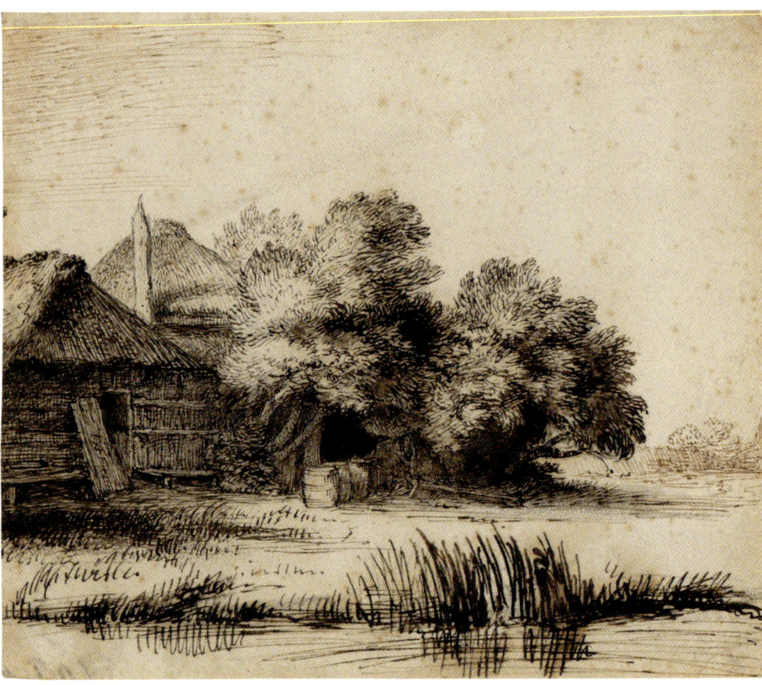

Fig. 9 Jacob Koninck, *Farmhouse with a Tall Haystack*, 1650s–60s. See p. 230 for full information.

Fig. 10 Pieter de With, *A Wooded Landscape with a Cottage*, late 1650s. See p. 233 for full information.



indicate that they probably served as taverns.[30] The landscape probably dates from the early 1650s, slightly later than *A Farm on the Amsteldijk(?)* (c. 1648–50), and is executed in a strikingly different technique.[31] In the latter, Rembrandt strove for a pictorial effect by contrasting the reserves of white paper, which suggest strong sunlight, with washes of two tones for the finely modulated shadows. He drew the cottages on the Schinkelweg with delicate, granular pen strokes on a sheet prepared with a light-gray wash. The broken lines and diffuse light suggested by the gray tone evoke a monochrome, overcast atmosphere.

Rembrandt's pupils followed his example in making lively ink and wash drawings of rustic buildings based on direct observation. The close view of the front of a cottage by Jacob Koninck (Fig. 9) is one of three drawings of the same house by the artist, all from a slightly different angle and with variant details, suggesting that he made them on separate visits.[32] With his characteristically profuse, dense penwork, Koninck conveys the textures of the weathered planks and wiry thatch, evokes the range of light and shade in the trees, and carefully describes incidental details, such as the barrels lined up near the doorway. Like Koninck, Pieter de With probably studied with Rembrandt in the early 1650s, and as noted above, drew some of the same sites as his master.[33] In his study of a farmstead comprised of two adjacent or conjoined houses surrounded by shrubs and trees in a flat, watery landscape, he takes a broad view of the site, with the buildings occupying only a corner of the right foreground (Fig. 10).[34] His technique – looping strokes for the foliage, parallel lines and cross-hatching for the roofs, and close attention to details such as the fenestration of the building and the tiny figure standing in front of it – is so similar to Koninck's that their hands have occasionally been confused.[35]

Abraham Furnerius, who studied under Rembrandt in the mid-1640s, is known today exclusively as a landscape draftsman who specialized in views of farmhouses and country roads.[36] The handling of the media in his *Landscape with Farmhouses* (Fig. 11) reflects that of Rembrandt's pictorial drawings of the late 1640s, such as *A Farm on the Amsteldijk(?)*.[37] Limiting the use of pen to the contours of the trees, buildings, and road, and relying on broadly applied washes for shading, Furnerius eschewed the descriptive detail that preoccupied De With and Koninck in favor of a more summary technique that conveys a general impression of light and shade at the site. Lievens similarly situated a farmhouse and adjacent buildings nestled within a stand of trees, although his prolific,

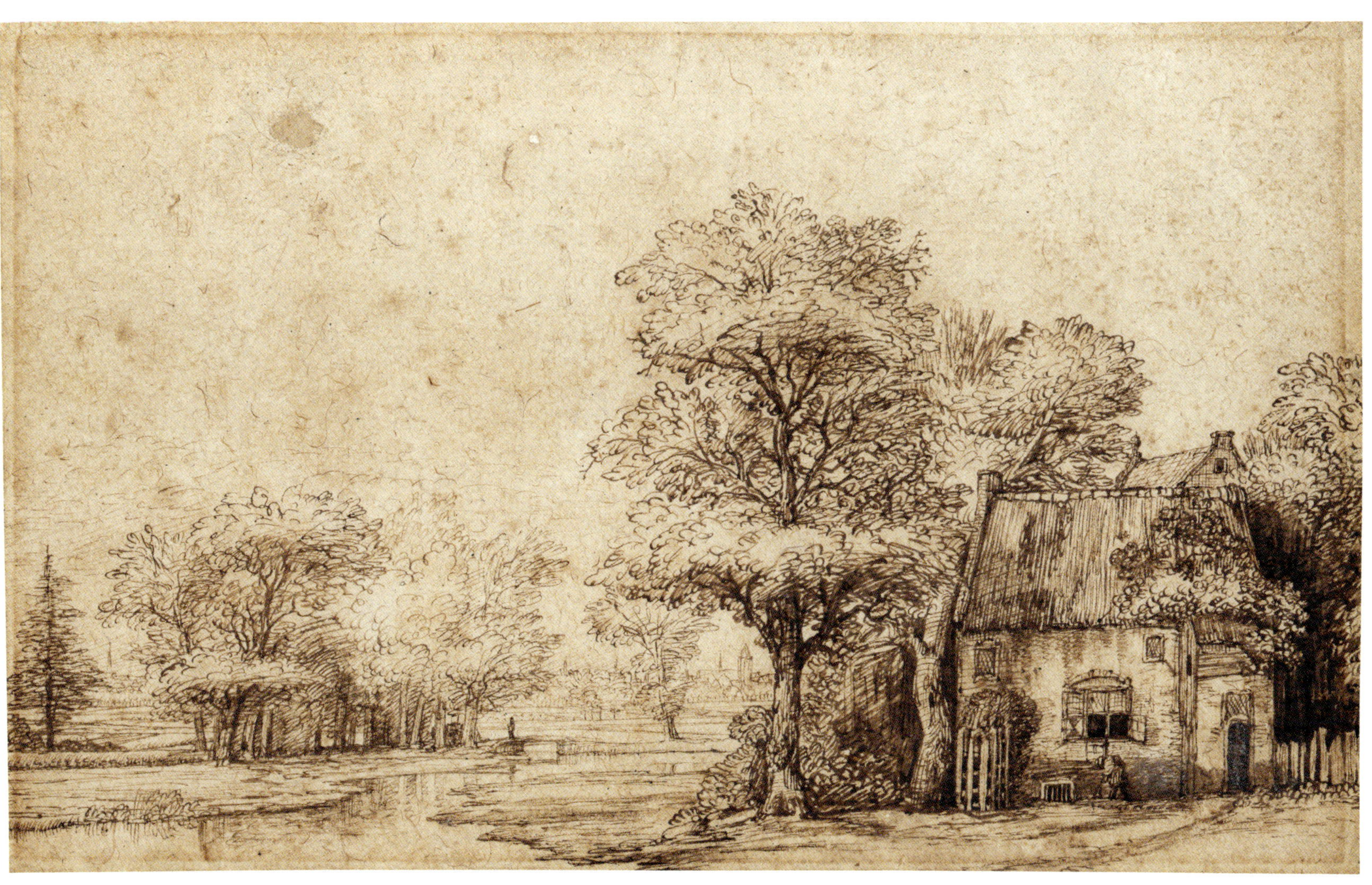

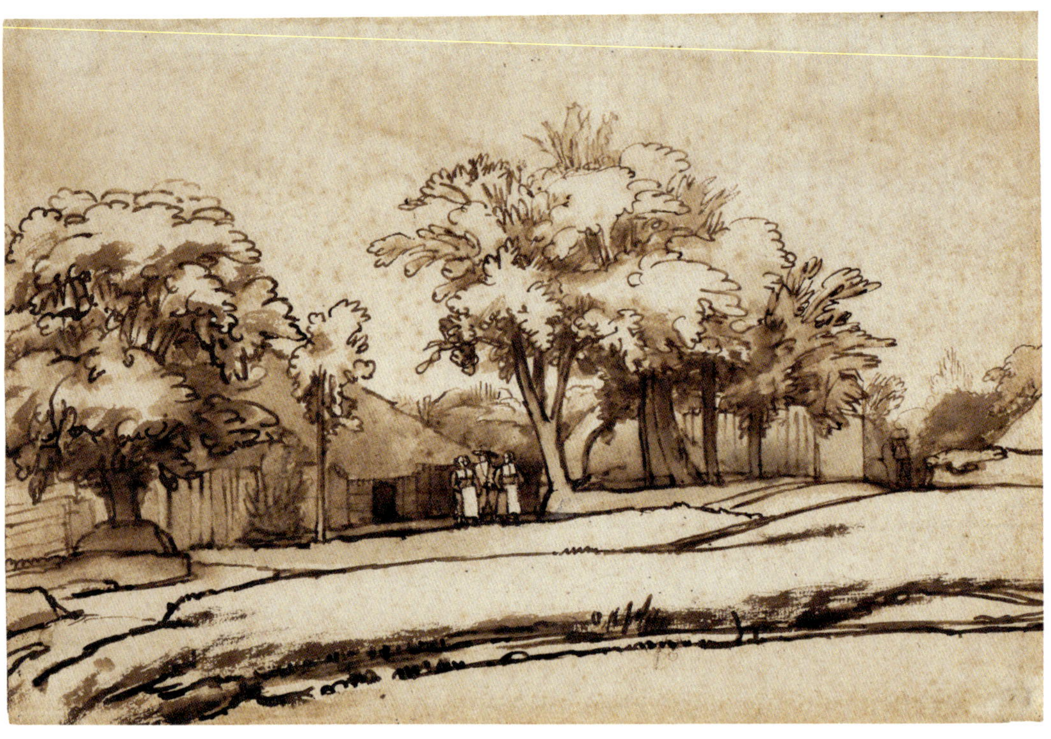

Fig. 11 Abraham Furnerius, *Landscape with Farmhouses*, c. 1650–54. See p. 229 for full information.

Fig. 12 Jan Lievens, *Cottage among Trees*, 1650s–60s. See p. 230 for full information.



performative hatching differs from Furnerius's looser handling of the pen (Fig. 12).[38] In this and other drawings of the 1650s and 1660s (see p. 42), Jan Lievens adapted the technique of Anthony van Dyck (1599–1641) and a Flemish compositional type that sets the subject within a forest interior, the trees growing beyond the upper limits of the picture space.[39] The property in Lievens's drawing looks less like a working farm than a country retreat, real or imagined. No animals are present, except for a resting dog; the fencing appears new; the chimney on the lower building might indicate that it is a detached kitchen, rather than a barn or shed; and the two relaxing figures, one of whom plays a musical instrument, establish a bucolic mood. The monogrammed, virtuoso drawing on a large sheet of expensive Asian paper must have been intended for sale to a collector.

While we know little about the connoisseurs who purchased drawings with rustic imagery, Jan van de Cappelle's (1626–1679) enormous collection surely included many that represented cottages, villages, and farmsteads.[40] The 277 landscape drawings by Rembrandt that belonged to Van de Cappelle – a significant proportion of all those listed in the inventory of the artist's possessions compiled in 1656, after he applied for bankruptcy protection – were probably acquired when Rembrandt's "paper art" was sold in 1658.[41] One of Van de Cappelle's portfolios housed 188 "sketches" of landscapes and another contained 89 "drawings" of landscapes, the latter presumably more finished or worked-up images.[42] Other documented owners of Rembrandt's landscape drawings include Lambert Doomer, who might have studied with Rembrandt around 1644,[43] and the collector plausibly identified as Rotterdam surgeon Johannes Furnerius (1582–1668), father of Abraham. Of the six Rembrandt landscapes owned by Dr. Furnerius, two were later acquired by Nicolaes Anthoni Flinck (1646–1723), son of Rembrandt's pupil Govert Flinck (1615–1660), who also owned both *A Farm on the Amsteldijk(?)* and *Houses on the Schinkelweg*.[44]

In the same decades that Dutch artists invented, and reinvented, the landscape to feature cottages and farmsteads, castles – real and imaginary, ruined and intact – also became a prominent motif for draftsmen and printmakers. While castles appear in the background of earlier works, including the *Small Landscapes* and *Views of the Environs of Brussels*, the second decade of the seventeenth century witnessed the invention of a new type of castle portrait, in which the building, often specified by a text or title, is not subordinate to

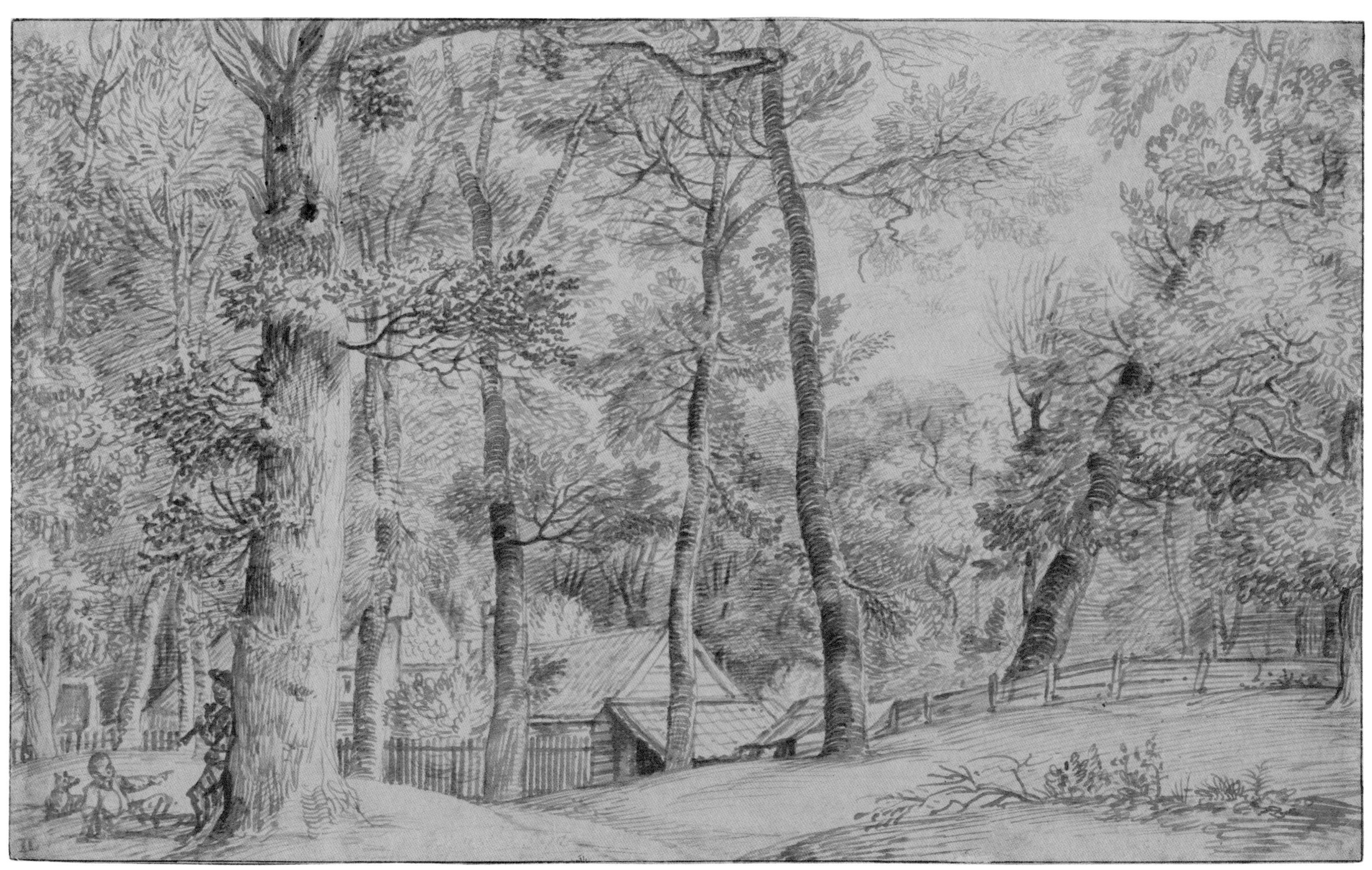

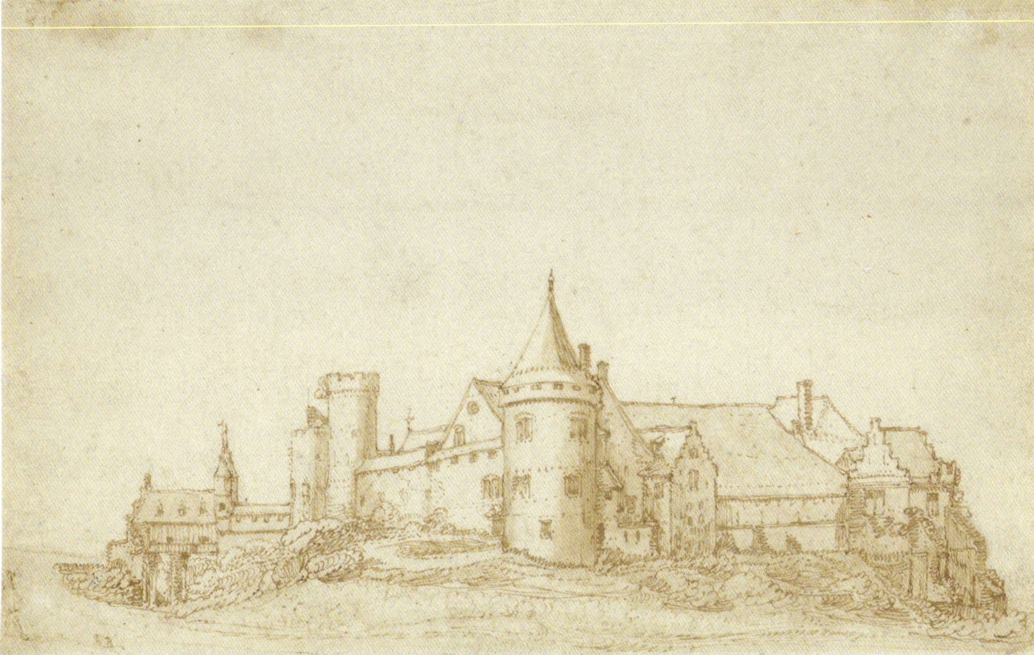

Fig. 13 Jan van de Velde II, *Keizersberg Castle in Leuven*, 1620s. See p. 232 for full information.



its surroundings, but the predominant element in the composition. In 1616, Jan van de Velde II produced a set of etchings of five castles and a monastery. Underscoring the historical and topographical interest of the prints, each building is identified by a title within the image. Patriotic associations with the struggle for independence from Spanish rule underlie the series: all six buildings suffered significant damage during the fighting, and Van de Velde shows them in their ruined state. One had belonged to Count Lamoraal van Egmont, whose execution in 1568 by the Duke of Alva, the Spanish general sent to quell religious and political unrest in the Netherlands, helped precipitate the Dutch Revolt.[45] When the prints appeared, the revolt was suspended under the Twelve Years' Truce, but its continuation was the subject of heated political debate. Buytewech's 1616 series *Various Landscapes* included close views of two castles near Haarlem – Huis te Kleef and Brederode – that had also been destroyed by Spanish forces. The following year, Visscher published a suite of four etchings of castles that, like Van de Velde's set, are portrait-like representations of specific houses identified by captions beneath the images.[46]

A few drawings of castles by Van de Velde have also survived. During a trip to the Southern Netherlands in the 1620s, he drew from life a detailed portrait of Keizersberg, the fourteenth-century stronghold of the Dukes of Brabant in Leuven (Fig. 13).[47] Having long outlived its purpose as a fortress and residence for the ducal family, the building was already neglected when Van de Velde visited and would soon be abandoned. The drawing's design and technique clearly affirm its topographical, documentary intent. Like the tiny figure in the lower left corner, the artist positioned himself close to the imposing edifice, and with refined penwork and light wash, precisely recorded its towers, gables, chimneys, walls, and fenestration while conveying an impression of the scale and additive character of the site. Van de Velde presumably made this study and a similar sketch of Merksem (Merxem) Castle near Antwerp, which probably dates from the same trip, with the intention of producing etchings of them, but neither appears in a print.[48]

By far the most comprehensive and innovative group of Dutch castle portraits was produced in 1646–47 by Roelant Roghman (1627–1692). At the age of nineteen, Roghman embarked on a campaign to document castles and manor houses in the provinces of Holland, Utrecht, and Gelderland. The project, mostly completed by the following year, eventually comprised some 245 drawings representing about 150 sites, all of which Roghman visited and sketched from life. More than 220 drawings survive, an invaluable record of an architectural and historical heritage that has largely disappeared (Figs. 14–15).[49] Even within the context of a developing interest in the history and topography of the newly autonomous Republic, Roghman's series was remarkably farsighted. Only in the late seventeenth and eighteenth centuries did Dutch antiquarians and artists such as Abraham Rademaker (1677–1735) and Abraham de Haen (1707–1748) continue the systematic visual documentation of the country's historic houses.[50]

We do not know who planned and underwrote the extensive travel required for the young draftsman to carry out this project, but he was presumably supported by a patron with antiquarian interests and extensive knowledge of Dutch castles.[51] Although the dimensions of the drawings differ, their media (usually gray wash and black chalk over a graphite sketch) and techniques are consistent, affirming that they were executed in a single, two- to three-year campaign.[52] That the series remained intact through the eighteenth century also supports the assumption of one original owner.

Roghman did not document only the most venerable houses associated with storied medieval families or events, although some certainly fit these criteria. His intention, according to one author, was to represent naturalistically the historic location – whether a ruin, an old building, or a new one – as it appeared when he visited. He was more interested in the antiquity of the site than the age or current condition of the structure.[53] This approach fostered the remarkably inventive compositional solutions that Roghman devised in these works. Sometimes he sat close by and chose a low viewpoint to convey the height and bulk of a house; other times he sequestered an unprepossessing ruin behind a haystack or stand of trees. In a few cases, he even positioned himself far away, showing the building and its surroundings as part of a panoramic landscape. In several instances, he made two or more drawings of a property from different viewpoints.

Whoever commissioned Roghman's series and presumably shared the drawings with fellow connoisseurs of the Republic's antiquities was probably not a member of the hereditary landed nobility. To be sure, many of the properties were still occupied by ancient families who passed them from generation to generation. Ameide, the building that dominates the horizon in Figure 14, was constructed around 1620 on the site of a much older castle. It belonged to Johan Wolfert van Brederode (1599–1655), a high-ranking nobleman whose family had held seigneurial rights to

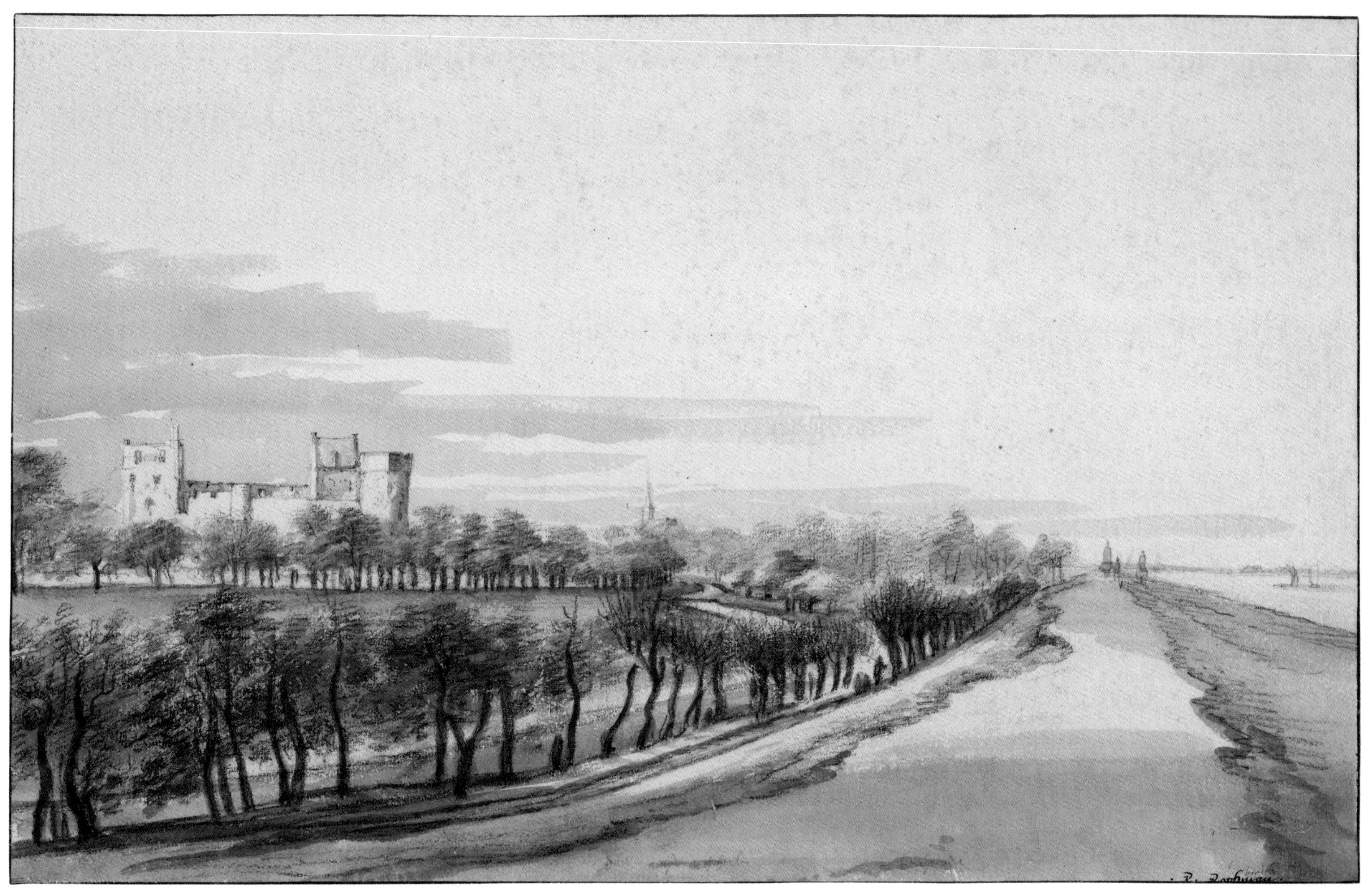

Fig. 14 Roelant Roghman, *Ameide Castle with Tienhoven in the Distance*, 1646–47. See p. 231 for full information; see also the detail on p. 122.

Fig. 15 Roelant Roghman, *Develstein Castle*, 1647. See p. 231 for full information.

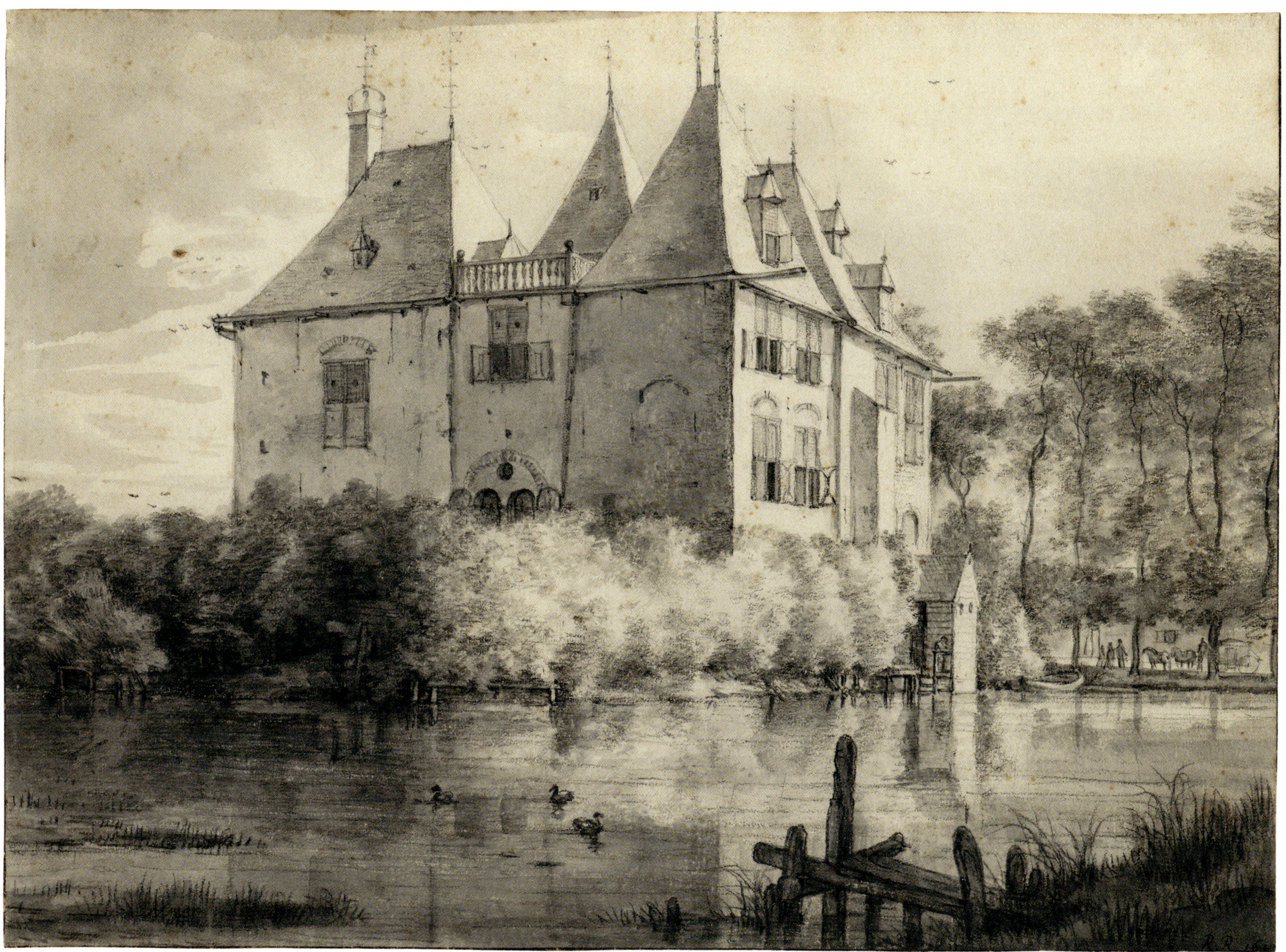

Fig. 16 Nicolaes Maes, *The Valkhof, Nijmegen, in an Imaginary Landscape*, 1650s. See p. 230 for full information.



the land for three hundred years. However, the growing interest in Dutch history and topography around the middle of the century was driven primarily by the urban mercantile and administrative elite, some of whom built or acquired country houses of their own: people like Dordrecht patrician Willem van Beveren (1556–1631), who purchased Develstein (Fig. 15) after it had been burned by Spanish troops in 1572 and rebuilt it as a country retreat. His son Cornelis (1591–1663), who owned the property when Roghman recorded it, served ten terms as burgomaster of Dordrecht and was a respected poet, diplomat, legal scholar, and authority on local history and antiquities.[54] He opened Develstein to a literary circle that included poet and politician Jacob Cats (1577–1660), physician Johan van Beverwijk (1594–1647), and painter Samuel van Hoogstraten (1627–1678), a former Rembrandt pupil with literary and social ambitions.[55]

While no other seventeenth-century draftsman undertook such an ambitious project as Roghman's series, many artists working on paper, especially those who responded in the middle decades of the century to collectors' developing interest in topographical material, represented castles and manor houses. In his drawing of Doorwerth Castle (see p. 182, Fig. P), Anthonie Waterloo (1609–1690), a landscape draftsman and printmaker who catered to this demand, opted to show the house from a distance, as Roghman did in his view of Ameide.[56] Waterloo's composition is less a portrait of the house than of its setting – the commanding, picturesque situation of the castle and its dependent structures rising above the flat landscape on the bank of the Lower Rhine, east of Arnhem. Yet its documentary purpose is the same as that of Roghman's *Ameide*. It probably dates from a journey Waterloo took through the Lower Rhine region in the 1650s that also yielded finished topographical drawings of Arnhem, Rhenen, Utrecht, and other towns.

In addition to these documentary, topographical works, Dutch landscape draftsmen produced imaginary views. Herman Saftleven (1609–1685), for example, made finished drawings of actual sites along the Rhine as well as invented "Rhenish" fantasies inspired by the steep picturesque hillsides, studded with castles, that line its banks.[57] Similarly, *The Valkhof, Nijmegen, in an Imaginary Landscape* (Fig. 16), one of the few landscape drawings attributable to Rembrandt pupil Nicolaes Maes (1634–1693), represents a made-up view based on a study from life.[58] On a trip to Nijmegen in the 1650s, Maes sketched the city's most prominent monuments: the castle Het Valkhof and a nearby tower, the Belvedere.

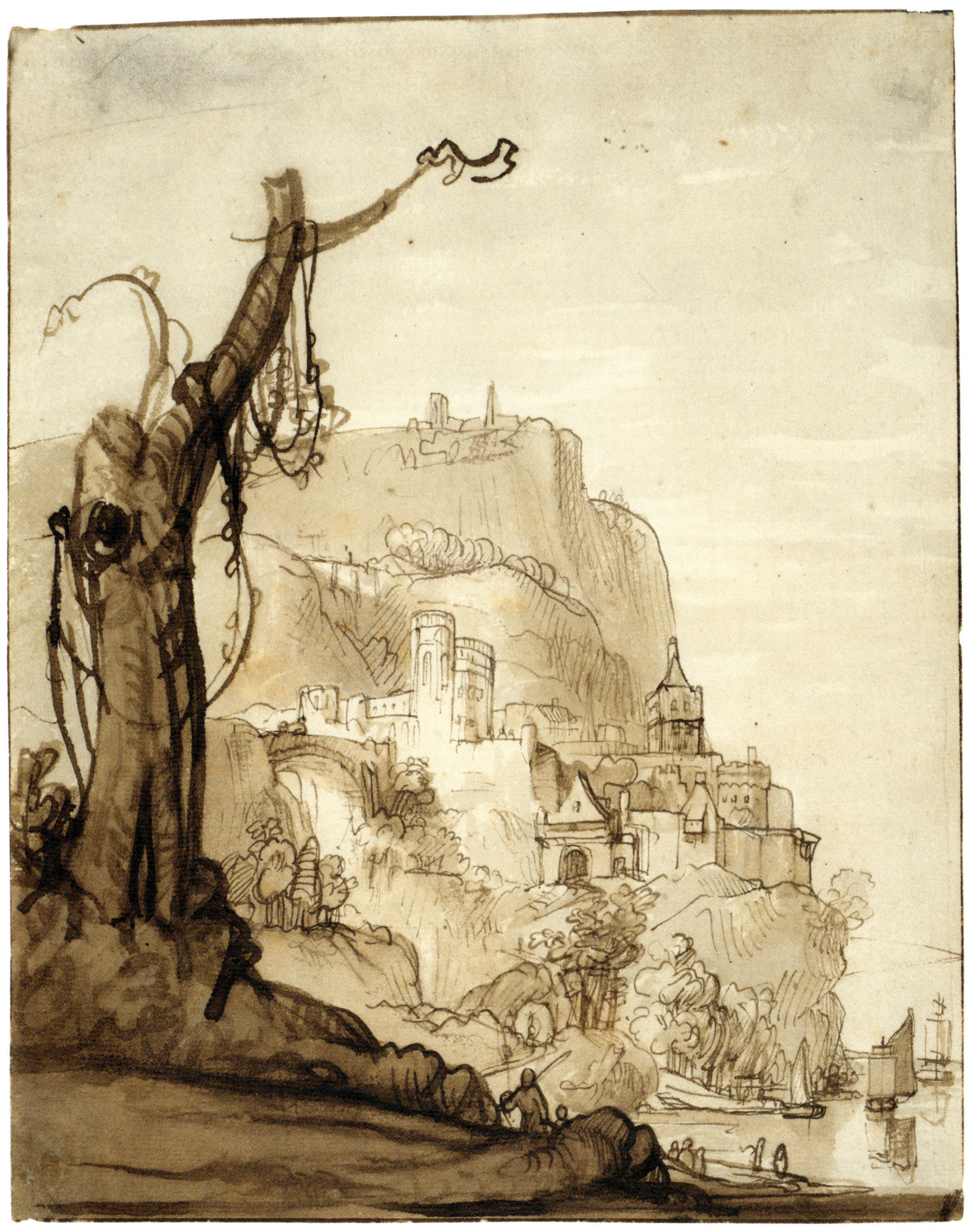

Spectacularly situated on a promontory above the Waal River, the medieval Valkhof was a favorite subject of Dutch landscape painters, including Maes's Dordrecht colleague Aelbert Cuyp (1620–1691).[59] One of Maes's studies, now in a European private collection, represents the castle and one of its portals, the Hoenderpoort, with a grove of trees and the Belvedere at left and some wooden houses at right.[60] That he sketched this view on the spot is affirmed by comparison with other drawings of the site and the artist's annotation on the sheet: *Belvedere met t hof tot Nimwegen* (Belvedere with the castle in Nijmegen).[61] At some later date, Maes referred to this study, or one very like it that has not survived, when composing the imaginary landscape on the Harvard sheet. Here, behind the dead tree that is the focus of the foreground, he incorporated architectural elements of the Valkhof in an invented setting in which the fortress, expanded by additional buildings and backed by towering cliffs, rises high above a river.

In addition to the many castles, cottages, and farm buildings damaged during the war (or that had fallen into ruin due to the accompanying disenfranchisement of the peasantry and depopulation of rural areas), the remains of various other structures were ubiquitous in the seventeenth-century countryside. Natural disasters, demographic changes, and even religious developments—including the official prohibition of Catholic institutions—left ancient walls and towers, churches, and former monasteries abandoned and isolated in the landscape.[62] In addition to the suite of ruined castles mentioned above, in 1616 Van de Velde published two other series that feature several landscapes in which abandoned, overgrown, and repurposed medieval gates or towers are the dominant motif.[63]

The currency of this imagery is reflected in a watercolor made around the same time by Hendrick Avercamp (1585–1634). A partially overgrown tower that has clearly outlasted its original function and context dominates the view (Fig. 17).[64] The tower stands high on a dike near a small lake with a spillway draining into a stream that widens to fill the foreground. A farmhouse abuts the tower, which evidently served as an extension of the family's home and livelihood. Makeshift signs above an entrance suggest that they operated a tavern on the lower floor. Several details betray the age and dereliction of the tower: a window hangs precariously from a single hinge, birds have nested in the roof, and greenery climbs the walls.

Saftleven recorded a very different type of ruin in the aftermath of a powerful storm that tore through the Netherlands on

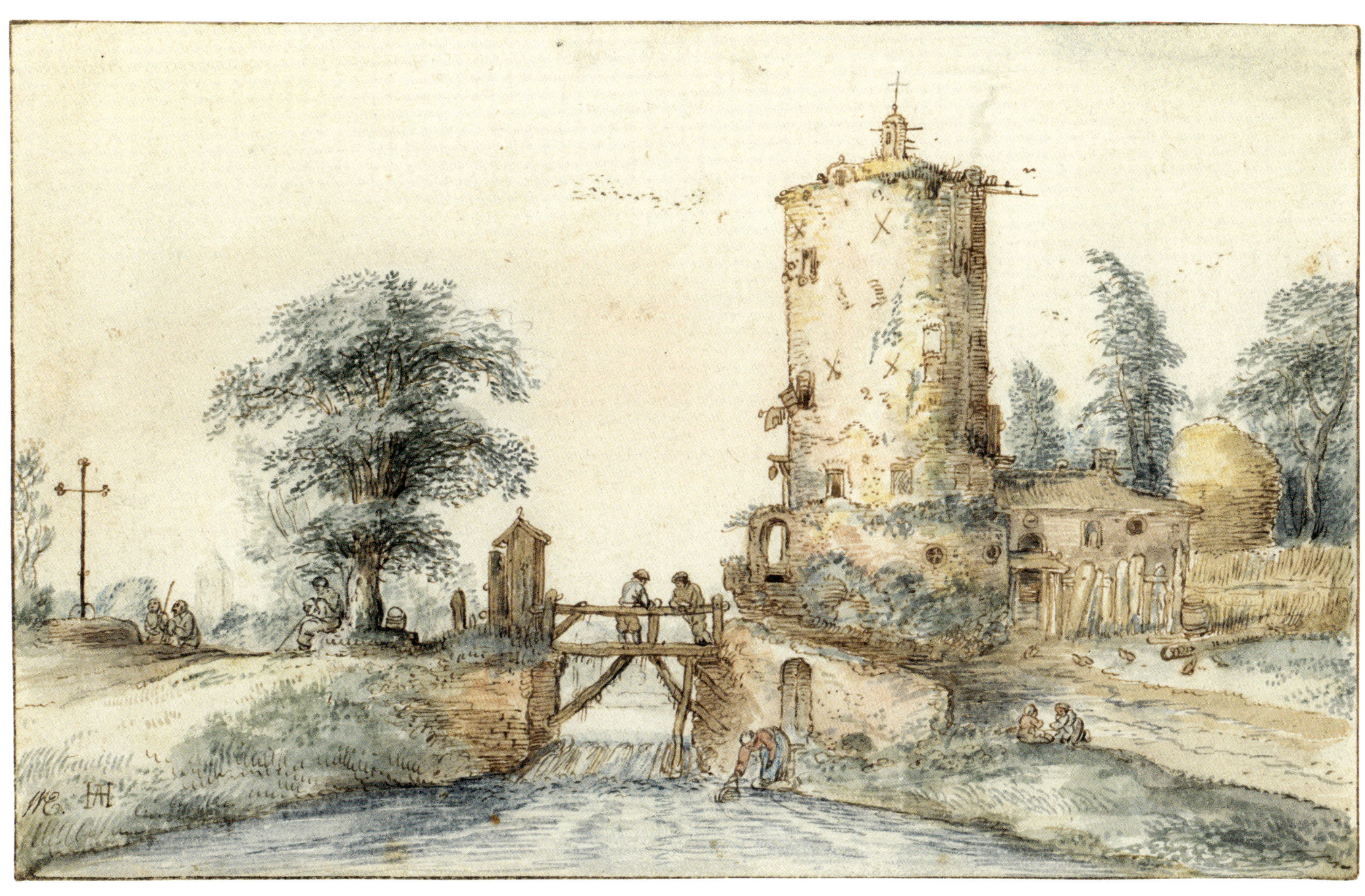

Fig. 17 Hendrick Avercamp, *Landscape with a Bridge and Tower*, c. 1615–20. See p. 228 for full information.

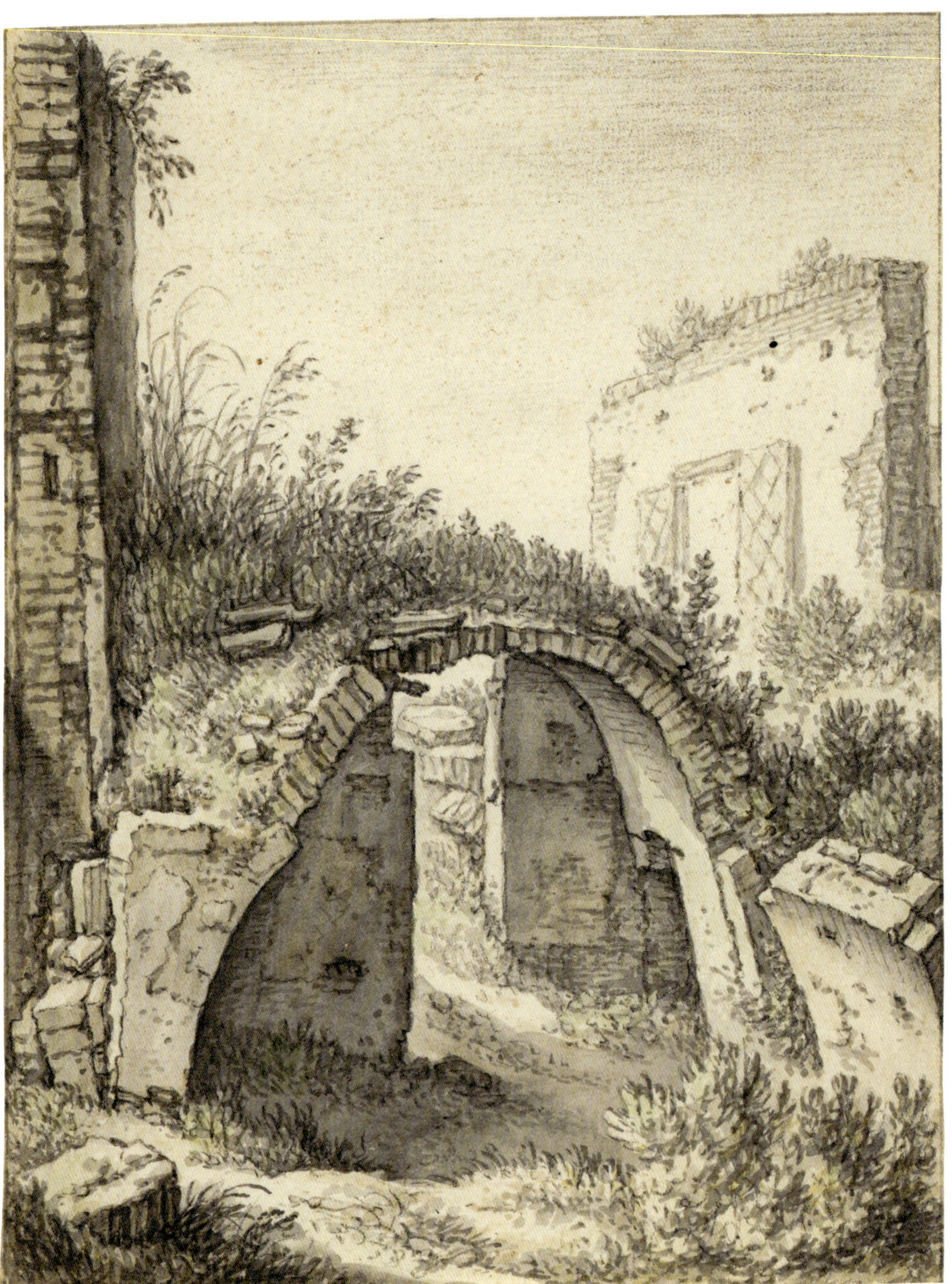

Fig. 18 Herman Saftleven, *Ruins in Utrecht by the Saint Jobsgasthuis,* 1674. See p. 232 for full information.



August 1, 1674 (Fig. 18). The storm inflicted particularly severe damage in Utrecht, where according to a contemporary newspaper report, "in a quarter of an hour most of the houses lost their facades and roofs" and the nave of the cathedral collapsed.[65] The destruction of the cathedral and innumerable other structures in the city was extensively documented by Saftleven in a series of some fifty drawings of vertical format.[66] On the verso of nearly all the drawings, the site is identified by an inscription in the artist's hand that begins *Dit op dander sijde getekent van Herman Saftleven is . . .* (This on the other side drawn by Herman Saftleven is . . .), followed by the location or building represented and the year 1674. Saftleven's inscription identifies the ruin in the Harvard work as *over St. Jop* (opposite or across from St. Job's).[67] Sint Jobsgasthuis (Saint Job's Inn) was a home for elderly indigent men located on the Vleutenseweg outside the Catharijne Poort, one of the main gates to the city.[68] Several other drawings in the series include Saint Job's and damaged buildings in the area.[69] Saftleven had previously produced numerous topographical studies in and around the city. In contrast to images of ruins by Breenbergh or Jan van de Velde that depicted sites that might have been centuries old, Saftleven's series documented ruins newly created by the storm. Drawings of buildings wrecked by catastrophic natural events, as opposed to war or the more gradual ravages of time, were novel in the seventeenth century, motivated not by nostalgia or curiosity about the past, but a desire to report on the present.

Drawings by seventeenth-century landscapists provide a comprehensive, nuanced, and stylistically inventive account of the varieties of human habitation in the Dutch countryside—some old, others newly constructed; some beautifully maintained, others in ruin; some directly connected to labor and productivity, others explicitly for leisure. A few types of studies, such as Saftleven's eyewitness record of the buildings damaged in the 1674 storm or Roghman's documentary series of castles, were recent innovations, while others developed traditions that originated in the sixteenth century. The continuous renewal of the rustic landscape, one of the principal motifs of Dutch landscape painting, unfolded—at least initially—in drawings.[70] Visscher refined his naturalistic, topographically based presentation of native scenery in his sketches from life some years before publishing his breakthrough series *Pleasant Places,* and Bloemaert began making his attractive studies of deteriorating farmhouses and barns nearly three decades before Bolswert popularized them in his lively etchings. Rembrandt's remarkable contribution to the rustic landscape – the subtly modulated evocation of sunlight and shadow and astonishing verisimilitude of the details and textures of weathered cottages – is best appreciated in drawings such as *A Farm on the Amsteldijk(?)* and *Houses on the Schinkelweg*. All these works constitute an interconnected picture of topographical, documentary, social, and aesthetic concerns that shape and inform our understanding of the Dutch countryside and the people who inhabited its vernacular structures.

William W. Robinson served as the Maida and George Abrams Curator of Drawings at the Harvard Art Museums from 1988 to 2015.

NOTES

1. William W. Robinson and Susan Anderson, *Drawings from the Age of Bruegel, Rubens, and Rembrandt: Highlights from the Collection of the Harvard Art Museums* (Cambridge, Mass.: Harvard Art Museums, 2016), 240–41, cat. 71; and Peter Schatborn and Erik Hinterding, *Rembrandt: The Complete Drawings and Etchings* (Cologne: Taschen, 2019), no. D546.
2. Walter S. Gibson, *Pleasant Places: The Rustic Landscape from Bruegel to Ruisdael* (Berkeley: University of California Press, 2000), xxvi–xxviii, 61–62; and Alexandra Onuf, *The "Small Landscape" Prints in Early Modern Netherlands* (London: Routledge, Taylor & Francis Group, 2018), 1–3.
3. Gibson, *Pleasant Places*, 20.
4. Ibid., 43, 62, 81; and Friedrich W.H. Hollstein, *Dutch and Flemish Etchings, Engravings, and Woodcuts, ca. 1450–1700*, vols. 33–34 (Amsterdam: Van Gendt, 1989), nos. 196–323.
5. Gibson, *Pleasant Places*, 27–49, 62, 81.
6. Franklin W. Robinson, ed., *Things of This World: A Selection of Dutch Drawings from the Collection of Maida and George Abrams* (Williamstown, Mass.: Sterling and Francine Clark Art Institute, 1972), 12, 40, 63, no. 23; and Curtis O. Baer, ed., *Seventeenth-Century Dutch Landscape Drawings and Selected Prints from American Collections* (Poughkeepsie, N.Y.: Vassar College Art Gallery, 1976), 14, 30–31, no. 10.
7. My thanks to Robert Fucci for suggesting the date (email to the author, October 9, 2019).
8. Thanks to Robert Fucci for pointing out that the only other squared drawing is in the Museum of Fine Arts, Boston (1988.432; email to the author, October 9, 2019).
9. Van de Velde's etching *Autumnus*, from a 1617 set of Seasons, shows a rain shower passing over a farmstead; Gibson, *Pleasant Places*, 125–28, Fig. 91.
10. E. A. de Klerk, "*De Teecken-Const*, een 17de eeuws Nederlands Traktaatje," *Oud Holland* 96 (1982): 51. Cited in ibid., 166.
11. Gibson, *Pleasant Places*, 164; and Walter S. Gibson, "Bloemaert's Privy: The Rustic Ruin in Dutch Art," in *Time and Transformation in Seventeenth-Century Dutch Art*, ed. Susan D. Kuretsky (Poughkeepsie, N.Y.: Frances Lehman Loeb Art Center, Vassar College; Sarasota, Fla.: John and Mable Ringling Museum of Art; Louisville, Ky.: J. B. Speed Art Museum, 2005), 68–69.
12. Jaap Bolten, "The Beginnings of Abraham Bloemaert's Artistic Career," *Master Drawings* 36 (1) (1998): 17–25; and Jaap Bolten, *Abraham Bloemaert, c. 1565–1651: The Drawings*, 2 vols. (Oegstgeest: J. Bolten, 2007), vol. 1, 5, 405–6, nos. 1336–1400, 406–15; vol. 2, 418–25, Figs. 1336–1400.
13. Karel van Mander, *The Lives of the Illustrious Netherlandish and German Painters, from the First Edition of the Schilder-Boeck (1603–1604)*, vol. 1, ed. and trans. Hessel Miedema (Doornspijk: Davaco Publishers, 1994–99), 450.
14. Robinson and Anderson, *Drawings from the Age of Bruegel, Rubens, and Rembrandt*, 49–51, cat. 8.
15. For the Bolswert series and the Visscher copies, see Marcel Roethlisberger, *Abraham Bloemaert and His Sons: Paintings and Prints*, 2 vols. (Doornspijk: Davaco Publishers, 1993), vol. 1, 195–200, nos. 230–49; vol. 2, Figs. 349–68. The plate reproduced in Figure 6 is no. 232.
16. Gibson, *Pleasant Places*, 162–64.
17. Peter C. Sutton, ed., *Prized Possessions: European Paintings from Private Collections of Friends of the Museum of Fine Arts, Boston* (Boston: Museum of Fine Arts, 1992), 202–3, no. 128, 38, pl. 35; and Peter C. Sutton, *The Martin and Kathleen Feldstein Collection* (privately published, 2020), 66–69, cat. 16.
18. Boudewijn Bakker, Mària van Berge-Gerbaud, Jan Peeters, and Erik Schmitz, *Landscapes of Rembrandt: His Favourite Walks* (Amsterdam: Stadsarchief/Gemeentearchief; Paris: Fondation Custodia, 1998), 58, 290–95; and Robinson and Anderson, *Drawings from the Age of Bruegel, Rubens, and Rembrandt*, 240–42, no. 71.
19. Bakker, Van Berge-Gerbaud, Peeters, and Schmitz, *Landscapes of Rembrandt*, 296–97.
20. Ibid., 245–46.
21. Ibid., 290–96, ills. 1, 2, 5, 7.
22. Ibid., 290–96; and Robinson and Anderson, *Drawings from the Age of Bruegel, Rubens, and Rembrandt*, 240–42, Fig. 1.
23. Bakker, Van Berge-Gerbaud, Peeters, and Schmitz, *Landscapes of Rembrandt*, 292–93, ill. 2.
24. Ibid., 101, 294–95, ills. 5, 6.
25. Ibid., 297; and Ronni Baer, ed., *Class Distinctions: Dutch Paintings in the Age of Rembrandt and Vermeer* (Boston: Museum of Fine Arts, 2015), 215.
26. See Rembrandt's separate study of this abandoned structure in the École des Beaux-Arts in Paris (Mu. 8914); Bakker, Van Berge-Gerbaud, Peeters, and Schmitz, *Landscapes of Rembrandt*, 293, ill. 3; and Schatborn and Hinterding, *Rembrandt*, no. D547.
27. Robinson and Anderson, *Drawings from the Age of Bruegel, Rubens, and Rembrandt*, 240, Fig. 1.
28. Even before the De With drawing came to light in 2009, Bakker, Van Berge-Gerbaud, Peeters, and Schmitz suggested in *Landscapes of Rembrandt* (at p. 297) that the dovecote and fishing nets might imply some hospitality functions.
29. Ibid., 306–7, 329–31; William W. Robinson, *Bruegel to Rembrandt: Dutch and Flemish Drawings from the Maida and George Abrams Collection* (Cambridge, Mass.: Harvard University Art Museums; London: British Museum; Paris: Institut Néerlandais; New Haven, Conn.: Yale University Press, 2002), 138–39, no. 56; and Schatborn and Hinterding, *Rembrandt*, no. D598.
30. Bakker, Van Berge-Gerbaud, Peeters, and Schmitz, *Landscapes of Rembrandt*, 62, 329–30.
31. Peter Schatborn dates *A Farm on the Amsteldijk(?)* to around 1648–50 and *Houses on the Schinkelweg* to roughly 1650–52; see Schatborn and Hinterding, *Rembrandt*, nos. D546, D598.
32. Robinson, *Bruegel to Rembrandt*, 140–41, no. 57. Koninck's other studies of the house are in Dresden and Haarlem; see Christian Dittrich and Thomas Ketelsen, *Rembrandt: Die Dresdener Zeichnungen* (Dresden: Staatliche Kunstsammlungen, Kupfersitch-Kabinett, 2004), 86–87, no. 20; and Michiel C. Plomp, *The Dutch Drawings in the Teyler Museum*, vol. 2, *Artists Born between 1575 and 1630* (Ghent: Snoeck Ducaju & Zoon; Doornspijk: Davaco Publishers, 1997), 211, no. 223. Nicolaes Anthoni Flinck (1646–1723), son of Rembrandt's pupil Govert Flinck (1615–1660), made an etching based on the Abrams drawing; see Robinson, *Bruegel to Rembrandt*, 140–41, no. 57, Fig. 2; and An van Camp, "The

Etchings by Drawings Collector Nicolaes Flinck," *Print Quarterly* 27 (4) (2010): 376–77, cat. 3.

33. Peter Schatborn, "Tekeningen van Rembrandt en Pieter de With," *Kroniek van het Rembrandthuis* (2005): 3, 6–8; and Peter Schatborn, "Getekende Landschappen van Pieter de With," in *De Verbeelde Wereld: Liber Amicorum voor Boudewijn Bakker*, ed. Jaap Evert Abrahamse, Marijke Carasso-Kok, and Erik Schmitz (Bussum: Thoth, 2008), 78–81.
34. Peter C. Sutton and William W. Robinson, *Drawings by Rembrandt, His Students, and Circle from the Maida and George Abrams Collection* (Greenwich, Conn.: Bruce Museum; Houston: Museum of Fine Arts; New Haven, Conn.: Yale University Press, 2011), 136–37, no. 50.
35. Peter Schatborn, "Getekende Landschappen van Pieter de With," 3.
36. Werner Sumowski, *Drawings of the Rembrandt School*, vol. 4 (New York: Abaris Books, 1981), 2167–312, nos. 984xx–1051axx.
37. Robinson, *Bruegel to Rembrandt*, 142–43, no. 58.
38. Ibid., 144–45, no. 59.
39. Arthur K. Wheelock, ed., *Jan Lievens: A Dutch Master Rediscovered* (Washington, D.C.: National Gallery of Art; Milwaukee: Milwaukee Art Museum; Amsterdam: Rembrandthuis; New Haven, Conn.: Yale University Press, 2008), 71–73, 239–40, 250.
40. Van de Cappelle's estate inventory is published in English translation by Margarita Russell, *Jan van de Cappelle 1624/6–1679* (Leigh-on-Sea, U.K.: F. Lewis, 1975), 48–57.
41. Peter Schatborn, "Van Rembrandt tot Crozat: Vroege verzamelingen met tekeningen van Rembrandt," *Nederlands Kunsthistorisch Jaarboek* 32 (1) (1981): 10–12.
42. On the distinction between *schetsen* (sketches) and *tekeningen* (drawings) in Van de Cappelle's inventory, see ibid., 6, 11.
43. Ibid., 10; and Peter Schatborn, *Rembrandt and His Circle: Drawings in the Frits Lugt Collection*, 2 vols. (Paris: Fondation Custodia; Bussum: Thoth, 2010), vol. 1, 23–24.
44. Jane Shoaf Turner and Robert-Jan te Rijdt, eds., *Home and Abroad: Dutch and Flemish Landscape Drawings from the John and Marine van Vlissingen Art Foundation* (Amsterdam: Rijksmuseum; Paris: Fondation Custodia; Curaçao: BCD Group N.V., 2015), 80. For the Rembrandt drawings, see Schatborn, "Van Rembrandt tot Crozat," 16–19. Those with farmsteads can be found in Schatborn and Hinterding, *Rembrandt*, nos. D527, D530, D536, D541, D543, D549. For the drawings of farmhouses by Abraham Furnerius that belonged to Nicolaes Flinck, see Sumowski, *Drawings of the Rembrandt School*, vol. 4, nos. 990xx–992xx, 1000xx.
45. Hollstein, *Dutch and Flemish Etchings, Engravings, and Woodcuts, ca. 1450–1700*, vols. 33–34, nos. 172–77; and H. W. M. van der Wyck, Wouter Th. Kloek, and J. W. Niemeijer, *De Kasteeltekeningen van Roelant Roghman*, 2 vols. (Amsterdam: Rijksmuseum; Alphen aan den Rijn: Canaletto, 1989–90), vol. 1, 55–57.
46. On Buytewech's series, see Friedrich W.H. Hollstein, *Dutch and Flemish Etchings, Engravings, and Woodcuts, ca. 1450–1700*, vol. 4 (Amsterdam: Menno Hertzberger, 1951), nos. 36–44. On Visscher's *Four Castles in Holland and Utrecht*, see Friedrich W.H. Hollstein, *Dutch and Flemish Etchings, Engravings, and Woodcuts, ca. 1450–1700*, vols. 38–39 (Amsterdam: Van Gendt, 1991), nos. 165–68.
47. Franklin W. Robinson, *Selections from the Collection of Dutch Drawings of Maida and George Abrams* (Wellesley, Mass.: Jewett Arts Center, Wellesley College, 1969), n.p., no. 44. Krista De Jonge, professor of architectural history at KU Leuven, suggested that Van de Velde's drawing might represent Keizersberg (An Zwollo, RKD – Netherlands Institute for Art History, The Hague, personal communication with the author, November 2002). A wood engraving by nineteenth-century Belgian printmaker Adolphe François Pannemaker (1822–1900) confirms this as the identity of the site; see the object information at https://www.erfgoedplus.be/details/24062A51.priref.1226.
48. Van de Velde's *Merksem Castle* is in the British Museum, London (1988,1001.2). My thanks to Robert Fucci, who called the drawing to my attention and identified the site (email to the author, October 9, 2019).
49. Van der Wyck, Kloek, and Niemeijer, *De Kasteeltekeningen van Roelant Roghman*, vol. 1, 34, 53, nos. 14, 33; and Robinson, *Bruegel to Rembrandt*, 154–57, nos. 64–65.
50. Van der Wyck, Kloek, and Niemeijer, *De Kasteeltekeningen van Roelant Roghman*, vol. 1, X; vol. 2, 73, 77, 101.
51. For candidates proposed as the original patron of the series, see ibid., vol. 1, 6–7; and Plomp, *The Dutch Drawings in the Teyler Museum*, 322–23.
52. Van der Wyck, Kloek, and Niemeijer, *De Kasteeltekeningen van Roelant Roghman*, vol. 2, 113.
53. Ibid., vol. 1, VIII.
54. A. J. van der Aa, *Biographisch woordenboek der Nederlanden. Deel 2. Eerste en tweede stuk* (Haarlem: J. J. van Brederode, 1854); available at https://www.dbnl.nl/tekst/aa__001biog02_01/aa__001biog02_01_0668.php#b0668 (accessed January 22, 2020).
55. Celeste Brusati, *Artifice and Illusion: The Art and Writing of Samuel van Hoogstraten* (Chicago: University of Chicago Press, 1995), 46; and Anne R. Larsen, *Anna Maria van Schurman, "The Star of Utrecht": The Educational Vision and Reception of a Savante* (London: Routledge, 2016), 46.
56. Robinson and Anderson, *Drawings from the Age of Bruegel, Rubens, and Rembrandt*, 318–20, cat. 97.
57. Wolfgang Schulz, *Herman Saftleven, 1609–1685: Leben und Werke: Mit einem kritischen Katalog der Gemälde und Zeichnungen* (Berlin: de Gruyter, 1982). For representative examples of Saftleven's topographical or "fantasy" views of the Rhine, see pp. 320, 372, cats. 724, 968.
58. Sutton and Robinson, *Drawings by Rembrandt, His Students, and Circle from the Maida and George Abrams Collection*, 92–93, no. 27; and William W. Robinson, "Landscape Drawings by Nicolaes Maes," *Een Kroniek voor Jeroen Giltay: Kroniek van het Rembrandthuis* (2012): 46.
59. Arthur K. Wheelock, Jr., ed., *Aelbert Cuyp* (Washington, D.C.: National Gallery of Art; London: Thames & Hudson, 2001), 58–61, nos. 33–34.
60. Robinson, "Landscape Drawings by Nicolaes Maes," 45–46, Fig. 4.
61. Three drawings from the early 1660s by Lambert Doomer show the Belvedere and Hoenderpoort; see Wolfgang Schulz, *Lambert Doomer: Sämtliche Zeichnungen* (Berlin: de Gruyter, 1974), nos. 181–82, 184, Figs. 91–92, 94.

62. Erik P. Löffler, "Ruins in the Netherlands: The Present Situation," in Kuretsky, *Time and Transformation in Seventeenth-Century Dutch Art*, 98–100.
63. Van de Velde's *Amenissimae aliquot requculae* is published in Hollstein, *Dutch and Flemish Etchings, Engravings, and Woodcuts, ca. 1450–1700*, vols. 33–34, nos. 232–91 (52 total); his *Vetustae Ruinae et Venustissimae aliquot Regiones* is nos. 216–31 (16 total). From the latter series, see, for example, *Ruined Round Tower in a Landscape* (no. 221) at http://hdl.handle.net/10934/RM0001.COLLECT.333456; and *Herder on a Bridge with a Ruined Tower* (no. 222) at http://hdl.handle.net/10934/RM0001.COLLECT.333458.
64. Robinson, *Bruegel to Rembrandt*, no. 7.
65. *Hollandsche Mercurius*, August 1674; quoted in Gerard van der Schrier and Rob Groenland, "A Reconstruction of 1 August 1674 Thunderstorms over the Low Countries," *Natural Hazards and Earth System Sciences* 17 (2017): 157–58.
66. Schulz, *Herman Saftleven, 1609–1685*, nos. 540–89.
67. Robinson, *Selections from the Collection of Dutch Drawings of Maida and George Abrams*, n.p., no. 61; and ibid., 274–84, nos. 540–92.
68. Baer, *Class Distinctions*, 236.
69. See Schulz, *Herman Saftleven, 1609–1685*, 277–78, 282–83, nos. 558–60, 582–83, 585.
70. Wolfgang Stechow, *Dutch Landscape Painting of the Seventeenth Century* (New York: Phaidon Publishers, 1966), 15–22.

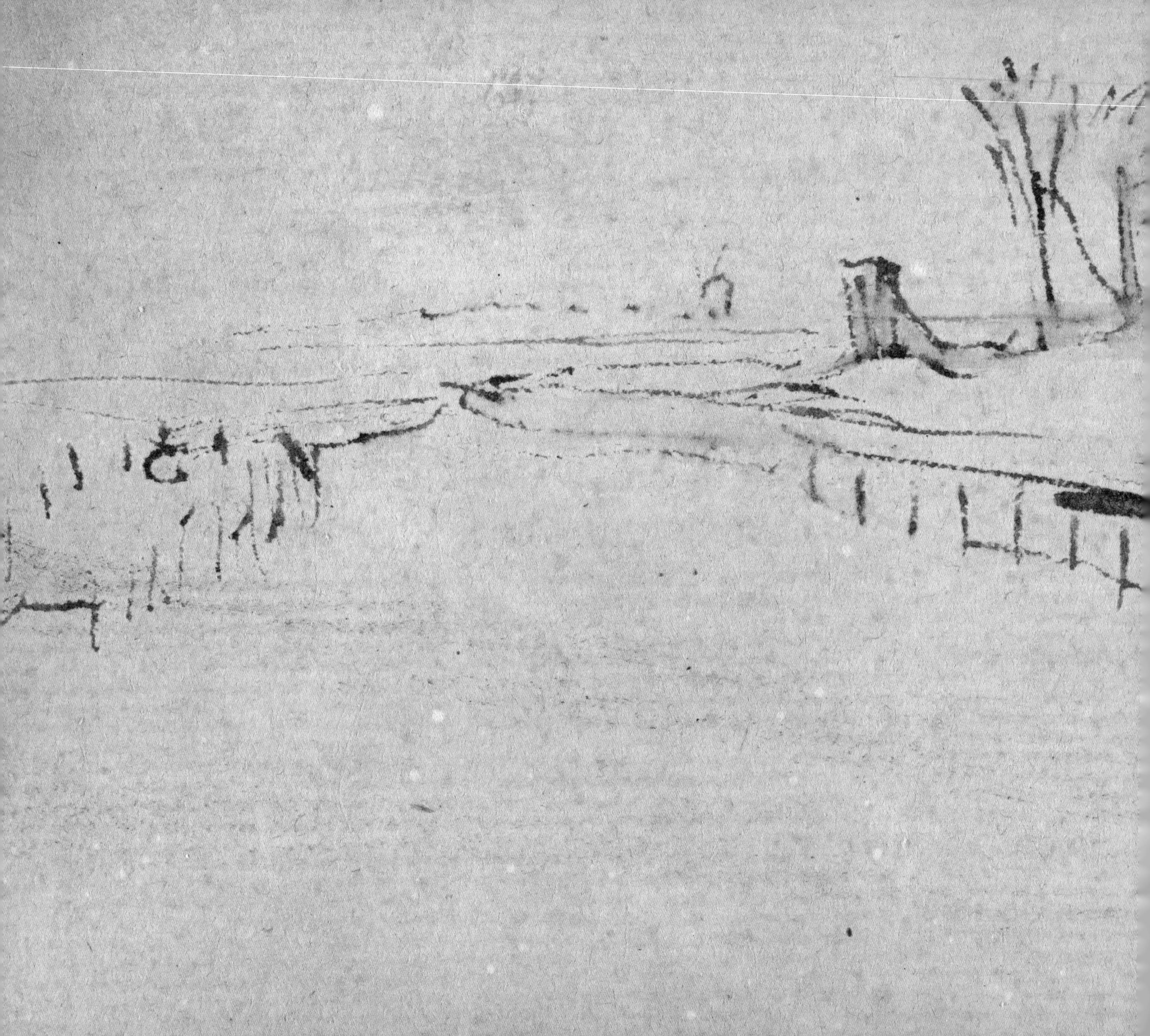

Rembrandt van Rijn
*Landscape with a Farmstead*,
c. 1650

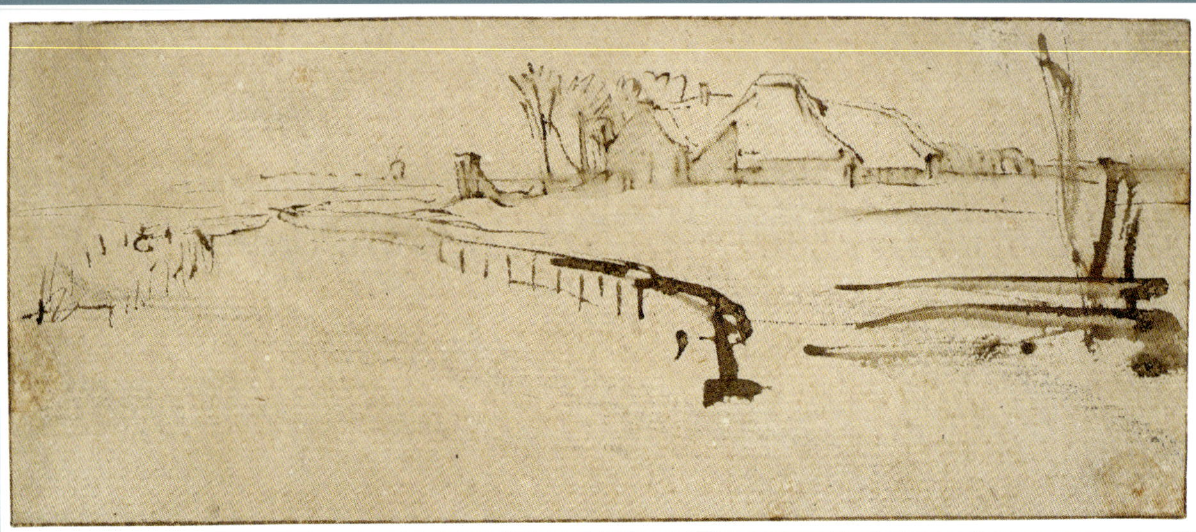

Fig. L Rembrandt van Rijn, *Landscape with a Farmstead,* c. 1650. See p. 231 for full information.

Rembrandt (1606–1669), the most famous of all Dutch draftsmen, explored rustic structures time and again as inspiration for innovative and creative explorations of atmosphere, texture, and light. In this drawing, he succinctly evokes these elements with effortless and minimal combinations of bold and sparing lines and judiciously placed areas of wash against the reserve of the paper. Through just a few strokes, he suggests a road, bordered by a fence and reeds, that passes by a farmstead before leading to a distant windmill. In its abbreviation, the sheet lacks sufficient identifiable details to situate it in a particular place. Despite this, Rembrandt's practice of drawing outdoors on walks in and around Amsterdam is evidenced by similar drawings by him and his cohort that can be compared with known dikes, localities, and structures and suggests that this sheet, too, was done from life. Yet Rembrandt's economy has allowed for varied interpretations: the bright areas of reserve, especially in the roofs and vast fields, were for many years thought to be snow, hence the longstanding title *Winter Landscape*. Given that the trees are in full foliage, however, the reserve may instead represent the strong sunlight of a summer's day.

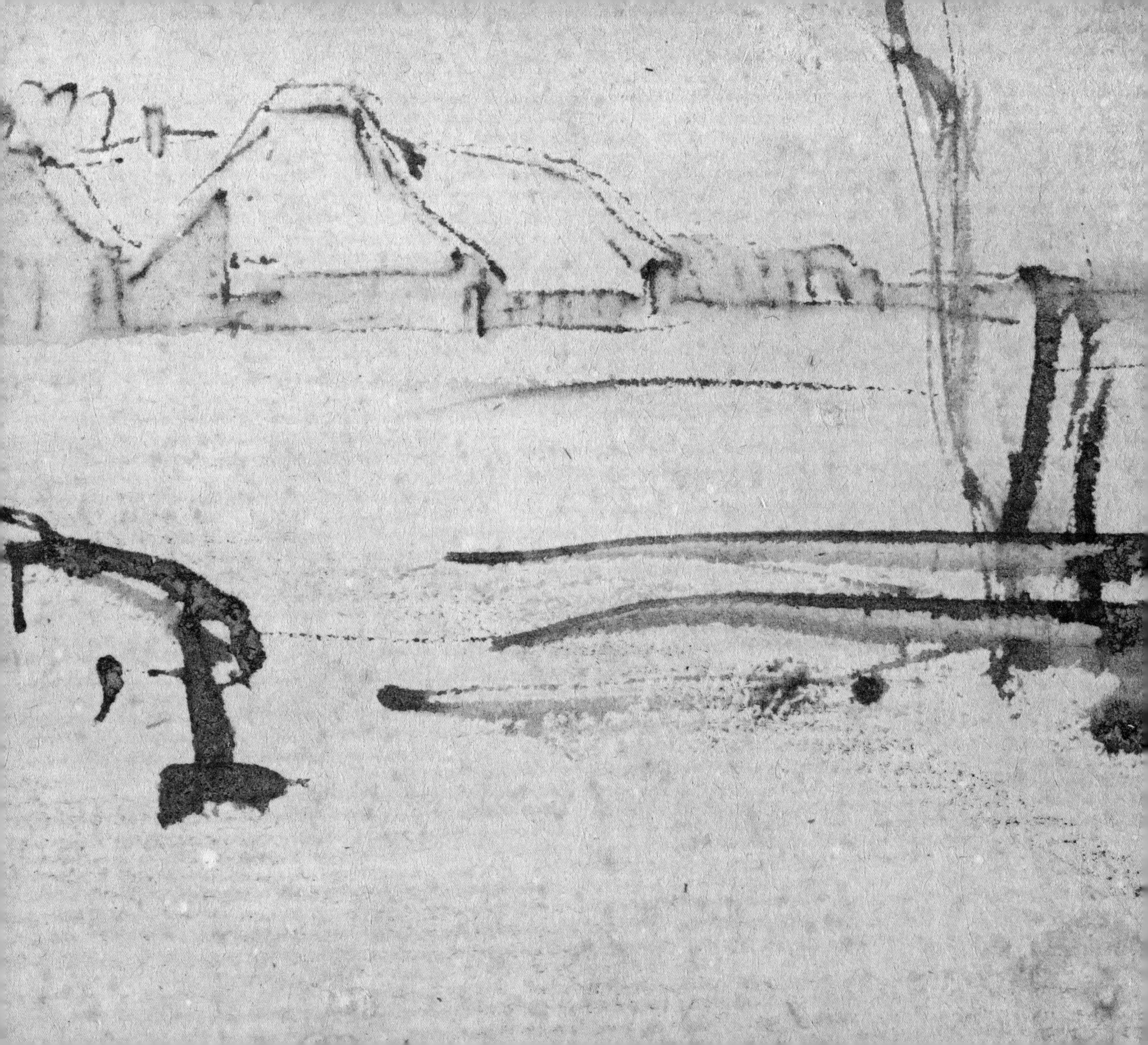

Jan de Bisschop
*Houses and a Well near Koudekerk,*
1650–55

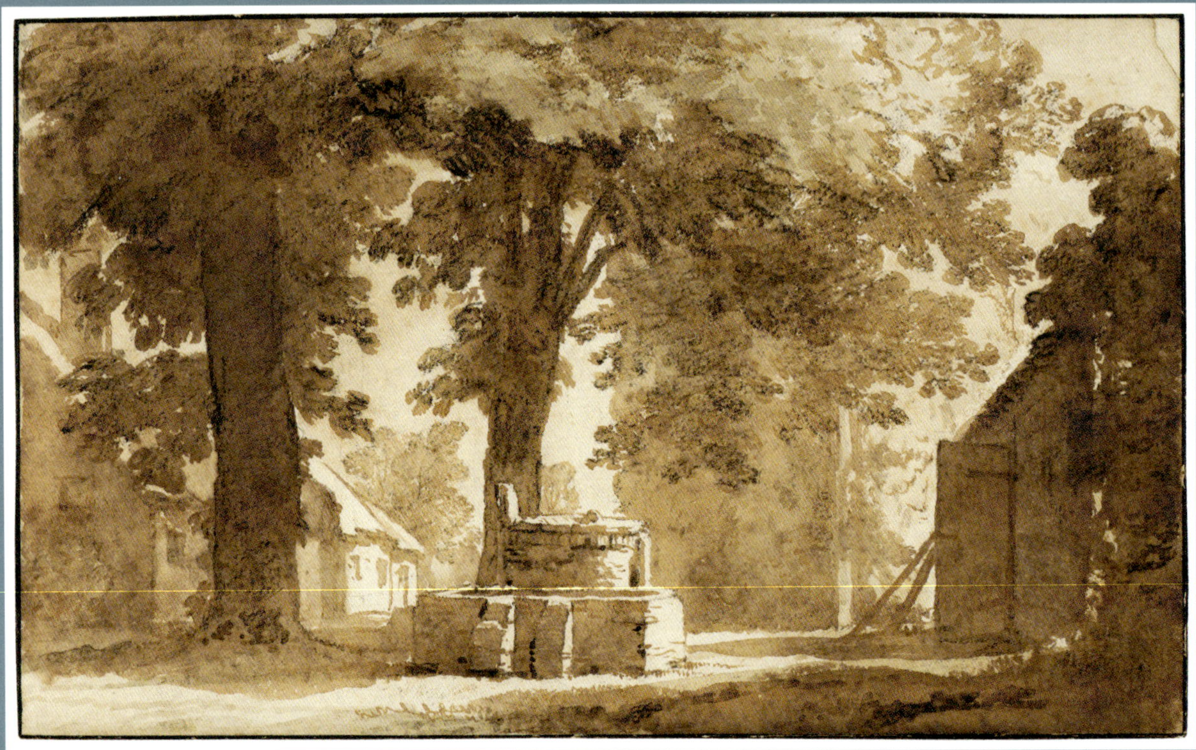

Fig. M Jan de Bisschop, *Houses and a Well near Koudekerk,* 1650–55. See p. 228 for full information.

Active during his adult years in The Hague, lawyer and amateur draftsman Jan de Bisschop (1628–1671) promoted a classicizing approach to art through his artistic output and his writings. In his *Paradigmata Graphices variorum artificum* of 1671, a treatise in which he reproduced Italian Renaissance drawings, he expressed a dim view of the Dutch favor for run-down, rustic structures and gnarled trees. Instead, when he adhered to the established preference for local scenes, he gravitated toward more unblemished subjects and rendered them with his trademark brown wash. He likely learned the technique – evocative of the warm light more commonly associated with views of the Apennine Peninsula – from Dutch Italianate artist Bartholomeus Breenbergh (see pp. 125–26) during his youth in Amsterdam.

De Bisschop inscribed the location depicted in *Houses and a Well near Koudekerk* on its verso, allowing us to situate the scene about nine and a half kilometers east of Leiden. He disguised the modest village structures with shadows and placed them at the margins of the composition as ancillary to the drawing's focus: a tidily maintained well. Highlighted by its central position, relative detail, and strong contrasts of light and shade, the well is further framed by its placement under two solid and towering trees. Through these tactics, De Bisschop added an important dimension to the more prevalent artistic approaches to vernacular scenery.

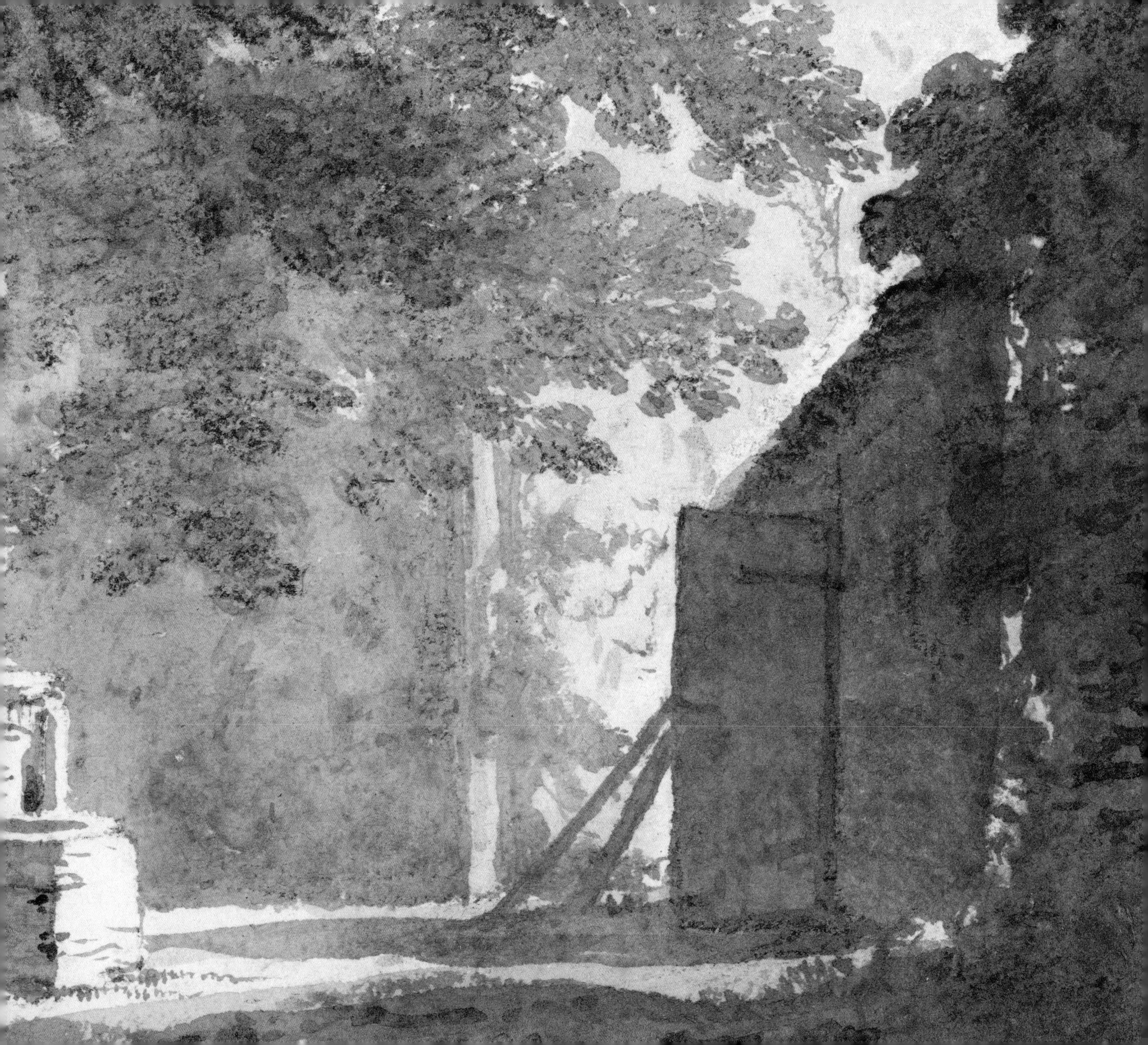

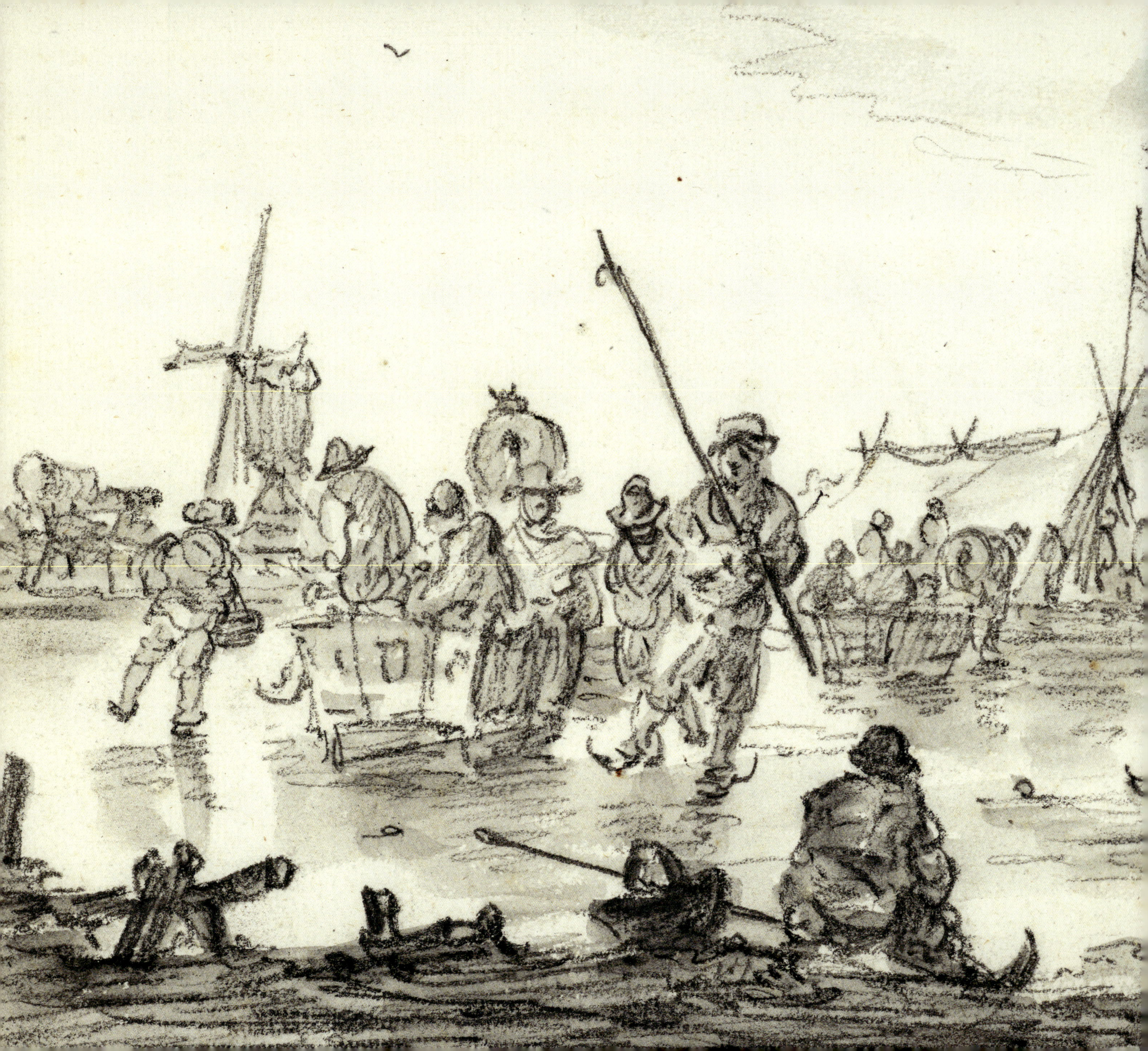

Jan van Goyen
*Landscape with Skaters*, 1653

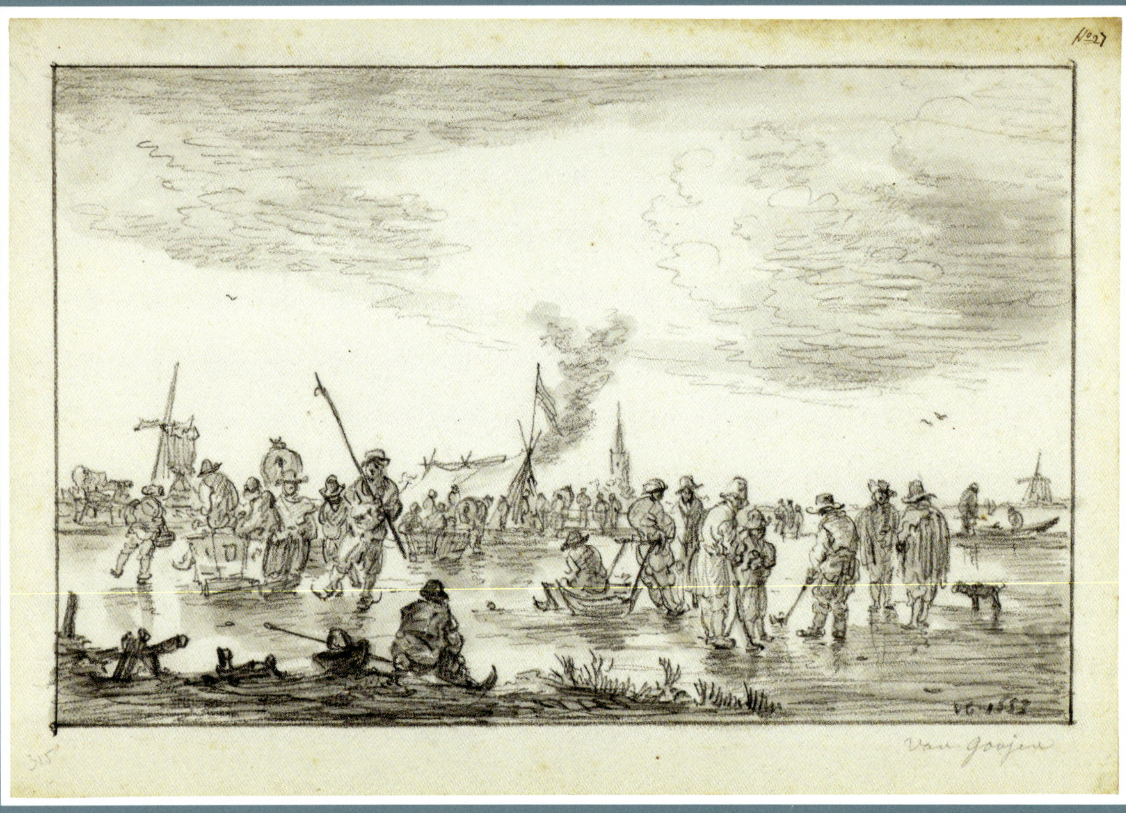

Fig. N Jan van Goyen, *Landscape with Skaters,* 1653. See p. 230 for full information.

In this drawing, executed in 1653 during a particularly prolific period of draftsmanship, Jan van Goyen (1596–1656) rapidly applied chalk lines to evoke the aesthetic of an observed sketch. The preserved wide margins, however, reveal carefully planned framing lines around a controlled, rectangular composition, indicating that the work was created for sale and survived the centuries in such immaculate condition within the leaves of an album.

Following the example of his last teacher, Esaias van de Velde (1587–1630), Van Goyen typically rendered his drawings in black chalk and gray wash. His apprenticeship and career brought him to many cities within the province of Holland, including Hoorn, Haarlem, Leiden, and The Hague. As we know from his large number of surviving sketchbooks, intact or disbanded, Van Goyen obsessively recorded the landscape around him, both on walks close to home and on trips farther afield. Here, however, he combined well-established and nonspecific conventional elements – the low horizon, windmills, a church tower, skaters, *kolf* players, sledges, and a hut for warmth and refreshment – with his remarkably energetic approach to line to capture a common wintertime experience from early modern Dutch life: the use of frozen waterways as a place for merriment and commerce. As is the case with other landscapes populated by many figures, the traditional categories of landscape and genre meet in a blend of the two.

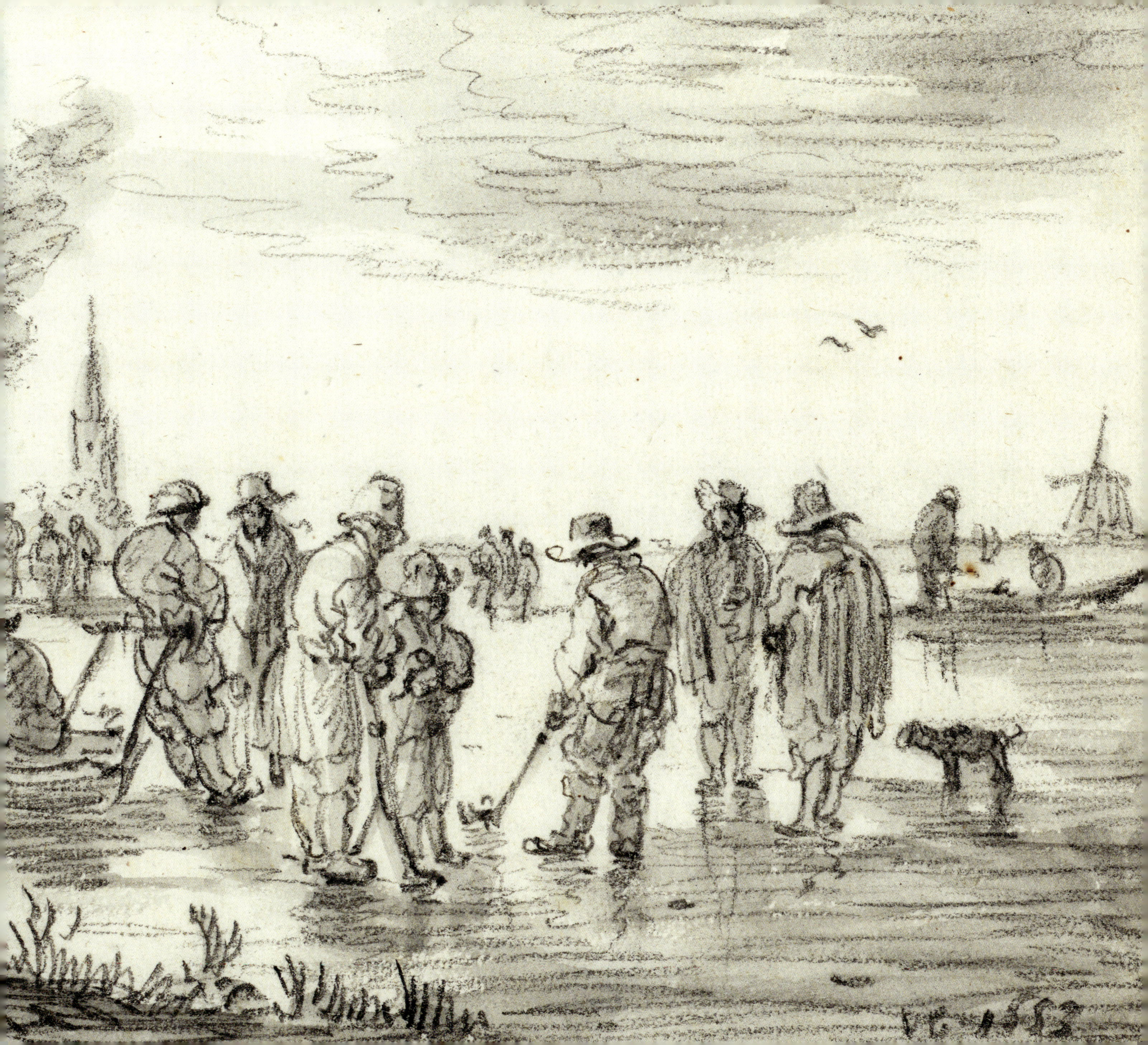

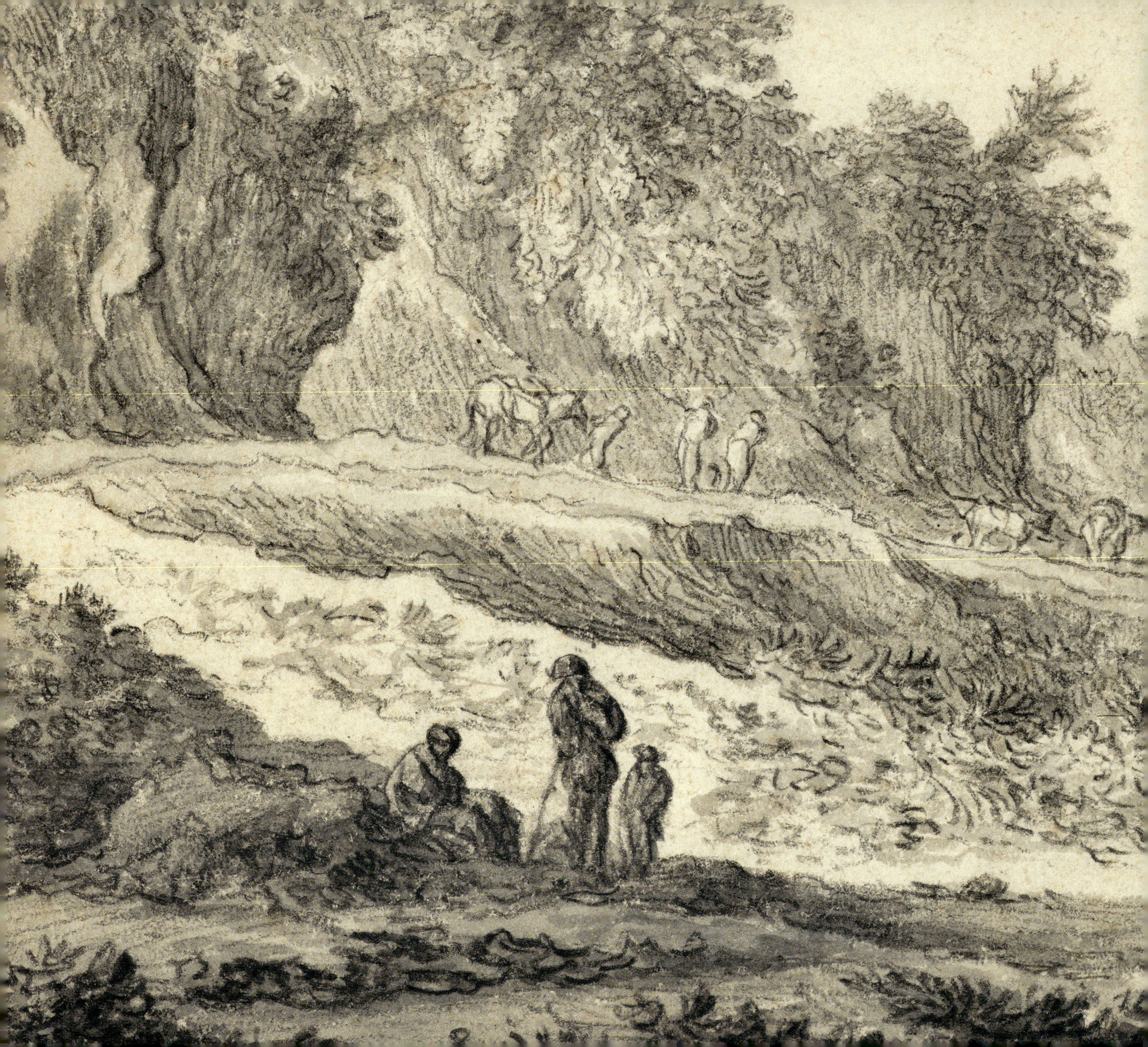

# Pieter de Molijn
## *A Panoramic Landscape*, c. 1659

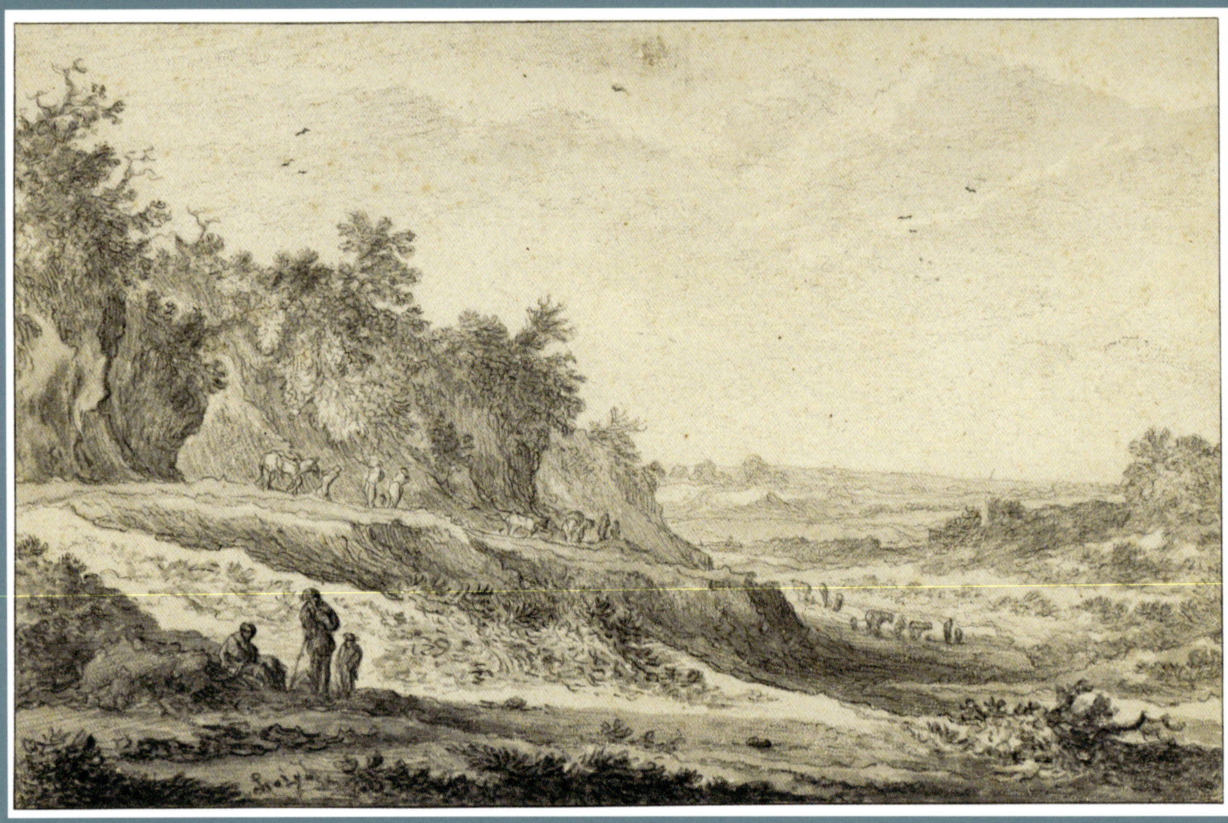

Fig. O Pieter de Molijn, *A Panoramic Landscape*, c. 1659. See p. 231 for full information.

This imaginary scene captures Pieter de Molijn's (1595–1661) distinctive approach to broad vistas of hilly, often barren terrain reminiscent of the dune area around Haarlem, but with no identifiable structures to situate us in a known place – or civilization at all. Active for virtually his entire career in Haarlem after a possible apprenticeship with Esaias van de Velde (1587–1630), De Molijn was poised to adopt and adapt landscape practices established by earlier generations. Here, he applied familiar devices to create depth and spatial recession, such as the combination of flat horizon and tall sky, alternating passages of light and dark, and the bending road framed on the left and right by solid, vertical elements that open to a distant vista.

Like Jan van Goyen (1596–1656), De Molijn employed black chalk and gray wash as his predominant choice of media, but his tremulous use of line often obscures landscape details to create a scene that is evocative and nonspecific. De Molijn's surviving corpus includes mostly finished drawings, often signed and dated, typically in either an oblong or roughly square format. The former, which he preferred toward the end of the 1650s and chose for this work, lent itself to the panoramic and mountainous views for which he is so well known.

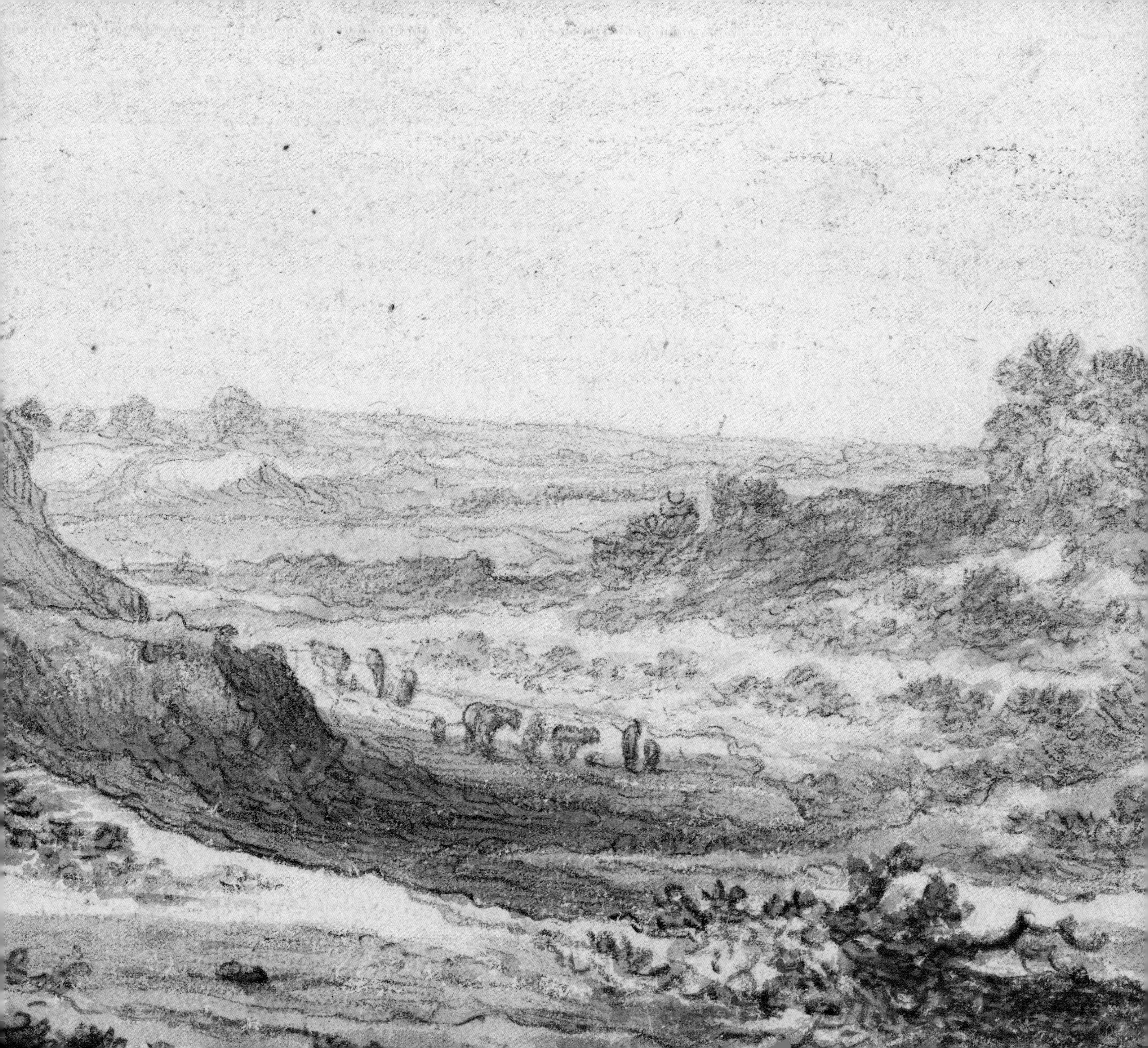

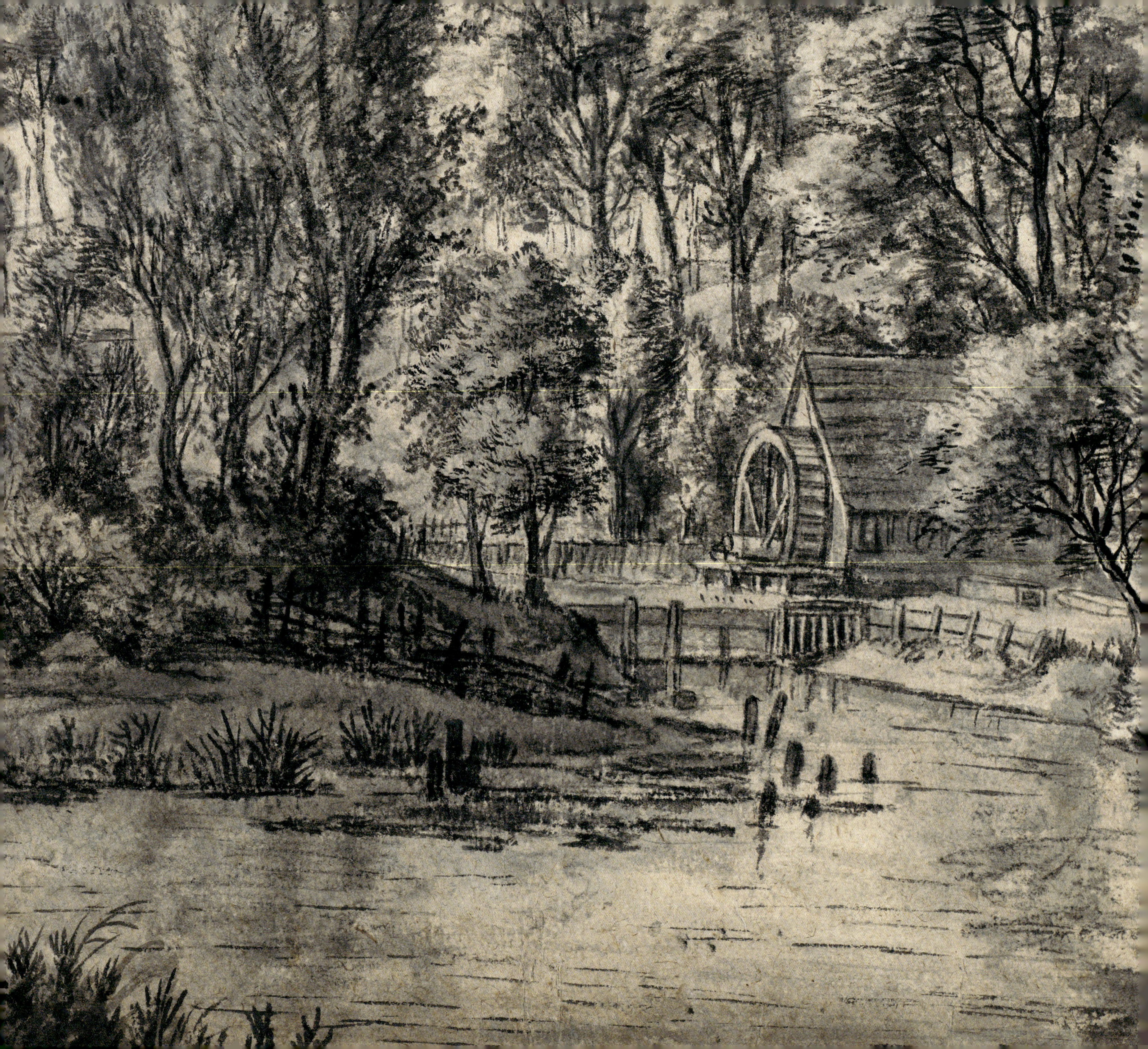

WET AND DRY

INTEGRATING DRAWING MATERIALS

*Anne Driesse*

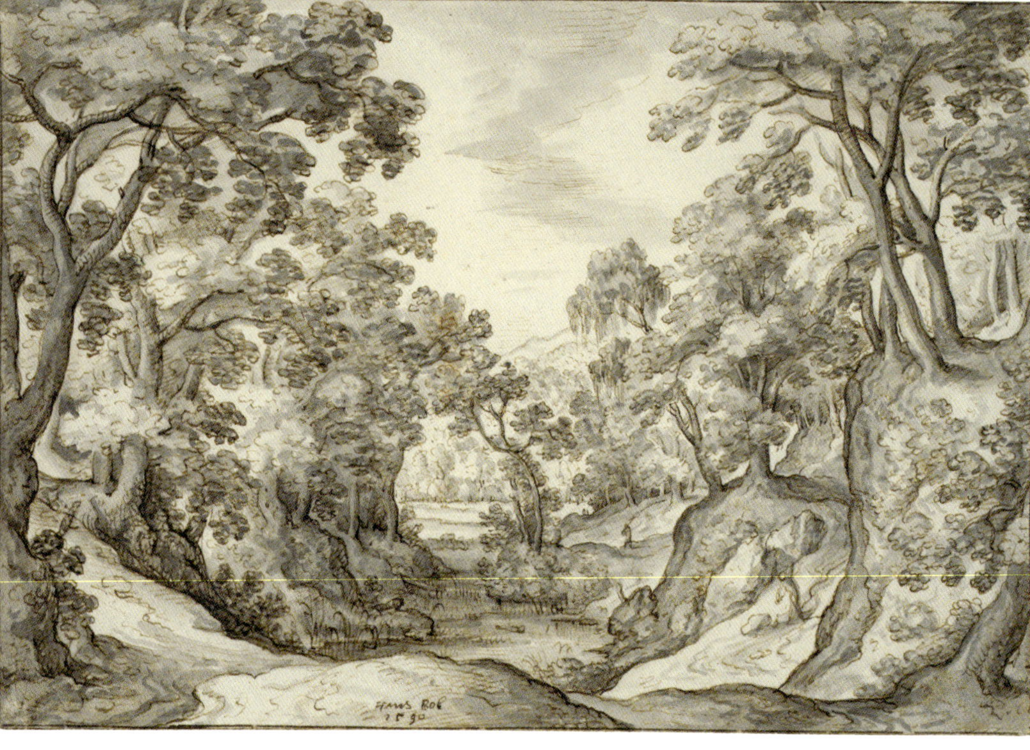

Fig. 1 Hans Bol, *Landscape with a Road near a Pond,* 1590. See p. 228 for full information.

Fig. 2 Detail of Bol's *Landscape with a Road near a Pond.*

Fig. 3 Infrared image of detail from Bol's *Landscape with a Road near a Pond.*

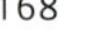
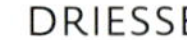


In the seventeenth century, Dutch draftsmen embraced newly available materials such as graphite, first mined in Europe in the 1560s, and Asian paper, introduced to the Netherlands by way of its expanding involvement in global trade. They also brought innovation to the way they prepared, applied, and combined materials that had long been used on the continent, among them laid paper, vellum, chalk, carbon-based and iron gall inks, and washes and watercolor made from natural pigments. This essay presents analyses of five drawings selected for their integration of media, often both wet and dry. The works are surprisingly complex, showing careful manipulation of materials, from paper supports to the finishing touches of chalk or graphite. Microscopic examination, multispectral imaging, and other non-destructive analytical techniques were employed to gain insight into the artists' working methods and choice of materials and to illuminate how those materials interact with one another.

The earliest of these sheets, Hans Bol's (1534–1593) *Landscape with a Road near a Pond* (1590), was executed in gray wash and brown ink on a sheet of off-white antique laid paper (Fig. 1). The faintest traces of a black chalk underdrawing appear along the horizon and in the contours of the trees at right. This extremely minimal underdrawing—visible only under high magnification[1]—contrasts with that of contemporary works, such as Paul Bril's *Wooded Landscape with Travelers* (see p. 32, Fig. C), where the underdrawing is well defined throughout. Over these lightly sketched chalk lines, Bol built up layers of transparent gray wash of various dilutions, then applied brown ink with pen to define features of the landscape.

Under infrared illumination,[2] only the broad brushstrokes of the carbon-based gray washes remain visible, while the ink lines disappear, as seen in the tree at upper right (Figs. 2–3). This strongly suggests that the brown ink is iron gall, of which transparency under infrared is a key identifying feature.[3] When fresh, iron gall ink produces a dark violet-gray color that oxidizes to an intense black and eventually turns brown over time, though the degree of fading and degradation depends on many factors, including atmospheric conditions, humidity, light, and the concentration and quantity of iron compounds.[4] Other visual characteristics of aged iron gall ink are generally identified as feathering of ink edges, a visible yellow halo around the ink lines when examined with ultraviolet light, and cracked and degraded paper areas under the darkest applied inks. Interestingly, the iron gall ink employed by Bol does not exhibit any of these characteristics. To

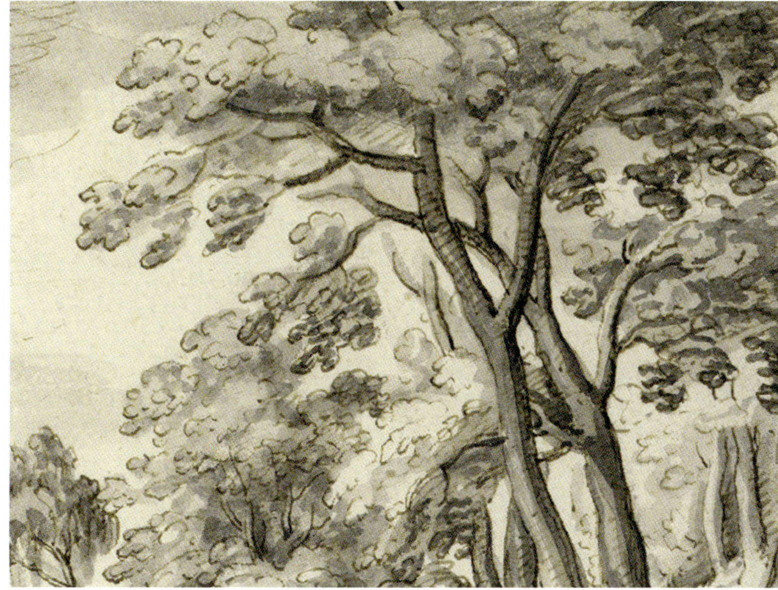

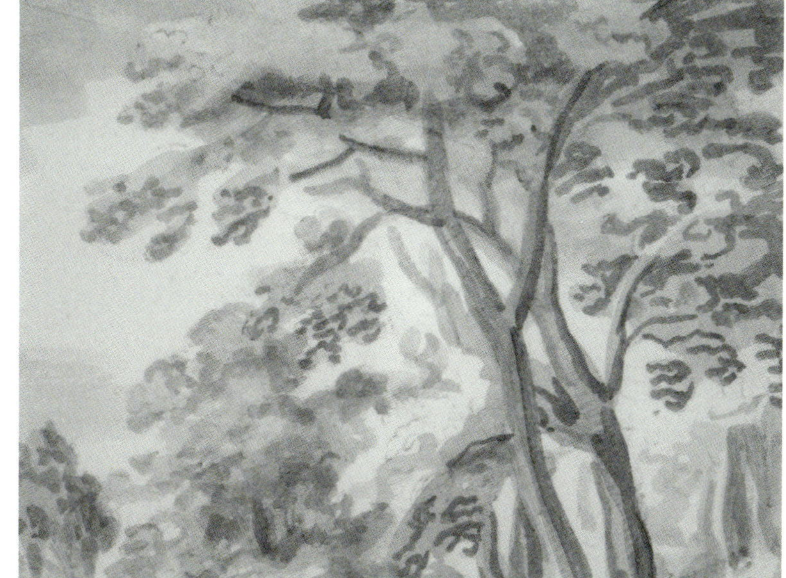

clarify this phenomenon, two areas of the tree along the left edge were analyzed with Attenuated Total Reflection Fourier Transform Infrared Spectroscopy (ATR-FTIR).[5] While the spectra produced from this analysis are consistent with iron gall ink, they also indicate the presence of calcium oxalates.[6] Calcium oxalates form when carbohydrates in the ink deteriorate. Their presence, along with the gelatin sizing of the paper (which reduces absorption), may have neutralized the natural acidity of the iron gall ink, thus preventing the ink from degrading the paper.[7] This may partially explain why the ink and paper of this drawing appear quite stable.

Upon close examination of the edges of the gray wash and brown ink lines, it is evident that the drawing was completed in multiple campaigns. The crisp edges of the wash layers clearly indicate that each was added over a completely dry layer, allowing the transparency of the under and upper layers to combine to achieve the overall color without the passage becoming too muddy. Similarly, if the iron gall ink was added while the gray wash or paper was even slightly damp, one would surely see feathering of the ink edges. Instead, we see no such feathering or blending of the ink and wash, indicating that the gray wash and paper were completely dry before the pen lines were added. Nor could Bol have applied the brown ink before adding the wash, as the water-soluble ink surely would have blurred upon contact with the diluted wash. We can conclude that Bol composed his drawing with brush and wash and then, only after establishing the general composition and tonal relationships, articulated the contours and details of the landscape features with pen and ink.

Abraham Bloemaert's (1566–1651) *Study of a Tree* (Fig. 4) is an exercise in the incorporation and manipulation of varied media to capture precise optical effects. It is executed on an off-white antique laid paper that bears a watermark of a double-headed eagle with the initials FB.[8] This points to the paper's manufacture in a Dutch-run papermill in France.[9] Bloemaert chose to work on the felt (rather than the wire) side of the paper, which offers an evenness to the drawing support.[10] He toned his paper with a light-brown wash, then rendered his drawing with rose and green watercolor, black chalk, and graphite, with final touches of white opaque highlights.

While watercolor[11] was commonly used as a delicate, restrained tint for drawings (see pp. 78, 143) and as a primary medium, usually in opaque form, for painterly compositions (see p. 38), Bloemaert integrated transparent watercolor, employing it alongside his other media. He also used the reductive watercolor

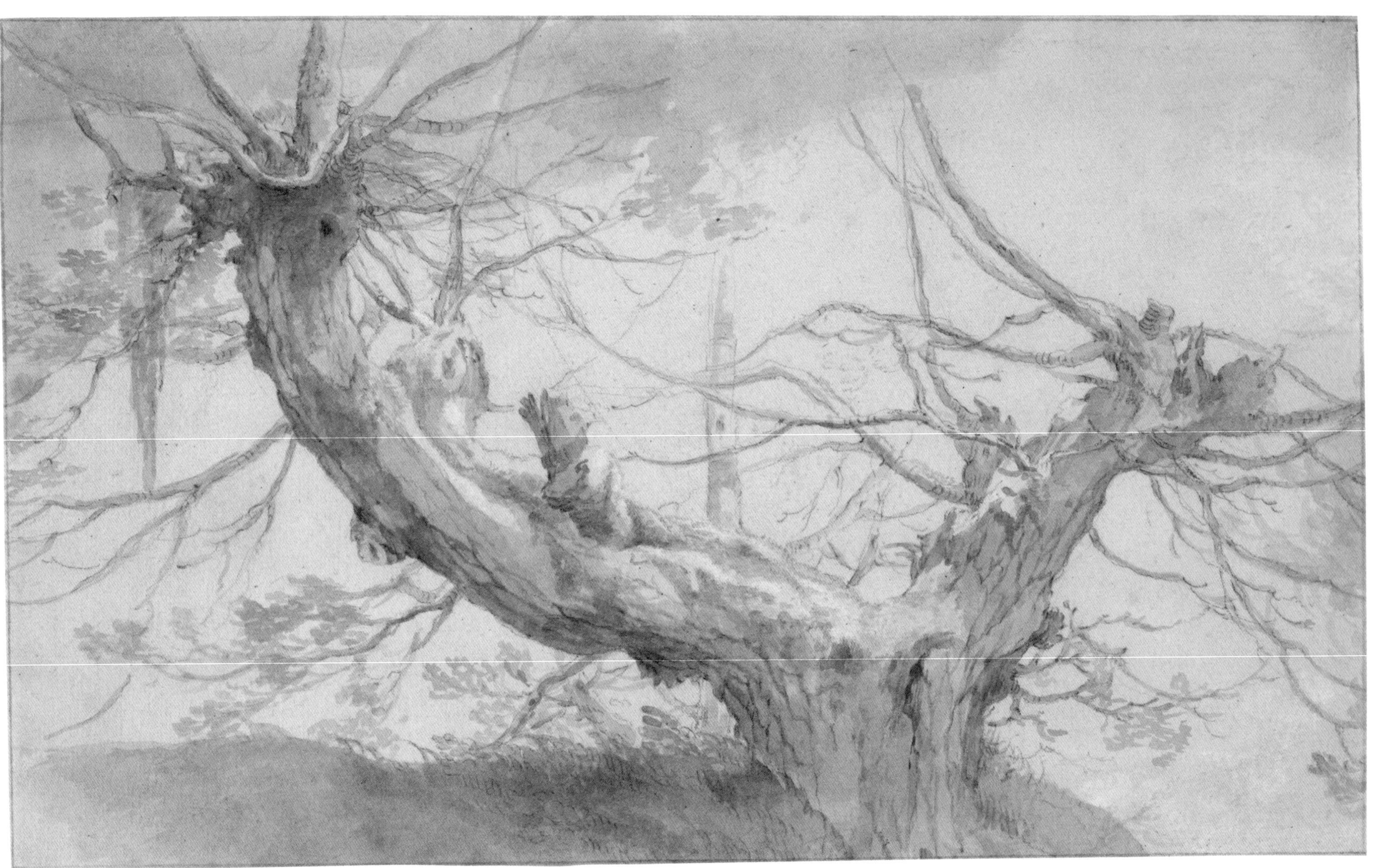

Fig. 4 Abraham Bloemaert, *Study of a Tree*, c. 1644–46. See p. 228 for full information.

Fig. 5 Detail of Bloemaert's *Study of a Tree*.

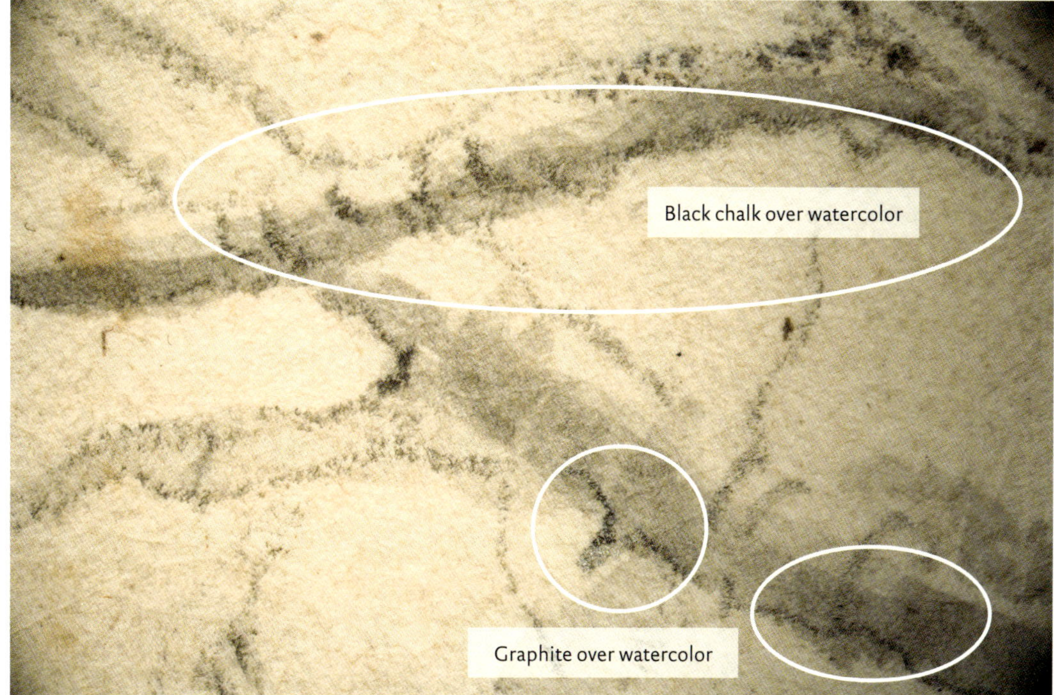




technique of scraping, ultimately removing some of the brown wash and paper to depict the roughened tree before adding touches of opaque white for highlights.

Black chalk[12] is the predominant dry medium in this study, applied both as a loose underdrawing and as a complement to the other media, but it is Bloemaert's use of graphite that is particularly notable. By the seventeenth century, Dutch draftsmen were increasingly employing graphite[13] alongside black chalk. Like chalk, graphite can sit on top of the paper surface or within the paper interstices, depending on the amount of pressure used. Bloemaert employed graphite together with the black chalk to create depth as well as to define the lights and darks of the tree. While the black chalk produces a rich, dark, and definite mark, the graphite yields a softer stroke and more subtle color, imparting a gray, silver appearance with a slight glint or sheen as it catches the light (Fig. 5). A similar interplay of graphite and black chalk can be seen in Roelant Roghman's (1627–1692) *Develstein Castle* (see p. 139).

Aelbert Cuyp's (1620–1691) *View of a Ploughed Field* (Fig. 6), dating to approximately the early 1640s and likewise executed on an off-white antique laid paper, exhibits a lightly sketched underdrawing in black chalk, which establishes the basic features of the composition. Unlike the drawing by Bol, broad washes of transparent color are applied next to, rather than on top of, one another to define the landscape. Cuyp then further developed his drawing with additional black chalk and watercolor.

A noticeable sheen appears on the black chalk lines along the left edge of the sheet and as a localized coating throughout the foreground (Fig. 7). This coating appears to sit on top of the paper without sinking into it. Not surprisingly, analysis revealed the presence of a gum, almost certainly gum arabic,[14] which Cuyp frequently applied to his drawings.[15] However, the gum coating in this work behaves quite differently than expected.

By the late seventeenth century, it was common for watercolorists to apply a final layer of gum arabic to their works to saturate colors, as Dirk Dalens III (1688–1753) did in his *Landscape with Rustic Scene* (p. 101). Cuyp's use of gum, by contrast, is always very localized and specific. In the Harvard drawing, the coating along the lower edge of the sheet suggests direct application with a brush, whereas the fluid treatment on the soft chalk lines at left, most evident in the tree branches, can be attributed to the chalk stick being soaked, or just briefly dipped, in the gum and then applied to the paper (Fig. 7).[16] Furthermore, the gum appears to flow over the

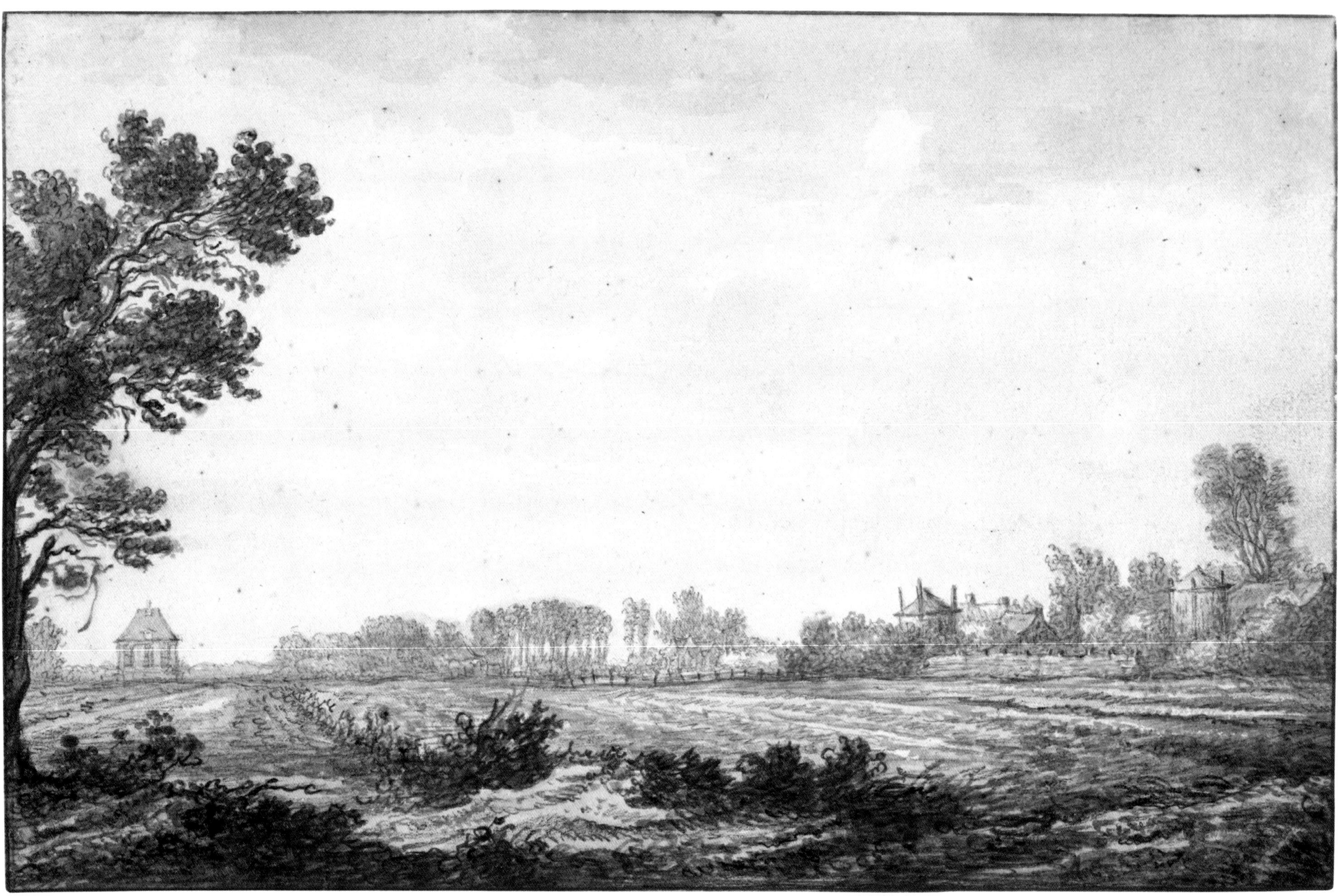

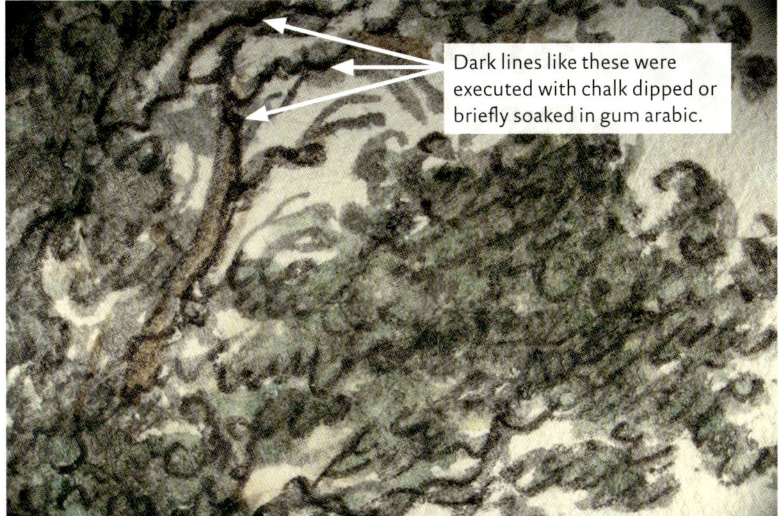


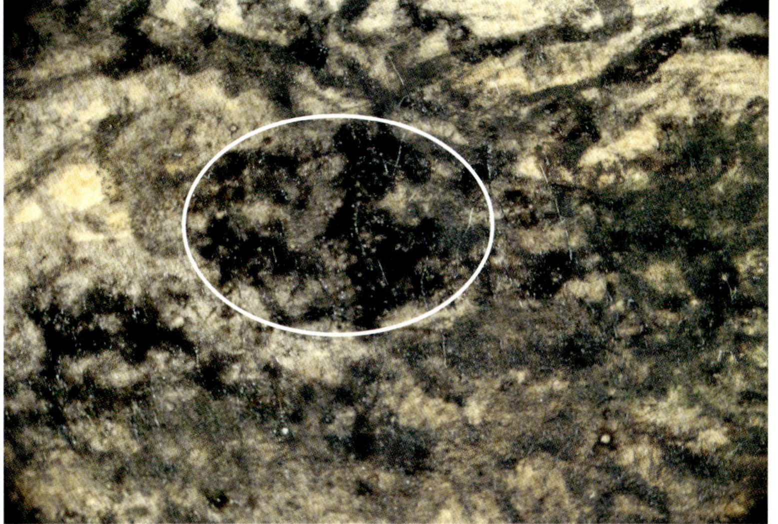

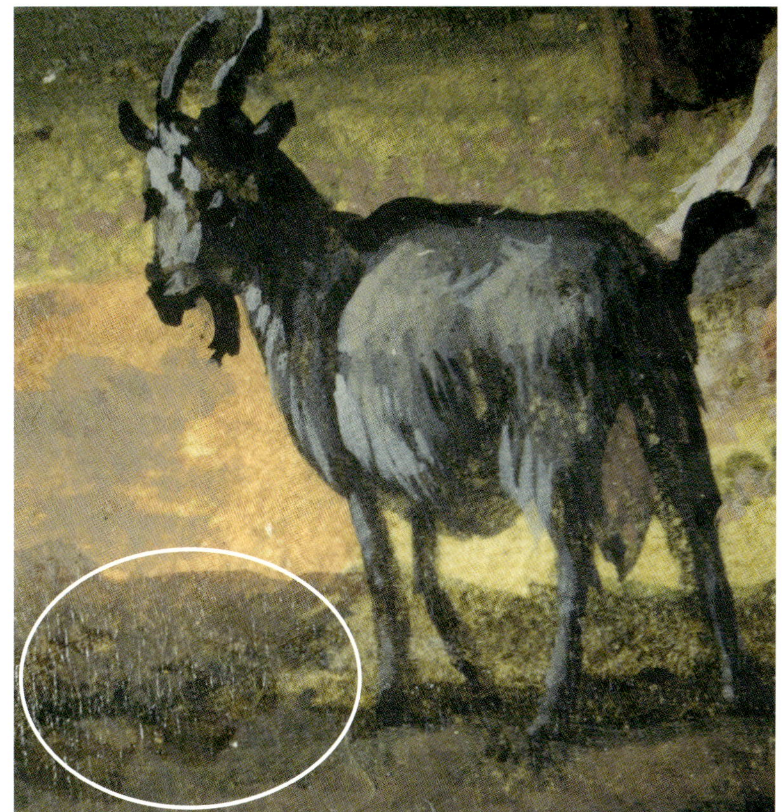

Fig. 6 Aelbert Cuyp, *View of a Ploughed Field*, c. 1639–42. See p. 229 for full information.

Fig. 7 Detail of Cuyp's *View of a Ploughed Field*.

Fig. 8 Detail of Cuyp's *View of a Ploughed Field*.

Fig. 9 Dirk Dalens III, *Landscape with Rustic Scene* (detail), c. 1725–35. See p. 229 for full information.

Fig. 10 Joris van der Haagen, *Forest Landscape*, c. 1640–60. See p. 230 for full information.

Fig. 11 Detail of Van der Haagen's *Forest Landscape.*



foliage with noticeable bubbles (Fig. 8), whereas the Dalens coating is cracked and crazed in a manner more typical of an aged gum coating (Fig. 9). While analysis indicates that both drawings have related spectra identifying gum arabic as the main component, there is an additional peak seen in the Cuyp spectra that could be associated with a protein-based substance, possibly an animal glue. Gum arabic used alone generally dries with a cracked pattern, so perhaps the addition of a protein allowed for a more fluid application and a bubbled drying pattern. This is further evidence of the care with which Cuyp prepared his materials to yield specific aesthetic effects.

Another drawing examined in this study, Joris van der Haagen's (1615–1669) *Forest Landscape* (Fig. 10), is executed in gray wash over a minimal black chalk underdrawing on off-white antique laid paper with a Dutch watermark.[17] Van der Haagen lightly sketched the horizon line and a few landscape features with black chalk to establish perspective, then developed the view in ink washes, saturating the paper with splotches of gray wash to capture the light of day. Black chalk defines the clouds, foliage, and rocky foreground.

It is clear through microscopic examination that this chalk is applied over the wash. If the wash were applied over the chalk, we would undoubtedly see some movement of the finer chalk particles and possibly settlement of those particles along the outer drying edge of each passage of wash. Instead, the black chalk leaves a clear, dark stroke with defined watercolor edges, which also indicates that the wash was completely dry prior to the chalk application (Fig. 11). Wielding black chalk much like Bol did iron gall ink, Van der Haagen completed his landscape with dry media, applying it as an *overdrawing* to define the areas of wash. Here, too, multiple campaigns necessitated planning and drying time.

In his *Grist Mills near Hamburg* from roughly 1660 (Fig. 12), Anthonie Waterloo (1609–1690) built up his landscape with alternating applications of wet and dry media. Starting with black chalk, he then applied broad passages of light-gray washes, followed by short intense brushstrokes of black ink for the leaves and tree trunks. A second layer of black chalk on top of the ink emphasizes the outlines of the landscape features, while short, horizontal graphite strokes in the foreground add a subtle, shimmery quality to the water. White chalk additions are visibly scattered over certain passages, but it is unclear whether these are corrections or highlights. Of central importance to the way these different materials interact is the paper.

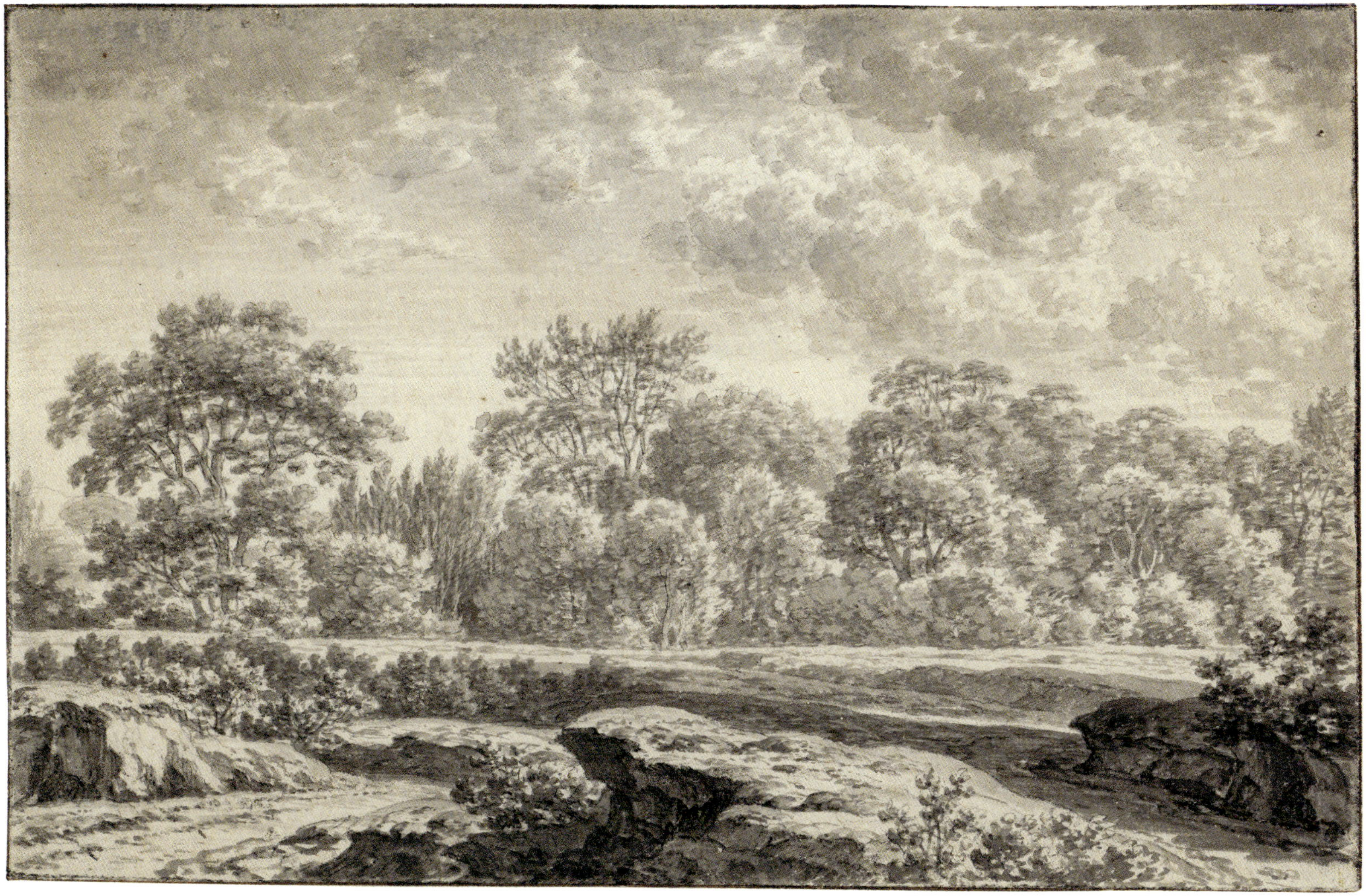

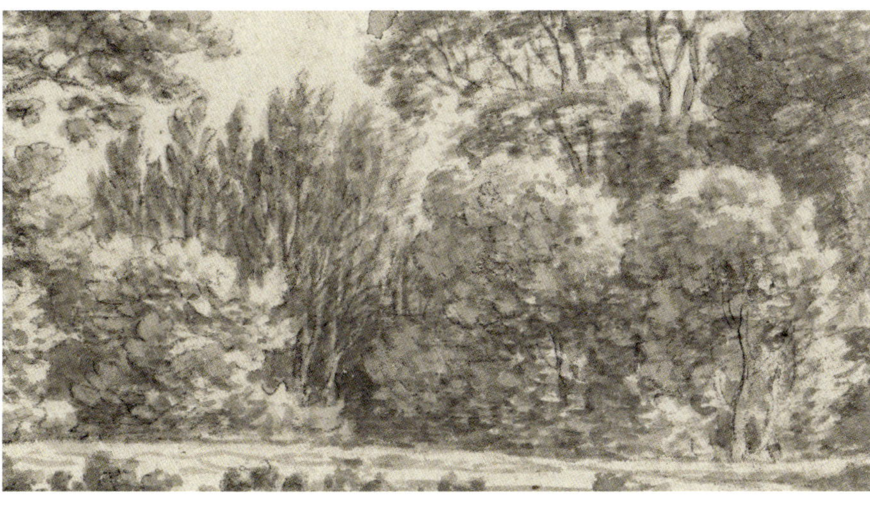

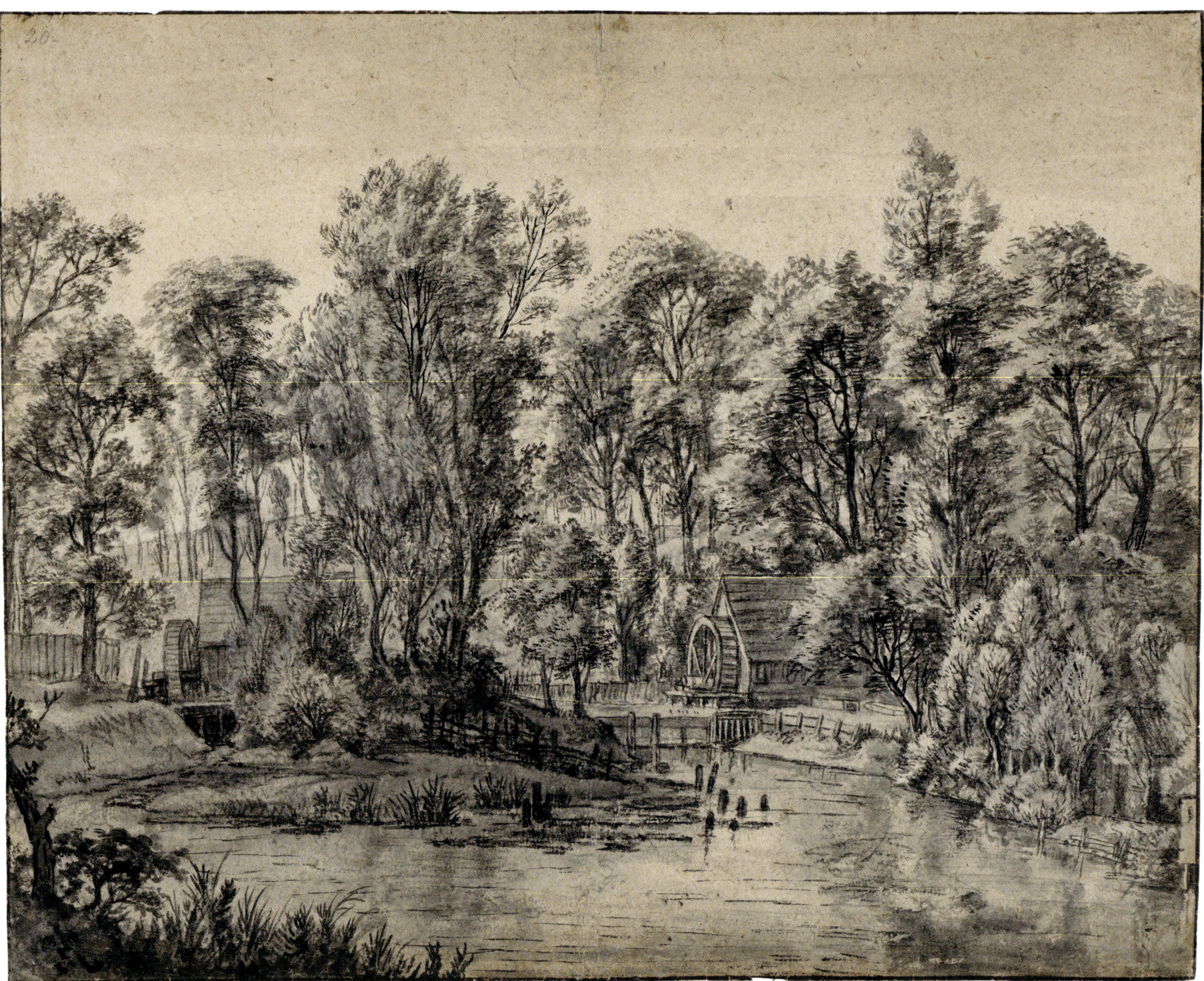

Fig. 12 Anthonie Waterloo, *Grist Mills near Hamburg*, c. 1660. See p. 233 for full information; see also the detail on p. 166.

Fig. 13 Transmitted light image of detail from Cuyp's *View of a Ploughed Field*.

Fig. 14 Transmitted light image of detail from Waterloo's *Grist Mills near Hamburg*.

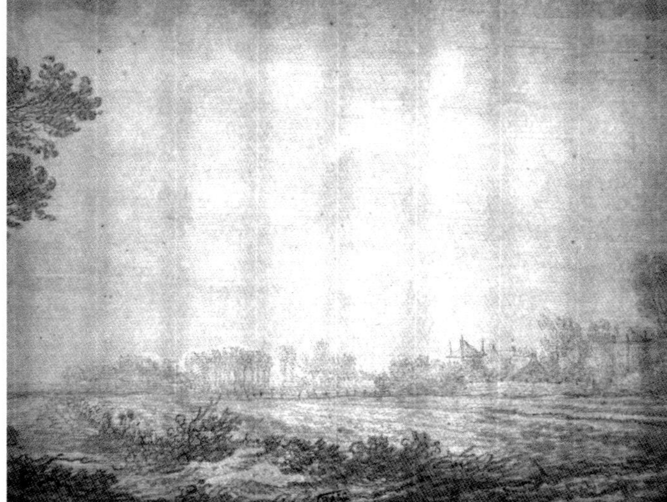

The other four drawings in this study are on off-white papers with fine laid and chain line patterns (see Fig. 13 for a transmitted light image of Cuyp's *Ploughed Field*). Like most writing papers, they are sized with gelatin to produce a surface that is relatively hard and smooth and therefore holds and retains the media applied to it. Waterloo, by contrast, executed his drawing on a tan paper with noticeable fibrous clumps and wood shives that produce a rough, uneven surface (Fig. 14).[18] Waterloo's paper is also unsized, resulting in a support that is soft and spongy—similar to a poor-quality wrapping paper—into which the media easily sinks.[19] Waterloo's interest in the technical and expressive role of paper is evident in the other two drawings by him in the present catalogue. An off-white antique laid paper is used for the precisely rendered *Landscape with Doorwerth Castle* (see p. 182, Fig. P), whereas a blue antique laid paper forms the middle tone of *A Forest at Twilight* (p. 99), lending the softness of the paper itself to the soft light of dawn or dusk. Conversely, the fibrous paper of *Grist Mills* seems purposefully chosen for its texture: as the brush glides over the paper, it leaves just enough media to suggest the rough tree bark.

The five drawings in this study reveal complex drawing practices characterized by creative combinations and manipulation of media. In each case, the artist's careful planning and knowledge of the working properties of his materials, including the paper, served his artistic vision. These drawings, like many others in the exhibition, were clearly not made on the spot in a single sitting. Yet despite being created, at least in large part, in the studio, they were informed by the practice of plein air drawing that was promoted in the period. To judge from the works examined here, this tradition played a significant role in inspiring artists to seek out new ways of manipulating their media to convey the visual experience of the outdoors.

Anne Driesse served as Senior Conservator of Works on Paper in the Straus Center for Conservation and Technical Studies at the Harvard Art Museums; she retired in 2020 and now works in private practice.

NOTES

1. A Leica Wild M10 microscope was used throughout this technical examination.
2. A video spectral comparator (VSC 8000) designed by Foster + Freeman was used to examine this group. Originally designed for forensic investigation of falsified documents, the VSC is routinely used to study works of art in the Straus Center paper lab. It consists of a main unit outfitted with several light sources and a camera, allowing for the examination of works under incident, raking, and transmitted light as well as infrared and ultraviolet illumination.
3. Carbon black and iron gall are two inks often associated with Old Master drawings and were increasingly used side by side from the beginning of the twelfth century. Carbon black ink is nearly pure amorphous carbon, which is collected from the condensed smoke produced by burning mineral oil, pitch, or resin. Microscopically, it is finely divided, uniform, and homogeneous. Rutherford J. Gettens and George L. Stout, *Painting Materials: A Short Encyclopaedia* (New York: Dover Publications, 1966), 124. Iron gall ink is made from tannin, or gallotannic acid, which is derived from oak gall nuts and is combined with iron sulphate to form ferrous gallatannate, then mixed with gum and water. Gettens and Stout, *Painting Materials*, 122. For a discussion of inks, see Jan Burandt, "An Investigation Toward the Identification of Traditional Drawing Inks," *Book and Paper Group Annual* 13 (1994): 9–16; Jane Colbourne, "A Survey of Methods Used in the Technical Examination and Analysis of Brown Inks," in *The Iron Gall Ink Meeting: Postprints, September 4th & 5th*, ed. A. Jean E. Brown (Rotterdam: University of Northumbria at Newcastle, 2001); and "The Iron Gall Ink Website," Cultural Heritage Agency of the Netherlands, https://irongallink.org/igi_index.html.
4. C. A. Baker, "A Comparison of Drawing Inks Using Ultraviolet and Infrared Light Examination Techniques," in *Applications of Science in the Examination of Works of Art: Proceedings of the Seminar, September 7–9, 1983*, ed. Pamela A. England and Lambertus van Zelst (Boston: The Research Laboratory, Museum of Fine Arts, 1985), 159–63.
5. Specular reflection FTIR is a non-contact, non-destructive method for chemically identifying organic materials. Attenuated Total Reflection (ATR-FTIR) requires an infrared transparent crystal to be placed on the surface being analyzed, with adjustable contact pressure that can be set to cause minimal damage to the object. Analysis was performed in the Straus Center under the guidance of Georgina Rayner, associate conservation scientist, and Arthur McClelland, principal scientist in Harvard's Center for Nanoscale Systems. CNS is a member of the National Nanotechnology Coordinated Infrastructure Network (NNCI), which is supported by the National Science Foundation under award no. 1541959.
6. Nuria Ferrer and M. Carme Sistach, "Analysis of Sediments on Iron Gall Inks in Manuscripts," *Restaurator: International Journal for the Preservation of Library and Archival Material* 34 (3) (2013): 175–93. Analysis was confined to non-destructive testing only. A more complete study of brown inks was undertaken in the Straus Center in 2020–21 to further identify and differentiate the various components of brown inks.
7. Thanks to Georgina Rayner for interpretation of results. See also Gesa Kolbe, "Gelatine in Historical Paper Production and as Inhibiting Agent for Iron-Gall Ink Corrosion on Paper," *Restaurator: International Journal for the Preservation of Library and Archival Material* 25 (1) (2004): 26–39.
8. Similar to Heawood #1300, Amsterdam 1644–66; Edward Heawood, *Watermarks, Mainly of the 17th and 18th Centuries*, Monumenta Chartae Papyraceae Historiam Illustrantia 1, ed. Émile Joseph Labarre (Hilversum: Paper Publications Society, 1950), 93.
9. W. A. Churchill, *Watermarks in Paper in Holland, England, France, Etc. in the XVII and XVIII Centuries and Their Interconnection* (Amsterdam: M. Hertzberger, 1967), 5, 7. Prior to the establishment of papermills in the Netherlands in the late seventeenth century, the Dutch imported paper from Italy, France, Switzerland, and Germany. French papers were preferred for drawing, and the well-established trade routes between France and Holland enabled the Dutch to import high-quality paper. In fact, many mills in the Angoumois region of France actually operated with Dutch capital and produced paper with Dutch watermarks. For a more thorough account of papermaking, see Dard Hunter, *Papermaking: The History and Technique of an Ancient Craft* (New York: Dover Publications, 1978).
10. Handmade paper will almost always have two discernible sides: felt and wire. The latter is the side in contact with the wire mold that is dipped into a pulp vat during papermaking. After the pulp has formed on top of the wire mold, it is pressed with felt to expel the water, then allowed to dry. Viewed with raking light, the imprint of the watermark and chain lines are visibly pronounced on the verso of Bloemaert's drawing support, indicating the impression of that side against the wire mold.
11. Watercolor is made from color obtained from minerals or plant materials, ground very fine and then mixed with small amounts of a binding medium, such as gum arabic or gum tragacanth, to form cakes. It is employed as an adjunct to drawing, usually in combination with pen or chalk.
12. Chalk is mined from natural deposits of carbon and clay. It is an earthy material comprised of short, round particles that produce soft and finely textured markings. Its color and working properties are determined by the amount of clay in the deposit. Chalk is well liked for its blackness, smoothness, tonality, and gradient shading; unlike charcoal, it cannot easily be erased or smudged. Gettens and Stout, *Painting Materials*, 285. See also George Keyes, "Esaias van de Velde and the Chalk Sketch," *Nederlands Kunsthistorisch Jaarboek* 38 (1987): 136–45.
13. Graphite is a naturally occurring mineral of almost pure carbon. It is a stable material and produces a metallic sheen due to its plate-like formation. The most well-known source of graphite was discovered in 1560 at Borrowdale, in Cumberland. Carlo James and Marjorie B. Cohn, *Old Master Prints and Drawings: A Guide to Preservation and Conservation* (Amsterdam: Amsterdam University Press, 1997), 64.
14. Analysis was carried out with ATR-FTIR. Gum arabic is a product of two species of acacia trees that grow in the Sahel region of Africa.

Most scholars believe that the substance is so named because it was via the ports of the Arabian Peninsula that Europeans first acquired it, though one researcher has offered a compelling alternative explanation, noting that the term "arabic" could derive from the word for "transparent" in the language of the Beja people in Sudan. Cited in O. H. M. Idris and G. M. Haddad, "Gum Arabic's (Gum Acacia's) Journey from Tree to End User," in *Gum Arabic*, ed. John F. Kennedy, Glyn O. Phillips, and Peter A. Williams (Cambridge: Royal Society of Chemistry, 2012), 3. Long valued for a variety of uses, gum arabic was discovered to be a prime thickening agent for textile dyes in the seventeenth century, spurring large-scale demand in Europe. Dorrit van Dalen, *Gum Arabic: The Golden Tears of the Acacia Tree* (Leiden: Leiden University Press, 2019), esp. 9–10, 59–60. Gum arabic is commonly used as a binder for ink and watercolor, and it can be employed as a medium in its own right to saturate or heighten certain colors or features. Ralph Mayer, *The Artist's Handbook of Materials and Techniques*, rev. ed. (New York: Viking Press, 1957), 405. See also Abdalbasit A. Mariod, "Chemical Properties of Gum Arabic," in *Gum Arabic: Structure, Properties, Application and Economics*, ed. Abdalbasit A. Mariod (San Diego: Elsevier Science & Technology, 2018), 67–73.

15. On Cuyp's use of gum arabic, see Egbert Haverkamp-Begemann, "The Beauty of Holland: Aelbert Cuyp as a Landscape Draftsman," in *Aelbert Cuyp*, ed. Arthur K. Wheelock, Jr. (Washington, D.C.: National Gallery of Art; London: Thames & Hudson, 2001), 77. See also p. 116, Fig. J in this volume, which exhibits touches of gum.
16. For recent discussions of the practice of dipping chalk or charcoal into gum arabic, see Carmen C. Bambach in Philippe Costamagna, Florian Härb, and Simonetta Prosperi Valenti Rodinò, eds., *Disegno, giudizio e bella maniera: Studi sul disegno italiano in onore di Catherine Monbeig Goguel* (Milan: Silvana Editoriale, 2005), 178–79; Julian Brooks, *Guercino: Mind to Paper* (Los Angeles: J. Paul Getty Museum, 2006), 23; and John Marciari, *Guercino: Virtuoso Draftsman* (New York: Morgan Library & Museum, 2019), 29–30. All cite a technical study by Marjorie Shelley, the Sherman Fairchild Conservator in Charge of Works on Paper at the Metropolitan Museum of Art, New York.
17. Similar to Heawood #2006, foolscap watermark with the initials PD, 1659–90; Heawood, *Watermarks, Mainly of the 17th and 18th Centuries*, 110.
18. In his nineteenth-century history of papermaking, Richard Herring wrote, "Paper participates in some sort of character of the country which makes it; the Venetian being neat, subtle and court like; the French light, slight, and slender; and the Dutch thick, corpulent and gross, sucking up the ink with sponginess thereof." Richard Herring, *Paper and Paper Making, Ancient and Modern*, 2nd ed. (London: Longman, Brown, Green, and Longmans, 1856), 34.
19. With the invention of the Hollander beater in the late seventeenth century, the Dutch became known for their fine, white papers, whose production grew into a major industry. *Papermaking—Art and Craft: An Account Derived from the Exhibition Presented in the Library of Congress, Washington, D.C., and Opened on April 21, 1968* (Washington, D.C.: Library of Congress, 1968), 23. The Hollander beater replaced stampers, which rub or fray linen rags to produce paper pulp. In contrast, the newer technology reduces rags to fibers by lacerating them with a series of blades attached to a wooden wheel. Hunter, *Papermaking*, 162. It is possible that the paper used by Waterloo is an early Dutch paper manufactured with stampers, which would explain the knots and clumps of fibers.

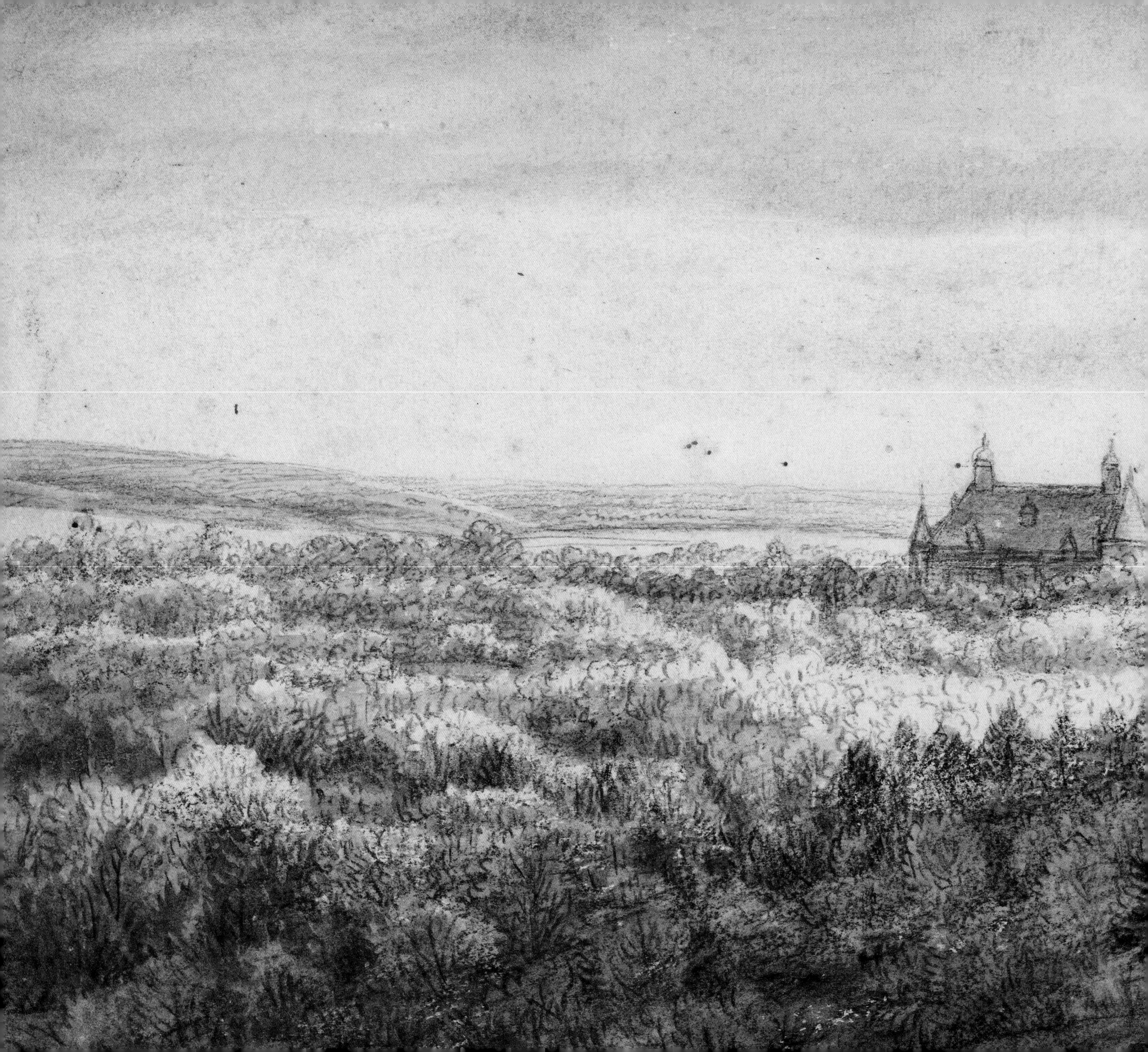

Anthonie Waterloo
*Landscape with Doorwerth Castle*,
c. 1650–70

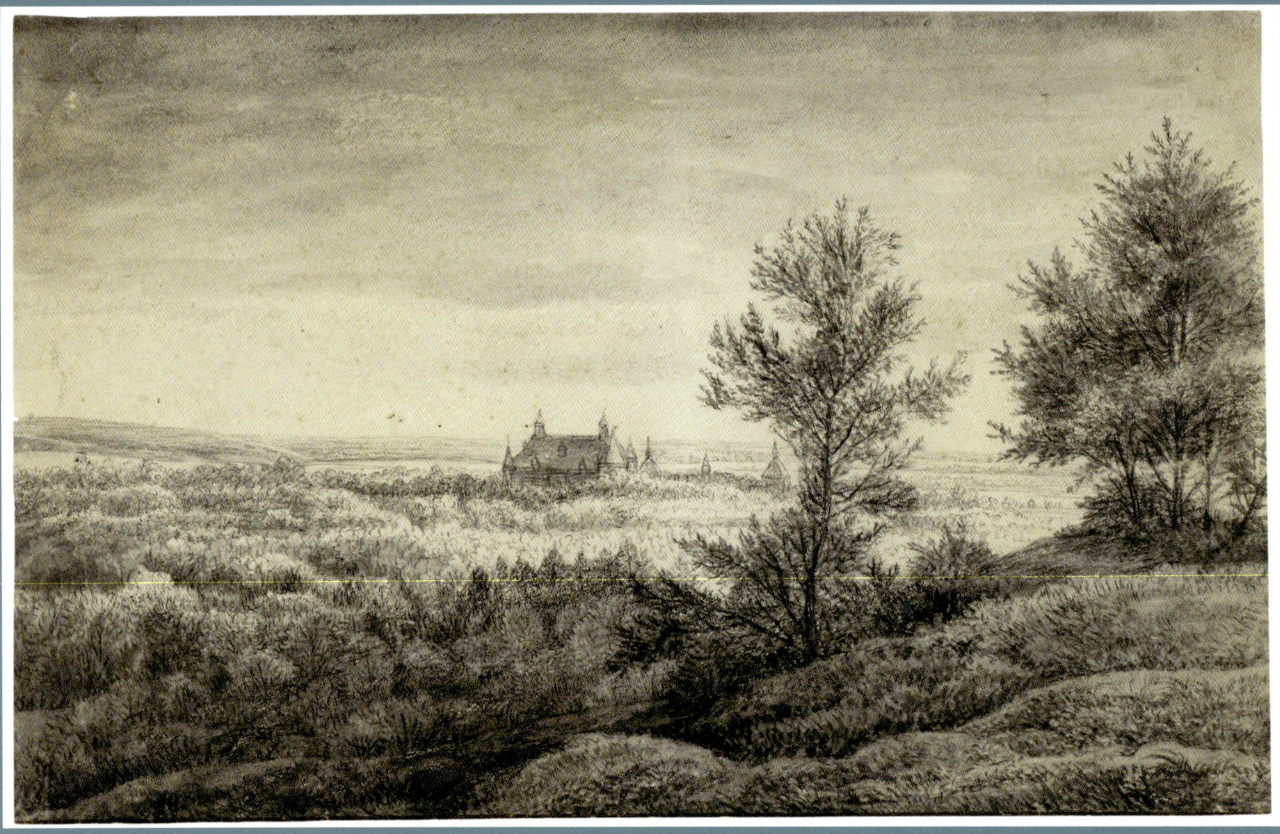

Fig. P Anthonie Waterloo, *Landscape with Doorwerth Castle*, c. 1650–70. See p. 233 for full information.

Anthonie Waterloo (1609–1690) traveled extensively after beginning his adult life and career in Amsterdam. His prolonged trip throughout northern Germany in the late 1650s resulted in a large number of well-documented sheets, as did his travels along the Lower Rhine, where he recorded scenes in and around cities from Utrecht to Cleves – including this drawing of Doorwerth Castle, which still stands today in a restored state outside of Arnhem. Identifiable by its distinctive roofline and turrets, Doorwerth is here placed amid its extensively wooded setting. The high vantage point allows for a broad panoramic expanse, including a view of the river and lands beyond. Waterloo provides a sense of scale to this broad vista with the placement of two tall trees atop a foreground hillock at right, one of which frames the rightmost turret with a concise, curved opening in its branches.

A virtuosic draftsman, Waterloo delighted in combining multiple media to brilliant effect, seen especially in his wooded views (as on p. 99). Here, he incorporates black chalk and gray wash with the lush qualities of charcoal to enhance the varied textures of the plants inhabiting this terrain, as well as the resulting atmospheric modulations from the alternating sunlight and shade of passing clouds. Combining recognizable detail with artistic prowess, *Doorwerth Castle* is a splendid example of the topographical landscape tradition as it had evolved at mid-century.

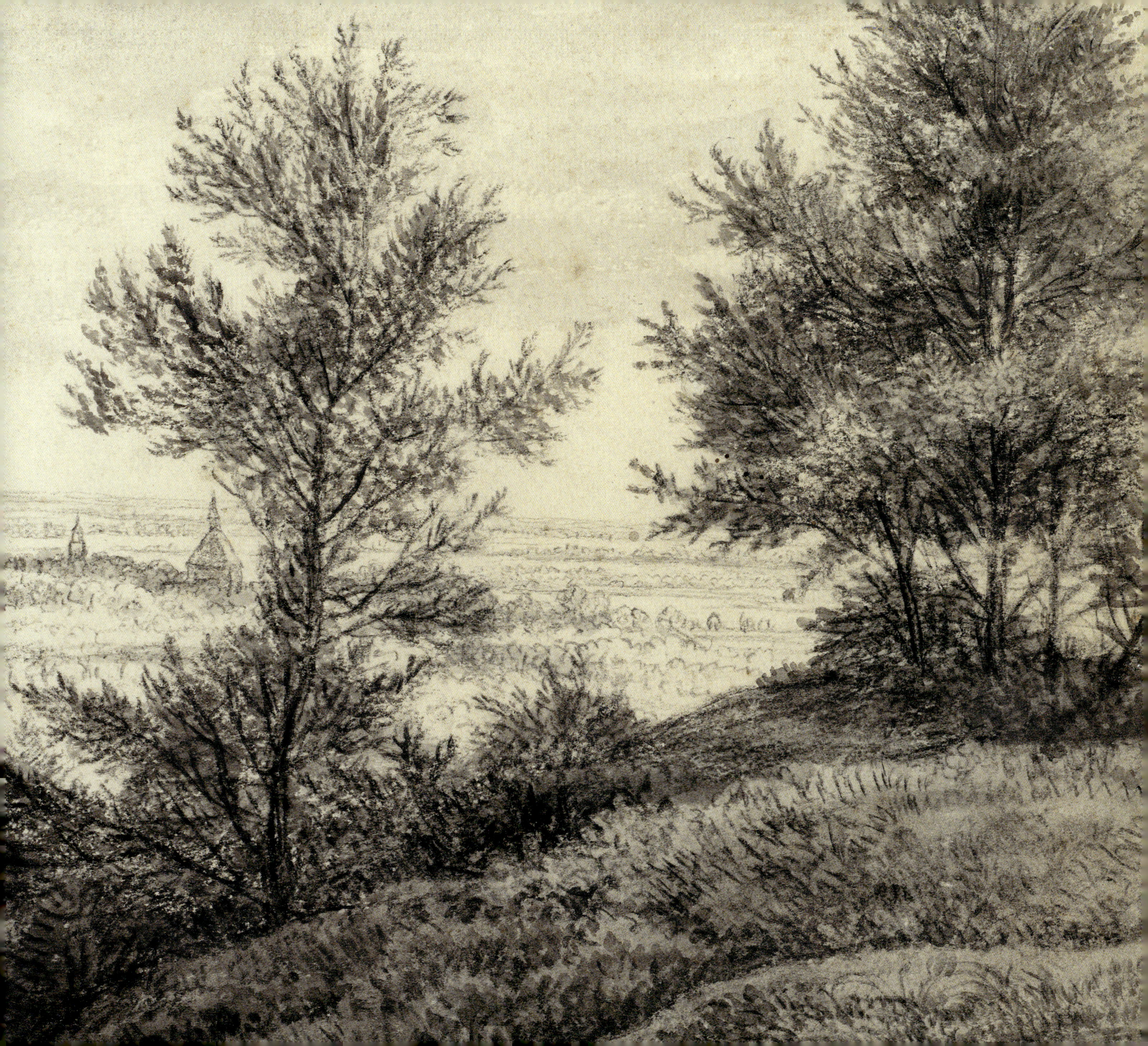

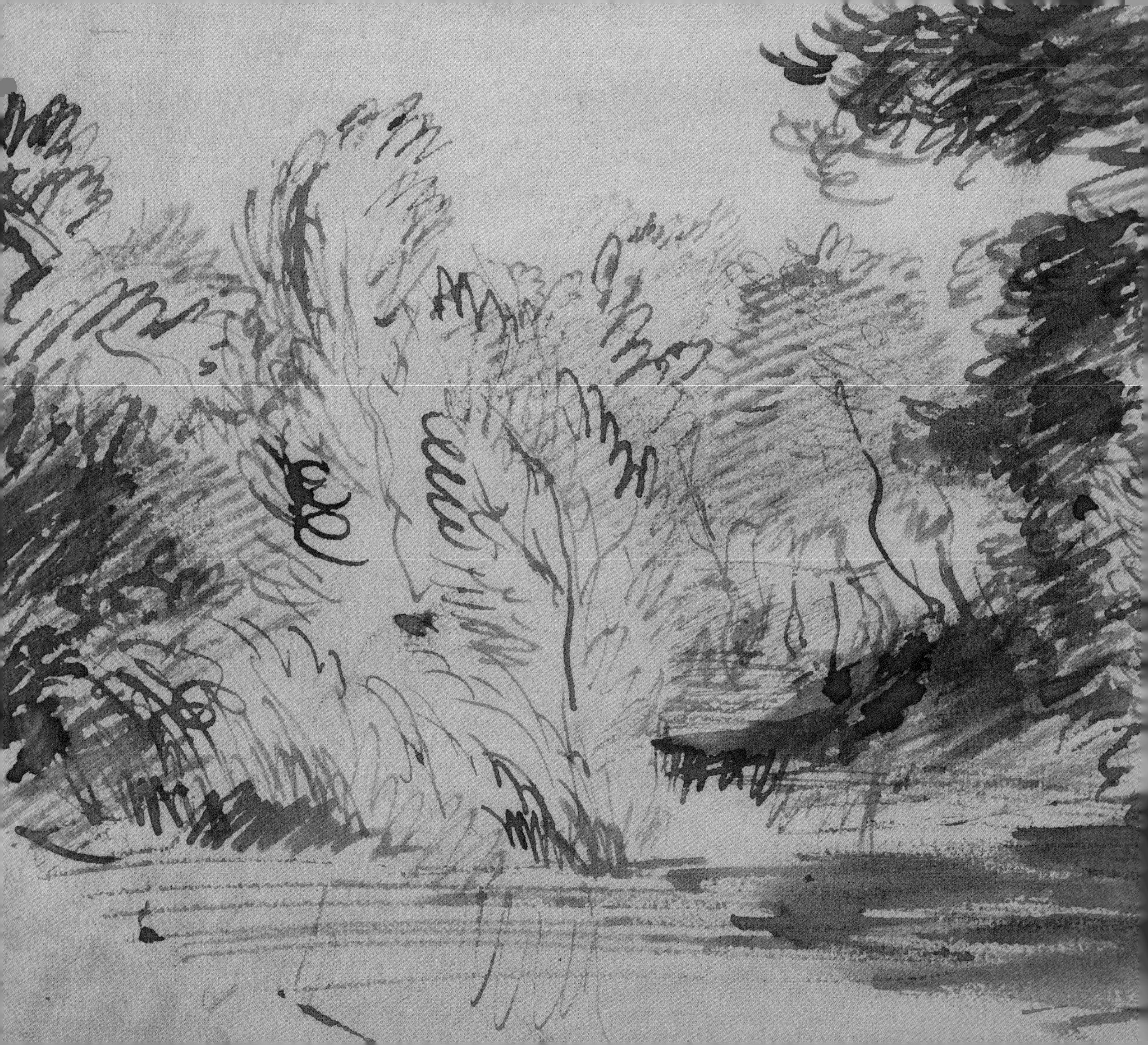

Jan Lievens

*Forest Landscape with a Pond*,

c. 1650–70

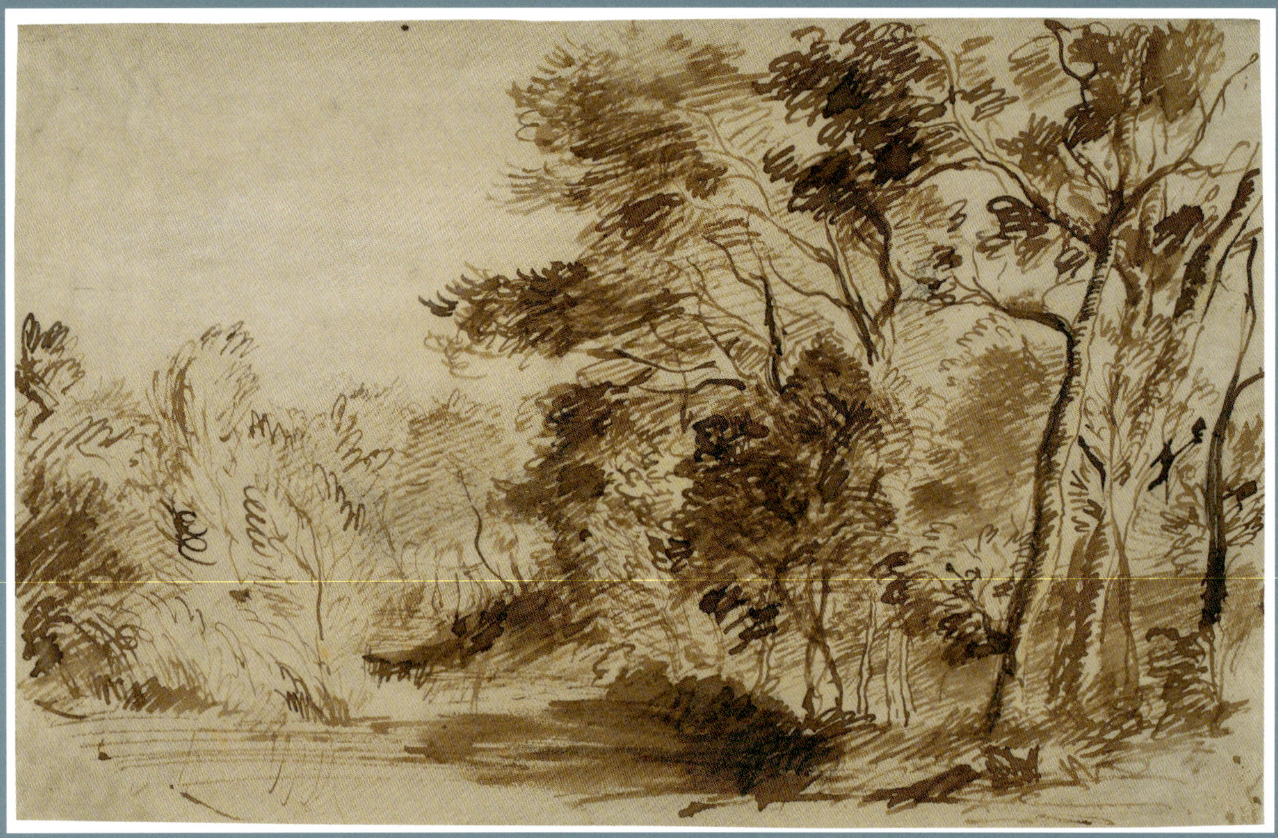

Fig. Q Jan Lievens, *Forest Landscape with a Pond*, c. 1650–70. See p. 230 for full information.

An associate of Rembrandt's (1606–1669) during their youthful years in Leiden, Jan Lievens (1607–1674) went on to forge a highly successful career as a history painter and portraitist. About half of his known drawings, however, are landscapes. Many of these are true tours de force of draftsmanship, often executed with a stiff reed pen on luxurious supports such as Asian paper or parchment (see p. 135). Others, no less masterful, were rendered more fluidly, possibly outdoors, for the artist's own purposes.

Drawn on antique laid paper prepared with brown wash, perhaps in imitation of Asian paper, *Forest Landscape with a Pond* likely belongs to the latter category, as it exhibits a quick approach to line that suggests a fleeting observation of tree branches bending in the wind. This strategy, together with the loose application of brown wash, recalls Anthony van Dyck's (1599–1641) landscape drawings, which Lievens must have seen during his years in London (1632–35), or even in Antwerp, where he lived for the next ten years. The watermark on this sheet dates it to his final three decades in Amsterdam, suggesting that Lievens absorbed Van Dyck's example and applied this approach even to a regional subject.

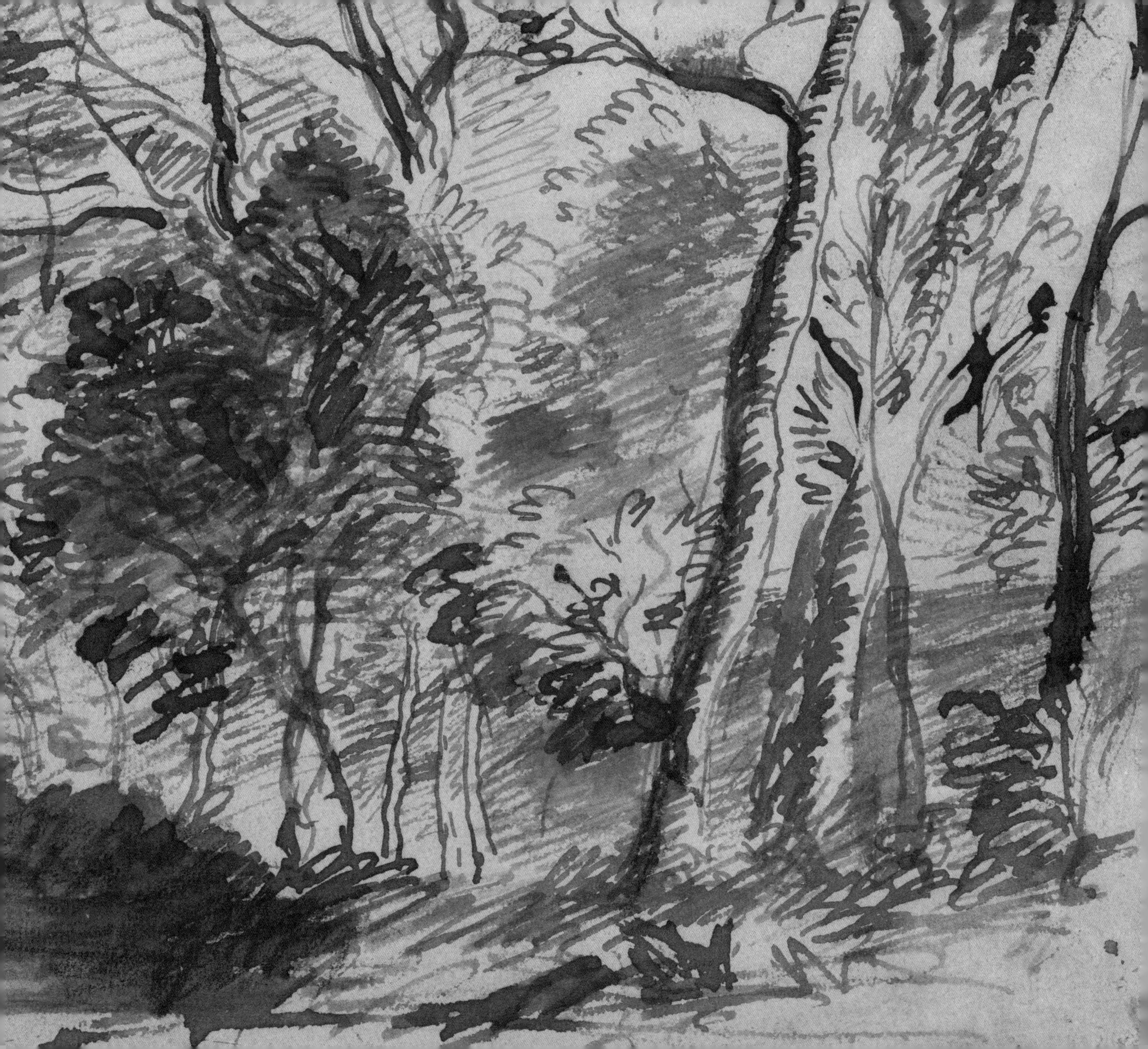

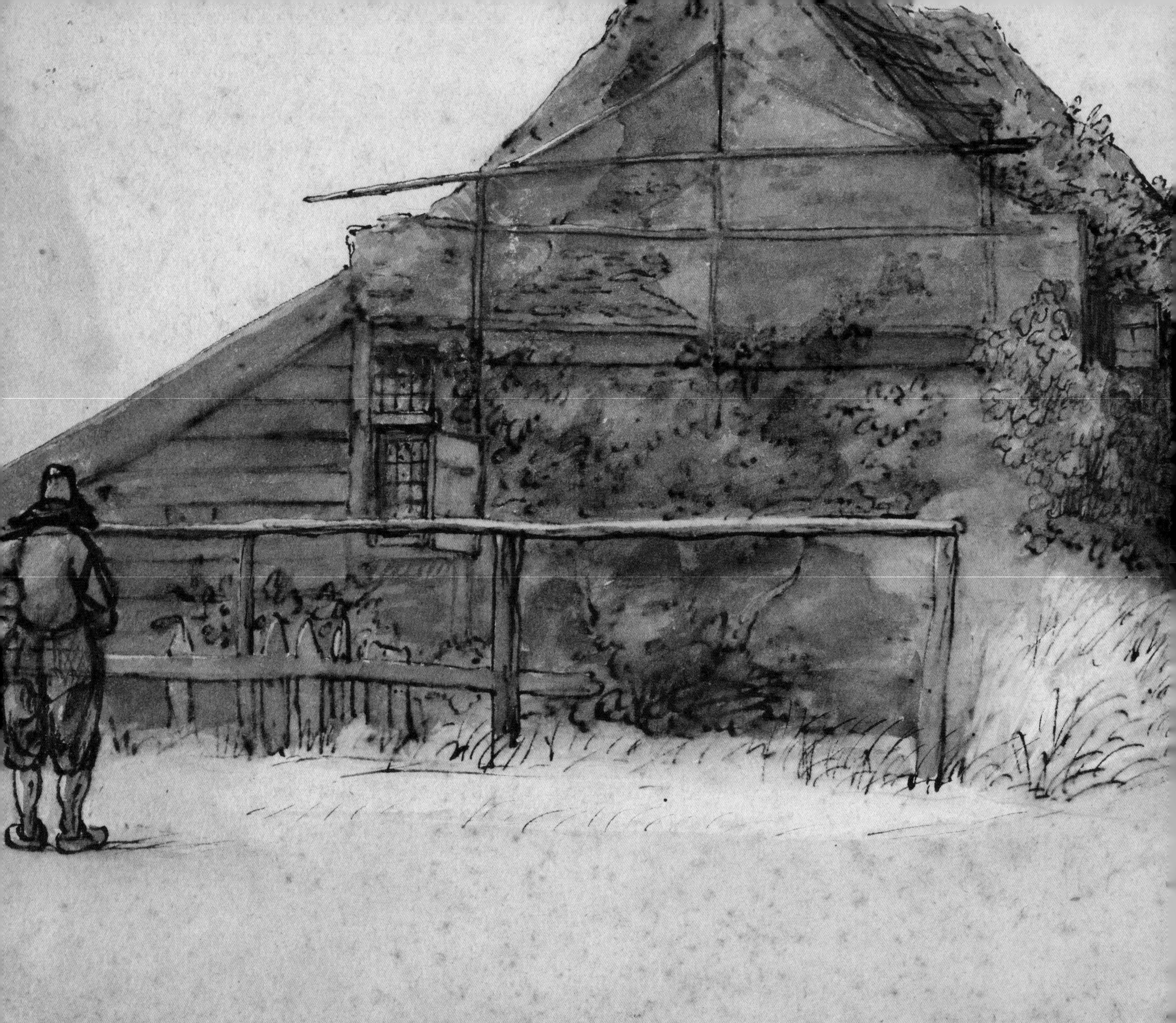

# Lambert Doomer
*Cottage with a Bleaching Yard*, 1660s

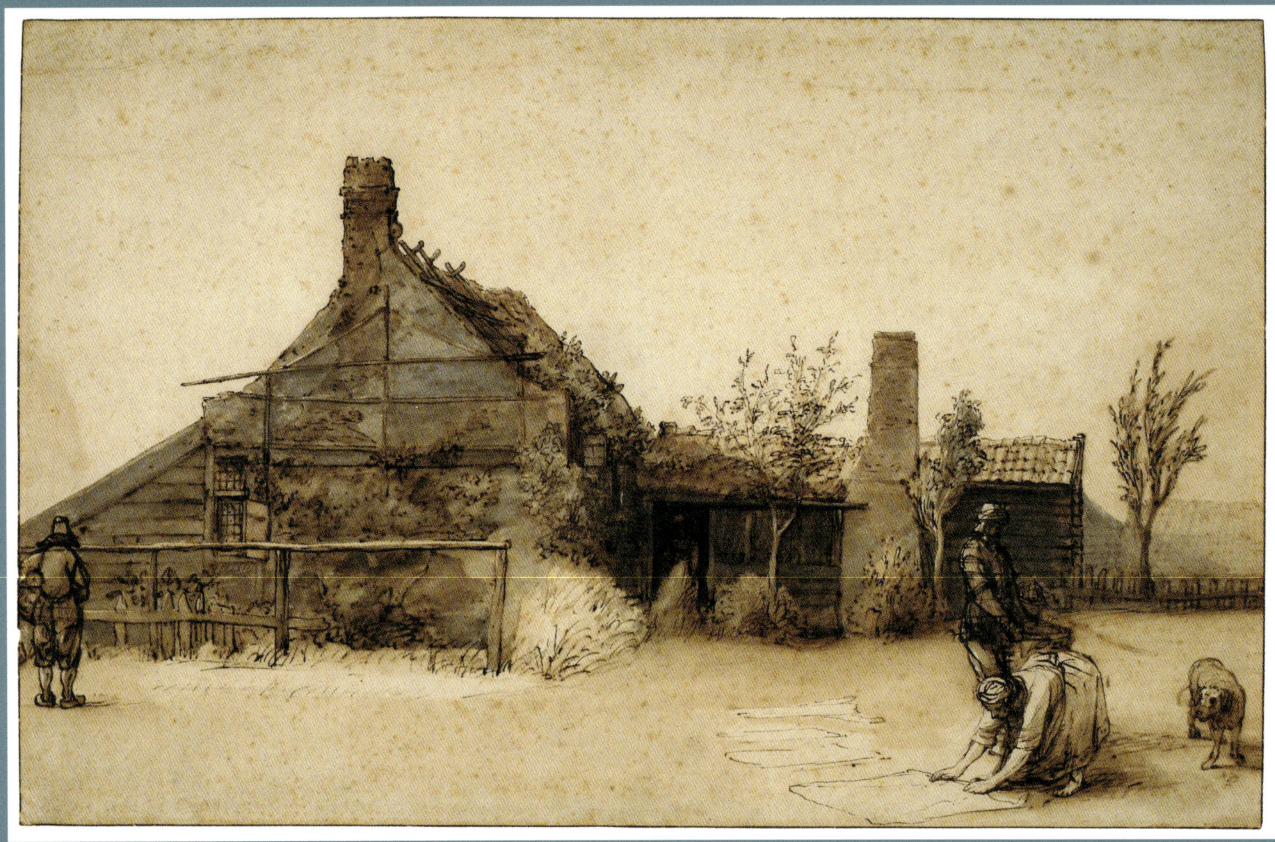

Fig. R Lambert Doomer, *Cottage with a Bleaching Yard*, 1660s. See p. 229 for full information.

In this luminous drawing of a humble cottage, Lambert Doomer (1624–1700) modulated his distinctively subtle blend of brown and gray wash with the addition of white opaque watercolor. Such evocative effects set him apart from the many other Rembrandt students and followers who were inspired by the master's interpretation of rustic architectural motifs. Although Doomer's personal connection to Rembrandt (1606–1669) remains uncertain, his surviving corpus of drawings, the overwhelming majority of them landscapes, attests to his intimate knowledge and appreciation of Rembrandt's own landscape sheets. Indeed, Doomer purchased five albums of drawings from Rembrandt's bankruptcy sales in 1657–58.

Active primarily in Amsterdam, Doomer traveled to France in the mid-1640s and along the Rhine into Germany in 1663. Although *Cottage* is neither dated nor inscribed and its structure unidentified, it is stylistically aligned with a group of drawings he produced during the latter trip. Despite the possibility that he saw this cottage on his journey eastward, the inclusion of the woman bleaching linen relates it to Dutch visual conventions surrounding the depiction of Haarlem, a stronghold in linen production.

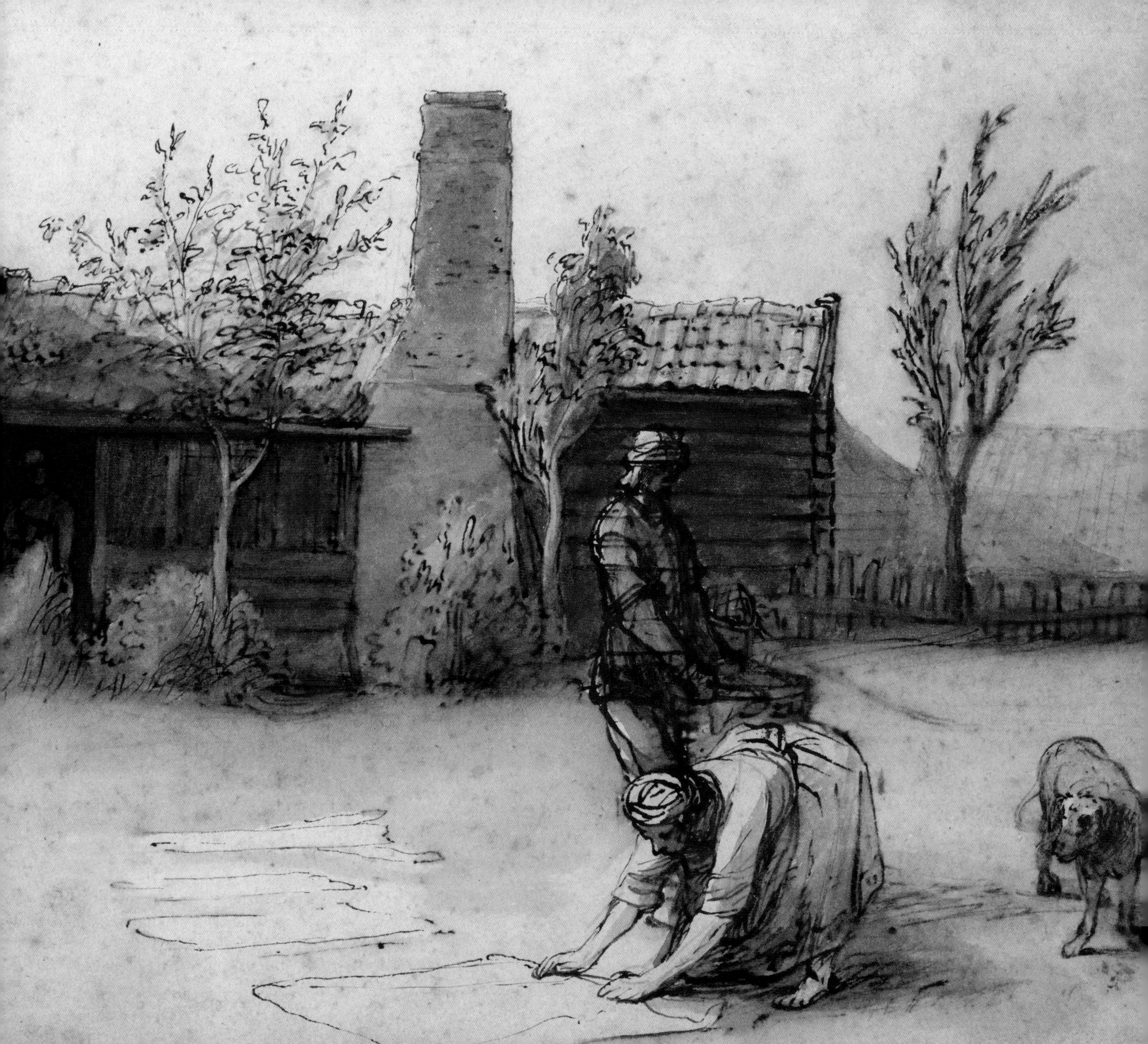

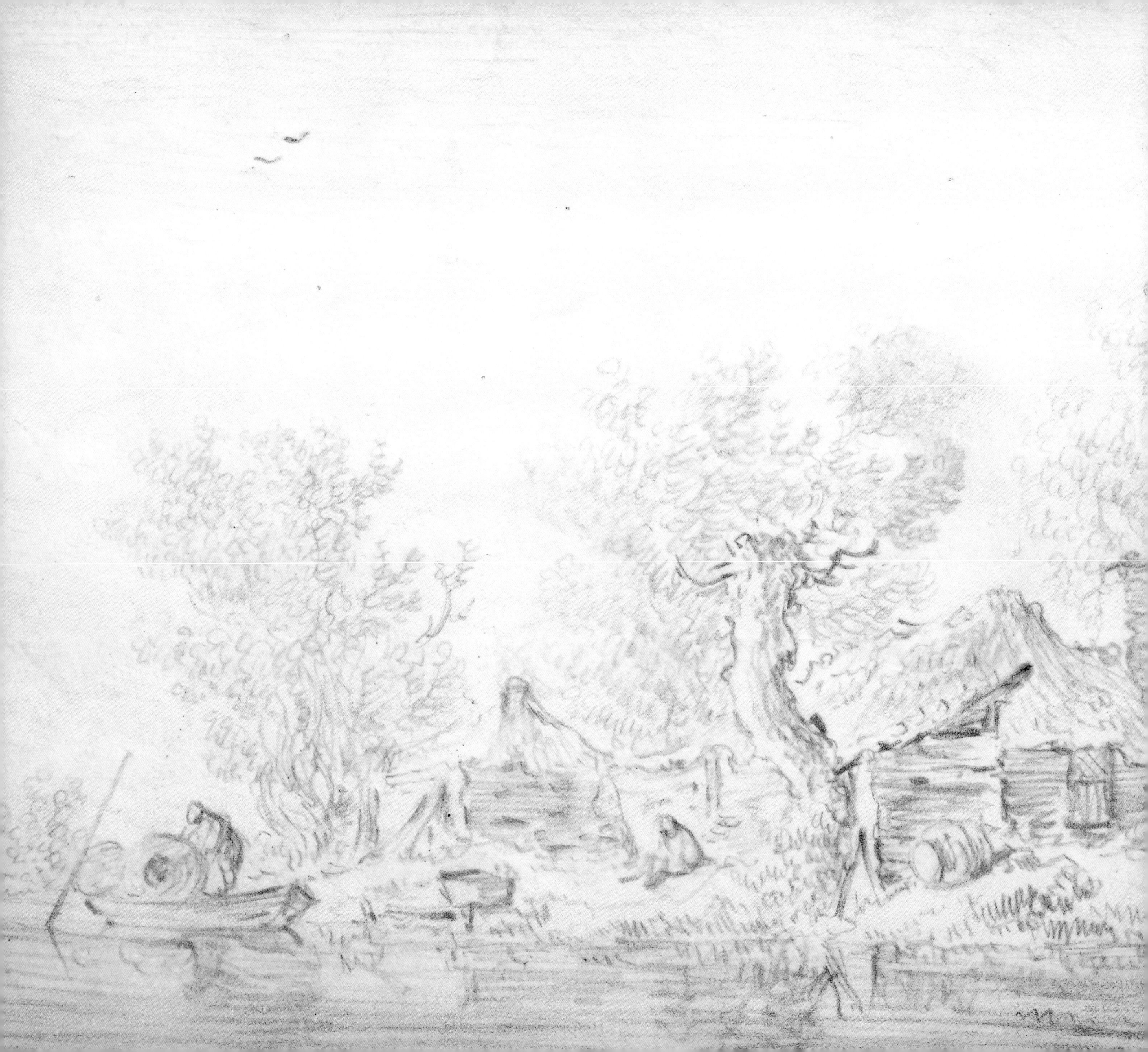

# DRAWINGS AS FRIENDS

*Joseph Leo Koerner*

*... così al vento ne le foglie levi si perdea la sentenza di Sibilla.*[1]

—Dante, *Paradiso* 33

Fig. 1 Rembrandt van Rijn, *Abraham Francen, Apothecary*, c. 1657. Etching, engraving, and drypoint with plate tone on vellum (the reverse of a mariner's chart), 15.6 × 20 cm. Harvard Art Museums/Fogg Museum, Gift of William Gray from the collection of Francis Calley Gray, G3277.



Landed long last in Italy, at Cumae, Aeneas ascends to a crater high on a volcanic hill, there to seek his father's ghost in Hades. At the crater's edge dwells a frenzied prophetess who should be his guide. But this sibyl, as she is called, refuses to speak or to explain her speech when asked; instead, she booms her cryptic oracles from the mouth of the cavern spontaneously, or scratches her prophecies on oak leaves that she then stacks in hidden corners of her cave, where, with the slightest draft, they scatter, confusing their testimony. In Virgil's telling, the sibyl will neither "link their shifted sense anew, / Nor reinvent her fragmentary song" (*Aeneid* 3.456–57).[2] Forewarned, Aeneas commands her to escort him personally through the underworld, the mazy paths of which are easy to enter but impossible to escape. To venture there alone would be irreversible, like the scattering of the sibyl's oracles.

Those wind-tossed leaves are a writer's nightmare: chapters, sentences, words get shuffled and the plot lost. For Virgil, composing in ten thousand tightly written lines the epic of Rome, such a fate would be a calamity – one he knew might befall his own poetry as it had other great books, such as Homer's *Iliad*. Soothsayers drew from these texts random lines called *sortes*, or lots, to foretell the future. And indeed, the *Aeneid* would eventually come to furnish *sortes Vergilianae*, its lines severed from their context to steer those seeking counsel. Writing thirteen centuries later, Dante fittingly presses Virgil into service as his prophetic guide in Hell, and at the end of his *Divine Comedy*, in the final vision of Heaven, the Christian poet returns to the ancient trope of the sibyl's scattered leaves as metaphor for his fading vision of God. Here, however, the outcome is reversed: in the depths of that divine realm, Dante sees "far down . . . lying / Bound up with love together in one volume [*in un volume*] / What through the universe in leaves is scattered" (*Paradiso* 33.ll.85–87).

Old Master drawings come to us like the sibyl's leaves: loose, fragile sheets inscribed with wondrous but often incomplete or inscrutable figures. Originally, they may have been bound together with other sheets in a sketchbook, or produced, one by one, as steps in an exercise or phases of a process whose outcome may no longer be discernable. Some passed directly from their maker to an admiring collector. Immediate signs of an artist's skill, such gathers are rare and nearly all were later dispersed. Prints – both series and single leaves (the latter sometimes called *Flugblätter*, literally "flying leaves," due to their mobility) – are also fragile. Only a tiny fraction of the countless images printed in Europe in the first few

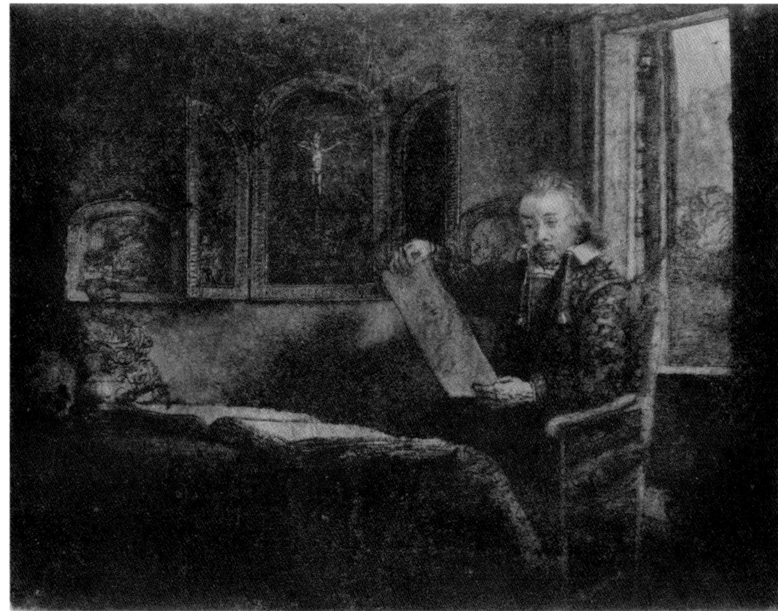



centuries following the birth of the medium survive. But there is strength in numbers, and not only because one out of many might endure. A drawing, as a singular, handmade work, can puzzle the intimate circle who sees it, its viewing an enactment of physical and social proximity, while a print, potentially present at thousands of locations, can gather disparate viewers into an expanded society of friends, encouraging collection, knowledge, and preservation. From the early years of the printing press, such images entered into networks of personal and professional associates, and beyond them, into a new collectivity that would come to be called the public.

While early modern appreciators of works on paper sometimes hung framed drawings and prints on their walls—Hendrick Avercamp's (1585–1634) *Winter Landscape* (see p. 112, Fig. I), for example, survives in its original seventeenth-century frame—they generally kept their treasures in bound albums or portfolios, often called books. Binding printed leaves was common, as was pasting prints and drawings down in albums, a practice to which the trimmed margins and ruled borders of most surviving older sheets attest.[3] In the Netherlands, however, works on paper were often inserted loosely within a portfolio or between an album's pages.[4] Collectors could remove sheets for viewing at will—an activity Rembrandt (1606–1669) depicts in his great etching of apothecary Abraham Francen (Fig. 1)—before carefully returning them to their rightful places within the album.[5] The order of an album was at once a personal choice, often made with a view to aesthetic presentation,[6] and a reflection of the categories according to which art was understood at a particular time.

Artists helped create these categories. At the turn of the sixteenth century, Albrecht Dürer (1471–1528) issued engravings and woodcuts that circulated in thousands of copies, making him the first world-famous living artist. Dürer published many of his works as series. The woodcuts *Apocalypse with Pictures* were issued as a book in 1498, with the biblical text—in German or in Latin, depending on the edition—printed with great care on the verso of the images. In 1511, he published the series again, in Latin only, but now with an elaborate figurative title page and in conjunction with two other woodcut series, the *Life of the Virgin* and the *Large Passion*. He called these "the three big books."[7] To his more illustrious patrons Dürer also gifted, in his words, "the whole of my works," by which he meant a complete set of his prints.[8] This is the first documented instance of an artist thinking of his output as a coherent and collectible whole, what would come to be termed an oeuvre.[9] Dürer shaped the market in which subsequent printmakers and collectors operated.

Printmakers continued to model the collection of their products by issuing them in unified groups. Later in the sixteenth century, from his Antwerp publishing house Aux Quatre Vents (literally, "To the Four Winds"), Netherlandish painter, etcher, and publisher Hieronymus Cock (1510–1570) issued most of the thousand-plus prints produced on his press in the form of series. Some of these reached back to traditional lists and enumerations: the Four Seasons, Seven Deadly Sins, Twelve Months, and so on. Others were looser and more open-ended. Pieter Bruegel the Elder's (1526/30–1569) twelve *Large Landscape* etching-engravings share the same size and format, and all feature dramatic vistas embellished by narratives, but Cock published them without a title page, perhaps so that each print could be purchased individually.[10] He issued the *Small Landscapes* (see p. 37) as a series of (probably) eighteen in 1559, followed by a second series of twenty-six in 1561,[11] demonstrating how accommodating and extendable such collections could be, the "many and very beautiful places" they capture (according to the first edition's title page) so engagingly ordinary that they might be discoverable and depictable anywhere, as if on an endless virtual walking tour. The buyers of such individual sets sometimes called them "books."[12] Bound either alone or with other series in albums and best enjoyed seated at a desk, they were stored in libraries together with bound and printed volumes.

An album composed entirely of landscape prints given to Harvard in 2000 by Robert M. Light contains complete series by Adam Perelle (1638–1695), Claes Jansz. Visscher (1587–1652), and Willem Buytewech (1591/92–1624). Marked *Livre de Peisage* on the spine, this gathering was probably compiled in France at the end of the seventeenth century. The ten etchings by Buytewech are among the most innovative works of Dutch art. Titled *Verscheyden Lantschapjes* (Various Landscapes), they amble from the ruins of Brederode Castle, near Haarlem, to the derelict chapel of Eik en Duinen in The Hague. In between, in six scenes of woods, cottages, and marshland, Buytewech enlists the power of etching to capture the mystery of the local environs. Tall trees energized as if by some inner force resemble, in their printed form, vegetal specimens pressed between the pages of a book. And the ground from which they rise – reduced, in the etchings, to a narrow band at the lower edge, just a few millimeters wide – expands vertiginously from shallow swamps pushed right up against the picture plane to vast pastures receding into a measureless distance (Fig. 2). Read in the *Livre* like poems on a page, these enigmatic prints revise our experience of the natural world, causing the close and familiar to seem exotic and strange.

Another album in the Harvard Art Museums, comprising 127 leaves assembled most likely in Flanders around 1600, binds between its covers five large and complete print sets (for a total of 97 prints), with eight original drawings mounted to blank leaves at the back of the album. Five of the drawings are by a follower of Flemish artist Hans Bol (see p. 38). Executed in brown ink and gray and colored wash over black chalk, these landscape views served as models for prints in a series engraved by Hans Collaert I (1525/30–1580) and published by Hans van Luyck. Titled *Views of the Environs of Brussels*, this extensive set of twenty-four plates is also included in the Harvard album.[13] Whoever assembled the album found it interesting to reunite this partial group of drawings with their printed incarnation. All incised, the drawings physically evidence how their transfer to the engraver's plate was achieved. While four of the drawings are in the same orientation as their corresponding prints, *View of Over Muelen* (Fig. 3)—the only one with its verso blackened for transfer—is reversed in the engraving (Fig. 4). It is possible these drawings were originally held loosely within the album's pages, such that each could be taken out and held next to its related print. Their inclusion suggests an interest in process and in the relation between copy and original. At the same time, the use of color, unusual in print designs but by all appearances autograph, suggests that these drawings were also intended as aesthetic objects in their own right.

Rare is the case of a group of master drawings originally created in a single volume and still preserved as such. The Abrams Album, also in the Harvard Art Museums, is a marvelous survival of this kind (Fig. 5).[14] A small oblong volume of fifty-two vellum leaves sewn together into a black leather binding, it was designed to be an album in the original sense of the word: a book consisting of blank, or white (Latin *albus*), pages waiting to be filled with signatures and souvenirs. In this instance, the album collects full-page drawings—forty-one of them—made directly on the bound vellum sheets. These are not exercises, studies, or project drawings, but finished works of art: thirty-six bear their maker's signature and ten include the year of their making, dates that range from 1635 to 1641. William W. Robinson has reconstructed the album's provenance. In brief, it came to Harvard as part of a gift from Maida and George Abrams, who purchased it (without auction and promising

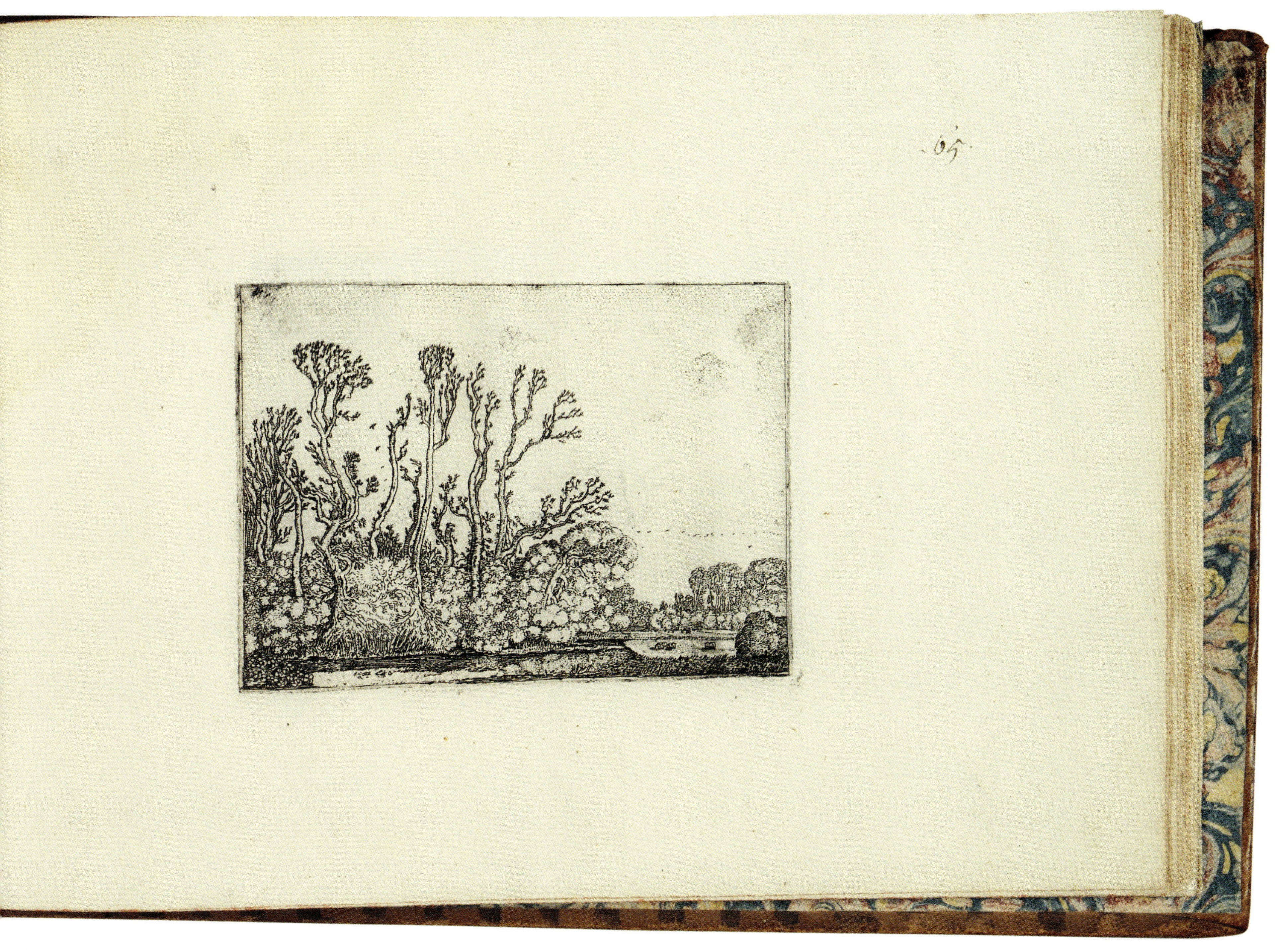


Fig. 2 Willem Buytewech, *Landscape with a Herd of Sheep near a Pond*, 1616. See p. 234 for full information.

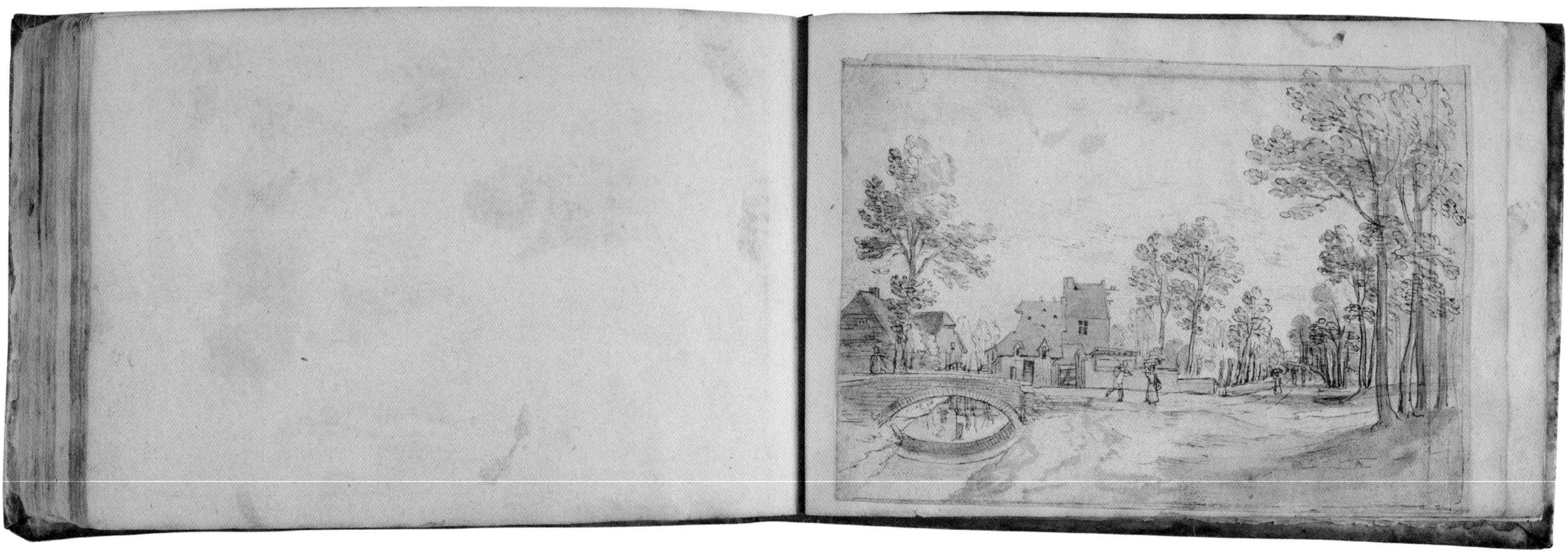

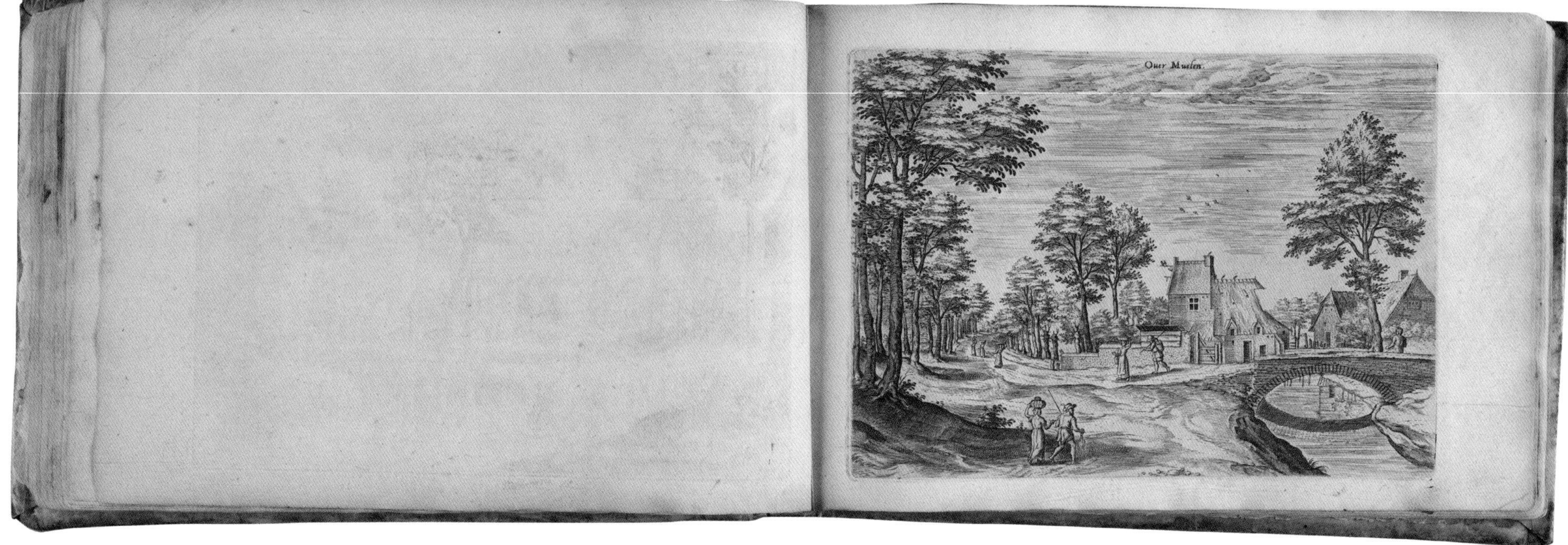
Ouer Muelen.

Fig. 3 Follower of Hans Bol, *View of Over Muelen*, c. 1575–80. See p. 228 for full information.

Fig. 4 Hans Collaert I, after a follower of Hans Bol, *View of Over Muelen*, c. 1575–80. See p. 234 for full information.

Fig. 5 Abrams Album, c. 1635–45. Bound album of 41 drawings on parchment. The Maida and George Abrams Collection, Fogg Art Museum, Harvard University, Cambridge, Massachusetts, 1999.123.1–53.

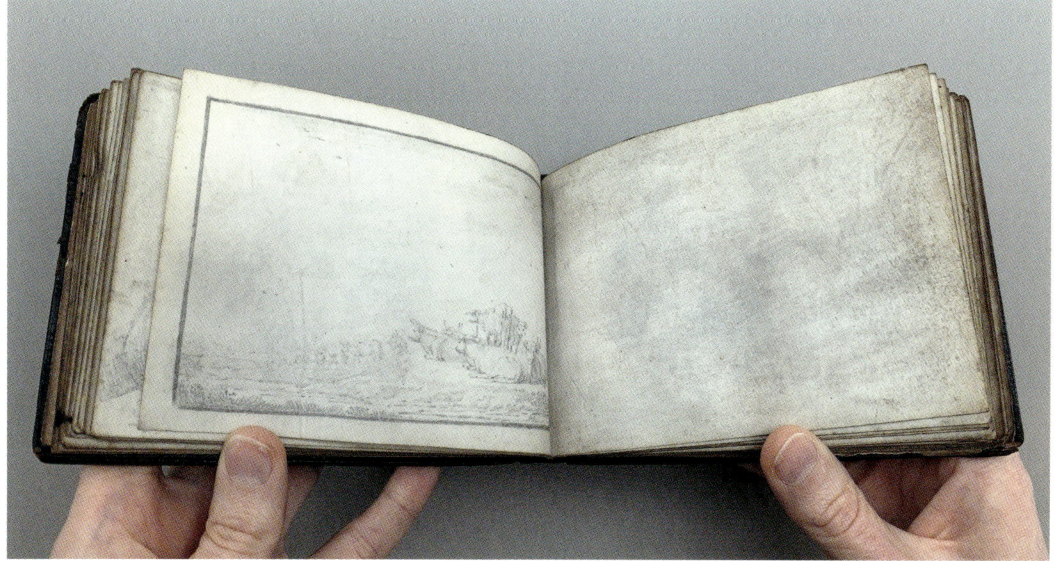



to keep it intact) at Sotheby's following its discovery in 1987 by a London bus conductor and its identification, by George Gordon, of the remarkable thing that it is. Where it lay the two centuries before it came to light remains unclear, but printed lot descriptions cut from an auction catalogue and pasted into the album's front cover suggest it was sold somewhere in the United Kingdom around 1800. Its binding links it further back, most likely to Pieter Spiering (c. 1595–1652), a renowned art dealer, connoisseur, and tapestry works director active in Delft and The Hague and with commercial connections to the Swedish court. Most of the twenty-seven identified artists represented in the volume were also active in Delft and The Hague, some of them apprentices of masters participating in the album. One Hendrik Verschuring (1627–1690) proudly noted on his page that he was only thirteen when he made his accomplished rendering of a horse in three-quarter view. The story the Abrams Album gives of its making is one of collective, competitive creativity, where talented local artists known personally to the album's owner treat the blank leaves as an open invitation.

The album tells this story without words. Except for the signatures and dates (and some upside-down script within one cryptic genre scene), there is nothing but visual imagery of a most diverse kind. Scenes of everyday life, animal studies, ornamental designs, still life, and (most numerously) landscapes appear bound together with scenes from classical myth and the Bible. The latter, which are in the minority, are not labeled and call for careful sleuthing to identify them. In a drawing of Abel giving sacrifice, the artist conceals the figure of Cain in a dense landscape background, and the album's two drawings of a person who, by her attributes, must be the goddess Diana require iconographic expertise for their identification. Although the album's contents are obviously linked by virtue of their form, and nearly all are executed in dry media (twenty-one in graphite and thirteen in black chalk), the overall impression is one of variety.

Holding the snug little volume in hand, turning its supple vellum pages, whose smoother "flesh side" was preferred over the "hair side" as the support for most of the drawings, one cannot but be struck by an expectation on the artists' part that their creations would be lovingly beheld. Already on the recto of folio 1, faint graphite lines conjure a bit of landscape and a human head, as if one of the participating draftsmen could hardly wait to get to work. But folio 2 sets the standard: there, Rotterdam painter Pieter de Bloot (1601/2–1658) details in black and red chalk a seated smoker who holds with

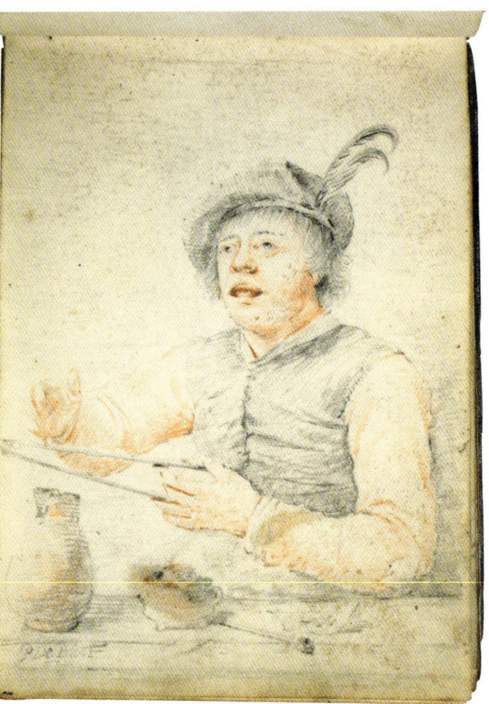

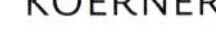

tongs a hot coal to light his pipe (Fig. 6). To properly appreciate the drawing, one must rotate the album 90 degrees. De Bloot lays further claim to his sheet by establishing along the whole of its bottom edge (when rotated) a wooden table. With its front edge flush with the picture plane and inscribed with the artist's name, the table fictively reinforces the vellum's vulnerable (because most fingered) fore edge. Meanwhile (De Bloot has engineered a sense of timing in his scene), the smoker reaches his tongs to the picture's limit, the burning coal threatening the album's foot edge—although his open-mouthed expression directed outward to the left affirms a virtual space beyond the material limits of the page.

Smoking was a popular motif among Dutch "low-life" genre painters—artists intent on grasping ordinary life through its crude embodiment by idle peasants, rowdy soldiers, and drunk and carousing figures on the margins. This was partly because smoking gave the subject something mentally and physically absorbing to do, making his or her gestures look candid because performed with a sort of rapt or intoxicated attention to the act itself. (In a state of distraction, De Bloot's smoker seems perhaps to have burnt his fingers on the hot tongs, hence his open mouth.) Along with the taste for sugar, addiction to tobacco fueled long-distance trade, and this had powerful reverberations for the Dutch, whose fortunes were made by global commerce and the exploitation that enabled it. But tobacco's pleasurable narcotic effects had special synergy with art, another luxury commodity that promised a transformative, out-of-body experience and trafficked in the smoky stuff of fantasy and dream.

Fictionally inebriated by De Bloot's *Seated Smoker*, the album's viewer turns the page to François van Knibbergen's (1596/97–after 1664) *Wooded Landscape* (Fig. 7). Returning the book to its natural landscape orientation, this artist claimed his territory by drawing with black chalk and establishing straight-edge framing lines around his composition. The stark difference between the first two drawings, and the freedom of each artist to treat the page as he wished, resets the character of the aesthetic experience. Whereas De Bloot's drawing and indeed each of the individual works that follow immerse us in their separate fictions, the album as a whole, by sampling these different narratives, conjures the fact of art itself—the arti*fact*, as it were. The initial observation of a smoker lighting his pipe becomes an exercise in recognizing the drawing's artistry and comparing it to other examples. Van Knibbergen's achievement is impressive partly because he does so much with so little.

Fig. 6 Pieter de Bloot, *Seated Smoker Holding Tongs*, 1634–41. Black and red chalk on parchment, 15.2 × 11 cm. The Maida and George Abrams Collection, Fogg Art Museum, Harvard University, Cambridge, Massachusetts, 1999.123.2.

Fig. 7 François van Knibbergen, *Wooded Landscape*, 1634–41. Black chalk on parchment, 11 × 15.2 cm. The Maida and George Abrams Collection, Fogg Art Museum, Harvard University, Cambridge, Massachusetts, 1999.123.3.

Fig. 8 Joris van der Haagen, *Mountain Landscape with a River and Distant City*, c. 1640–42. Graphite on parchment, 11 × 15.2 cm. The Maida and George Abrams Collection, Fogg Art Museum, Harvard University, Cambridge, Massachusetts, 1999.123.48.

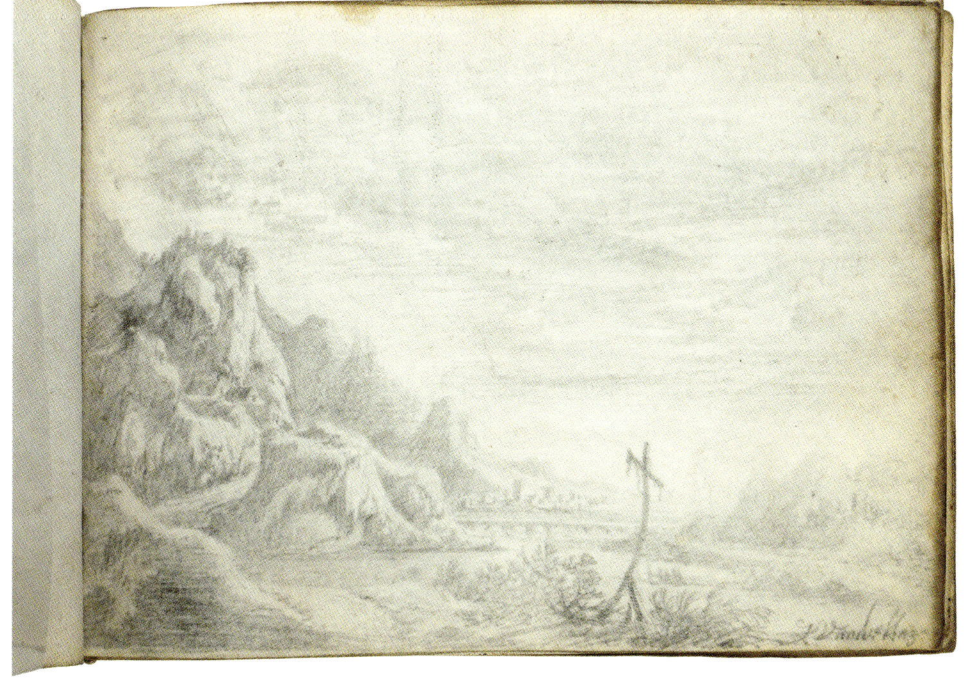

Drawn delicately in black chalk, an expressive pair of feathery trees at left give way to an atmospheric prospect of woods and clearings that guide the eye in a shallow curve back to the trees in the foreground again. There, through minute blanks on either side of the right tree's shaded trunk, the artist suggests an infinite horizon. It is a trick played by several landscape drawings in the album, where one of the tiniest bits of sketching conjures an immensity. On folio 48, Joris van der Haagen (1615–1669) allows a crooked wayside cross to gesture theatrically toward an infinity both spiritual and real: sketched on a thin sliver of vellum and shown dwarfed by towering peaks and backed by vast expanses, the great city in the distance measures the drawing's make-believe reach (Fig. 8). And even if this mountain gives way, with the turn of a page, to Willem van Aelst's (1627–after 1683) powerfully proximate and tangible *Vanitas Still Life*, the space-engendering capabilities of graphite and black chalk remain in play. The Preacher may be right that "all is vanity," but not that therefore "the eye is not satisfied with seeing" (Eccles. 1:3, 10), for drawing has created something wondrously new.

The album's oblong shape is naturally formatted for landscape views, and indeed, more than a third of the drawings are landscapes. Leafing through the book thus allows a kind of imaginative travel, the small album miraculously evoking a wide world to explore. Each page rewards close, sustained scrutiny. On folio 20, Leonaert Bramer (1596–1674) created his arresting portrait of Diana asleep in a forest, her bow and quiver dormant beside her (Fig. 9). Because she slumbers, the nude body of the formidable goddess of the hunt lies immobile, passive, and available, a condition Bramer exploits by detailing her shadowed but anatomically elucidated backside. Casting the viewer into the role of an unseen voyeur, the artist gives him (the implied male beholder) more to see than just the nude. He surrounds Diana with attributes that, in order to be identified, awaken the viewer's recollections of classical myth, and he envelops her in pleasant natural surroundings that, casually perused, cause each return to the nude sleeper to feel that much more intimate and intense, since she has not budged in the time that has lapsed, nor will she soon. Within these supplementary zones of entertainment, Bramer includes a surprise. Much closer to her than we, yet easy to overlook, a bearded satyr stares lustfully at the sleeping goddess. That the viewer is not the only voyeur is the least of his astonishments. Bramer startles us with the awareness that his drawing itself, and not just its erotic subject, jealously demands scrutiny, since it harbors more shady secrets than she.

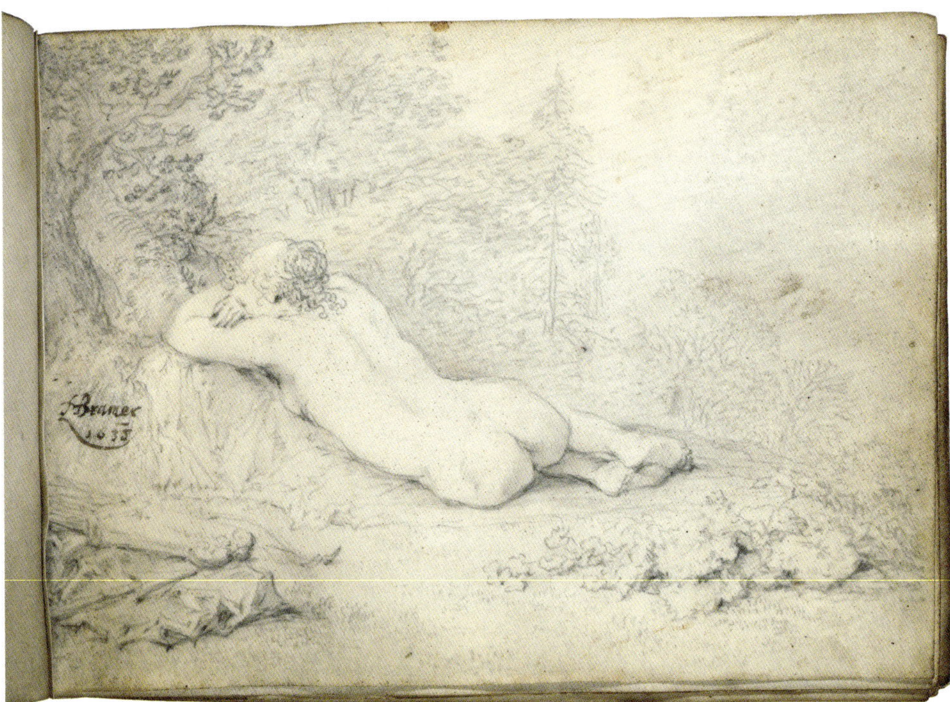

Fig. 9 Leonaert Bramer, *Sleeping Diana Spied upon by a Satyr*, 1635. Graphite on parchment, 11 × 15.2 cm. The Maida and George Abrams Collection, Fogg Art Museum, Harvard University, Cambridge, Massachusetts, 1999.123.20.



Signed and dated 1635, this drawing must be one of the album's earliest. Artists evidently filled the pages not consecutively but willfully, with Bramer claiming sheets both in the middle (fol. 20) and toward the beginning, where he sketched a genre scene of a couple singing (fol. 6). Each artist likewise took the liberty of drawing whatever he so desired, or what he believed himself to be especially good at. The young Verschuring boasts his precocious talents through his well-drawn horse; established landscapist Jan van Goyen (1596–1656) offers his signature subject rendered in his signature style. In 1637, Van Goyen drew two landscapes on widely separated leaves (fols. 8 and 45), perhaps recognizing that the album's strength would be in its diversity, which would develop in time through intervening drawings to come. Although he portrays ordinary bits of local landscape, Van Goyen creates drama out of the diversity of his own means: by applying more pressure to the black chalk, he captures the fugitive quiddity of ordinary things (a tree, a boat, a ruined hovel) while also dazzling with the sheer calligraphic beauty of his line (Fig. 10). Some artists seem to respond to what comes before or after their chosen leaf. A drawing rendered upside down on the verso of an album leaf—an anonymous sketch of a monster's head that looks like a design for metalwork—precedes an elaborate portrayal of Medusa (fol. 42; Fig. 11). The two seem interconnected, though in an associative way, recalling the head of Medusa's placement as the decorative aegis on Athena's metallic shield upon the gorgon's defeat. However we choose to understand its relation to the ornamental monster, Emanuel de Witte's (1617–1692) *Medusa* relates playfully with us. The snake-haired woman with the petrifying gaze turns her back to her viewers, but keeps us nervous and alert nonetheless.

Each of the album's drawings rewards vigilance in its own way. Simon de Vlieger's (1600/1601–1653) sketch of a coastal landscape with ships offshore might easily be passed over as a marine view typical of the artist's output—until one lingers on the rocks in the foreground (Fig. 12). Their striation conjures a multiplying host of human faces. Animating the dangerous shore like heaped-together victims of Medusa, these faces are also, potentially, accidental forms, images "made by chance" in accordance with what natural historians contended and collectors of curiosities celebrated: that nature herself could produce works of art.[15] Robinson has suggested that De Vlieger referenced a published engraving of the Swedish coast that gives a boulder a human face.[16] With his ties to Sweden, the album's owner might have appreciated De Vlieger's drawing all the

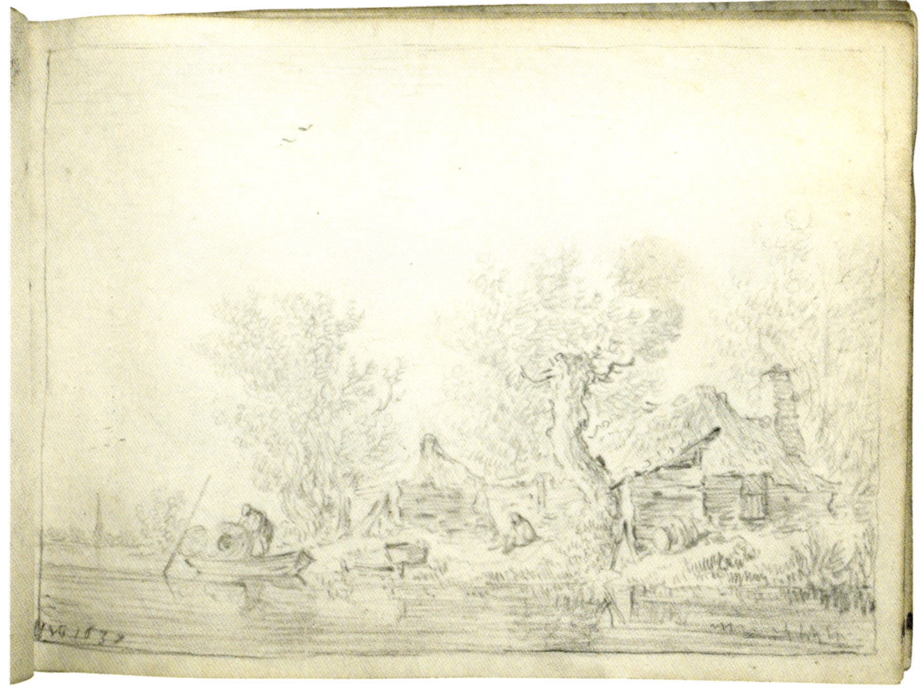

Fig. 10 Jan van Goyen, *River Landscape with Cottage*, 1637. Black chalk on parchment, autograph framing line in black chalk, 11 × 15.2 cm. The Maida and George Abrams Collection, Fogg Art Museum, Harvard University, Cambridge, Massachusetts, 1999.123.8. (For a detail of this drawing, see p. 192.)



more. Not only do the monstrous faces project onto landscape the semblance of a person; they also personalize the drawing, allowing it to speak to Spiering in ways that indicate a special bond, like a secret handshake or password shared between artist and collector.

The Abrams Album has rightly been called a "friendship book," or *album amicorum* (in the Latin cultivated by this type of object's devotees). Originating in the mid-sixteenth century, most probably in the Lutheran regions of Germany, friendship albums consisted of blank vellum or paper pages intended to be filled by the owner's acquaintances with signatures, mottos, coats of arms, song snippets, and biblical, classical, or proverbial texts.[17] Some early *alba amicorum* were printed books featuring adages framed in ornamental borders and illustrated with woodcut prints, but with blank pages added at the beginning and end, or carefully interleaved. A work favored for such treatment was Andrea Alciato's *Emblemata* (1531). It usefully exemplified the combination of text, image, and symbol that friends might deposit on the empty leaves. Many thousands of such friendship books survive – the British Museum holds about five hundred. Their beginnings lie in the careers of German students who, encouraged to move from university to university over the course of their education, collected signatures, advice, and mementos from teachers and students encountered along the way. Such albums, called *Stammbücher*, served as vehicles of self-representation for the owners and their friends, a place where ego comes to light through amicable bonds with others.

In the period, friendship modeled new associations among individuals, relations independent of the old bonds of family, marriage, and fealty. Elevating nobility of spirit over mobility of blood, the cult of friendship fostered networks of like-minded persons that would give rise to the more expansive collectivities of citizenship and the public sphere. Comparing friendship books to current social networking media, Bronwen Wilson writes that the *album amicorum* is "both a virtual collection of individuals and a real one, a space in which a public is assembled and imagined."[18] Conceived as portraits of friendship, many of these albums give ample space to visual images. The most famous example is the one kept by Antwerp humanist and cartographer Abraham Ortelius (1527–1598), with its scores of printed and drawn portraits and allegories and its eulogy to Bruegel, who died in 1569, about five years before the album was initiated, and was therefore unable to decorate a page.[19] In another, assembled in the 1560s by Jacob Heyblocq (1623–1690), Haarlem painter Jan de Bray (c. 1627–1697) portrays

Fig. 11 Emanuel de Witte, *Medusa*, early 1640s. Graphite on parchment, autograph framing line in graphite, 15.2 × 11 cm. The Maida and George Abrams Collection, Fogg Art Museum, Harvard University, Cambridge, Massachusetts, 1999.123.42.

Fig. 12 Simon de Vlieger, *Coastal Landscape with Anthropomorphic Rocks*, c. 1634–38. See p. 233 for full information.



himself looking out at the viewer across a chess game that has been pushed aside. "What is man alone?" asks De Bray in an accompanying inscription. "He cannot play chess, so if I find no friend, my game begone."[20]

Aristotle wrote that "love for a soulless thing is not called friendship, since there is no mutual loving."[21] Addressing the book owner directly, De Bray seems to lament that, however heartfelt they may be, material inscriptions cannot reciprocate as friends, and the project of the *album amicorum*, like the chess match, might just as well be tossed. But here and in the Abrams Album, the game lives on through the friends' mutual affection for a certain kind of unresponsive object. Treated amicably, giving more the more the viewer gives, the drawing is a sort of friend.[22] The Abrams Album binds persons and drawings together into a single volume. A collector, connoisseur, and collaborator (through his work in the tapestry trade), Spiering was as dependent on artists as they were on him. His book, an *album artistorum*,[23] passed to the future the reciprocity it originally performed, recently to the friends it found in Maida and George Abrams, and through them, to generations to come.

Generational reciprocity is also expressed in the album from roughly 1600 discussed above (see Figs. 3–4). The drawing mounted to this album's final leaf features a sketch by an unidentified hand representing what seems to be an allegory of Peace and Restraint. Catherine Levesque, who accepted this reading, further argued that Collaert's landscape prints, capturing the charm of local scenery, relate more generally to the theme of peace by expressing territorial pride in dangerous times.[24] Leafing through the rest of this remarkable volume, assembled in the wake of the Dutch Revolt and amid continued war, and observing its diverse contents – depictions of birds of the world, architectural and perspectival demonstrations, pleasant landscape views – I was struck by what seemed a puzzling inclusion: the *Disasters of the Jewish Nation*, a series of twenty-two prints engraved by Philips Galle (1537–1612) after designs by Maarten van Heemskerck (1498–1574). Yet the group gains significance through its adjacency to the landscapes.

The series' title page portrays Heemskerck in the form of a bronze portrait bust balanced precariously in a niche. Its text announces that the prints form a "little book" (*libellus*) that, by remembering the past, can serve as an example for the future. The past recalled is a calamitous one: the mostly Old Testament story of destruction, death, and disaster that befell the Jewish people either through human failure, in the form of hubris and

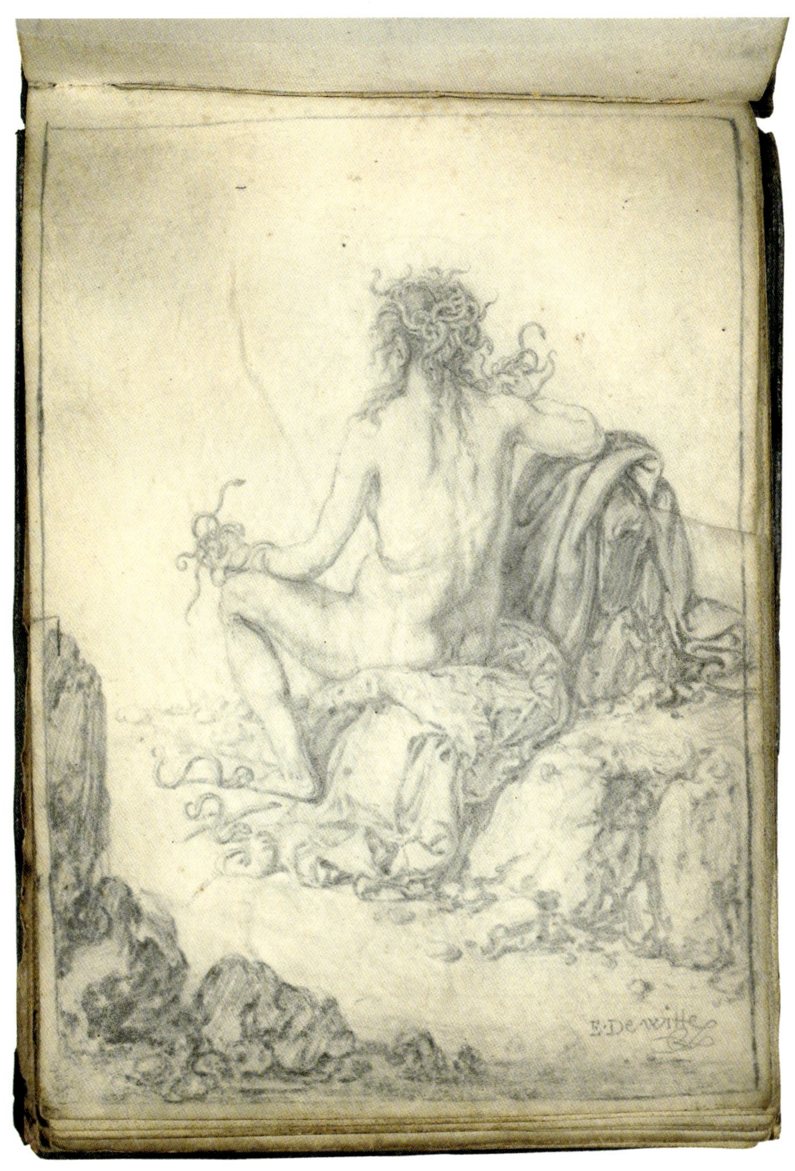

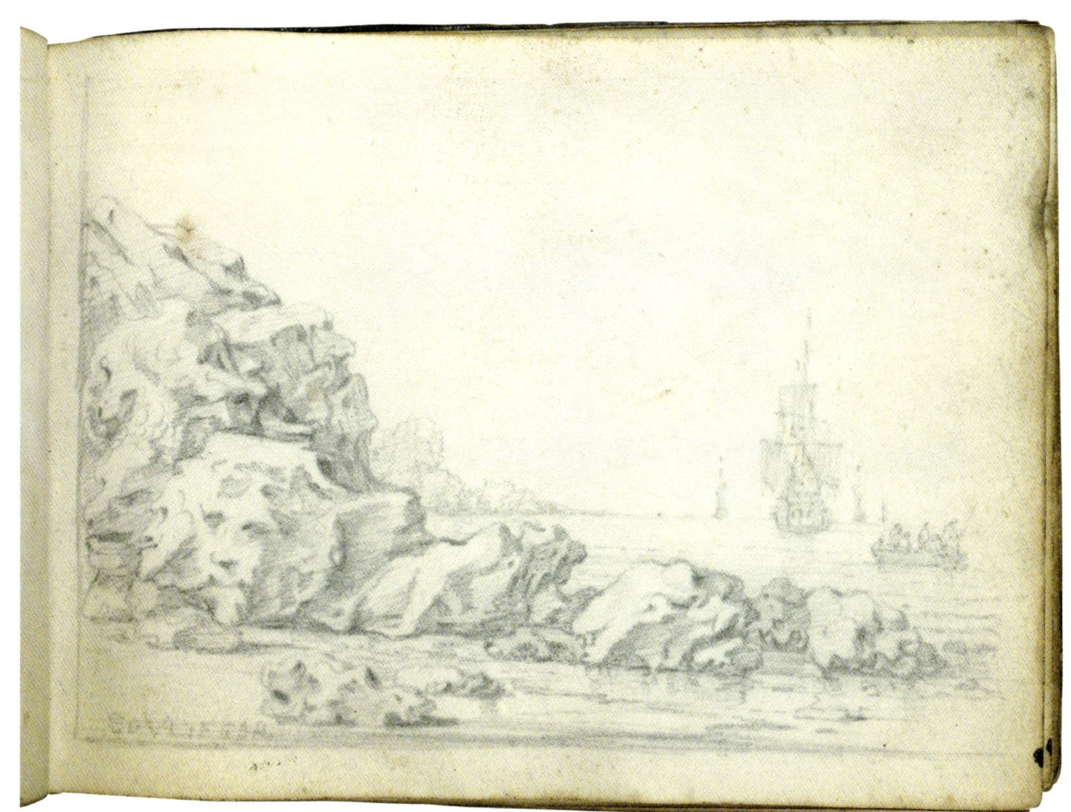

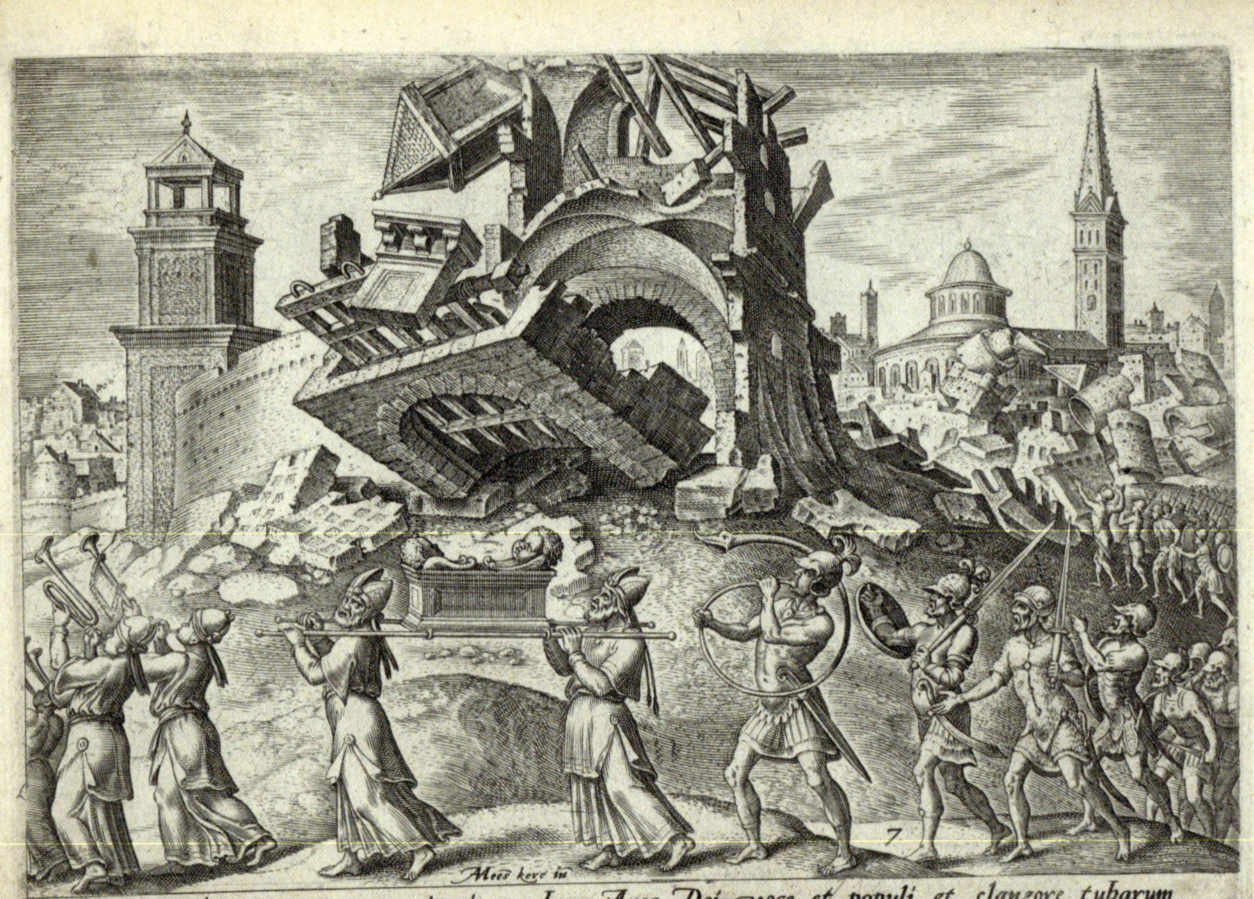


*Corruit Hiericho totam cum circuit vrbem Arca Dei, voce et populi, et clangore tubarum*

Fig. 13 Philips Galle, after Maarten van Heemskerck, *The Destruction of Jericho*, 1569. Engraving, 14.2 × 20.1 cm. Harvard Art Museums/Fogg Museum, The Kate, Maurice R. and Melvin R. Seiden Purchase Fund and Richard Norton Memorial Fund, M22176.



idolatry, or through violence arriving from outside, at the hands of enemy peoples or a wrathful God. Heemskerck's compositions are masterpieces of orderly disorder, with towers, temples, and statues toppling, cities burning, and victims fleeing, but all rendered expertly in single-point perspective and with an antiquarian's eye for past architectural forms.[25] Published in Antwerp in 1569, three years after Protestant iconoclasts submitted a huge proportion of the city's church art to violent destruction, the series must have had topical relevance, perhaps (again) preaching the virtues of peace and restraint during times of violence. But within the series' grim procession of disasters there appear several different forms of cultural survival.

The penultimate engravings picture in two steps Christ's coming into the world, completing the list of Jewish calamities as the New Testament completes the Old: the Adoration of the Shepherds, its ruinous setting signaling the end of the Jewish era, and the Adoration of the Magi, by contrast in a fabulous intact edifice, expressing through futuristic spiral architecture the advent of a new age. The final engraving confirms this familiar, still troubling successionist perspective, whereby Christ at once fulfills and annuls the exclusive Old Covenant, inaugurating a new era but condemning the unconverted Jews—uniquely among nations—to interminable disaster and ultimate damnation.

But an engraving from earlier in the series suggests a less triumphalist model of historical continuity. Heemskerck's *The Destruction of Jericho* (Fig. 13) features a spectacular, quasi-stop-action view of the city crumbling, but in the foreground two priests hurry the Ark of the Covenant to safety in some new homeland elsewhere. Whether miraculously rescued from ruin or captured, appropriated, and disfigured as "spoils of war," the past comes to us only in fragments. Like the sibyl's leaves, these fragments might never quite be gathered "by love" (Dante) into a single, beatific whole. Each era must instead improvise its own provisional friendship album of the past.

Joseph Leo Koerner is the Victor S. Thomas Professor of the History of Art and Architecture at Harvard University.

NOTES

1. "Even thus upon the wind in the light leaves / Were the soothsayings of the Sibyl lost." Dante Alighieri, *Paradiso*, trans. Henry Wadsworth Longfellow (Leipzig: Bernard Tauchnitz, 1867). Further translations of the text in this essay are also from this edition.
2. Virgil, *The Aeneid of Virgil*, trans. Theodore C. Williams (Boston: Houghton Mifflin, 1910). On the peculiarities of sibyllic communication, see Emily Gowers, "Virgil's Sibyl and the 'Many Mouths' Cliché," *Classical Quarterly* 55 (2005): 170–82, with bibliography.
3. Anthony Griffiths, "The Archaeology of the Print," in *Collecting Prints and Drawings in Europe, c. 1500–1750*, ed. Christopher Baker, Caroline Elam, and Genevieve Warwick (Aldershot, U.K., and Burlington, Vt.: Ashgate, in association with the *Burlington Magazine*, 2003), 9–11.
4. For more information on how drawings were housed and organized in eighteenth-century Dutch collections, see Michiel C. Plomp, *Hartstochtelijk Verzameld* (Paris: Fondation Custodia; Bussum: Thoth, 2001), esp. 72–91.
5. This is suggested by the numeration systems and inventories of early collectors, for example Valerius Röver (1686–1739).
6. Marjorie B. Cohn, *A Noble Collection: The Spencer Albums of Old Master Prints* (Cambridge, Mass.: Fogg Art Museum, 1992), 41.
7. Hans Rupprich, ed., *Dürer: Schriftlicher Nachlass*, vol. 1 (Berlin: Deutscher Verein für Kunstwissenschaft, 1956–69), 162.
8. Ibid., 148. On the early collecting of works by Dürer, see Jeffrey Chipps Smith, "The Early Collecting of Dürer's Prints," in *Prayer Nuts, Private Devotion, and Early Modern Art Collecting*, ed. Evelin Wetter and Frits Scholten (Riggisberg: Abegg-Stiftung, 2017), 141–55.
9. Dürer was also one of the first to archive other artists' drawings, such as those he procured from the Colmar workshop of the deceased Martin Schongauer (c. 1450–1491), where they would have functioned as a valuable stockpile of designs. These drawings entered, through Dürer, a novel kind of assemblage: Dürer's careful ingathering of his own drawings, unsold prints, woodblocks, engraved and etched plates, and literary and theoretical writings, together with collected works by the masters who formed him (Schongauer, for example) or communicated with him (such as Raphael). Intended for posterity, Dürer's *Nachlass* did not survive intact. Split between his wife and brother, with some material kept by his friend Willibald Pirckheimer, the curated residue soon dispersed. Subsequent artists followed this practice, and their studio contents often suffered the same fate when no clear artistic heir presented him or herself – most famously the Kantoor of Peter Paul Rubens. On the medium of paper as an invitation to artists "to keep other people's drawings," see Caroline O. Fowler, *The Art of Paper: From the Holy Land to the Americas* (New Haven, Conn.: Yale University Press, 2019), 83–85.
10. Nadine M. Orenstein, ed., *Pieter Bruegel the Elder: Drawings and Prints* (New York: Metropolitan Museum of Art; Rotterdam: Museum Boijmans van Beuningen, 2001), 121.
11. The number of prints contained in each series is the subject of debate. The traditional view is that there were fourteen prints in the first series and thirty in the second. However, on the basis of an inventory compiled by Cock's widow and early collections of the series, Alexandra Onuf has cautiously proposed the eighteen/twenty-six division. See Alexandra Onuf, *The "Small Landscape" Prints in Early Modern Netherlands* (London: Routledge, Taylor & Francis Group, 2018), 205–12.
12. Ibid., 62.
13. On Collaert's *Views*, see Stefaan Hautekeete, "De la ville à la campagne: L'image du Brabant dans les dessins topographiques du xvie siècle," in *Le peintre et l'arpenteur: Images de Bruxelles et de l'ancien duché de Brabant*, ed. Véronique van de Kerckhof et al. (Brussels: Royal Museums of Fine Arts of Belgium; Tournai: Dexia Banque, 2000), 47–56.
14. The album is meticulously described and analyzed in William W. Robinson, "The Abrams Album: An *Album Amicorum* of Dutch Drawings from the Seventeenth Century," *Master Drawings* 53 (Spring 2015): 3–58. See, most recently, Michael Zell, *Rembrandt, Vermeer, and the Gift in Seventeenth-Century Dutch Art* (Amsterdam: Amsterdam University Press, 2021), 193. For reproductions of the drawings in the album, see the object page on the Harvard Art Museums website, https://hvrd.art/o/294019.
15. Horst W. Jansen, "The 'Image Made by Chance' in Renaissance Thought," in *De Artibus opuscula XL: Essays in Honor of Erwin Panofsky*, vol. 1, ed. Millard Meiss (New York: New York University Press, 1961), 254–66; and Horst Bredekamp, *The Lure of Antiquity and the Cult of the Machine: The Kunstkammer and the Evolution of Nature, Art and Technology*, trans. Allison Brown (Princeton, N.J.: Markus Wiener Publishers, 1995), 13–14.
16. Robinson, "The Abrams Album," 16.
17. The term first appeared in 1714 in a French dictionary, though it originated in the Roman word for the blank wall on which public messages were posted; see Hans Bots, Giel van Gemert, and P. J. A. N. Rietbergen, *L'album amicorum de Cornelis de Glarges 1599–1683* (Amsterdam: Holland University Press, 1975), vii, ix; and Bronwen Wilson, "Social Networking: The 'Album amicorum' and Early Modern Public Making," in *Beyond the Public Sphere: Opinions, Publics, Spaces in Early Modern Europe*, ed. Massimo Rospocher (Bologna: Il Mulino, 2012), 205. On the *album amicorum* generally, see Robert Keil and Richard Keil, *Die Deutschen Stammbücher des sechzehnten bis neunzehnten Jahrhunderts* (Berlin: G. Grote, 1893); Max Rosenheim, "The Album Amicorum," *Archaeologia, or Miscellaneous Tracts Relating to Antiquity* 62 (1910): 251–308; and Kees Thomassen, *Alba amicorum: Vijf eeuwen vriendschap op papier gezet* (The Hague: G. Schwartz/SDU Uitgeverij/Rijksmuseum Meermanno-Westreenianum/Museum van het Boek, 's-Gravenhage, 1990). On friendship albums with drawings, see (with up-to-date bibliography) Giovanna Sapori, "L'*album amicorum* come libro di disegni: Alcuni esempi tra Cinquecento e Seicento (Venius, Ortelius, Abrams, Heyblocq)," in *Libri e album di disegni 1550–1800: Nuove prospettive metodologiche e di esegesi storico-critica*, ed. Vita Segreto (Rome: De Luca, 2018), 99–110.
18. Wilson, "Social Networking," 207
19. Jean Puraye, ed., *Amicorum Abraham Ortelius*, 2 vols. (Antwerp: Brill, 1967–68). The earliest dated entry (fol. 6r) is from January 1574.

20. J. A. Gruys and Kees Thomassen, eds., *The Album Amicorum of Jacob Heyblocq* (Zwolle: Waanders, 1998), 248–49.
21. Aristotle, *Nicomachean Ethics*, trans. Terence Irwin (Indianapolis: Hackett Publishing Company, 1985), 8.1155a23.
22. On the objects "*sort of* answering back," see Miguel Tamen, *Friends of Interpretable Objects* (Cambridge, Mass.: Harvard University Press, 2001), 2 and passim.
23. Sapori, "*L'album amicorum*," 110.
24. Catherine Levesque, *Journey through Landscape in Seventeenth-Century Holland: The Haarlem Print Series and Dutch Identity* (University Park: Pennsylvania State University Press, 1994), 41.
25. On the antiquarian nature of the series, see Dagmar Eichberger, "Framing Warfare and Destruction in Sixteenth-Century Netherlandish Prints: The *Clades Judaeae Gentis* Series by Maarten van Heemskerck," in *Disaster, Death, and the Emotions in the Shadow of the Apocalypse, 1400–1700*, ed. Jennifer Spinks and Charles Zika (London: Palgrave Macmillan, 2016), 236.

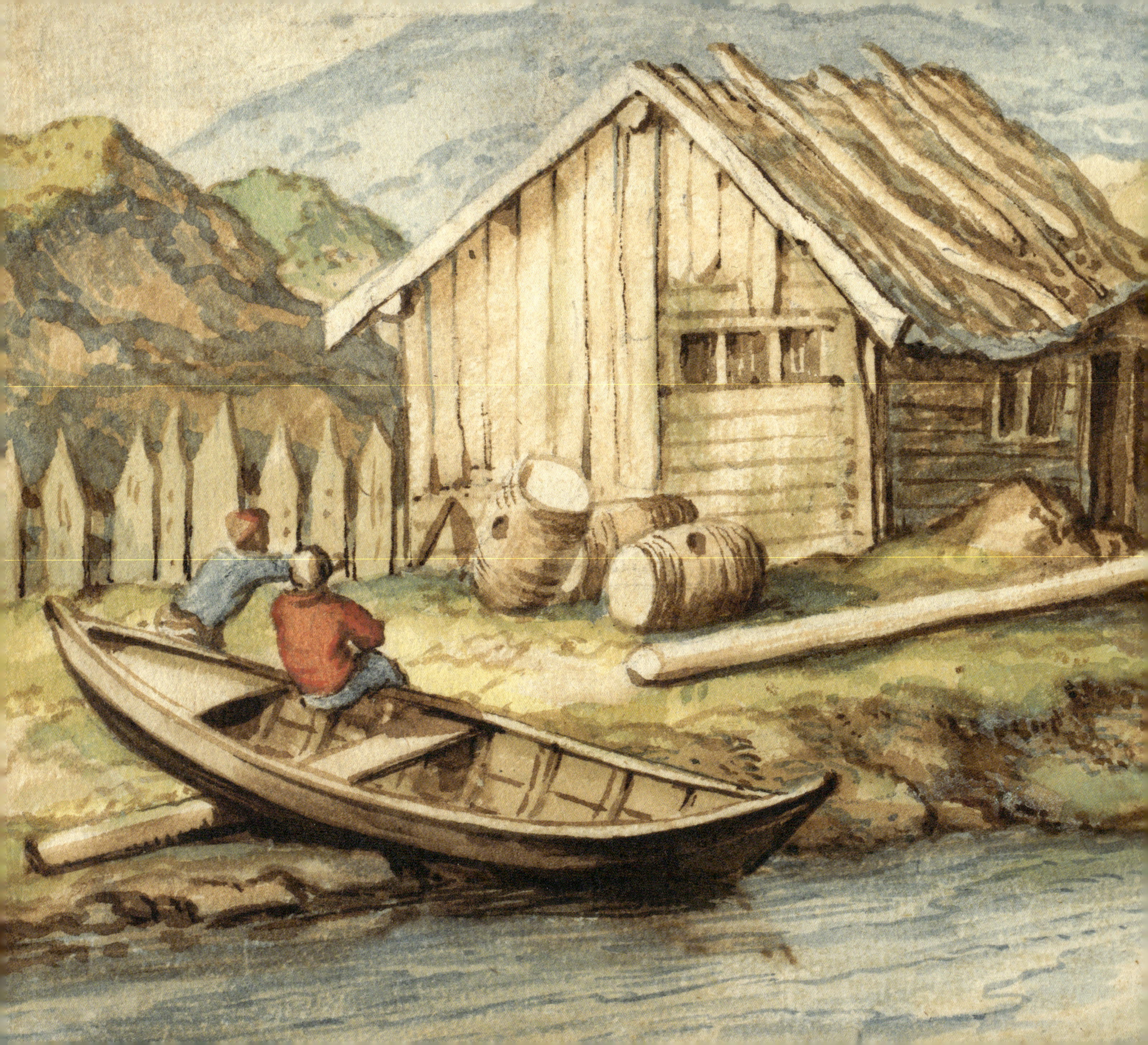

## Allart van Everdingen
## *A Scandinavian Landscape*, 1660s

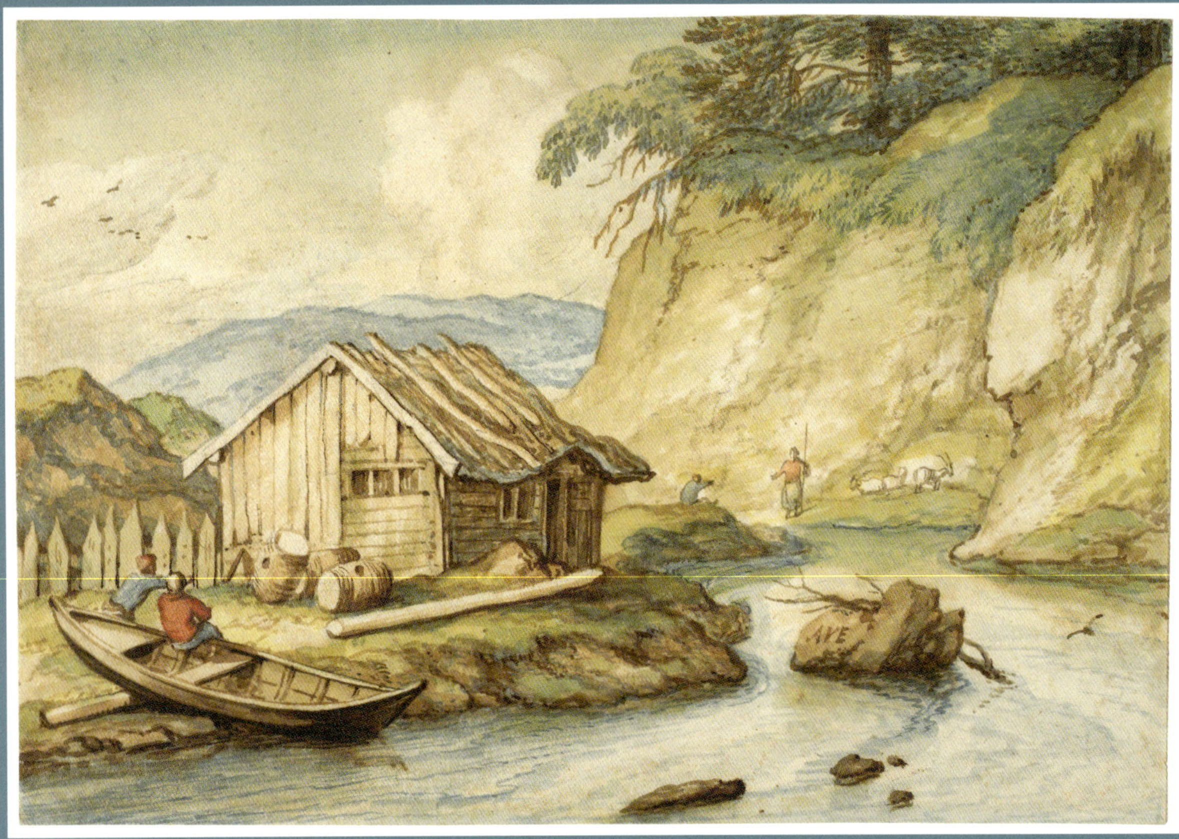


Fig. S Allart van Everdingen, *A Scandinavian Landscape,* 1660s. See p. 229 for full information.

With a striking combination of transparent watercolor and fluidly applied brown ink, Allart van Everdingen (1621–1675) captured the intricate details of a modest wooden structure, river embankments, and foliage against the atmospheric perspective of a far-off mountain view. A finished drawing complete with the artist's monogram on the rock at right, this sheet is undoubtedly a studio work based on sketches made years earlier, during his travels to Norway and Sweden in 1644. The drawing features scenery that, for Dutch viewers, would have been recognizably foreign but at the same time familiar in its focus on quotidian life centered around a rustic dwelling.

After returning from his travels, Everdingen spent time in Haarlem from 1645 to 1652 before settling in Amsterdam, where he made this sheet in the 1660s as part of a group of sixteen watercolors of similar dimensions depicting either Nordic or Dutch views. During his lifetime, Dutch artists traveling to Italy – or those otherwise inspired by representations of the Italian *campagna* and its characteristic light – dominated cross-cultural networks in the development of landscape. Everdingen's application of the Dutch visual vocabulary to Nordic views speaks further to these currents of artistic exchange.

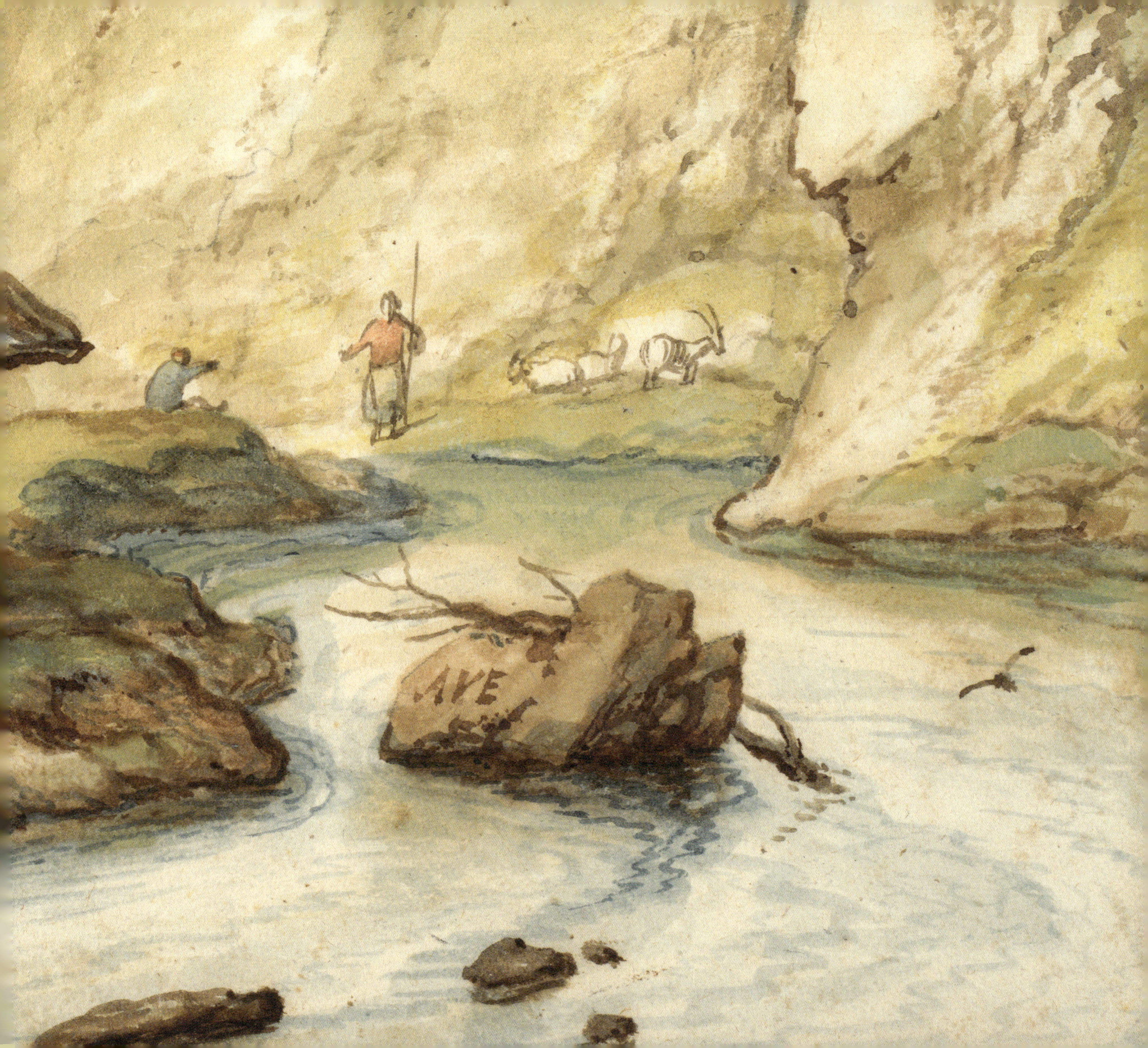
AVE

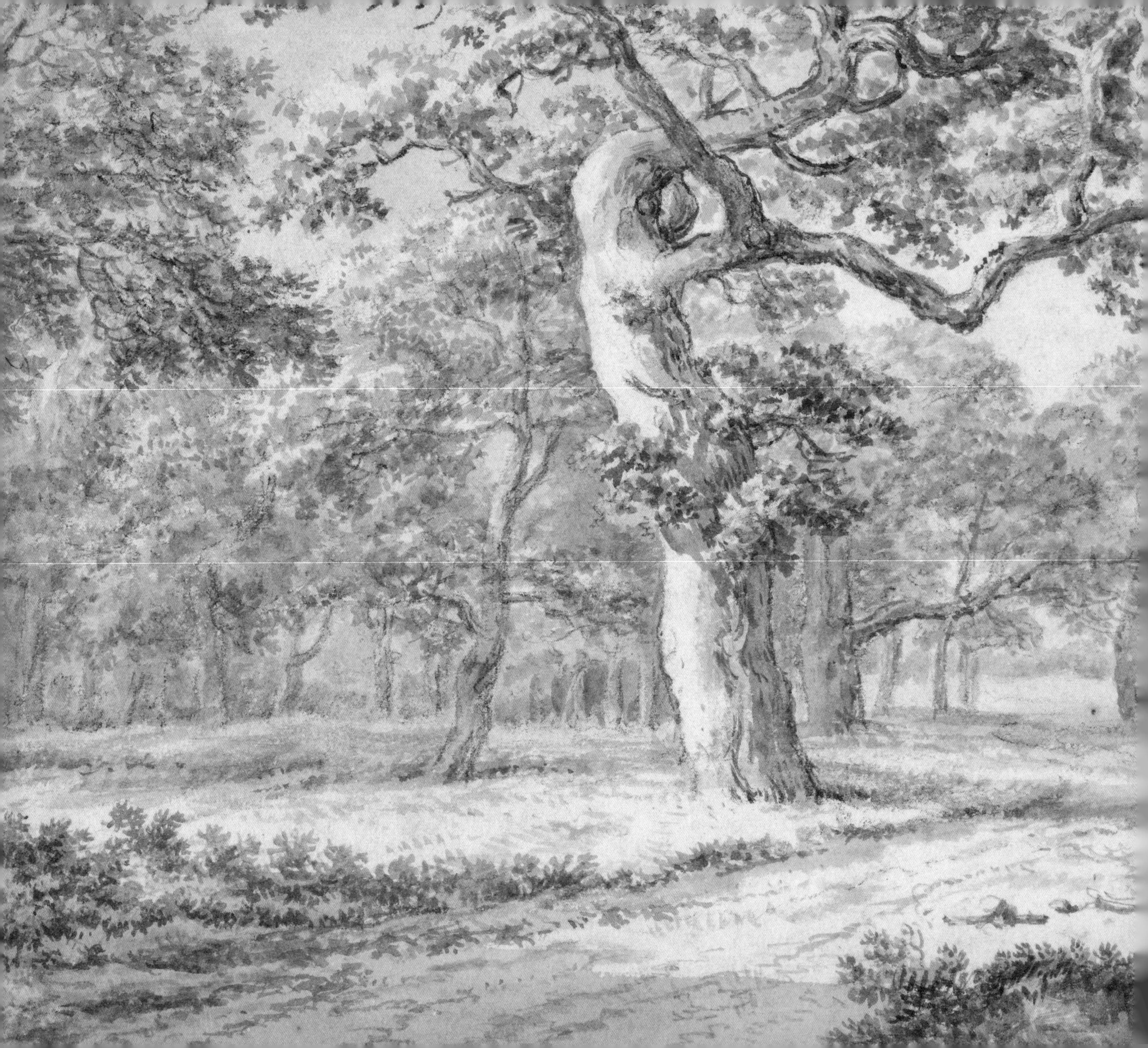

Jacob van Ruisdael

*Two Large Oaks and Two Deer at the Edge of a Wood*, c. 1670

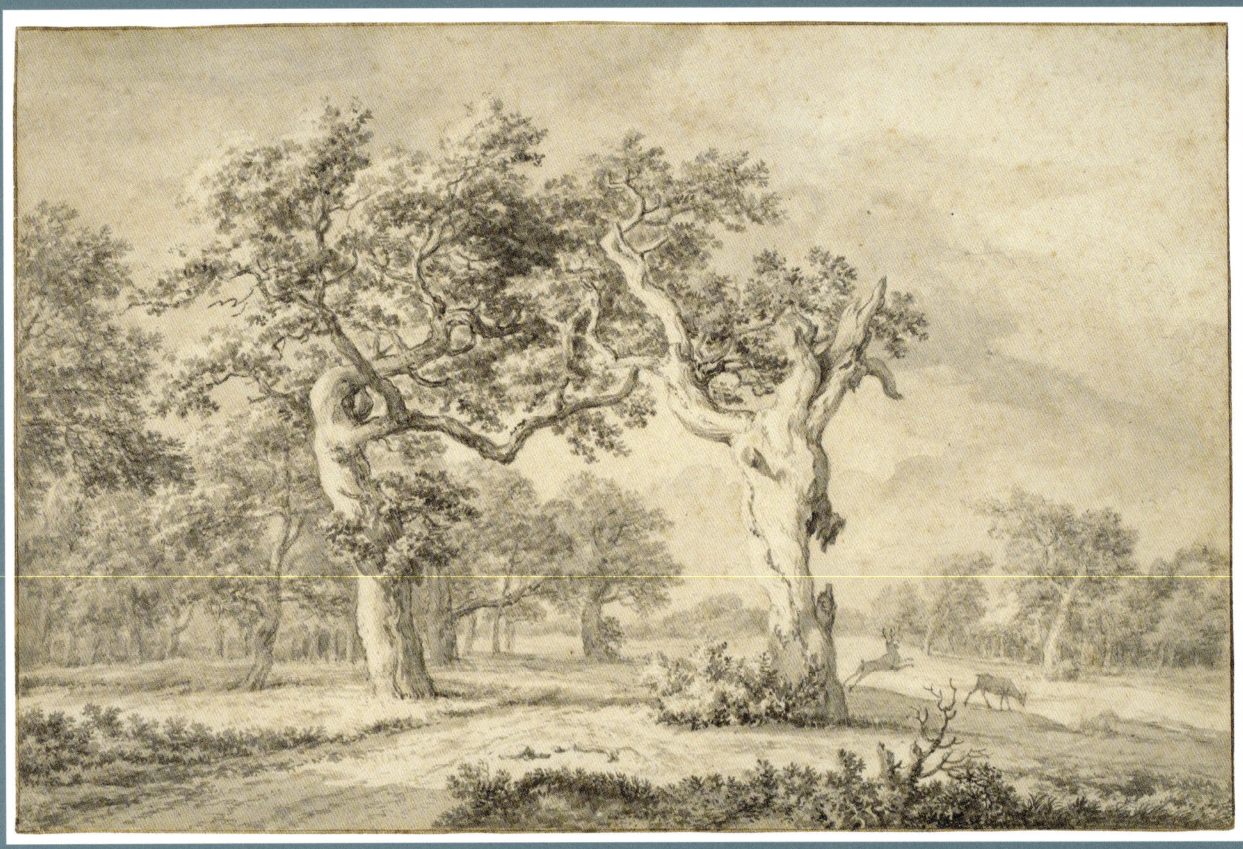

Fig. T Jacob van Ruisdael, *Two Large Oaks and Two Deer at the Edge of a Wood*, c. 1670. See p. 232 for full information.

Suggestive of the interaction between humanity and nature, two gnarled oaks, large in scale, dominate the center of this sheet as they form an arch over a path that is absent of figures. Active primarily in Haarlem and Amsterdam, Jacob van Ruisdael (1628/29–1682), preeminent landscapist of the seventeenth century in paintings, drawings, and prints, created this composition in black chalk and gray wash as an extremely fine, polished, and detailed example of his finished approach to drawn landscape. An early owner of this sheet, the well-known eighteenth-century collector Sybrand Feitama (1694–1758), recorded in his inventory that the drawing entered his family's collection around 1690, identifying the location as *'t Haagsche Bosch* (The Hague Woods), a forest preserved close to the city. Though the location cannot securely be identified today, that it was thought to be such so close to the drawing's creation implies that the claim is highly probable. It also leads one to wonder how many other localities depicted in landscapes, now appearing more generalized to us, were once appreciated for their easily recognized place or evocation thereof—in this case, a naturally occurring forest controlled by man.

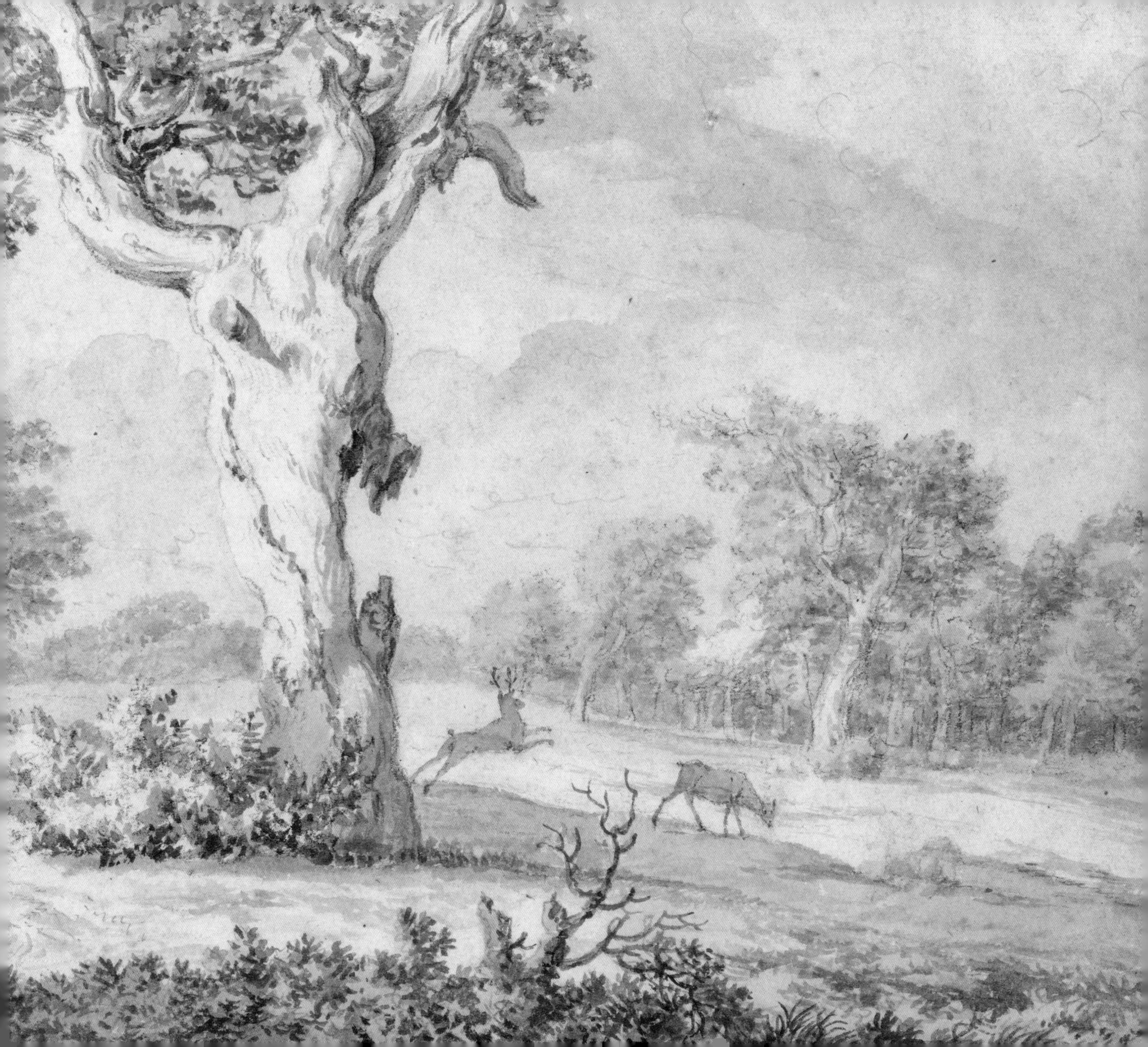

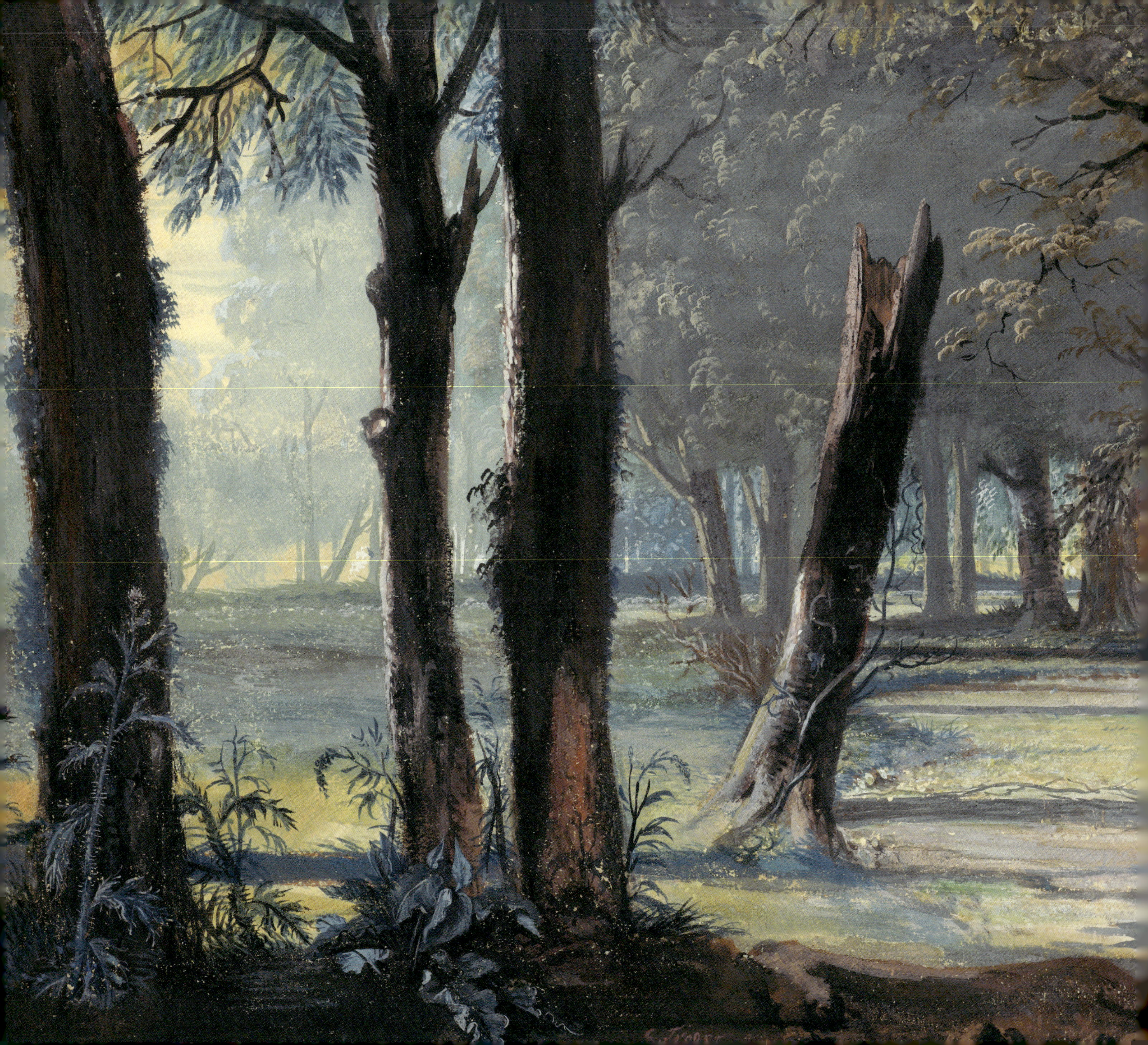

Cornelis Troost

*A Park Scene*, 1740s

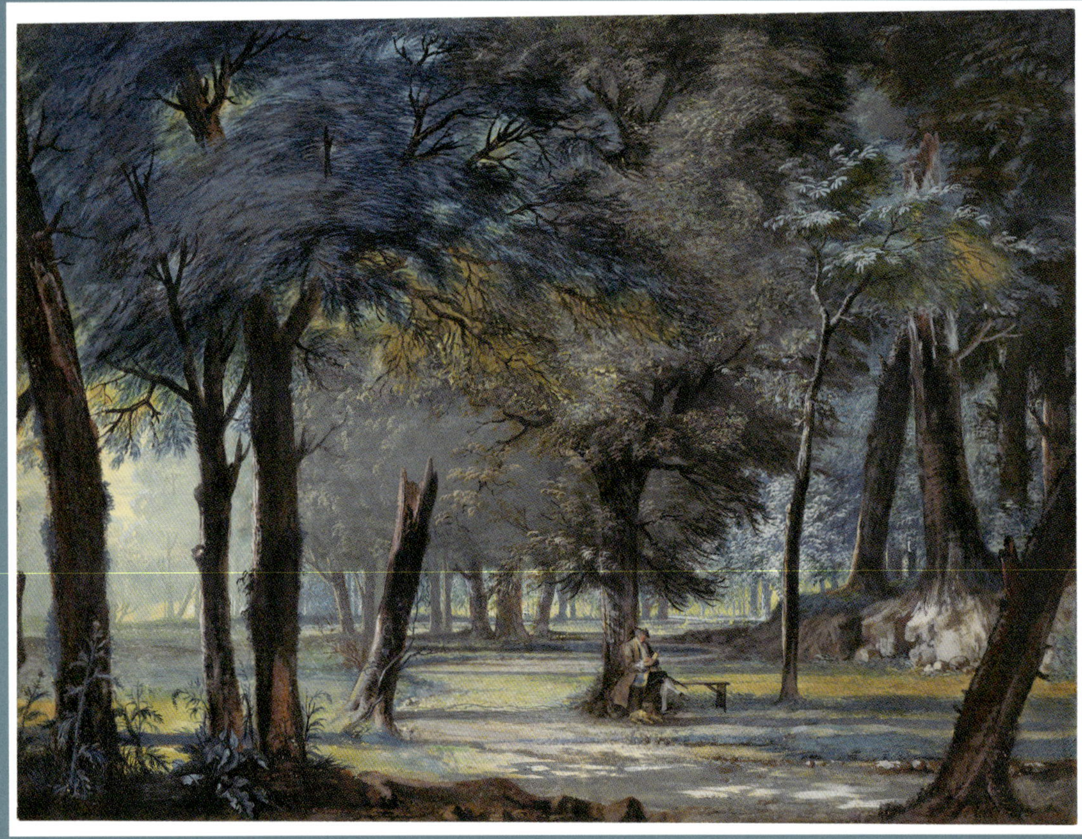

Fig. U Cornelis Troost, *A Park Scene,* 1740s. See p. 232 for full information.

In this eighteenth-century drawing, hazy sunshine filters through towering trees to touch a seated man reading, alone save his dog on a forested path. The bench on which he sits suggests a park as his surroundings, a place for urban respite that gained popularity in the period. Garden design could feature tightly groomed elements, but could also preserve or recall natural settings like the one seen here.

Trained as an actor, Cornelis Troost (1696–1750) became Amsterdam's premier figural artist, known mostly for his depictions of theatrical subjects in a manner not unlike his British contemporary William Hogarth (1697–1764). Unlike his representations of outdoor theatrical scenes, in which park settings serve as backdrops, here Troost embraces landscape by emphasizing the towering trees, some fallen, in reference to earlier conventions. Following Dutch draftsmen of the late seventeenth century who revived opaque watercolor as a landscape medium, Troost applies it to this sheet in a feathery approach similar to his pastels; with a palette of yellows and blues, he depicts the layers of branches and boughs as dappled light plays across their leaves. Also a nod to the past, the seated man recalls the long visual tradition of lone figures situated in a landscape, presumably evoking the form of leisure that Karel van Mander (1548–1606) encouraged artists to undertake at the dawn of the seventeenth century.

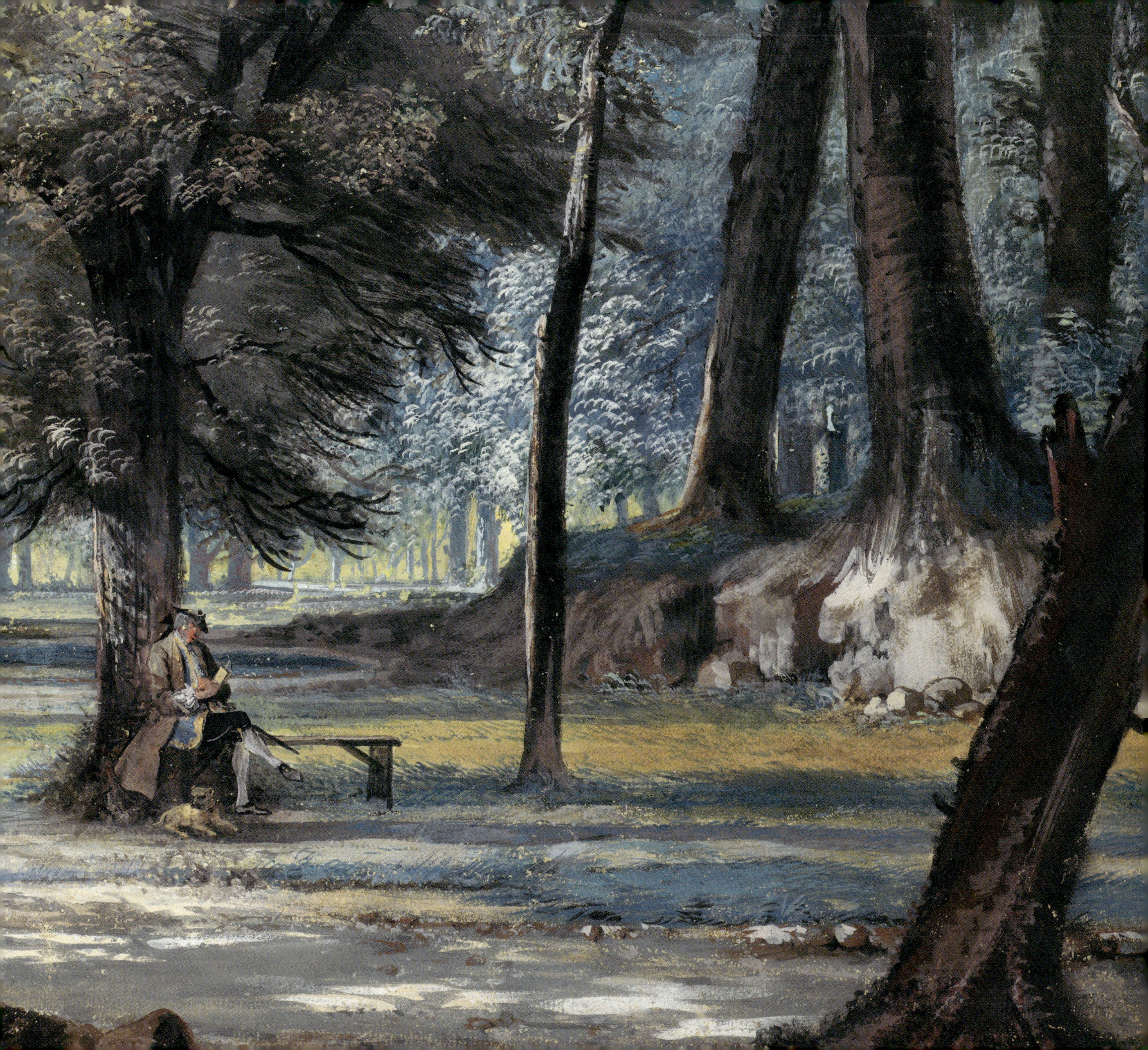

# AFTERWORD

*George S. Abrams*



In the early 1960s, Maida and I were fortunate to spend some time with Paul Sachs. By then, he was well known among art scholars and collectors for his many years as deputy director of the Fogg Art Museum and professor of fine arts at Harvard – and he was also an extraordinary collector in his own right. Those who knew him, particularly those who launched their careers through his widely popular Museum Course, appreciated him for his passion for art, his empathetic and personal interest in those who came into his orbit, and his ability to keenly observe and discuss all aspects of drawings.

I remember very well the Saturday morning when Professor Sachs first visited our home to view the drawings in the collection we were forming. He first took in the framed works on display, making helpful comments – some supportive, some less appreciative. Then we went through solander boxes of drawings rotated off view. He shared some of his collecting stories and gave us tips on where to find good sources of drawings. Toward the end, he said, "I can see you're People Collectors." People Collectors, we wondered? Sachs went on: "I have found that people who love and collect drawings often tend to fall into two broad groups – those who like drawings depicting people and their lives, and those who like drawings depicting landscapes and the distant world around them. And you are clearly People Collectors."

We were a bit taken aback. We'd never thought about our collection in that way, but once he said it, we knew he was right. We had a preponderance of figure studies, studies of heads, genre scenes, and topics from history, but only a few landscapes. We set out to rectify the situation. What serious collector wants such an imbalance?

By then we were concentrating almost solely on Dutch drawings. As with the rest of our collection, Maida and I taught ourselves about landscape draftsmen primarily by reading numerous books, looking at drawings in print rooms across Europe, and developing relationships with scholars, other collectors, and members of the trade. Rembrandt's landscapes captivated us, of course, but in the early days we dismissed the idea of ever being able to afford one. Jan van Goyen, among others, had a wonderfully distinctive style, and we found we could trace his development in landscape drawings from his early to middle period to his wonderful late group of drawings made in the 1650s. We became interested in his contemporaries,

Pieter de Molijn and Allart van Everdingen among them. And we thought in terms of the influence of the greatest sixteenth-century Netherlandish artists, Pieter Bruegel the Elder and a few of the next generation, such as Hans Bol and Paul Bril. However, the highly innovative landscape practitioners in early seventeenth-century Netherlands stirred us most: Jan and Esaias van de Velde, Hendrick Avercamp, Claes Jansz. Visscher, and especially Cornelis Vroom.

Vroom's *Landscape with a Road and a Fence* (see p. 75) captured my imagination for its stunningly intricate technique and powerful, evocative composition, and remains to this day one of my favorite drawings ever acquired. It came up for auction in Munich in 1972, and I asked Boston-based drawings dealer Bob Light to bid for me with an agreed-upon limit. These were the days before cell phones and e-mail, and overseas calls were rarely made. I had to wait until Bob was back stateside to learn the results. I called anxiously several times on the day he was scheduled to return, finally reaching him in the afternoon. "What happened?" I asked with excitement and impatience. "You won't believe what happened," Bob said. The Vroom had gone for an astronomical sum, almost three times my top bid. "Who is the crazy person who paid that much money?" I asked incredulously. "You were," came the reply. I had always known Bob was a good dealer, but then I realized he had become a great dealer. He was right to push my limits, and I have never regretted it.

When a selection of eight of Chatsworth's finest Rembrandt landscapes came up for sale in 1984, we realized our dream of owning one. That sale was a turning point for the relatively quiet Old Master drawings world: Christie's was swarming with press and people wanting to watch in person, and TV cameras were present inside and outside the auction house. We had to push our way through the crowds blocking the entrance and eventually made our way into the main auction room and found our seats. There were two other full auxiliary rooms, and throughout the auction there was substantial bidding from all three spaces – no telephone bidding back then. Fortunately, the work we wanted most, *A Farm on the Amsteldijk(?)* (p. 124), was positioned toward the end of the sale and next to last in the group of eight Rembrandts. We hoped that many of the top bidders, including Ian Woodner, Gene Thaw, John Gaines, the Getty, and other major museums, would have already exhausted their resources by the time the drawing came up, and that is exactly what happened. Not that it came cheap, of course! But we couldn't let it go; we loved Rembrandt's masterful shorthand in details such as the cow and the small wake running behind the swimming duck—and when the hammer came down, surprisingly, it was ours.

And then, even though we didn't think so at the time, our luck continued in a strange way. Our drawing was blocked from export by the British license review board three times over the next year and a half. Originally, twenty-seven Chatsworth drawings were denied export licenses by the review board. By the time of the final decision, they had released all but three of the Rembrandt landscapes, including ours. Not only did this give us time to put together the money to pay for it, but the dollar had substantially improved against the pound in the interim. Then one morning I received a call from John Rowlands, keeper of prints and drawings at the British Museum, who told me that the board had finally granted a license for my drawing, preventing the export of only one Rembrandt landscape (bought by the Getty Museum). I asked him if I could pick up the license and drawing the next day and bring it home, and he said that was possible. I quickly made a reservation to fly from Boston to London that night. And indeed, I brought the drawing back from London two days later. Maida and I didn't want to take the chance the board would somehow change its mind.

But sometimes good fortune smiles without such expense or complex delays. In 1992, I purchased an anonymous sixteenth-century landscape drawing on blue paper. It captivated me with its beautifully drawn trees that recede into a broad panorama, executed in the three tones of the blue paper, brown ink, and white opaque watercolor. Acquiring the drawing was difficult, with a second claimant in the picture, and I was a little unsettled by having to spend much more than I believed a drawing by an unidentified artist should cost. Actually, I was a little angry at myself for being unable to resist it. So I put it in a solander box and tried to forget about my inability to control myself. Some months later, during one of his visits to the house, Bill Robinson pulled the drawing out and asked me about it. I made some kind of grumpy and noncommittal answer. But he had something on his mind and asked if he could take it to the Fogg to have a photograph made, to then send to Hans Mielke, the eminent German art historian and drawings scholar. Mielke called Bill two weeks later and excitedly exclaimed that the drawing was by Pieter Bruegel the Elder, "perhaps his very best landscape!" (p. 24, Fig. A). As Mielke was very ill with cancer, he made a request to see the original drawing as soon as possible, and Bill and I flew to Berlin with it a week later to show him. Mielke was in a Berlin hospital and allowed only one visitor at a time; Bill took the drawing in to him first, and I went in second. He was very moved by the drawing. Unfortunately, he passed away shortly thereafter, but surprisingly he had been able to find enough time to include it in his posthumously published catalogue raisonné of Bruegel's drawings.

Every one of my drawings has a story, and I can describe only a few of my favorite landscapes here. Even though my heart is still with drawings of people, I have come to embrace the nuances of landscape as I have acquired these sheets over the years. When I look at our landscapes on the whole, I am pleased to see such high quality paired with significant breadth and depth over the long seventeenth century. I am particularly proud of our holdings by the early landscape draftsmen who flourished between 1600 and 1630, a fascination of ours, as I am of the group by Rembrandt, his students, and contemporaries, which we set out to collect with purpose and intent. Who would have thought that Paul Sachs's first visit to our home almost sixty years ago would have triggered our careful accumulation of Dutch landscape drawings? Harvard certainly owes him a debt for his foundational enthusiasm and tremendous bequest of his own phenomenal drawings, which successive curators and directors have built upon to maintain Harvard's status as a premier destination for drawings study in the United States. This splendid exhibition and catalogue are just the latest manifestation of that continuum, for which I am grateful. In addition to her support of this project, particularly striking to me at this time is director Martha Tedeschi's commitment to drawings as a central part of the Harvard Art Museums' efforts to teach, show, and entice the next generation and beyond of students, scholars, collectors, and dealers – or indeed, anyone captured by the magic of these works.

## DRAWINGS

**Hendrick Avercamp**
**(Amsterdam 1585–1634 Kampen)**

*Landscape with a Bridge and Tower*, c. 1615–20
Brown ink and watercolor over graphite on off-white antique laid paper
13.5 × 21.6 cm
Maida and George Abrams Collection, Boston, Long-term loan to the Harvard Art Museums, 1.2018.203
Illustrated p. 143

*Landscape with a Fisherman*, 1620s
Brown ink and watercolor over graphite on off-white antique laid paper, framing lines in brown and black ink
19.3 × 29.2 cm
Maida and George Abrams Collection, Boston, Long-term loan to the Harvard Art Museums, 1.2018.202
Illustrated p. 78

*A Winter Landscape*, late 1620s
Brown and black ink, transparent and opaque watercolor, and gray wash over graphite on two sheets of antique laid paper, partial framing line in graphite, mounted overall
18.2 × 28.7 cm
The Maida and George Abrams Collection, Fogg Art Museum, Harvard University, Cambridge, Massachusetts, Gift of George Abrams in appreciation of Charles J. Egan, Jr., Harvard Class of 1954, 2014.409
Illustrated p. 112

**Gerrit Battem**
**(Rotterdam 1636–1684 Rotterdam)**

*Landscape with Hunters*, c. 1665–84
Opaque watercolor with touches of transparent watercolor on off-white antique laid paper, framing line in brown ink
22.4 × 36.7 cm
Maida and George Abrams Collection, Boston, Long-term loan to the Harvard Art Museums, 1.2018.207
Illustrated p. 81

**Jan de Bisschop**
**(Amsterdam 1628–1671 The Hague)**

*Houses and a Well near Koudekerk*, 1650–55
Brown ink, brown and gray wash, and black chalk on off-white antique laid paper, framing line in black ink
9.5 × 15.8 cm
The Maida and George Abrams Collection, Fogg Art Museum, Harvard University, Cambridge, Massachusetts, 1999.129
Illustrated p. 156

**Abraham Bloemaert**
**(Gorinchem 1566–1651 Utrecht)**

*A Dilapidated Farmhouse*; verso: *Walls of a Farmhouse*, c. 1595–1605
Brown ink, brown and gray wash, pink and green transparent watercolor, and white opaque watercolor over black chalk on off-white antique laid paper, framing line in brown ink
16.1 × 21.4 cm
The Maida and George Abrams Collection, Fogg Art Museum, Harvard University, Cambridge, Massachusetts, 1999.130
Illustrated p. 128

*Study of a Tree*, c. 1644–46
Gray wash with black chalk and graphite, green and rose transparent watercolor, scraping, and traces of white opaque watercolor on off-white antique laid paper, toned with brown wash, framing lines in graphite and gray wash
16.3 × 26.9 cm
Harvard Art Museums/Fogg Museum, Friends of the Fogg Art Museum Fund, 1957.100
Illustrated p. 170

**Hans Bol**
**(Mechelen 1534–1593 Amsterdam)**

*The Outskirts of a Village with Peasants*, 1589
Opaque and transparent watercolor over traces of black chalk and graphite on antique laid paper mounted overall to wood panel, framing lines in shell gold and dark-red opaque watercolor
11.1 × 15 cm
Harvard Art Museums/Fogg Museum, The Kate, Maurice R. and Melvin R. Seiden Special Purchase Fund in honor of Virginia Deknatel and in memory of Lucy Rowland, Paul J. Sachs Memorial Fund, Marian H. Phinney Fund, Agnes Mongan Purchase Fund, Drawing Department Acquisition Fund, and Drawing Department Discretionary Fund, and through the generosity of an anonymous donor, David Giles Carter, the DBH Foundation, and the B. Walter and Geraldine E. Sterenfeld Foundation, 2001.54
Illustrated p. 38

*Abraham and the Angels*, 1589
Opaque and transparent watercolor over traces of black chalk on antique laid paper mounted overall to wood panel, traces of framing lines in shell gold and dark-red opaque watercolor
11.2 × 15.3 cm
Harvard Art Museums/Fogg Museum, The Kate, Maurice R. and Melvin R. Seiden Special Purchase Fund in honor of Joseph Koerner and Margaret Koster, 2004.75
Illustrated p. 38

*Landscape with a Road near a Pond*, 1590
Brown ink and gray wash over traces of black chalk on off-white antique laid paper, framing line in brown ink
14.6 × 21.1 cm
The Maida and George Abrams Collection, Fogg Art Museum, Harvard University, Cambridge, Massachusetts, Promised gift, 1.2018.29
Illustrated p. 168

**Follower of Hans Bol**
**(Mechelen 1534–1593 Amsterdam)**

*View of Over Muelen*, c. 1575–80
Mounted to a page of an album containing 8 drawings and 97 prints in a plain vellum binding, 16th–17th century
Brown ink and gray, rose, and yellow wash over black chalk, incised, on off-white antique laid paper, inside framing line in black chalk (at top, right, and partially at bottom), outside framing line in brown ink (at top, right, and bottom)
14.5 × 21.5 cm
Harvard Art Museums/Fogg Museum, The Kate,

Maurice R. and Melvin R. Seiden Purchase Fund and Richard Norton Memorial Fund, 1993.170
Illustrated p. 200

**Bartholomeus Breenbergh**
**(Deventer 1598–1657 Amsterdam)**

*Ruins in a Landscape*, 1620s
Brown ink and brown and gray wash on off-white antique laid paper, framing line in brown ink
26.1 × 38.8 cm
Maida and George Abrams Collection, Boston, Long-term loan to the Harvard Art Museums, 2.2020.3
Illustrated p. 125

**Paul Bril**
**(Antwerp or Breda 1553/54–1626 Rome)**

*Wooded Landscape with Travelers*, 1600
Brown ink and brown and gray wash over black chalk on off-white antique laid paper, framing lines in black ink over black chalk
18.2 × 27.3 cm
The Maida and George Abrams Collection, Fogg Art Museum, Harvard University, Cambridge, Massachusetts, Promised gift, 1.2018.216
Illustrated p. 32

**Pieter Bruegel the Elder**
**(Breda[?] 1526/30–1569 Brussels)**

*Wooded Landscape with a Distant View toward the Sea*, 1554
Brown ink, brown wash, and white opaque watercolor over black chalk on blue antique laid paper
26 × 34.4 cm
The Maida and George Abrams Collection, Fogg Art Museum, Harvard University, Cambridge, Massachusetts, 1999.132
Illustrated p. 24

**Aelbert Cuyp**
**(Dordrecht 1620–1691 Dordrecht)**

*View of a Ploughed Field*, c. 1639–42
Watercolor, black chalk, and a modified gum arabic on off-white antique laid paper, framing line in brown ink
16.2 × 25.1 cm
Maida and George Abrams Collection, Boston, Long-term loan to the Harvard Art Museums, 1.2018.222
Illustrated p. 172

*View of Rhenen*, c. 1642–46
Black chalk, brown and gray wash, green transparent watercolor, white opaque watercolor, and touches of gum arabic on off-white antique laid paper
17.8 × 49.8 cm
Harvard Art Museums/Fogg Museum, Gift of John S. Newberry, Jr., given in honor of Paul J. Sachs's 70th birthday, 1949.33
Illustrated p. 116

**Dirk Dalens III**
**(Amsterdam 1688–1753 Amsterdam)**

*Landscape with Rustic Scene*, c. 1725–35
Opaque watercolor with gum arabic on off-white antique laid paper, framing line in black ink and shell gold
38.1 × 28.5 cm
The Maida and George Abrams Collection, Fogg Art Museum, Harvard University, Cambridge, Massachusetts, Promised gift, 1.2018.48
Illustrated p. 101

**Lambert Doomer**
**(Amsterdam 1624–1700 Amsterdam)**

*Cottage with a Bleaching Yard*, 1660s
Brown ink, brown wash, and gray wash mixed with white opaque watercolor over graphite on off-white antique laid paper, framing line in brown ink
22.7 × 36.1 cm
Harvard Art Museums/Fogg Museum, Bequest of Frances L. Hofer, 1979.51
Illustrated p. 190

*View of Rouen with Mont Sainte-Catherine*, early 1670s
Brown ink, brown and gray wash, green transparent watercolor, and touches of white chalk on the sheet of an account book, framing line in black ink and partial framing line in brown ink (at bottom)
24 × 41.3 cm
The Maida and George Abrams Collection, Fogg Art Museum, Harvard University, Cambridge, Massachusetts, Gift of George Abrams in memory of Edward M. Kennedy, Harvard Class of 1954, 2011.516
Illustrated p. 88

**Allart van Everdingen**
**(Alkmaar 1621–1675 Amsterdam)**

*A Scandinavian Landscape*, 1660s
Transparent watercolor and brown ink over graphite on off-white antique laid paper, remnants of a framing line in brown ink
15.3 × 22.4 cm
The Maida and George Abrams Collection, Fogg Art Museum, Harvard University, Cambridge, Massachusetts, 1999.139
Illustrated p. 214

**Abraham Furnerius**
**(Rotterdam 1628–1654 Rotterdam)**

*Landscape with Farmhouses*, c. 1650–54
Brown ink and brown wash with white opaque watercolor over black chalk on off-white antique laid paper, partial framing line in brown ink
17.8 × 26.9 cm
Maida and George Abrams Collection, Boston, Long-term loan to the Harvard Art Museums, 1.2018.237
Illustrated p. 134

**Jan van Goyen**
**(Leiden 1596–1656 The Hague)**

*Landscape with the Hospital for Lepers outside Haarlem*, c. 1628–30
Brown ink on off-white antique laid paper, framing lines in brown ink
10.7 × 18.3 cm
Maida and George Abrams Collection, Boston, Long-term loan to the Harvard Art Museums, 1.2018.248
Illustrated p. 44

*Landscape with Cottages and Figures*, c. 1650
Black chalk and gray wash on off-white antique laid paper
9.7 × 15.8 cm
Harvard Art Museums/Fogg Museum, Bequest of Marian H. Phinney, 1962.40
Illustrated p. 43

*On the Seashore*, 1652
Black chalk and gray wash on off-white antique laid paper, framing line in black chalk
14.3 × 21.7 cm
Harvard Art Museums/Fogg Museum, Bequest of Meta and Paul J. Sachs, 1965.204
Illustrated p. 49

*Landscape with Skaters*, 1653
Black chalk and gray wash on off-white antique laid paper, framing lines in black chalk
20.5 × 30.1 cm
Maida and George Abrams Collection, Boston, Long-term loan to the Harvard Art Museums, 1.2018.250
Illustrated p. 160



**Joris van der Haagen (Arnhem or Dordrecht 1615–1669 The Hague)**

*Forest Landscape*, c. 1640–60
Black chalk and gray wash on off-white antique laid paper, framing lines in brown ink and black chalk
19.3 × 30.7 cm
The Maida and George Abrams Collection, Fogg Art Museum, Harvard University, Cambridge, Massachusetts, 1999.147
Illustrated p. 175

**Valentijn Klotz (Maastricht c. 1650–1721 The Hague)**

*View of the Katelijnepoort in Mechelen*, 1674
Brown ink and gray wash over black chalk on off-white antique laid paper, framing line in brown ink, mounted overall
15.2 × 20 cm
Harvard Art Museums/Fogg Museum, Purchase through the generosity of an anonymous donor in honor of Robert M. Light, 1997.202
Illustrated p. 94

**Jacob Koninck (Amsterdam c. 1614/15–by 1666 Amsterdam)**

*Farmhouse with a Tall Haystack*, 1650s–60s
Brown ink and brown wash with scraping over black chalk with a touch of gray wash on off-white antique laid paper
15.4 × 18.3 cm
Maida and George Abrams Collection, Boston, Long-term loan to the Harvard Art Museums, 1.2018.258
Illustrated p. 132

**Jan Lievens (Leiden 1607–1674 Amsterdam)**

*Cottage among Trees*, 1650s–60s
Brown ink on toned Asian paper, mounted overall to a sheet of off-white antique laid paper, framing line in dark-black ink
22.3 × 37 cm
The Maida and George Abrams Collection, Fogg Art Museum, Harvard University, Cambridge, Massachusetts, Promised gift, 1.2018.101
Illustrated p. 135

*Forest Landscape with a Pond*, c. 1650–70
Brown ink, brown wash, black chalk, and later touches of white chalk on light-tan antique laid paper prepared with light-tan wash, partial framing line in black chalk (at upper edge)
22 × 35.6 cm
The Maida and George Abrams Collection, Fogg Art Museum, Harvard University, Cambridge, Massachusetts, Gift of George Abrams in memory of Professor Seymour Slive, 2014.410
Illustrated p. 186

*Forest Interior with Draftsman*, 1664–65
Brown ink over traces of black chalk on off-white antique laid paper, framing line in dark-brown ink
24 × 36.2 cm
Maida and George Abrams Collection, Boston, Long-term loan to the Harvard Art Museums, 1.2018.260
Illustrated p. 42

*Landscape with a Distant View of Haarlem*, 1664–65
Brown ink over traces of black chalk on off-white antique laid paper, framing line in brown ink
23.3 × 35.7 cm
Maida and George Abrams Collection, Boston, Long-term loan to the Harvard Art Museums, 1.2018.261
Illustrated p. 48

**Nicolaes Maes (Dordrecht 1634–1693 Amsterdam)**

*View of Dordrecht*, 1653–60
Brown ink, brown wash, and touches of white opaque watercolor on light-tan antique laid paper
12.3 × 25.7 cm
Harvard Art Museums/Fogg Museum, Bequest of Frances L. Hofer, 1979.210
Illustrated p. 47

*The Valkhof, Nijmegen, in an Imaginary Landscape*, 1650s
Brown ink, brown and pale brown-gray wash, and touches of white opaque watercolor over traces of black chalk on off-white antique laid paper, framing line in brown ink
25.3 × 20.7 cm
The Maida and George Abrams Collection, Fogg Art Museum, Harvard University, Cambridge, Massachusetts, 2008.255
Illustrated p. 141

**Master of the Small Landscapes (active Southern Netherlands c. 1560)**

*Women Bleaching Linen near a Walled Town*, c. 1560
Two kinds of brown ink over black chalk on off-white antique laid paper, lined with Asian paper
13.4 × 20.5 cm
Harvard Art Museums/Fogg Museum, The Kate, Maurice R. and Melvin R. Seiden Special Purchase Fund, 1994.137
Illustrated p. 28

**Pieter de Molijn (London 1595–1661 Haarlem)**

*Travelers on a Country Road*, 1654
Black chalk and gray wash on beige antique laid paper, framing line in black chalk
14.9 × 19.5 cm
Maida and George Abrams Collection, Boston,

Long-term loan to the Harvard Art Museums, 1.2018.268
Illustrated p. 80

*A Panoramic Landscape*, c. 1659
Black chalk and gray wash on off-white antique laid paper, mounted overall
18.8 × 29.9 cm
The Maida and George Abrams Collection, Fogg Art Museum, Harvard University, Cambridge, Massachusetts, Gift of George Abrams in memory of Roger Sonnabend, Harvard Business School Class of 1949, 2011.514
Illustrated p. 164

**Isaac de Moucheron**
**(Amsterdam 1667–1744 Amsterdam)**

*Wooded Landscape with Bathers*, c. 1700
Black ink and gray wash on off-white antique laid paper, framing lines in black ink
20.2 × 32.5 cm
Harvard Art Museums/Fogg Museum, Gift of Kathryn K. and William W. Robinson in honor of Seymour and Zoya Slive, 2013.42
Illustrated p. 96

*Landscape with a Formal Garden*, c. 1700
Black ink and gray wash on off-white antique laid paper, framing lines in black ink
20 × 31 cm
Harvard Art Museums/Fogg Museum, The Kate, Maurice R. and Melvin R. Seiden Special Purchase Fund in memory of Joseph Pulitzer and in honor of Emily Pulitzer, 2004.93
Illustrated p. 96

*A Shepherd with His Flock Sheltering from a Storm among Antique Ruins*, c. 1700
Black ink and gray wash on off-white antique laid paper, framing lines in black ink
20 × 31.2 cm
Harvard Art Museums/Fogg Museum, William W. Robinson Fund, 2019.107
Illustrated p. 97

*Man Leading a Horse by a Pond in a Stormy, Wooded Landscape*, c. 1700
Black ink, gray wash, and white opaque watercolor on off-white antique laid paper, framing lines in black ink
20.8 × 31.5 cm
The Maida and George Abrams Collection, Fogg Art Museum, Harvard University, Cambridge, Massachusetts, Gift of George Abrams in memory of Milton Gwirtzman, Harvard Class of 1954, 2011.518
Illustrated p. 97

**Jan Pynas**
**(Alkmaar 1581/82–1631 Amsterdam)**

*A Mountainous Landscape with an Arched Bridge over a River*, 1605–7
Brown ink and gray wash over traces of black chalk on off-white antique laid paper, framing line in dark-brown ink
14.3 × 19.1 cm
Maida and George Abrams Collection, Boston, Long-term loan to the Harvard Art Museums, 1.2018.277
Illustrated p. 85

**Rembrandt van Rijn**
**(Leiden 1606–1669 Amsterdam)**

*A Farm on the Amsteldijk(?)*, c. 1648–50
Brown ink, brown wash, and white opaque watercolor on off-white antique laid paper
10.9 × 22.1 cm
The Maida and George Abrams Collection, Fogg Art Museum, Harvard University, Cambridge, Massachusetts, Gift of George Abrams in memory of Maida Abrams, 2004.181
Illustrated p. 124

*Landscape with a Farmstead ("Winter Landscape")*, c. 1650
Brown ink, pale brown wash, and incidental marks in black chalk on off-white antique laid paper, prepared with light rose-brown wash, mounted overall, framing line in brown ink
6.7 × 16 cm
Harvard Art Museums/Fogg Museum, Bequest of Charles A. Loeser, 1932.368
Illustrated p. 152

*Houses on the Schinkelweg*, c. 1650–52
Brown ink on off-white antique laid paper prepared with gray wash, partial framing line in brown ink
10 × 22.8 cm
Maida and George Abrams Collection, Boston, Long-term loan to the Harvard Art Museums, 1.2018.279
Illustrated p. 131

*View of Mariakerk in Utrecht from the South*, c. 1652
Brown ink and later gray wash and later touches of graphite on off-white antique laid paper, prepared with a brownish-gray wash(?), framing line in brown ink
11.3 × 18.7 cm
Harvard Art Museums/Fogg Museum, Kelsey S. McDonald Fund, 1951.130
Illustrated p. 45

**Roelant Roghman**
**(Amsterdam 1627–1692 Amsterdam)**

*Ameide Castle with Tienhoven in the Distance*, 1646–47
Black chalk and gray wash with graphite on off-white antique laid paper, framing lines in dark-brown ink
30.3 × 48.5 cm
Maida and George Abrams Collection, Boston, Long-term loan to the Harvard Art Museums, 1.2018.281
Illustrated p. 138

*Develstein Castle*, 1647
Gray wash and black chalk with scratchwork and touches of graphite on off-white antique laid paper, framing line in brown ink
35.2 × 49 cm
The Maida and George Abrams Collection, Fogg Art Museum, Harvard University, Cambridge, Massachusetts, Promised gift, 1.2018.147
Illustrated p. 139

*Wooded Landscape with Riders and Dogs*, 1660s
Watercolor, brown ink, and black chalk on beige antique laid paper, framing lines in brown ink
15.2 × 22.7 cm
Maida and George Abrams Collection, Boston, Long-term loan to the Harvard Art Museums, 1.2018.282
Illustrated p. 92

**Jacob van Ruisdael**
**(Haarlem 1628/29–1682 Amsterdam)**

*Trees and a Cottage at the Edge of a Road*, c. 1648–55
Black chalk on light-tan antique laid paper, framing lines in brown ink and black chalk

15.3 × 19.7 cm
The Maida and George Abrams Collection, Fogg Art Museum, Harvard University, Cambridge, Massachusetts, 2008.251
Illustrated p. 46

*The Kamperbuitenpoort in Amersfoort*, c. 1650
Black chalk on beige antique laid paper, framing line in brown ink and partial framing line in black chalk
14.2 × 20 cm
The Maida and George Abrams Collection, Fogg Art Museum, Harvard University, Cambridge, Massachusetts, Promised gift, 1.2018.149
Illustrated p. 46

*Two Large Oaks and Two Deer at the Edge of a Wood*, c. 1670
Black chalk and gray wash with touches of graphite on off-white antique laid paper, framing line in brown ink
20.5 × 32 cm
Maida and George Abrams Collection, Boston, Long-term loan to the Harvard Art Museums, 1.2018.283
Illustrated p. 218



**Abraham Rutgers
(Amsterdam 1632–1699 Amsterdam)**

*Dike on a River*, 1686–87
Brown ink and brown wash over traces of black chalk on off-white antique laid paper, partial framing line in brown ink
11.8 × 20 cm
Maida and George Abrams Collection, Boston, Long-term loan to the Harvard Art Museums, 1.2018.284
Illustrated p. 79

**Franchoys Ryckhals
(Middelburg 1609–1647 Middelburg)**

*Landscape with Trees and a View to the Distance*, c. 1632
Black chalk on off-white antique laid paper, framing line in dark-brown ink
19.7 × 29.5 cm
The Maida and George Abrams Collection, Fogg Art Museum, Harvard University, Cambridge, Massachusetts, Promised gift, 1.2018.153
Illustrated p. 50

**Herman Saftleven
(Rotterdam 1609–1685 Utrecht)**

*Ruins in Utrecht by the Saint Jobsgasthuis*, 1674
Black chalk and gray, brown, green, and yellow transparent watercolor on off-white antique laid paper, framing line on three sides in gray ink
19.4 × 15 cm
The Maida and George Abrams Collection, Fogg Art Museum, Harvard University, Cambridge, Massachusetts, 1999.168
Illustrated p. 144

**Cornelis Troost
(Amsterdam 1696–1750 Amsterdam)**

*A Park Scene*, 1740s
Opaque watercolor on off-white antique laid paper, partial framing line in black ink
43.2 × 59 cm
Maida and George Abrams Collection, Boston, Long-term loan to the Harvard Art Museums, 1.2018.293
Illustrated p. 222

**Esaias van de Velde
(Amsterdam 1587–1630 The Hague)**

*Shepherds and Sheep before a Rock*, c. 1615–16
Brown ink on white antique laid paper, prepared with red chalk wash, mounted overall on antique laid paper
7.3 × 16.7 cm
Harvard Art Museums/Fogg Museum, Bequest of Frances L. Hofer, 1979.62
Illustrated p. 66

*Farms and a Dovecote by a Frozen River*; verso: *River Scene with a Ferry*, c. 1617–18
Black chalk on off-white antique laid paper
18.5 × 30.5 cm
The Maida and George Abrams Collection, Fogg Art Museum, Harvard University, Cambridge, Massachusetts, Gift of George Abrams in honor of Egbert Haverkamp-Begemann, 2015.169
Illustrated p. 41

**Jan van de Velde II
(Rotterdam[?] 1593–1641 Enkhuizen)**

*A Farmhouse in the Trees*, c. 1620
Brown ink and brown wash with traces of black chalk on off-white antique laid paper, squared and numbered for transfer in black chalk, partial framing line in brown ink
15.9 × 20.3 cm
The Maida and George Abrams Collection, Fogg Art Museum, Harvard University, Cambridge, Massachusetts, Promised gift, 1.2018.187
Illustrated p. 127

*Keizersberg Castle in Leuven*, 1620s
Brown ink and brown wash over graphite on off-white antique laid paper
18.9 × 30.7 cm
The Maida and George Abrams Collection, Fogg Art Museum, Harvard University, Cambridge, Massachusetts, 1999.176
Illustrated p. 136

**Adriaen van de Venne
(Delft 1589–1662 The Hague)**

*Spring*, 1622
Brown ink, gray wash, and white opaque watercolor, incised, on off-white antique laid paper, framing line in black ink
10.5 × 14 cm
The Maida and George Abrams Collection, Fogg Art Museum, Harvard University, Cambridge, Massachusetts, 1999.178
Illustrated p. 70

**Paulus van Vianen
(Utrecht 1570–1613 Prague)**

*A Village Street in Primolano*, 1607
Brown ink and gray-brown and blue wash over traces of black chalk on off-white antique laid paper, framing line in brown ink
16.1 × 20 cm
Harvard Art Museums/Fogg Museum, Gift of Maida and George S. Abrams in memory of Jakob Rosenberg, 1993.246
Illustrated p. 62

**Claes Jansz. Visscher
(Amsterdam 1587–1652 Amsterdam)**

*View of Houtewael*; verso: *Trunk of an Alder Tree and a Grassy Bank by a Pool*, c. 1607–8
Brown ink on off-white antique laid paper, framing lines in brown ink
14.3 × 18.6 cm
Maida and George Abrams Collection, Boston,

Long-term loan to the Harvard Art Museums, 1.2018.304
Illustrated p. 58

**Simon de Vlieger**
**(Rotterdam 1600/1601–1653 Weesp)**

*Coastal Landscape with Anthropomorphic Rocks*, c. 1634–38
Drawn on a page of an album containing 52 leaves of parchment in a black leather stationer's binding, 17th century
Graphite on parchment
11 × 15.2 cm
The Maida and George Abrams Collection, Fogg Art Museum, Harvard University, Cambridge, Massachusetts, 1999.123.11
Illustrated p. 207

*A Port Town*, late 1630s
Black chalk and gray wash on off-white antique laid paper, mounted overall to another sheet of antique laid paper, framing lines in brown ink and black chalk and partial framing line in black ink
19.8 × 31.3 cm
Maida and George Abrams Collection, Boston, Long-term loan to the Harvard Art Museums, 1.2018.306
Illustrated p. 82

*Landscape with Trees by a River*, c. 1645–53
Black and white chalk and gray wash on blue antique laid paper, framing line in black ink
26.7 × 44 cm
Harvard Art Museums/Fogg Museum, Purchase through the generosity of David Giles Carter, Eric Greenleaf, an anonymous donor and the Grenville L. Winthrop Frame Fund, 1999.66
Illustrated p. 120

*View of Weesp*, c. 1649–53
Black chalk and gray wash on off-white antique laid paper, some incised lines in lower half of added strip (at right)
39.3 × 67.9 cm
The Maida and George Abrams Collection, Fogg Art Museum, Harvard University, Cambridge, Massachusetts, 2008.250
Illustrated p. 51

**Cornelis Vroom**
**(Haarlem[?] 1590/92–1661 Haarlem)**

*River Landscape*, c. 1622–23
Brown ink with touches of gray ink on beige antique laid paper, framing line in brown ink
18.1 × 24.2 cm
Maida and George Abrams Collection, Boston, Long-term loan to the Harvard Art Museums, 1.2018.308
Illustrated p. 108

*Landscape with a Road and a Fence*, 1631
Brown ink over graphite on off-white antique laid paper
19.2 × 25.2 cm
The Maida and George Abrams Collection, Fogg Art Museum, Harvard University, Cambridge, Massachusetts, Gift of George Abrams in memory of Robert M. Light, 2020.209
Illustrated p. 75

**Anthonie Waterloo**
**(Lille 1609–1690 Utrecht)**

*Landscape with Doorwerth Castle*, c. 1650–70
Black chalk, charcoal, gray wash, and some white opaque watercolor on off-white antique laid paper, partial framing line in brown ink (at bottom)
25.2 × 40.5 cm
The Maida and George Abrams Collection, Fogg Art Museum, Harvard University, Cambridge, Massachusetts, 1999.180
Illustrated p. 182

*Grist Mills near Hamburg*, c. 1660
Black ink and gray wash with black chalk and white opaque watercolor over black chalk and traces of graphite on off-white antique laid paper, framing line in brown ink
44.3 × 55.8 cm
The Maida and George Abrams Collection, Fogg Art Museum, Harvard University, Cambridge, Massachusetts, 2008.252
Illustrated p. 176

*A Forest at Twilight*, c. 1675–85
Black and white chalk, charcoal, and gray wash on blue antique laid paper, autograph framing line in charcoal
28.3 × 23 cm
Harvard Art Museums/Fogg Museum, Bequest of Meta and Paul J. Sachs, 1965.219
Illustrated p. 99

**Cornelis Claesz. van Wieringen**
**(Haarlem 1575/77–1633 Haarlem)**

*Coastal View with Ships, Crag with Castle, and Bridge*, 1600–1610
Brown ink on beige antique laid paper, mounted, framing lines in brown ink, partially trimmed at upper edge
14.7 × 19.4 cm
Maida and George Abrams Collection, Boston, Long-term loan to the Harvard Art Museums, 1.2018.314
Illustrated p. 83

**Pieter de With**
**(? c. 1635–1689 or later ?)**

*A Wooded Landscape with a Cottage*, late 1650s
Brown ink with touches of opaque white watercolor on beige antique laid paper, mounted overall, partial framing line in brown ink
15 × 24.5 cm
Maida and George Abrams Collection, Boston, Long-term loan to the Harvard Art Museums, 1.2018.315
Illustrated p. 133

## PRINTS AND PRINTED VOLUMES

**Carel Allard**
**(Amsterdam 1648–c. 1709 Amsterdam)**

*Nova tabula Indiae orientalis*, c. 1706
From *Atlas minor sive tabulae geographicae proecipuorum regnorum regionum, insularum, provinciarum, etc* (Amsterdam: J. Cóvens & C. Mortier, c. 1706)
Hand-colored etching with engraving on off-white antique laid paper
58.4 × 36.8 cm
Harvard Map Collection, Harvard College Library, GEN MA 18.10.2 pf*

**Jan van Brosterhuysen**
**(Leiden c. 1596–1650 Breda)**
**after**
**Frans Post**
**(Haarlem 1612–1680 Haarlem)**

*View of Olinda*, 1647
From Caspar Barlaeus's *Rervm per octennivm in Brasilia et alibi nuper gestarum, sub præfectura illustrissimi comitis I. Mavritii, Nassoviæ, &c. comitis, nunc Vesaliæ gubernatoris & equitatus fœderatorum Belgii Ordd. sub Avriaco ductoris, historia* (Amsterdam: Joan Blaeu, 1647)
Etching on off-white antique laid paper
47 × 65 cm
Houghton Library, Harvard University, SA 5860.5*
Illustrated p. 87

**Willem Buytewech**
**(Rotterdam 1591/92–1624 Rotterdam)**

*Landscape with a Herd of Sheep near a Pond*, 1616
Bound within an album containing 76 landscape prints in a mottled calf binding bearing on its spine the title *Livre de Peisage*, 17th–early 18th century
Etching on off-white antique laid paper, state i/iii
Plate: 8.9 × 12.8 cm; sheet: 19.3 × 28.7 cm
Harvard Art Museums/Fogg Museum, Light-Outerbridge Collection, Gift of Robert M. Light, M24417.65
Illustrated pp. 198–99



**Hans Collaert I**
**(Brussels 1525/30–1580 Antwerp)**
**after**
**Follower of Hans Bol**
**(Mechelen 1534–1593 Amsterdam)**
**Published by Hans van Luyck**
**(probably Antwerp c. 1518–after 1580 Antwerp)**

*View of Over Muelen*, c. 1575–80
Bound within an album containing 8 drawings and 97 prints in a plain vellum binding, 16th–17th century
Engraving on off-white antique laid paper, only state
Plate: 13.8 × 20.1 cm; sheet: 16.3 × 25.2 cm
Harvard Art Museums/Fogg Museum, The Kate, Maurice R. and Melvin R. Seiden Purchase Fund and Richard Norton Memorial Fund, M22209
Illustrated p. 200

**Joannes van Doetecum**
**(Deventer 1528/32–1605 Haarlem)**
**or**
**Lucas van Doetecum**
**(active Southern Netherlands 1554–1579/89)**
**after**
**Master of the Small Landscapes**
**(active Southern Netherlands c. 1560)**
**Published by Theodoor Galle**
**(Antwerp 1571–1633 Antwerp)**

*Fields and a Village Road, with a Post Mill*, 1559–61, third edition printed c. 1612
Etching and engraving on off-white antique laid paper
Plate: 13.2 × 19.6 cm; sheet: 18.1 × 29.1 cm
Harvard Art Museums/Fogg Museum, Light-Outerbridge Collection, Richard Norton Memorial Fund, M24515

**Hendrick Goltzius**
**(Mühlbracht 1558–1617 Haarlem)**

*Landscape with a Farmhouse*, c. 1597–98
Woodcut printed in black ink on blue antique laid paper, highlighted with white opaque watercolor, state i/ii
Block: 11.5 × 14.3 cm; sheet: 12.1 × 15 cm
Harvard Art Museums/Fogg Museum, Gray Collection of Engravings Fund, G7448

**Possibly Simon Novellanus**
**(active second half 16th century)**
**after**
**Pieter Bruegel the Elder**
**(Breda[?] 1526/30–1569 Brussels)**
**Published by Joris Hoefnagel**
**(Antwerp 1542–1600 Vienna)**

*River Landscape with Mercury and Psyche*, c. 1595
Etching and engraving on off-white antique laid paper, state i/ii
Plate: 27.7 × 34.6 cm; sheet: 28.4 × 35.2 cm
Harvard Art Museums/Fogg Museum, Gift of Hope R. Edison '56 in memory of Julian I. Edison '51, MBA '53, 2019.143

**Adriaen van Ostade**
**(Haarlem 1610–1685 Haarlem)**

*The Anglers*, c. 1653
Etching on off-white antique laid paper, state iv/vi
11.4 × 16.5 cm
Harvard Art Museums/Fogg Museum, Gift of Melvin R. Seiden, S5.20.2

*The Anglers*, c. 1653
Etched copper plate
11.8 × 16.9 cm
Maida and George Abrams Collection, Boston

**Magdalena de Passe**
**(Cologne 1600–1640 Utrecht)**
**after**
**Paul Bril**
**(Antwerp or Breda 1553/54–1626 Rome)**
**Published by Crispijn van de Passe**
**(Arnemuiden 1564–1637 Utrecht)**

*Landscape with Trees and Town*, c. 1615–30
Engraving on off-white antique laid paper, only state
Plate: 22.4 × 26.1 cm; sheet: 22.3 × 26.9 cm
Harvard Art Museums/Fogg Museum, Light-Outerbridge Collection, Purchase through the generosity of Margaret D. Carroll, M24624

**Rembrandt van Rijn**
**(Leiden 1606–1669 Amsterdam)**

*The Three Trees*, 1643
Etching, engraving, and drypoint on off-white antique laid paper, only state
Image: 20.5 × 27.7 cm; mounting sheet: 27.4 × 35 cm
Harvard Art Museums/Fogg Museum, Gift of William Gray from the collection of Francis Calley Gray, G3264

**Geertruydt Roghman**
**(Amsterdam 1625–1657 Amsterdam)**
**after**
**Roelant Roghman**
**(Amsterdam 1627–1692 Amsterdam)**
**Published by Claes Jansz. Visscher**
**(Amsterdam 1587–1652 Amsterdam)**

*The Bridge to Maersen*, 1645–48
Etching on off-white antique laid paper, only state
Plate: 13.2 × 22.6 cm; image: 11.6 × 21.9 cm; sheet: 16 × 25.3 cm
Harvard Art Museums/Fogg Museum, Light-Outerbridge Collection, Acquisition Fund for Prints, M24642

**Jacob van Ruisdael**
**(Haarlem 1628/29–1682 Amsterdam)**

*A Forest Marsh with Travelers on a Bank*, c. 1652
Etching and drypoint on off-white antique laid paper, state iii/iv
Plate: 19.5 × 28 cm; image: 18.5 × 27.2 cm; sheet: 20 × 28.7 cm
Harvard Art Museums/Fogg Museum, Light-Outerbridge Collection, Gift of Robert M. Light and Acquisition Fund for Prints, M26584

**Esaias van de Velde**
**(Amsterdam 1587–1630 The Hague)**

*Path at Right Leading to a Village*, 1615–16
Etching on off-white antique laid paper, state ii/v
Plate: 8.8 × 18.2 cm; sheet: 9.7 × 19 cm
Harvard Art Museums/Fogg Museum, Light-Outerbridge Collection, Alpheus Hyatt Purchase Fund, M24763

*Landscape with a Brewery*, 1615–16
Etching on off-white antique laid paper, state ii/v
Plate: 8.7 × 17.6 cm; sheet: 9.1 × 18 cm
Harvard Art Museums/Fogg Museum, Light-Outerbridge Collection, Alpheus Hyatt Purchase Fund, M24765

**Jan van de Velde II**
**(Rotterdam[?] 1593–1641 Enkhuizen)**
**Published by Claes Jansz. Visscher**
**(Amsterdam 1587–1652 Amsterdam)**

*March*, 1618
Etching and engraving on off-white antique laid paper, only state
Image: 25.9 × 35.7 cm; sheet: 27.2 × 35.6 cm
Harvard Art Museums/Fogg Museum, Light-Outerbridge Collection, Purchase through the generosity of the Fanny and Leo Koerner Charitable Trust, M24819

**Claes Jansz. Visscher**
**(Amsterdam 1587–1652 Amsterdam)**
**after**
**Boëtius Adamsz. Bolswert**
**(Bolsward c. 1580–1633 Antwerp)**
**after**
**Abraham Bloemaert**
**(Gorinchem 1566–1651 Utrecht)**

*Man with Two Pails Walking Back to a Farmhouse*, 1620
Etching on off-white antique laid paper, only state
Plate: 10.5 × 15.1 cm; sheet: 20 × 29.4 cm
Harvard Art Museums/Fogg Museum, Light-Outerbridge Collection, Acquisition Fund for Prints, M24863

# BIBLIOGRAPHY




Aa, A. J. van der. *Biographisch woordenboek der Nederlanden. Deel 2. Eerste en tweede stuk.* Haarlem: J. J. van Brederode, 1854.

Abrams, George. "Forum: Cornelis Vroom, Gentle Poet of Landscape." *Drawings* 8 (4) (1986): 78–79.

Ackley, Clifford, et al. *From Michelangelo to Rembrandt: Master Drawings from the Teyler Museum*. Exh. cat. New York: Pierpont Morgan Library; Chicago: Art Institute of Chicago, 1989.

Adams, Ann Jensen. "Competing Communities in the 'Great Bog of Europe': Identity and Seventeenth-Century Dutch Landscape Painting." In *Landscape and Power*, ed. W. J. T. Mitchell. 2nd ed. Chicago: University of Chicago Press, 2002.

Alighieri, Dante. *Paradiso*. Trans. Henry Wadsworth Longfellow. Leipzig: Bernard Tauchnitz, 1867.

Alpers, Svetlana. *The Art of Describing: Dutch Art in the Seventeenth Century*. Chicago: University of Chicago Press, 1983.

Alsteens, Stijn. "The Atlas Blaeu-Van der Hem of the Austrian National Library." *Master Drawings* 48 (1) (Spring 2010): 105–20.

Alsteens, Stijn, and Hans Buijs. *Paysages de France: Dessinés par Lambert Doomer et les artistes hollandais et flamands des XVIe et XVIIe siècles*. Paris: Fondation Custodia, 2008.

Ampzing, Samuel. *Beschryvinge ende lof der stad Haerlem in Holland. In rijm bearbeyd: ende met veele oude en nieuwe stucken buyten dicht uyt verscheyde kronijken, handvesten, brieven, memorien ofte geheugenissen, ende diergelijke schriften verklaerd, ende bevestigd.* Haarlem: Adriaan Roman, 1628.

Antonov, Oleg, et al. *Le Musée Pouchkine: Cinq cents ans de dessins de maîtres*. Exh. cat. Paris: Fondation Custodia, 2019.

Aristotle. *Nicomachean Ethics*. Trans. Terence Irwin. Indianapolis: Hackett Publishing Company, 1985.

Baarsen, Reinier, Robert-Jan te Rijdt, and Frits Scholten. *Netherlandish Art in the Rijksmuseum 1700–1800*. Zwolle: Waanders; Amsterdam: Rijksmuseum, 2006.

Baer, Curtis O., ed. *Seventeenth-Century Dutch Landscape Drawings and Selected Prints from American Collections*. Exh. cat. Introduction by Susan Donahue Kuretsky. Poughkeepsie, N.Y.: Vassar College Art Gallery, 1976.

Baer, Ronni, ed. *Class Distinctions: Dutch Painting in the Age of Rembrandt and Vermeer*. Exh. cat. Boston: Museum of Fine Arts, 2015.

Baker, C. A. "A Comparison of Drawing Inks Using Ultraviolet and Infrared Light Examination Techniques." In *Applications of Science in the Examination of Works of Art: Proceedings of the Seminar, September 7–9, 1983*, ed. Pamela A. England and Lambertus van Zelst, 159–63. Boston: The Research Laboratory, Museum of Fine Arts, 1985.

Bakker, Boudewijn. *Landscape and Religion from Van Eyck to Rembrandt*. Trans. Diane Webb. Farnham, U.K.: Ashgate, 2012.

———. "Points of View: Recent Studies on Dutch Landscape Painting." In *The Ashgate Research Companion to Dutch Art of the Seventeenth Century*, ed. Wayne Franits. New York: Routledge, 2016.

Bakker, Boudewijn, and Huigen Leeflang. *Nederland naar 't leven: Landschapsprenten uit de Gouden Eeuw*. Exh. cat. Amsterdam: Museum het Rembrandthuis, 1993.

Bakker, Boudewijn, Mària van Berge-Gerbaud, Jan Peeters, and Erik Schmitz. *Landscapes of Rembrandt: His Favourite Walks*. Exh. cat. Amsterdam: Stadsarchief/Gemeentearchief; Paris: Fondation Custodia, 1998.

Barlaeus, Caspar. *The History of Brazil under the Governorship of Count Johan Maurits of Nassau, 1636–1644*. Trans. and ed. Blanche T. van Berckel-Ebeling Koning. Gainesville: University Press of Florida, 2011.

———. *Rerum per octennium in Brasilia et alibi nuper gestarum, sub praefectura illustrissimi comitis I. Mauritii, Nassoviae, &c. comitis, nunc Vesaliae gubernatoris & equitatis foederatorum Belgii Ordd. Sub Avriaco ductoris, historia.* Amsterdam: Blaeu, 1647.

Barrell, John. *The Dark Side of the Landscape: The Rural Poor in English Painting, 1730–1840*. Cambridge: Cambridge University Press, 1980.

Barringer, Tim, and Elizabeth Kornhauser. *Thomas Cole's Journey: Atlantic Crossings*. Exh. cat. New York: Metropolitan Museum of Art, 2018.

Bartilla, Stefan. "Die Wildnis: Visuel Neugier in der Berg- und Waldlandschaften und ihres Naturbegriffs um 1600." Ph.D. diss., Albert-Ludwigs-Universität Freiburg, 2000.

Bartsch, Tatjana. *Maarten van Heemskerck: Römische Studien zwischen Sachlichkeit und Imagination*. Munich: Hirmer, 2019.

Bass, Marisa Anne. *Insect Artifice: Nature and Art in the Dutch Revolt*. Princeton, N.J.: Princeton University Press, 2019.

Bavel, Bas van. *Manors and Markets: Economy and Society in the Low Countries, 500–1600*. New York: Oxford University Press, 2010.

Beck, Hans-Ulrich. *Jan van Goyen, 1596–1656: Ein Oeuvreverzeichnis*. 4 vols. Amsterdam: Van Gendt (vols. 1–2); Doornspijk: Davaco (vols. 3–4), 1972–91.

———. *Pieter Molyn, 1595–1661: Katalog der Handzeichnungen*. Doornspijk: Davaco, 1998.

Benesch, Otto. *The Drawings of Rembrandt*. Enlarged and ed. Eva Benesch. London: Phaidon Press, 1973.

———. *The Drawings of Rembrandt: A Critical and Chronological Catalogue*. London: Phaidon Press, 1954–57.

Berge, Mària van, et al. *Willem Buytewech*. Exh. cat. Rotterdam: Museum Boymans-Van Beuningen; Paris: Institut neerlandais, 1974.

Berge-Gerbaud, Mària van. *Rembrandt et son école: Dessins de la Collection Frits Lugt*. Exh. cat. Paris: Fondation Custodia, 1997.

Bieleman, Jan. *Five Centuries of Farming: A Short History of Dutch Agriculture, 1500–2000*. Wageningen: Wageningen Academic Publishers, 2010.

Biesboer, Peter. "George Keyes, 'Cornelis Vroom, marine and landscape artist' (book review)." *Simiolus* 10 (3) 1978: 210.

Bisanz-Prakken, Marian. *Drawings from the Albertina: Landscape in the Age of Rembrandt.*

Exh. cat. New York: The Drawing Center; Fort Worth, Tex.: Kimbell Art Museum; Alexandria, Va.: Art Services International, 1995.

Bisschop, Jan de. *Paradigmata graphices variorum artificum*. Hagae-Comitis: N. Visscher, 1671.

Bleyerveld, Yvonne, Albert J. Elen, and Judith Niessan. *Bosch to Bloemaert: Early Netherlandish Drawings in Museum Boijmans Van Beuningen, Rotterdam*. Exh. cat. Paris: Fondation Custodia; Bussum: Thoth, 2014.

Bleyerveld, Yvonne, and Ilja M. Veldman. *The Netherlandish Drawings of the 16th Century in Teylers Museum*. Exh. cat. Haarlem: Teylers Museum; Leiden: Primavera Press, 2016.

Bleyerveld, Yvonne, et al. *Netherlandish Drawings of the Fifteenth and Sixteenth Centuries: Artists Born before 1581*. Online catalogue. Museum Boijmans Van Beuningen, Rotterdam, 2012. https://www.boijmans.nl/en/collection/research/netherlandish-drawings-of-the-fifteenth-and-sixteenth-centuries.

Blom, Philipp. *Nature's Mutiny: How the Little Ice Age of the Long Seventeenth Century Transformed the West and Shaped the Present*. New York: Liveright Publishing Corporation, 2019.

Bol, Laurens J. *Adriaen Pietersz. van de Venne: Painter and Draughtsman*. Doornspijk: Davaco, 1989.

Bolten, Jaap. *Abraham Bloemaert, c. 1565–1651: The Drawings*. 2 vols. Oegstgeest: J. Bolten, 2007.

———. "The Beginnings of Abraham Bloemaert's Artistic Career." *Master Drawings* 36 (1) (1998): 17–25.

Boogaart, Ernst van den. "A Well-Governed Colony: Frans Post's Illustrations in Caspar Barlaeus's History of Dutch Brazil." *Rijksmuseum Bulletin* 59 (3) (2011): 236–71.

Boogert, Bob van den, et al. *Buiten tekenen in Rembrandts tijd*. Exh. cat. Amsterdam: Museum Het Rembrandthuis, 1998.

Bots, Hans, Giel van Gemert, and P. J. A. N. Rietbergen. *L'album amicorum de Cornelis de Glarges 1599–1683*. Amsterdam: Holland University Press, 1975.

Brandon, Pepijn. "The Armed Forces." In *The Cambridge Companion to the Dutch Golden Age*, ed. Helmer J. Helmers and Geert H. Janssen. Cambridge: Cambridge University Press, 2018.

Brandon, Pepijn, et al., eds. *De Slavernij in Oost en West: Het Amsterdam Onderzoek*. Amsterdam: Uitgeverij Het Spectrum, 2020.

Braun, Georg, and Franz Hogenberg. *Civitates orbis terrarium. Cities of the World: 230 Colour Engravings which Transformed Urban Cartography, 1572–1617*. Ed. Stephan Füssel. Cologne: Taschen, 2015.

Bredekamp, Horst. *The Lure of Antiquity and the Cult of the Machine: The Kunstkammer and the Evolution of Nature, Art and Technology*. Trans. Allison Brown. Princeton, N.J.: Markus Wiener Publishers, 1995.

Bredius, Abraham. "Het schetsboek van Jacob de Wet." *Oud Holland* 37 (1919): 215–22.

———. "De schilder Johannes van de Cappelle." *Oud Holland* 10 (3) (1892): 26–40.

Breitbarth-van der Stok, M. H. "Josua de Grave, Valentinus Klotz en Barnardus Klotz." *Bulletin van de Koninklijke Nederlandse Oudheidkundige Bond* 68 (1969): 93–115.

Brooks, Julian. *Guercino: Mind to Paper*. Exh. cat. Los Angeles: J. Paul Getty Museum, 2006.

Broos, B. P. J. "'Notitie der Teekeningen van Sybrand Feitama': De boekhouding van drie generaties verzamelaars van oude Nederlandse tekenkunst." *Oud Holland* 98 (1984): 13–39.

———. "'Notitie der Teekeningen van Sybrand Feitama,' II: 'verkocht, verhandeld, vereerd, geruiled en overgedaan.'" *Oud Holland* 99 (1985): 110–54.

———. "'Notitie der Teekeningen van Sybrand Feitama,' III: de verzameling van Sybrand I Feitama (1620–1701) en van Isaac Feitama (1666–1709)." *Oud Holland* 101 (1987): 171–217.

Broos, B. P. J., and Marijn Schapelhouman. *Nederlandse Tekenaars geboren tussen 1600 en 1660*. Amsterdam: Amsterdams Historisch Museum, 1993.

Brown, Christopher, ed. *Dutch Landscape: The Early Years, Haarlem and Amsterdam 1590–1650*. Exh. cat. London: The National Gallery, 1986.

Brugerolles, Emmanuelle, ed. *L'age d'or du paysage hollandais: Cabinet des dessins de Jean Bonna*. Exh. cat. Paris: École nationale supérieure des beaux-arts, 2014.

Brusati, Celeste. *Artifice and Illusion: The Art and Writing of Samuel van Hoogstraten*. Chicago: University of Chicago Press, 1995.

Buell, Lawrence. *The Future of Environmental Criticism: Environmental Crisis and Literary Imagination*. Malden, Mass.: Blackwell Publishing, 2005.

Buijs, Hans, and Ger Luijten, eds. *Goltzius to Van Gogh: Drawings and Paintings from the P. & N. de Boer Foundation*. Exh. cat. Paris: Fondation Custodia; Bussum: Uitgeverij Thoth, 2014.

Buijsen, Edwin. *Between Fantasy and Reality: 17th-Century Dutch Landscape Painting*. Exh. cat. Tokyo: Station Gallery; Baarn: De Prom, 1993.

———. "De schetsboeken van Jan van Goyen." In *Jan van Goyen*, ed. Christiaan Vogelaar, 22–37. Leiden: Stedelijk Museum De Lakenhal, 1996.

Buis, Jaap. *Historia forestis: Nederlandse bosgeschiedenis*. 2 vols. Utrecht: H & S, 1985.

Burandt, Jan. "An Investigation Toward the Identification of Traditional Drawing Inks." *Book and Paper Group Annual* 13 (1994): 9–16.

Camp, An van. "The Etchings by Drawings Collector Nicolaes Flinck." *Print Quarterly* 27 (4) (2010): 371–81.

Carriveau, Gary W., and Marjorie Shelley. "A Study of Rembrandt Drawings Using X-Ray Fluorescence." *Nuclear Instruments and Methods in Physics Research* 193 (1–2) (1982): 297–301.

Cats, Jacob. *Houwelyck, dat is De gansche gelegentheyt des echten-staets*. Middelburg: 1625.

Churchill, W. A. *Watermarks in Paper in Holland, England, France, Etc. in the XVII and XVIII Centuries and Their Interconnection*. Amsterdam: M. Hertzberger, 1967.

Cohn, Marjorie. "An Interpretation of Four Woodcut Landscapes by Hendrick Goltzius." *Print Quarterly* 31 (2) (June 2014): 144–54.

———. *A Noble Collection: The Spencer Albums of Old Master Prints*. Exh. cat. Cambridge, Mass.: Fogg Art Museum, 1992.

———. *Wash and Gouache: A Study of the Development of the Materials of Watercolor*. Cambridge, Mass.: Center for Conservation and Technical Studies, Fogg Art Museum, 1977.

Colbourne, Jane. "A Survey of Methods Used in the Technical Examination and Analysis of Brown Inks." In *The Iron Gall Ink Meeting: Postprints, September 4th & 5th, 2000*, ed. A. Jean E. Brown. Rotterdam: University of Northumbria at Newcastle, 2001.

Corrêa do Lago, Pedro. *Frans Post, 1612–1680: Catalogue Raisonné*. Milan: 5 Continents; Woodbridge, U.K.: ACC Distribution, 2007.

Corrêa do Lago, Pedro, and Blaise Ducos. *Frans Post: Le Brésil à la cour de Louis XIV*. Exh. cat. Paris: Musée du Louvre; Milan: 5 Continents Editions, 2005.

Corrigan, Karina H., et al., eds. *Asia in Amsterdam: The Culture of Luxury in the Golden Age*. Exh. cat. Salem, Mass.: Peabody Essex Museum; Amsterdam: Rijksmuseum; New Haven, Conn.: Yale University Press, 2015.

Costamagna, Philippe, Florian Härb, and Simonetta Prosperi Valenti Rodinò, eds. *Disegno, giudizio e bella maniera: Studi sul disegno italiano in onore di Catherine Monbeig Goguel*. Milan: Silvana Editoriale, 2005.

DaCosta Kaufmann, Thomas. *Court, Cloister, and City: The Art and Culture of Central Europe, 1450–1800*. Chicago: University of Chicago Press, 1995.

———. *Drawings from the Holy Roman Empire, 1540–1680: A Selection from North American Collections*. Exh. cat. Princeton, N.J.: Art Museum, Princeton University; Washington, D.C.: National Gallery of Art; Pittsburgh: Museum of Art, Carnegie Institute, 1982.

———. *Toward a Geography of Art*. Chicago: University of Chicago Press, 2004.

Dalen, Dorrit van. *Gum Arabic: The Golden Tears of the Acacia Tree*. Leiden: Leiden University Press, 2019.

Dam, Petra van, and Mijla van Tielhof. *Waterstaat in stedenland, Het Hoogheemraadschap van Rijnland voor 1857*. Utrecht: Matrijs, 2006.

Dams, Britt. "Elias Herckmans: A Poet at the Borders of Dutch Brazil." *Intersections* 14 (2010): 19–38.

Davies, Alice. *Allart van Everdingen, 1621–1675: First Painter of Scandinavian Landscape: Catalogue Raisonné of Paintings*. Doornspijk: Davaco, 2001.

———. *The Drawings of Allart van Everdingen: A Complete Catalogue, Including the Studies for Reynard the Fox*. Doornspijk: Davaco, 2007.

Deursen, A. Th. van. *Een Dorp in de Polder: Graft in de zeventiende eeuw*. Amsterdam: Bert Bakker, 1994.

Dittrich, Christian, and Thomas Ketelsen. *Rembrandt: Die Dresdener Zeichnungen*. Exh. cat. Dresden: Staatliche Kunstsammlungen, Kupfersitch-Kabinett, 2004.

Dumas, Charles. "Dirk Dalens III en zijn bronnen." *Kunstschrift* 41 (6) (1997): 32–37.

Dumas, Charles, and Robert-Jan te Rijdt. *Kleur en Raffinement: Tekeningen uit de Unicornio collectie*. Exh. cat. Amsterdam: Museum het Rembrandthuis; Dordrecht: Dordrechts Museum; Zwolle: Waanders, 1994.

Duparc, Frederik J. *Landscape in Perspective: Drawings by Rembrandt and His Contemporaries*. Exh. cat. Montreal: Montreal Museum of Fine Arts; Cambridge, Mass.: Arthur M. Sackler Museum, Harvard University, 1988.

Eeghen, Christopher P. van. "Simon de Vlieger as a Draftsman, I: The Pen Drawings." *Master Drawings* 44 (1) (Spring 2006): 3–47.

———. "Simon de Vlieger as a Draftsman, II: Chalk Drawings Other than Pure Landscapes." *Master Drawings* 49 (2) (Summer 2011): 179–221.

———. "Simon de Vlieger as a Draftsman, III: His Chalk Drawings and Their Connections to Works by Anthonie van Waterloo." *Master Drawings* 53 (3) (Autumn 2015): 313–42.

Eichberger, Dagmar. "Framing Warfare and Destruction in Sixteenth-Century Netherlandish Prints: The *Clades Judaeae Gentis* Series by Maarten van Heemskerck." In *Disaster, Death, and the Emotions in the Shadow of the Apocalypse, 1400–1700*, ed. Jennifer Spinks and Charles Zika. London: Palgrave MacMillan, 2016.

Emmer, Pieter C., and Wim Klooster. "The Dutch Atlantic, 1600–1800: Expansion without Empire." *Itinerario* 23 (2) (1999): 48–69.

Ferrer, Nuria, and M. Carme Sistach. "Analysis of Sediments on Iron Gall Inks in Manuscripts." *Restaurator: International Journal for the Preservation of Library and Archival Material* 34 (3) (2013): 175–93.

Foucault, Michel. *Security, Territory, Population: Lectures at the Collège de France, 1977–78*. Ed. Michel Senellart. Trans. Graham Burchell. Basingstoke, U.K.: Palgrave Macmillan, 2007.

Fowler, Caroline O. *The Art of Paper: From the Holy Land to the Americas*. New Haven, Conn.: Yale University Press, 2019.

Freedberg, David. *Dutch Landscape Prints of the Seventeenth Century*. London: British Museum, 1980.

Frijhoff, Willem, and Marijke Spies. *1650: Bevochten Eendracht*. The Hague: Sdu Uitgevers, 1999.

Fucci, Robert. "Arcadia Unbound: Early Dutch Landscape Prints and the *Amenissimae aliquot regiunculae* of 1616 by Jan van de Velde II." *Art in Print* 4 (5) (January–February 2015): 17–22.

———. "Landscape into History: The Early Printed Landscape Series by Jan van de Velde II (1593–1641)." Ph.D. diss., Columbia University, 2018.

Gaudio, Michael. *Sound, Image, Silence: Art and Aural Imagination in the Atlantic World*. Minneapolis: University of Minnesota Press, 2019.

Gelder, J. G. van. *Jan van de Velde, 1593–1941, teekenaarschilder*. 's-Gravenhage: M. Nijhoff, 1933.

Gelder, J. G. van, and Ingrid Joost. *Jan de Bisschop and His Icones & Paradigmata: Classical Antiquities and Italian Drawings for Artistic Instruction in Seventeenth-Century Holland*. Doornspijk, Davaco: 1985.

Gelder, J. G. van, and J. M. de Groot. *Aelbert Cuyp en zijn familie, Schilders te Dordrecht: Gerrit Gerritz. Cuyp, ca. 1565–1644, Jacob Gerritz. Cuyp, 1594–1651/52, Benjamin Gerritz. Cuyp, 1612–1652, Aelbert Cuyp, 1620–1691; Schilderijen, Tekeningen*. Exh. cat. Dordrecht: Dordrechts Museum, 1977.

Gerszi, Teréz. *Paulus van Vianen: Handzeichnungen*. Hanau: Verlag Werner Dausien, 1982.

Gettens, Rutherford J., and George L. Stout. *Painting Materials: A Short Encyclopaedia*. New York: Dover Publications, 1966.

Gibson, Walter S. "Bloemaert's Privy: The Rustic Ruin in Dutch Art." In *Time and Transformation in Seventeenth-Century Dutch Art*, ed. Susan D. Kuretsky. Exh. cat. Poughkeepsie, N.Y.: Frances Lehman Loeb Art Center, Vassar College; Sarasota, Fla.: John and Mable Ringling Museum of Art; Louisville, Ky.: J. B. Speed Art Museum, 2005.

———. *Pleasant Places: The Rustic Landscape from Bruegel to Ruisdael*. Berkeley: University of California Press, 2000.

Giltaij, Jeroen. "A Newly Discovered Seventeenth-Century Sketchbook." *Simiolus* 31 (2007): 81–93.

———. "De Tekeningen van Jacob van Ruisdael." *Oud Holland* 94 (1980): 141–208.

Glotfelty, Cheryll, and Harold Fromm. *The Ecocriticism Reader: Landmarks in Literary Ecology*. Athens: University of Georgia Press, 1996.

Gnann, Achim. *Rembrandt: Landschaftszeichnungen, Landscape Drawings*. Petersberg, Germany: Michael Imhof Verlag, 2021.

Gobin, Anuradha. "Picturing Liminal Spaces and Bodies: Rituals of Punishment and the Limits of Control at the Gallows Field." *RACAR* 43 (1) (2018): 7–24.

Goeree, Willem. *Inleydinge tot de Al-ghemeene Teycken-Konst*. Middelburg: 1668.

———. *Willem Goeree: Inleydinge tot de Al-ghemeene Teycken-Konst: Een Kritische Geannoteerde Editie*. Ed. Michael W. Kwakkelstein. Leiden: Primavera Press, 1998.

Göttler, Christine, and Mia M. Mochizuki, eds. *Unruly Landscapes: Producing, Picturing, and Embodying Nature*. Forthcoming.

Gowers, Emily. "Virgil's Sibyl and the 'Many Mouths' Cliché." *Classical Quarterly* 55 (2005): 170–82.

Griffiths, Anthony. "The Archaeology of the Print." In *Collecting Prints and Drawings in Europe, c. 1500–1750*, ed. Christopher Baker, Caroline Elam, and Genevieve Warwick. Aldershot, U.K., and Burlington, Vt.: Ashgate, in association with the *Burlington Magazine*, 2003.

Groesen, Michiel van. *Amsterdam's Atlantic: Print Culture and the Making of Dutch Brazil*. Philadelphia: University of Pennsylvania Press, 2017.

———. "Heroic Memories: Admirals of Dutch Brazil in the Rise of Dutch National Consciousness." In *The Legacy of Dutch Brazil*, ed. Michiel van Groesen. New York: Cambridge University Press, 2014.

———, ed. *The Legacy of Dutch Brazil*. New York: Cambridge University Press, 2014.

———. *The Representations of the Overseas World in the De Bry Collection of Voyages*. Leiden: Brill, 2008.

Groot, Erlend de, and Peter van der Krogt, eds. *The Atlas Blaeu-Van der Hem of the Austrian National Library*. 7 vols. 't Goy-Houten: HES & DE GRAAF Publishers, 1996–2008.

Gruys, J. A., and Kees Thomassen, eds. *The Album Amicorum of Jacog Heyblocq*. Zwolle: Waanders, 1998.

Haitsma Mulier, Eco O.G. "De eerste Hollandse stadsbeschrijvingen uit de zeventiende eeuw (dl. 2)." *De zeventiende eeuw* 9 (1993): 97–111.

Handschke, Ulrike. *Die flämische Waldlandschaft: Anfänge und Entwicklungen im 16. und 17. Jahrhundert*. Worms: Wernersche Verlagsgesellschaft, 1988.

Hasselt, Carlos van. *Rembrandt and His Century: Dutch Drawings of the Seventeenth Century from the Collection of Frits Lugt*. Exh. cat. New York: Pierpont Morgan Library; Paris: Institut neerlandais, 1977.

Hautekeete, Stefaan. "De la ville à la campagne: L'image du Brabant dans les dessins topographiques du xvie siècle." In *Le peintre et l'arpenteur: Images de Bruxelles et de l'ancien duché de Brabant*. Tournai: Dexia Banque, 2000.

———. "New Insights into the Working Methods of Hans Bol." *Master Drawings* 50 (3) (2012): 329–56.

Haverkamp-Begemann, Egbert. "The Beauty of Holland: Albert Cuyp as Landscape Draftsman." In *Aelbert Cuyp*, ed. Arthur K. Wheelock, Jr. Washington, D.C.: National Gallery of Art, 2001.

———. *Fifteenth- to Eighteenth-Century European Drawings: Central Europe, The Netherlands, France, England*. The Robert Lehman Collection 7. New York: Metropolitan Museum of Art, 1999.

———. "Joos van Liere." In *Pieter Bruegel und seine Welt*, ed. Otto von Simson and Matthias Winner. Berlin: Mann, 1979.

———. *Willem Buytewech*. Amsterdam: H. Hertzberger, 1959.

Heawood, Edward. *Watermarks, Mainly of the 17th and 18th Centuries*, ed. Émile Joseph Labarre. Monumenta Chartae Papyraceae Historiam Illustrantia 1. Hilversum: Paper Publications Society, 1950.

Helmus, Liesbeth, ed. *Pieter Saenredam, het Utrechtse werk*. Exh. cat. Utrecht: Centraal Museum, 2000.

Hendrix, Harald. "The Rise of a Proto-Tourist Infrastructure in Late Sixteenth-Century Rome and Naples." In *Artes Apodemicae and Early Modern Travel Culture, 1550–1700*, ed. Karl A.E. Enenkel and Jan L. de Jong. Leiden: Brill, 2019.

Hendrix, Lee. *Noir: The Romance of Black in 19th-Century French Drawings and Prints*. Exh. cat. Los Angeles: J. Paul Getty Museum, 2015.

Herckenhoff, Paulo, et al., eds. *O Brasil e os holandeses, 1630–1654*. Exh. cat. São Paulo: Banco Real, 1999.

Herckmans, Elias. *Der zee-vaert lof*. Amsterdam: Jacob Wachter, 1634.

Herring, Richard. *Paper and Paper Making, Ancient and Modern*. 2nd ed. London: Longman, Brown, Green, and Longmans, 1856.

Hochstrasser, Julie Berger. "Inroads to Seventeenth-Century Dutch Landscape Painting." *Nederlands Kunsthistorisch Jaarboek* 48 (1997): 192–221.

Hoeksema, Robert J. "Three Stages in the History of Land Reclamation in the Netherlands." *Irrigation and Drainage* 56 (S1) (December 2007): 113–26.

Hollstein, Friedrich W.H. *Dutch and Flemish Etchings, Engravings and Woodcuts, ca. 1450–1700*. Amsterdam: M. Hertzberger, 1949–2010.

Honig, Elizabeth Alice. "Country Folk and City Business: A Print Series by Jan van de Velde II."

*Art Bulletin* 78 (3) (September 1996): 511–26.

Hoogstraten, Samuel van. *Inleyding tot de Hooge Schoole der Schilderkonst*. Rotterdam: Fransois van Hoogstraeten, 1678.

Hoppenbrouwers, Peter, and Jan Luiten van Zanden, eds. *Peasants into Farmers?: The Transformation of the Rural Economy in the Low Countries (Middle Ages–19th Century) in Light of the Brenner Debate*. Turnhout: Brepols, 2001.

Hunter, Dard. *Papermaking: The History and Technique of an Ancient Craft*. New York: Dover Publications, 1978.

Idris, O. H. M., and G. M. Haddad. "Gum Arabic's (Gum Acacia's) Journey from Tree to End User." In *Gum Arabic*, ed. John F. Kennedy, Glyn O. Phillips, and Peter A. Williams. Cambridge: Royal Society of Chemistry, 2012.

Israel, Jonathan I. *The Dutch Republic: Its Rise, Greatness, and Fall, 1477–1806*. Rev. ed. Oxford: Clarendon Press, 1995.

James, Carlo, and Marjorie B. Cohn. *Old Master Prints and Drawings: A Guide to Preservation and Conservation*. Amsterdam: Amsterdam University Press, 1997.

Jansen, Horst W. "The 'Image Made by Chance' in Renaissance Thought." In *De Artibus opuscula XL: Essays in Honor of Erwin Panofsky*, vol. 1, ed. Millard Meiss. New York: New York University Press, 1961.

Jellema, Renske, and Michiel C. Plomp. *Episcopius: Jan de Bisschop (1628–1671): Advocaat en Tekenaar*. Exh. cat. Amsterdam: Museum het Rembrandthuis; Zwolle: Waanders, 1992.

Kahn-Gerzon, B. S. "Biografische gegevens over Anthonie Waterloo." *Oud Holland* 106 (2) (1992): 94–98.

Keil, Robert, and Richard Keil. *Die Deutschen Stammbücher des sechzehnten bis neunzehnten Jahrhunderts*. Berlin: G. Grote, 1893.

Kerckhof, Véronique van de, et al., eds. *Le peintre et l'arpenteur: Images des Bruxelles et de l'ancien duché de Brabant*. Exh. cat. Brussels: Royal Museums of Fine Arts of Belgium; Tournai: Dexia Banque, 2000.

Keyes, George. *Cornelis Vroom: Marine and Landscape Artist*. 2 vols. Alphen aan den Rijn: Canaletto, 1975.

———. "Cornelisz Claesz. van Wieringen." *Oud Holland* 93 (1) (1979): 1–46.

———. *Esaias van de Velde, 1587–1630*. Doornspijk: Davaco Publishers, 1984.

———. "Esaias van de Velde and the Chalk Sketch." *Nederlands Kunsthistorisch Jaarboek* 38 (1987): 136–45.

Keyes, George S., et al. *Mirror of Empire: Dutch Marine Art of the Seventeenth Century*. Exh. cat. Minneapolis: Minneapolis Institute of Arts; Toledo, Ohio: Toledo Museum of Art; Los Angeles: Los Angeles County Museum of Art; Cambridge: Cambridge University Press, 1990.

Klerk, E. A. de. "*De Teecken-Const*, een 17de eeuws Nederlands Traktaatje." *Oud Holland* 96 (1982): 16–56.

Kloek, Wouter, and Bert W. Meijer, eds. *Bruegel, Rubens et leurs contemporains: Dessins nordiques du Musee des Offices a Florence*. Exh. cat. Paris: Fondation Custodia, Collection Frits Lugt; Florence: Gabinetto Disegni e Stampe degli Uffizi, 2008.

Koerner, Joseph Leo. *Caspar David Friedrich and the Subject of Landscape*. 2nd ed. London: Reaktion Books, 2009.

Kolbe, Gesa. "Gelatine in Historical Paper Production and as Inhibiting Agent for Iron-Gall Ink Corrosion on Paper." *Restaurator: International Journal for the Preservation of Library and Archival Material* 25 (1) (2004): 26–39.

Kuretsky, Susan D. "Dutch Ruins: Time and Transformation." In *Time and Transformation in Seventeenth-Century Dutch Art*, ed. Susan D. Kuretsky. Exh. cat. Poughkeepsie, N.Y.: Frances Lehman Loeb Art Center, Vassar College; Sarasota, Fla.: John and Mable Ringling Museum of Art; Louisville, Ky.: J. B. Speed Art Museum, 2005.

———, ed. *Time and Transformation in Seventeenth-Century Dutch Art*. Exh. cat. Poughkeepsie, N.Y.: Frances Lehman Loeb Art Center, Vassar College; Sarasota, Fla.: John and Mable Ringling Museum of Art; Louisville, Ky.: J. B. Speed Art Museum, 2005.

Kwakkelstein, Michael W. "Boticelli, Leonardo, and a Morris Dance." *Print Quarterly* 15 (1) (1998): 3–14.

Lambert, Audrey M. *The Making of the Dutch Landscape: An Historical Geography of the Netherlands*. London: Seminar Press Ltd, 1971.

Larsen, Anne R. *Anna Maria van Schurman, "The Star of Utrecht": The Educational Vision and Reception of a Savante*. London: Routledge, 2016.

Leeflang, Huigen. "Dutch Landscape, the Urban View: Haarlem and Its Environs in Literature and Art, 15th–17th Century." *Nederlands Kunsthistorisch Jaarboek* 48 (1997): 52–115.

Levesque, Catherine. *Journey through Landscape in Seventeenth-Century Holland: The Haarlem Print Series and Dutch Identity*. University Park: Pennsylvania State University Press, 1994.

Liess, Reinhard. *Jan Vermeer van Delft, Pieter Bruegel d. A., Rogier van de Weyden: Drei Studien zur niederlandischen Kunst*. Gottingen: V&R Unipress, 2004.

———. "Die kleinen Landschaften Pieter Bruegels d. A. im Lichte seines Gesamtwerk." *Kunsthistorisches Jahrbuch Graz* 18 (3) (1982).

———. "Die kleinen Landschaften Pieter Bruegels d. A. im Lichte seines Gesamtwerks, Part 1." *Kunsthistorisches Jahrbuch Graz* 15–16 (1979–80): 1–116.

Löffler, Erik P. "Ruins in the Netherlands: The Present Situation." In *Time and Transformation in Seventeenth-Century Dutch Art*, ed. Susan D. Kuretsky. Exh. cat. Poughkeepsie, N.Y.: Frances Lehman Loeb Art Center, Vassar College; Sarasota, Fla.: John and Mable Ringling Museum of Art; Louisville, Ky.: J. B. Speed Art Museum, 2005.

———. "A Subject of the Small Landscapes Series Identified." *Print Quarterly* 28 (2011): 46–49.

Lugt, Frits. *Wandelingen met Rembrandt in en om Amsterdam*. Amsterdam: P.N. van Kampen, 1915.

Luijten, Ger, Ariane van Suchtelen, Reinier Baarson, and Walter Kloek, eds. *Dawn of the Golden Age: Northern Netherlandish Art, 1580–1620*. Exh. cat. Amsterdam: Rijksmuseum, 1993.

Luijten, Ger, Peter Schatborn, William W. Robinson, and Arthur K. Wheelock. *Drawings for Paintings in the Age of Rembrandt*. Exh. cat. Washington, D.C.: National Gallery of Art, 2016.

Mallory, Sarah. "Memory Spaces and Far Away Places: Mauritius, Golden Age Myths, and the Origins of Dutch Landscape." In *Dutch Golden Age(s): The Shaping of a Cultural Community*, ed. Jan Blanc. Gouden Eeuw: New Perspectives on Dutch Seventeenth-Century Art 1. Turnhout: Brepols, 2021.

Mander, Karel van. *Den grondt der edel vry schilder-const*. Ed. Hessel Miedema. Utrecht: Haentjens Dekker & Gumbert, 1973.

———. *The Lives of the Illustrious Netherlandish and German Painters, from the First Edition of the Schilder-Boeck (1603–1604)*. 6 vols. Ed. and trans. Hessel Miedema. Doornspijk: Davaco, 1994–99.

———. *Het Schilder-Boeck*. Haarlem: Paschier van Wesbvach, 1604.

Marciari, John. *Guercino: Virtuoso Draftsman*. Exh. cat. New York: Morgan Library & Museum, 2019.

Mariod, Abdalbasit A. "Chemical Properties of Gum Arabic." In *Gum Arabic: Structure, Properties, Application and Economics*, ed. Abdalbasit A. Mariod. San Diego: Elsevier Science & Technology, 2018.

Mayer, Ralph. *The Artist's Handbook of Materials and Techniques*. Rev. ed. New York: Viking Press, 1957.

Mayhew, Timothy David, Margo Ellis, and Supapan Seraphin. "Natural Black Chalk in Traditional Old Master Drawings." *Journal of the American Institute for Conservation* 49 (2) (2010): 83–95.

Meijer, Fred G. *Franchoys Ryckhals: Een Zeeuwse meester uit de Gouden Eeuw*. Exh. cat. Zieriksee: Stadhuismuseum; Zwolle: WBOOKS, 2019.

Merula, Paullus. *Placaten ende ordonnancien op 't stuck van de wildernissen*. The Hague: Beuckel Cornelisz. Nieulant, 1605.

Meuwissen, Daantje. "Attributing the Berlin Sketchbook to Cornelis Anthonisz." *Simiolus* 39 (2017): 15–43.

Mielke, Hans, ed. *Pieter Bruegel d. A. als Zeichner*. Exh. cat. Berlin: Staatliche Museen zu Berlin, Preussischer Kulturbesitz, 1975.

———. *Pieter Bruegel: Die Zeichnungen*. Turnhout: Brepols, 1996.

Miller, Angela. *The Empire of the Eye: Landscape Representation and American Cultural Politics, 1825–1875*. Ithaca, N.Y.: Cornell University Press, 1993.

Mitchell, C. Ainsworth. "Characteristics of Pigments in Early Pencil Writing." *Nature* 105 (2627) (1920): 12–14.

Mitchell, W. J. T., ed. *Landscape and Power*. 2nd ed. Chicago: University of Chicago Press, 2002.

*The New Hollstein Dutch and Flemish Etchings, Engravings and Woodcuts, 1450–1700*. Vol. 5: *The Van Doetecum Family*, part 1, compiled by Henk J. Nalis. Rotterdam: Koninklijke van Poll, 1998.

*The New Hollstein Dutch and Flemish Etchings, Engravings and Woodcuts, 1450–1700*. Vol. 15: *The Collaert Dynasty*, compiled by Ann Diels and Marjolein Leesberg. 8 parts. Ouderkerk aan den Ijssel: Sound and Vision Publishers, 2005–6.

Nguyen, Kristina Hartzer. "The Made Landscape: City and Country in Seventeenth-Century Dutch Prints." *Harvard University Art Museums Bulletin* 1 (1) (Autumn 1992): 7–40.

Nibbering, Jacobus. "Identificatie van een tekening van Jan van Goyen." *Oud Holland* 105 (1991): 41–43.

Niemeijer, J. W. *Aquarelles hollandaises du XVIIIe siecle du Cabinet des Dessins du Rijksmuseum d'Amsterdam*. Paris: Institut Néerlandais; Amsterdam: Rijksmuseum; Zwolle: Waanders, 1990.

———. *Cornelis Troost, 1696–1750*. Assen: Van Gorcum, 1973.

———. "Varia Topografica IV Een album met Utrechtse gezichten door Abraham Rutgers." *Oud Holland* 79 (1964): 127–30, 134.

Nierop, Henk van. "The Anatomy of Society." In *Class Distinctions: Dutch Painting in the Age of Rembrandt and Vermeer*, ed. Ronni Baer. Exh. cat. Boston: Museum of Fine Arts, 2015.

———. *Treason in the Northern Quarter: War, Terror, and the Rule of Law in the Dutch Revolt*. Trans. J. C. Grayson. Princeton, N.J.: Princeton University Press, 2009.

Oberhuber, Konrad. *Die Kunst der Graphik IV. Zwischen Renaissance und Barock: Das Zeitalter von Bruegel und Bellange*. Exh. cat. Vienna: Graphische Sammlung Albertina, 1967.

Onnekink, David, and Gijs Rommelse. *The Dutch in the Early Modern World: A History of a Global Power*. Cambridge: Cambridge University Press, 2019.

Onuf, Alexandra. *The "Small Landscape" Prints in Early Modern Netherlands*. London: Routledge, Taylor & Francis Group, 2018.

Orenstein, Nadine M., ed. *Pieter Bruegel the Elder: Drawings and Prints*. Exh. cat. New York: Metropolitan Museum of Art; Rotterdam: Museum Boijmans van Beuningen, 2001.

Ortelius, Abraham, and Jean Puraye. *Album Amicorum*. Facsimile ed. Trans. Jean Puraye with Marie Delcourt. Gulden Passer 45–46. Antwerp: Nederlandsche Boekhandel, 1967.

Papenbrock, Martin. *Landschaften des Exils: Gillis van Coninxloo und die Frankenthaler Maler*. Cologne: Böhlau, 2001.

*Papermaking—Art and Craft: An Account Derived from the Exhibition Presented in the Library of Congress, Washington, D.C., and Opened on April 21, 1968*. Washington, D.C.: Library of Congress, 1968.

Patrizio, Andrew. *The Ecological Eye: Assembling an Ecocritical Art History*. Rethinking Art's Histories. Manchester: Manchester University Press, 2019.

Plomp, Michiel C. *The Dutch Drawings in the Teyler Museum*. Vol. 2: *Artists Born between 1575 and 1630*. Ghent: Snoeck Ducaju & Zoon; Doornspijk: Davaco Publishers, 1997.

———. *Hartstochtelijk Verzameld*. Paris: Fondation Custodia; Bussum: Thoth, 2001.

Price, J. L. "Water and Land." In *The Cambridge Companion to the Dutch Golden Age*, ed. Helmer J. Helmers and Geert H. Janssen. Cambridge: Cambridge University Press, 2018.

Puraye, Jean, ed. *Amicorum Abraham Ortelius*. 2 vols. Antwerp: Brill, 1967–68.

Reznicek, E. K. J. "Drawings by Hendrick Goltzius, Thirty Years Later: Supplement to the 1961 Catalogue Raisonné." *Master Drawings* 31 (3) (Autumn 1993): 215–78.

———. *Die Zeichnungen von Hendrick Goltzius*. 2 vols. Utrecht: Haentjens Dekker & Gumbert, 1961.

Robinson, Franklin W., ed. *Fresh Woods and Pastures New: Seventeenth-Century Dutch Landscape*

*Drawings from the Peck Collection*. Exh. cat. Chapel Hill: Ackland Art Museum, University of North Carolina at Chapel Hill, 1999.

———. *Selections from the Collection of Dutch Drawings of Maida and George Abrams*. Exh. cat. Wellesley, Mass.: Jewett Arts Center, Wellesley College, 1969.

———. *Seventeenth-Century Dutch Drawings from American Collections*. Exh. cat. Washington, D.C.: National Gallery of Art; Denver: Denver Art Museum; Fort Worth, Tex.: Kimbell Art Museum; Washington, D.C.: International Exhibitions Foundation, 1977.

———, ed. *Things of This World: A Selection of Dutch Drawings from the Collection of Maida and George Abrams*. Exh. cat. Williamstown, Mass.: Sterling and Francine Clark Art Institute, 1972.

Robinson, William W. "The Abrams Album: An *Album Amicorum* of Dutch Drawings from the Seventeenth Century." *Master Drawings* 53 (1) (Spring 2015): 3–58.

———. *Bruegel to Rembrandt: Dutch and Flemish Drawings from the Maida and George Abrams Collection*. Exh. cat. Cambridge, Mass.: Harvard University Art Museums; London: British Museum; Paris: Institut Néerlandais; New Haven, Conn.: Yale University Press, 2002.

———. "Landscape Drawings by Nicolaes Maes." *Een Kroniek voor Jeroen Giltay: Kroniek van het Rembrandthuis* (2012): 42–47.

———. *Seventeenth-Century Dutch Drawings: A Selection from the Maida and George Abrams Collection*. Exh. cat. Cambridge, Mass.: Harvard University Art Museums; Amsterdam: Rijksmuseum; Vienna: Graphische Sammlung Albertina; New York: Pierpont Morgan Library; Lynn, Mass.: H. O. Zimman, 1991.

Robinson, William W., and Susan Anderson. *Drawings from the Age of Bruegel, Rubens, and Rembrandt: Highlights from the Collection of the Harvard Art Museums*. Cambridge, Mass.: Harvard Art Museums, 2016.

Robinson, William W., et al. *Drawings from the Age of Bruegel, Rubens, and Rembrandt: The Complete Collection Online*. Ed. Susan Anderson. https://www.harvardartmuseums.org/publications/special-collections/drawings-from-the-age-of-bruegel-rubens-and-rembrandt-the-complete-collection-online.

Roelofs, Pieter, ed. *Hendrick Avercamp: Master of the Ice Scene*. Exh. cat. Trans. Lynne Richards. Amsterdam: Rijksmuseum; Washington, D.C.: National Gallery of Art, 2010.

Roethlisberger, Marcel. *Abraham Bloemaert and His Sons: Paintings and Prints*. 2 vols. Doornspijk: Davaco Publishers, 1993.

———. *Bartholomäus Breenbergh: Handzeichnungen*. Berlin: De Gruyter, 1969.

Rosenheim, Max. "The Album Amicorum." *Archaeologia, or Miscellaneous Tracts Relating to Antiquity* 62 (1910): 251–308.

Royalton-Kisch, Martin. *Catalogue of Drawings by Rembrandt and His School in the British Museum*. 2010. https://www.britishmuseum.org/collection/term/BIB6822.

———. *Drawings by Rembrandt and His Circle in the British Museum*. Exh. cat. London: British Museum Press, 1992.

———. *The Light of Nature: Landscape Drawings and Watercolours by Van Dyck and His Contemporaries*. Exh. cat. Antwerp: Rubenshuis; London: British Museum, 1999.

Rupprich, Hans, ed. *Dürer: Schriftlicher Nachlass*. Berlin: Deutscher Verein für Kunstwissenschaft, 1956–69.

Russell, Margarita. *Jan van de Cappelle 1624/6–1679*. Leigh-on-Sea, U.K.: F. Lewis, 1975.

Sadkov, Vadim, et al. *Netherlandish, Flemish and Dutch Drawings of the XVI–XVIII Centuries; Belgian and Dutch Drawings of the XIX–XX Centuries*. Amsterdam: Foundation for Cultural Inventory, 2010.

Said, Edward. "Invention, Memory, and Place." In *Landscape and Power*, ed. W. J. T. Mitchell. 2nd ed. Chicago: University of Chicago Press, 2002.

Sapori, Giovanna. "L'*album amicorum* come libro di disegni: Alcuni esempi tra Cinquecento e Seicento (Venius, Ortelius, Abrams, Heyblocq)." In *Libri e album di disegni 1550–1800: Nuove prospettive metodologiche e di esegesi storico-critica*, ed. Vita Segreto. Rome: De Luca, 2018.

Saywell, Edward. "Behind the Line: The Materials and Techniques of Old Master Drawings." *Harvard University Art Museums Bulletin* 6 (2) (1998): 7–39.

Schapelhouman, Marijn. "The Drawings, Reflections on an Oeuvre." In *Hendrick Avercamp: Master of the Ice Scene*, ed. Pieter Roelefs. Exh. cat. Amsterdam: Rijksmuseum; Washington, D.C.: National Gallery of Art, 2009.

———. "A Note on the Pleasures of Traveling in Former Time." In *Home and Abroad: Dutch and Flemish Landscape Drawings from the John and Marine van Vlissingen Art Foundation*, ed. Jane Shoaf Turner and Robert-Jan te Rijdt. Exh. cat. Amsterdam: Rijksmuseum; Paris: Fondation Custodia; Curaçao: BCD Group N.V., 2015.

———. *Rembrandt and the Art of Drawing*. Amsterdam: Rijksmuseum, 2006.

Schapelhouman, Marijn, and Peter Schatborn. *Land & Water: Dutch Drawings from the 17th Century in the Rijksmuseum Print Room*. Zwolle: Waanders, 1987.

Schatborn, Peter. *Drawings by Rembrandt, His Anonymous Pupils and Followers*. Catalogue of the Dutch and Flemish Drawings in the Rijksprentenkabinet, Rijksmuseum, Amsterdam 4. 's-Gravenhage: Staatsuitgeverij, 1985.

———. *Drawn to Warmth: 17th-Century Dutch Artists in Italy*. Exh. cat. Amsterdam: Rijksmuseum; Zwolle: Waanders, 2001.

———. "Getekende landschappen van Pieter de With." In *De Verbeelde Wereld: Liber Amicorum voor Boudewijn Bakker*, ed. Jaap Evert Abrahamse, Marijke Carasso-Kok, and Erik Schmitz. Bussum: Thoth, 2008.

———. "The Importance of Drawing from Life—Some Preliminary Notes." In *Seventeenth-Century Dutch Drawings: A Selection from the Maida and George Abrams Collection*, by William W. Robinson. Cambridge, Mass.: Harvard University Art Museums; Amsterdam: Rijksmuseum; Vienna: Graphische Sammlung Albertina; New York: Pierpont Morgan Library; Lynn, Mass.: H. O. Zimman, 1991.

———. *Old Drawings, New Names: Rembrandt and His Contemporaries*. Exh. cat. Amsterdam: Rembrandthuis Museum; Varik: De Weideblik, 2014.

———. *Rembrandt and His Circle: Drawings in the Frits Lugt Collection*. 2 vols. Paris: Fondation Custodia; Bussum: Thoth, 2010.

———. "Tekeningen van de gebroeders Jan en Jacob Pynas 1. Jan Pynas." *Bulletin van het Rijksmuseum* 44 (1) (1996): 37–54.

———. "Tekeningen van Rembrandt en Pieter de With." *Kroniek van het Rembrandthuis* (2005): 2–13.

———. "Van Rembrandt tot Crozat: Vroege verzamelingen met tekeningen van Rembrandt." *Nederlands Kunsthistorisch Jaarboek* 32 (1) (1981): 1–54.

———. "Wolfgang Schulz, Lambert Doomer: Samtliche Zeichnungen (book review)." *Simiolus* 9 (1) (1977): 48–55.

Schatborn, Peter, and E. Ornstein-Van Slooten. *Jan Lievens, 1607–1674: Prenten & Tekeningen*. Exh. cat. Amsterdam: Het Museum, 1988.

Schatborn, Peter, and Erik Hinterding. *Rembrandt: The Complete Drawings and Etchings*. Cologne: Taschen, 2019.

Schmidt, Benjamin. "The Dutch Atlantic: From Provincialism to Globalism." In *Atlantic History: A Critical Appraisal*, ed. Jack P. Greene and Philip D. Morgan. Oxford: Oxford University Press, 2009.

———. *Innocence Abroad: The Dutch Imagination and the New World, 1570–1670*. Cambridge: Cambridge University Press, 2001.

———. *Inventing Exoticism: Geography, Globalism, and Europe's Early Modern World*. Philadelphia: University of Pennsylvania Press, 2015.

Schneider, Hans, and Rudolf E.O. Ekkart. *Jan Lievens: Sein Leben und seine Werke*. Amsterdam: Israël, 1973.

Schoemaker, Laurens M. "Jacob van Ruisdael tekent de Kamperbuitenpoort in Amersfoort." In *Connoisseurship: Essays in Honour of Fred G. Meijer*, ed. Charles Dumas. Leiden: Primavera Press, 2020.

———. "A Little Street in Harderwijk by Jacob van Ruisdael." *RKD Bulletin* 1 (2016): 3–10.

Schrier, Gerard van der, and Rob Groenland. "A Reconstruction of 1 August 1674 Thunderstorms over the Low Countries." *Natural Hazards and Earth System Sciences* 17 (2017): 157–70.

Schulz, Wolfgang. *Herman Saftleven, 1609–1685: Leben und Werke: Mit einem kritischen Katalog der Gemälde und Zeichnungen*. Berlin: de Gruyter, 1982.

———. *Lambert Doomer: Sämtliche Zeichnungen*. Berlin: de Gruyter, 1974.

Scott, Emily Eliza, and Kirsten Swenson. *Critical Landscapes: Art, Space, Politics*. Oakland: University of California Press, 2015.

Silver, Larry. "Albrecht Altdorfer and the German Wilderness Landscape." *Simiolus* 13 (1) (1983): 4–43.

———. *Peasant Scenes and Landscapes: The Rise of Pictorial Genres in the Antwerp Art Market*. Philadelphia: University of Pennsylvania Press, 2012.

Sint Nicolaas, Eveline, et al. *Slavery: The Story of João, Wally, Oopjen, Paulus, Van Bengalen, Surapati, Sapali, Tula, Dirk, Lohkay*. Exh. cat. Amsterdam: Rijksmuseum, 2021.

Sliggers, Bert, Jr. *Dagelijckse aentekeninge van Vincent Laurensz van der Vinne*. Haarlem: Fibula-Van Dishoeck, 1979.

Slive, Seymour. *Jacob van Ruisdael: A Complete Catalogue of His Paintings, Drawings, and Etchings*. New Haven, Conn.: Yale University Press, 2001.

———. *Rembrandt Drawings*. Los Angeles: J. Paul Getty Museum, 2009.

Smith, Jeffrey Chipps. "The Early Collecting of Dürer's Prints." In *Prayer Nuts, Private Devotion, and Early Modern Art Collecting*, ed. Evelin Wetter and Frits Scholten. Riggisberg: Abegg-Stiftung, 2017.

Spicer, Joaneath. "A Pictorial Vocabulary of Otherness: Roelandt Saverij, Adam Willarts, and the Representation of Foreign Coasts." *Nederlands Kunsthistorisch Jaarboek* 48 (1997): 22–51.

Stechow, Wolfgang. *Dutch Landscape Painting of the Seventeenth Century*. New York: Phaidon Publishers, 1966.

Stilgoe, John R. "Landschaft and Linearity: Two Archetypes of Landscapes." *Environmental Review: ER* 4 (1) (1980): 2–17.

Stubbe, Lotte, and Wolf Stubbe. *Um 1660 auf Reisen gezeichnet. Anthonie Waterloo, 1610–1690: Ansichten aus Hamburg, Altona, Blankenese, Holstein, Bergedorf, Lüneberg, und Danzig-Olivia*. Hamburg: Christians Verlag, 1983.

Suchtelen, Ariane van, and Arthur K. Wheelock. *Dutch Cityscapes of the Golden Age*. Exh. cat. The Hague: Royal Picture Gallery Mauritshuis; Washington, D.C.: National Gallery of Art, 2008.

Sumowski, Werner. *Drawings of the Rembrandt School*. 10 vols. New York: Abaris Books, 1979–92.

———. "Observations on Jan Lievens' Landscape Drawings." *Master Drawings* 18 (4) (1980): 370–73.

Sutton, Elizabeth. *Capitalism and Cartography in the Dutch Golden Age*. Chicago: University of Chicago Press, 2015.

———. *Early Modern Dutch Prints of Africa*. Farnham, U.K., and Burlington, Vt.: Ashgate, 2012.

———. "Possessing Brazil in Print, 1630–54." *Journal of Historians of Netherlandish Art* 5 (1) (Winter 2013). DOI: 10.5092/jhna.2013.5.1.3.

Sutton, Peter C., ed. *Masters of 17th-Century Dutch Landscape Painting*. Exh. cat. Amsterdam: Rijksmuseum; Boston: Museum of Fine Arts; Philadelphia: Philadelphia Museum of Art, 1987.

———, ed. *Prized Possessions: European Paintings from Private Collections of Friends of the Museum of Fine Arts, Boston*. Exh. cat. Boston: Museum of Fine Arts, 1992.

Sutton, Peter C., and William W. Robinson. *Drawings by Rembrandt, His Students, and Circle from the Maida and George Abrams Collection*. Exh. cat. Greenwich, Conn.: Bruce Museum; Houston: Museum of Fine Arts; New Haven, Conn.: Yale University Press, 2011.

Swan, Claudia. "*Ad vivum, naer het leven*, from the life: Defining a mode of representation." *Word & Image* 11 (4) (October–December 1995): 353–72.

———. *Rarities of These Lands: Art, Trade, and Diplomacy in the Dutch Republic*. Princeton, N.J.: Princeton University Press, 2021.

Tamen, Miguel. *Friends of Interpretable Objects*. Cambridge, Mass.: Harvard University Press, 2001.

Thomassen, Kees. *Alba amicorum: Vijf eeuwen vriendschap op papier gezet*. The Hague: G. Schwartz/SDU Uitgeverij/Rijksmuseum Meermanno-Westreenianum/Museum van het Boek, 's-Gravenhage, 1990.

Turner, Jane Shoaf. *Rembrandt's World: Dutch Drawings from the Clement C. Moore Collection*. Exh. cat. New York: Morgan Library & Museum, 2012.

Turner, Jane Shoaf, and Robert-Jan te Rijdt, eds. *Home and Abroad: Dutch and Flemish Landscape Drawings from the John and Marine van Vlissingen Art Foundation*. Exh. cat. Amsterdam: Rijksmuseum; Paris: Fondation Custodia; Curaçao: BCD Group N.V., 2015.

Veldman, Ilja M. *Images for the Eye and Soul: Function and Meaning in Netherlandish Prints (1450–1650)*. Leiden: Primavera Press, 2006.

Verbeek, Hans. "Gerrit Battem, constrijk schilder (1636–1684)." Ph.D. diss., Universiteit Leiden, 1982.

———. *Travels through Town and Country: Dutch and Flemish Landscape Drawings, 1550–1830*. Exh. cat. Haarlem: Teylers Museum, 2000.

Virgil. *The Aeneid of Virgil*. Trans. Theodore C. Williams. Boston: Houghton Mifflin, 1910.

Vries, Jan de. *Barges and Capitalism: Passenger Transportation in the Dutch Economy, 1632–1839*. Utrecht: HES Publishers, 1981.

———. "The Dutch Rural Economy and the Landscape." In *Dutch Landscape: The Early Years, Haarlem and Amsterdam 1590–1650*, ed. Christopher Brown. Exh. cat. London: The National Gallery, 1986.

———. *The Dutch Rural Economy in the Golden Age, 1500–1700*. New Haven, Conn.: Yale University Press, 1974.

———. "The Transition to Capitalism in a Land without Feudalism." In *Peasants into Farmers?: The Transformation of the Rural Economy in the Low Countries (Middle Ages–19th Century) in Light of the Brenner Debate*, ed. Peter Hoppenbrouwers and Jan Luiten van Zanden. Turnhout: Brepols, 2001.

Walraven-Schipper, Meta. "De Landschappen van Dirk Dalens III (1688–1753) in de achttiende-eeuwse decoratieve." 2 parts. Ph.D. diss., Rijksuniversiteit Leiden, 1996.

Watrous, James. *The Craft of Old-Master Drawings*. Madison: University of Wisconsin Press, 1957.

Wedde, Nina. *Isaac de Moucheron (1667–1744): His Life and Works with a Catalogue Raisonné of His Drawings, Watercolors, Paintings, and Etchings*. New York: Peter Lang, 1996.

Welcker, Clara Johanna. *Hendrick Avercamp, 1525–1634, bijgenaamd "De Stomme Van Campen," en Barent Avercamp, 1612–1679, "Schilders tot Campen."* Doornspijk: Davaco, 1979.

Weststeijn, Arthur. "Republican Empire: Colonialism, Commerce and Corruption in the Dutch Golden Age." *Renaissance Studies* 26 (4) (September 2012): 491–509.

Wetering, Ernst van de. "Verdwenen tekeningen en het gebruik van afwisbare tekenplankjes en *tafeletten*." *Oud Holland* 105 (1991): 210–27.

Wheelock, Arthur K., Jr., ed. *Aelbert Cuyp*. Exh. cat. Washington, D.C.: National Gallery of Art; London: Thames & Hudson, 2001.

———, ed. *Jan Lievens: A Dutch Master Rediscovered*. Exh. cat. Washington, D.C.: National Gallery of Art; Milwaukee: Milwaukee Art Museum; Amsterdam: Rembrandthuis; New Haven, Conn.: Yale University Press, 2008.

Whited, Tamara L., et al. *Northern Europe: An Environmental History*. Santa Barbara, Calif.: ABC-CLIO, 2005.

Williams, Raymond. *The Country and the City*. New York: Oxford University Press, 1973.

Wilmers, Catharina C.S. *De getekende stad: Utrecht in oude tekeningen, 1550–1900*. Utrecht: Matrijs, 2005.

Wilson, Bronwen. "Social Networking: The 'Album amicorum' and Early Modern Public Making." In *Beyond the Public Sphere: Opinions, Publics, Spaces in Early Modern Europe*, ed. Massimo Rospocher. Bologna: Il Mulino, 2012.

Wood, Christopher S. *Albrecht Altdorfer and the Origins of Landscape*. Rev. ed. London: Reaktion Books, 2014.

Wood Ruby, Louisa. *Paul Bril, the Drawings*. Brussels: Brepols, 1999.

Wyck, H. W. M. van der, Wouter Th. Kloek, and J. W. Niemeijer. *De Kasteeltekeningen van Roelant Roghman*. Exh. cat. 2 vols. Amsterdam: Rijksmuseum; Alphen aan den Rijn: Canaletto, 1989–90.

Zell, Michael. "A Leisurely and Virtuous Pursuit: Amateur Artists, Rembrandt, and Landscape Representation in Seventeenth-Century Dutch Holland." *Nederlands Kunsthistorisch Jaarboek* 54 (2003): 334–68.

———. *Rembrandt, Vermeer, and the Gift in Seventeenth-Century Dutch Art*. Amsterdam: Amsterdam University Press, 2021.

# IMAGE CREDITS

All photographs were supplied by the owners of the works of art, who hold the copyright thereto, and are reproduced with permission.

All images of objects from Harvard collections and archives © 2022 President and Fellows of Harvard College.

Additional credits:

"Introduction"
Susan Anderson

Figs. 1–2: Maps created by Scott Walker, Digital Cartography Specialist, Harvard Map Collection

"On the Spot: The Appeal of the Local"
Yvonne Bleyerveld

Fig. 1: © KBR (Royal Library of Belgium); Fig. 2: © Trustees of the British Museum; Fig. 5: © Museum Boijmans Van Beuningen

"Shifting Terrain: Environmental Change, Global Expansion, and the Drawn Landscape"
Joanna Sheers Seidenstein

Figs. 9, 13: Rijksmuseum, Amsterdam; Fig. 11: Houghton Library, Harvard College Library Imaging Services

"Farmsteads, Castles, Ruins: The Rustic Landscape and the Presence of the Past"
William W. Robinson

Fig. 7: © The Frick Collection

"Wet and Dry: Integrating Drawing Materials"
Anne Driesse

Figs. 3, 5, 7–9, 11, 13–14: Technical images by Anne Driesse

"Drawings as Friends"
Joseph Leo Koerner

Figs. 2–5: Courtesy of Penley Knipe

This book is published in conjunction with the exhibition *Crossroads: Drawing the Dutch Landscape*, on view at the Harvard Art Museums, Cambridge, Massachusetts, from May 21 through August 14, 2022.



Published by
Harvard Art Museums
32 Quincy Street
Cambridge, MA 02138-3847
harvardartmuseums.org

Distributed by
Yale University Press
302 Temple Street
PO Box 209040
New Haven, CT 06520-9040
yalebooks.com/art

Managing Editor: Micah Buis
Editors: Sarah Kuschner, Cheryl Pappas
Design Manager: Zak Jensen
Designers: Angela Lorenzo, Adam Sherkanowski

Typeset in Hollander and Documenta Sans
by Tina Henderson
Printed on Symbol Tatami
Printed in Belgium by Graphius

ISBN: 978-0-300-26382-4
Library of Congress Control Number: 2021943104

Cover image: Cornelis Vroom, *Landscape with a Road and a Fence* (detail), 1631. See p. 233 for full information.